DON QUIJOTE
IN WORLD LITERATURE

GARLAND REFERENCE LIBRARY
OF THE HUMANITIES
(VOL. 187)

DON QUIJOTE
IN WORLD LITERATURE
A Selective, Annotated Bibliography

Don Quijote (1894–1970): A Selective,
Annotated Bibliography, Volume III

Dana B. Drake

GARLAND PUBLISHING, INC. • NEW YORK & LONDON
1980

Library of Congress Cataloging in Publication Data

Drake, Dana B
  Don Quijote in world literature.

  (Garland reference library of the humanities ; v. 187)
  "Don Quijote (1894–1970): a selective, annotated
bibliography, volume III."
  Includes indexes.
  1. Cervantes Saavedra, Miguel de, 1547–1616—
Bibliography. I. Title.
Z8158.D694 [PQ6337]   016.863'3   79-7926
ISBN 0-8240-9542-1

Printed on acid-free, 250-year-life paper
Manufactured in the United States of America

To Professor Werner P. Friederich
for his inspiration, advice, and many kind words
over the past fifteen years.

CONTENTS

Acknowledgments   xi

Introduction   xiii

Explanatory Note   xix

I   ***Don Quijote* in World Literature**
    Editions and Translations   3
    The Reasons for the *Quijote's* Importance   5
    The Critical Reception of the *Quijote*   16
    The Influence of the *Quijote* on the Later Novel   19
    Theatrical, Poetic, and Cinematographic
        Interpretations of the *Quijote*   26

II   ***Don Quijote* in Spain**
    General   33
    Seventeenth-Century Spain   34
    Eighteenth-Century Spain   37
    Nineteenth-Century Spain
        General   38
        Pérez Galdós   42
        Marcelino Menéndez y Pelayo   54
    The Generation of 1898
        General   55
        "Azorín"   57
        Miguel de Unamuno   58
    Twentieth-Century Spain   60

III ***Don Quijote* in France**
    General   65
    Seventeenth-Century France   69
    Eighteenth-Century France   73

Nineteenth-Century France 76
Twentieth-Century France 84

IV   *Don Quijote* in Italy
      General 87
      Seventeenth-Century Italy 89
      Eighteenth-Century Italy 92
      Nineteenth-Century Italy 92
      Twentieth-Century Italy 96

V   *Don Quijote* in England
      General 99
      Seventeenth-Century England 107
      Eighteenth-Century England
          General 120
          Henry Fielding 123
          Tobias Smollett 135
          Lewis Theobald 136
          John Bowle 138
          Laurence Sterne 139
          Other Writers 141
      Nineteenth-Century England
          Charles Dickens 144
          Sir Walter Scott 149
          Lewis Carroll 150
          Other Writers 152
      Twentieth-Century England 154

VI   *Don Quijote* in Germany
      General 157
      Seventeenth-Century Germany 164
      Eighteenth-Century Germany 167
      Nineteenth-Century Germany 168
      Twentieth-Century Germany 175

VII   *Don Quijote* in Russia
      General 179
      Nineteenth-Century Russia 187
      Twentieth-Century Russia 193

V.III *Don Quijote* **in Latin America**

General 197
Argentina 201
Brazil 205
Chile 207
Colombia 209
Cuba 210
Ecuador 211
Mexico 215
Nicaragua 216
Uruguay 216
Venezuela 217

IX *Don Quijote* **in the United States**

General 219
Eighteenth-Century United States 221
Nineteenth-Century United States 223
Twentieth-Century United States 227

X *Don Quijote* **in Other Countries**

Eastern Europe and the Balkans 233
China 237
The Low Countries 238
Portugal 239
Scandinavia 243

Indexes

Author Index 245
Subject Index 251

ACKNOWLEDGMENTS

To the many professors, students, and librarians for their help and patience. Particular appreciation is expressed to Sterling A. Stoudemire, William A. McKnight, John J. Allen, Joseph R. Jones, and Manuel Durán for their kind and wise suggestions. To Sonia de Lama, Arthur Ramírez, Dennis Nazak, and Edith Smargon for assistance in preparing various entries. To Ralph Anderson for his help in revising the Introduction. And, most of all, to my typist, Mrs. Lewis Whitescarver, for her determination and fortitude.

INTRODUCTION

This volume is the third step in our efforts to encompass leading criticism of the *Quijote*. The first volume was published in 1974 (*North Carolina Studies in the Romance Languages and Literatures*, number 138), and the second in 1978 (Ediciones Universal, Miami, Florida). During the preparation of these two volumes, a logical division of the collected material indicated that all bibliographical entries dealing with the influence of the *Quijote* on a given country or on a specific author (together with leading works which treat the critical reception of Cervantes' masterpiece in a given land) should appear as a distinct entity. Therefore, this third volume.

In our previous two bibliographies we have dealt with such matters as the literary influences on Cervantes' masterpiece, the philosophy of the *Quijote*, and the style and structure of that novel. We also summarized various works which are concerned with the changing interpretation of the *Quijote* over the centuries. The reader will observe that several works from this last-mentioned group are repeated in this third volume, since the critical interpretation of Cervantes' novel ties in closely with the influence of the *Quijote* on later creative writers. Indeed, various works summarized here are concerned with both the critical reception of that novel, as well as its interpretation by novelists, poets, and playwrights.

Perhaps it would be wise to recapitulate in general terms the history of *Quijote* interpretation. In the early seventeenth century Cervantes' novel was treated as a jest book, a strictly comic work with a comic hero. Later in that century, especially in France, it came to be regarded as an example of fine satire, as opposed to low or bitter satire. In eighteenth-century England, with Motteux, there began a process of identification with the Knight of the Sad Countenance. The German Romanticists of the early nineteenth century, following the sympathetic approach of the English, developed a symbolistic school of *Quijote* interpretation in which the Don became the representative of idealism and the Squire the personification of materialism. In the latter part of the nineteenth century the Knight became, in the minds of some, a battler for political liberty, a struggler against all oppression. This tendency to exalt or even deify Cervantes' hero reached a peak in 1905 with Unamuno's *Vida de Don Quijote y Sancho* and Rubén Darío's "Lentanías de Nuestro Señor Don Quijote." Following this feverish pitch of *Quijotismo* a more sober and balanced approach has slowly evolved. Critics have come to note again the Don's faults: his childishness and his all-absorbing interest in his own fame and glory. With the increased popularity of Existentialism after World War II various critics have concluded that the *Quijote* is a study in identity crisis or a problem of self-fulfillment in society. What future interpretations are in store for us no one knows.

We of course realize that this summary excludes certain approaches. Over the centuries not all were carried away with the tendency to obscure the Knight's faults. Various critics, one should also note, have taken a "simplistic" view (that the *Quijote* is merely an attack on the decadent chivalresque novel). Others have even treated that novel as a pessimistic work which attacks not only had literature but also all human enthusiasm. But to return to the principal subject of this third volume: the effect of *Don Quijote* on later creative writing.

As the size of the present work indicates, there is a vast amount of material dealing with the influence of Cervantes' masterpiece on later poets, playwrights, and novelists. The use of Cervantine material by English dramatists of the seventeenth century has received the attention of numerous critics. It was first noted by Gerard Langbaine in 1691, in his *Account of the English Dramatick Poets* (see 256). The profound effect of the *Quijote* on English novelists of the eighteenth century has also been a popular topic of investigation, and Fielding, Sterne, and Smollett have often been cited as disciples of Cervantes in their creation of lovable eccentrics patterned after the Don. A considerable block of critical material regarding nineteenth-century

English writers is concerned with the influence of Cervantes on Charles Dickens, Sir Walter Scott, and Lewis Carroll.

In France, playwrights of the seventeenth century often drew upon the *Quijote* for material, and there were various French satirical novels of that epoch and later which were based on Cervantes' masterpiece. As for the influence of the *Quijote* on the modern French novel, great attention has been devoted to its effect on Flaubert, especially on his *Madame Bovary* and *Bouvard et Pécuchet*.

In Spain there have been numerous plays based on the *Quijote*; these have been cataloged and analyzed on various occasions. There was also a vague Cervantine influence on the Spanish novel of the seventeenth and eighteenth centuries. However, those writing on the influence of Cervantes on the Spanish novel have devoted their main attention to the impact of the *Quijote* on nineteenth- and twentieth-century writers such as Pérez Galdós, Unamuno, Azorín, and Ayala.

Cervantes' tale of the Knight and the Squire was, of course, of profound effect on German critics, dramatists, and novelists, particularly in the late eighteenth and early nineteenth centuries. Goethe, Schiller, Tieck, Heine, Wieland, and numerous other Germans have been studied for Cervantine influence on their plots, characters, or technique.

Russia, too, was affected by the *Quijote*, especially in the nineteenth century. Pushkin, Gogol, and Dostoevski have frequently been pointed out as followers of Cervantes in their use of a multitude of characters, their presentation of an idealistic or eccentric hero, or their general approach to writing.

Various critics have examined the use of the *Quijote* by writers in the New World. In North America its effect on Brackenridge, Melville, and Twain has been frequently noted, and recently the story of the Knight has been successfully adapted to the stage in the lovely musical drama *Man of La Mancha*, by Dale Wasserman. In Latin America, the influence of Cervantes has been even greater. Critics have often pointed out the use of Cervantine material or techniques by such writers as Alberdi, Montalvo, Hernández, Sarmiento, Gallegos, and Güiraldes.

The reader will observe, also, that various articles deal with the effect of the *Quijote* on the literature of other countries, e.g., Italy, Greece, Portugal, Holland, Sweden, Rumania, Yugoslavia, and even China. The reader may thus conclude that the influence of the *Quijote* on later writing has been considerable. Cervantes' characters and episodic material have indeed been drawn upon in innumerable instances, and his ironic style has been imitated by many writers.

Unfortunately, however, many of the works here examined and summarized tend to focus on a limited area, such as the influence of one specific episode of the *Quijote* on a particular writer. To give the reader a broader picture of the overall impact of Cervantes' masterpiece, we have been careful to set up, at the beginning, a section devoted to the general importance of the *Quijote* for world literature. The reader is particularly referred to those works which seek to determine the true contributions of Cervantes' masterpiece, why it is a lasting work, and why it was such an important step in the development of the modern novel: Robert Alter (8), Américo Castro (13), Dámaso Alonso (7), Harry Levin (21–22), Maurice Shroder (24), Leo Spitzer (25), Pedro Salinas (23), and Herman Wouk (28). Was it the universal or symbolic nature of his two protagonists? Was it the writer's new authorial attitude? Or, instead, was it that his masterpiece is the first imaginative treatment of everyday affairs? Was it his masterful use of details? Could it be that it was Cervantes' willingness to deal with basic moral and philosophical questions? Was Cervantes really the first to discover that the human being is a very complex creature? Was it the author's masterful depiction of a man struggling to fulfill himself in his environment? Could it instead have been Cervantes' skillful portrayal of the age-old problem of appearances and reality, or the description of the conflict between real life and the imagination? Could it have been his good-hearted humor? The reader will observe that there is by no means a unanimity of opinion on these fundamental questions.

We originally chose the post–1894 period as the time-span to be covered by this volume, as well as by the two previous volumes, because Leopoldo Rius (4), at the turn of the century, had already presented numerous excerpts from critical studies of the

Quijote up to 1894, or slightly thereafter. It was our intention, when we began, to adhere strictly to the year 1894 as the beginning date of our bibliographies. During the course of our ten-year investigation, however, we came across several interesting pre–1894 items which were not examined by Rius, and we have felt it proper to include such earlier items (whether or not noted by Rius) where they are helpful in completing a particular phase of our study. For example, D'Ovidio, in 1885, appears to have initiated the question of the influence of the *Quijote* on Manzoni. Hence D'Ovidio's work (210) is included in our section on Italy.

In regard to the stated cut-off date of 1970, let the following be said. This bibliographical series was begun in 1968, and at that time the year 1970 seemed a logical stopping point for our studies. However, as time went by and new material appeared, it became apparent that the termination date originally chosen for our earlier volumes would no longer be tenable. To adhere strictly to that date would have required the exclusion of such works as Gerhart Hoffmeister's *Spanien und Deutschland* (342), 1976, one of the most practical studies devoting attention to the influence of the *Quijote* in Germany.

We have endeavored to make this present volume as comprehensive and accurate as possible, using available bibliographical material. First, we have sought to include all leading works on the influence of the *Quijote* on the writers and critics of a given country. Secondly, we have attempted to present all leading works known to us on the adaptations of Cervantes' novel. Finally, it is our intention to offer here the numerous books, theses, and articles on the influence of *Don Quijote* on individual writers. We have not, however, attempted to include various items dealing with a particular translation of Cervantes' masterpiece. Also, various items have not been included because they were overly general in nature and did not add significantly to the subject. Other items we have no doubt merely overlooked. For such omissions we beg the reader's indulgence and hope that what we have included will be of some practical benefit to the investigator in search of material concerning the influence of *Don Quijote* on later writing.

For the convenience of the reader we have divided the material into several categories. First we present as an orientation to Cervantes' masterpiece a general section which crosses national boundaries and presents the overall influence of the *Quijote*, its numerous translations and adaptations, and various theories as to why it was of such significance to the present-day novel. Next we divide the material geographically, summarizing works which treat the influence of the *Quijote* in Spain, France, Italy, England, Germany, Russia, Latin America, and the United States. A final section discusses the Knight in other lands. These categories are subdivided, at times by century and at times by country. Where the material on a particular writer (e.g., Fielding) is very abundant, a special subcategory is provided. We hope the arrangement chosen will facilitate the study of a given problem. The subject index at the end of this volume may aid the student in locating additional citations to authors, themes, or works mentioned throughout this bibliography, where they would not normally be expected.

One final word regarding this meagre effort of ours: we approach the chosen theme with humility, realizing that no work of this nature can be complete. Again we ask the reader's indulgence for any oversight or other error which we have committed. Our best to you all in your study of the influence of the *sin par* Miguel de Cervantes Saavedra on later creative writing.

DANA B. DRAKE
Associate Professor of Spanish
Department of Foreign Languages
and Literatures
Virginia Polytechnic Institute
and State University
Blacksburg, Virginia 24061

EXPLANATORY NOTE

An effort has been made to summarize the material using the author's own words. Where an editorial paraphrase was necessary we have set the material off with brackets. In the bibliographical headnote itself we have sought to follow the system recommended by Kate L. Turabian in the fourth edition of *A Manual for Writers of Term Papers, Theses, and Dissertations*, 1973. In the case of certain articles summarized we have been unable to establish the month of publication or other bibliographical data.

DON QUIJOTE
IN WORLD LITERATURE

I.   *DON QUIJOTE* IN WORLD LITERATURE

Editions and Translations

1. Colón, Germán. *Die ersten romanischen und germanischen*
    Übersetzungen des "Don Quijote." Bern: Francke Ver-
    lag, 1974. Pp. 121.

    [Colón points out problems in translating the *Quijote*,
    especially with such words as "ingenioso." The early
    Italian, French, English, German, and Dutch versions
    are briefly discussed, and the strong points and weak-
    nesses of each version are noted. Chapter 16, Part I,
    of the *Quijote* is presented in the above languages, along
    with the original Spanish version of the 1605 *princeps*
    edition. At the end of this work the modern Catalan
    and modern Portuguese versions of Chapter 16, Part I,
    are set forth.]

2. Fitz Gerald, Thos. A. "Cervantes' Popularity Abroad."
    Modern Language Journal 32 (1948):171-178.

    [Fitz Gerald lists the editions of the *Quijote* in the
    various languages, noting, for example, that there are,
    as of the date of his article, 455 Spanish editions,
    394 English editions, 321 French editions, 76 German
    editions, 80 Italian editions, and 30 Dutch editions.
    He states that about 40 per cent of the Spanish editions
    were published outside of Spain, 85 having been printed
    in England or America.]

3. Palau y Dulcet, Antonio. *Manual del librero hispano-*
    americano. Vol. III (C-Comyn), pp. 391-471. Barce-
    lona-Madrid: A. Palau, 1950.

[Palau y Dulcet lists numerous editions of the *Quijote* and other Cervantine works, including translations. Critical comments on each edition are furnished.]

4. Rius y de Llosellas, Leopoldo. *Bibliografía crítica de las obras de Miguel de Cervantes Saavedra*. Madrid: M. Murillo, 1895-1905. 3 vols.

   [Rius' lengthy work presents not only translations but also adaptations and critical material.]

5. Simón Díaz, José. *Bibliografía de la literatura hispánica*. Volume VIII, pp. 3-442. Madrid: C.S.I.C., 1970.

   [Pages 17-19 of this work contain a list of the Spanish editions of Cervantes' complete works. Pages 27-84 list separate editions of the *Quijote*. Translations of Cervantes' works are presented at pages 144-254. Abundant critical material is also found in this volume, pages 314-397. The diffusion and influence of Cervantes' *obras* are examined by country, pp. 422-430. Several items listed here dealing with the impact of the *Quijote* on a particular country could not be located in time for summary and inclusion in our bibliography: (1) Langdarech, A.M. "Cervantes en la poesía centroamericana," in his *Estudios literarios*, pp. 222-234. San Salvador, 1959; (2) Barahona Vega, Clemente. *Cervantes en el Folklore chileno*. Santiago de Chile: Imp. San Buenaventura, 1915; (3) Guevara, Darío. *La sabiduría de Sancho en la novela ecuatoriana*. Quito: Talleres Gráficos "Minerva," 1965; (4) Iriazoz, Antonio, *Don Quijote en Francia*. 1960; (5) Thomas, Henry. "Inglaterra ante Miguel de Cervantes." *Escorial*, 2ª época, 19 (1949): 233 et seq.; (6) Vegas Castillo, M. "Cervantes y Don Quijote de la Mancha en el Perú." *La Peruanidad* 2 (1942):767-774; (7) Carmona, Ángel. "Rusia y el alma de Don Quijote." *La Jirafa*, núm. 9, pp. 1-14; (8) Pinski, Leonid. "Cervantes en Rusia." *Literatura Soviética*, núm. 4 (1966):175-181; (9) *Miguel de Cervantes Saavedra. Bibliografía de las obras traducidas al ruso y ensayos críticos, 1763-1957*. Moscow: Biblioteca de Estado de Literaturas Extranjeras de la U.R.S.S. Edit. de la Cámara del Libro, 1959. Pp. 130.]

6. Suñé Benages, Juan, and Suñé Fonbuena, Juan. *A Critical Bibliography of Editions of Don Quijote printed between 1605 and 1917 and continued down to 1937 by Suñé Benages and edited by J.D.M. Ford and C.T. Keller*.

Cambridge, Mass.: Harvard University Press, 1939.
Pp. xvii + 72.

[This item is summarized in Volume Two of this bibliography (item 311, pp. 203-204). The compilers of this
work furnish various tables prior to the main body of
the bibliography. One table is entitled "Resumen de las
Ediciones del *Quijote* publicadas desde 1605 hasta 1937,"
which lists the number of editions of *Don Quijote* in
each language. Another table indicates the cities in
which the Spanish editions were published, both inside
and outside Spain. Another table considers all the editions in all languages, and reveals that France has produced more editions, 316, than Spain, 311. The arrangement of the main body of the text is by the language in
which the edition is published. The arrangement within
each language is chronological. The "critical" element
varies from a brief skeletal reference to completely
detailed quotations.]

The Reasons for the *Quijote*'s Importance

7. Alonso, Dámaso. "La novela española y su contribución
   a la novela realista moderna." *Cuadernos del Idioma*,
   no. 1 (1965), pp. 17-43. [English version: "The
   Spanish Contribution to the Modern European Novel."
   Cahiers d'Histoire Mondiale 6 (1961):878-897.]

   [Dámaso Alonso traces the history of Spanish realism
   and points out the innovations of the *Cid*, *El Libro de
   Buen Amor*, the *Celestina*, *Tirante el Blanco*, and the
   Quijote. Under Cervantes' contributions the following
   are observed: (1) his realization that we are all mixed
   beings, and his generalization and universalization of
   his image of this alloy into two figures, the Knight and
   the Squire, a total representation of the human soul;
   (2) Cervantes brings *things*, details, into the novel to
   create an atmosphere of reality; (3) the masterful use
   of dialog, not only between two people but among several,
   each person revealing his personality as he speaks;
   (4) Cervantes' sense of humor, largely arising out of
   his use of mixed characters, is lightly joking, something
   unknown in the European novel of his day.]

8. Alter, Robert. *Partial Magic, The Novel as a Self-
   Conscious Genre.* Berkeley, Los Angeles and London:

University of California Press, 1975.   Pp. xvi + 248.
[See especially Chapter I: "The Mirror of Knighthood
and the World of Mirrors," pp. 1-29.]

The novel begins out of an erosion of belief in the
authority of the written word, and it begins with Cervantes. He was the first to see in the mere fictionality
of fictions the key to the predicament of a whole culture, and to use this awareness centrally in creating
a new fiction of his own. One measure of Cervantes'
genius is the fact that he is the initiator of both traditions of the novel; his juxtaposition of high-flown
literary fantasies with grubby actuality pointing the
way to the realists, his zestfully ostentatious manipu-
lation of the artifice he constructs setting a precedent
for all the self-conscious novelists to come.

The intuition of life that, beginning with Cervantes,
crystallized in the novel is profoundly paradoxical:
the novelist lucidly recognizes the ways man may be pain-
fully frustrated and victimized in a world with no fixed
values or ideals, without even a secure sense of what is
real and what is not, yet through the exercise of an
autonomous art the writer boldly asserts the freedom of
consciousness itself. The imagination, then, is alter-
nately, or even simultaneously, the supreme instrument
of human realization and the eternal snare of delusion
of a creature doomed to futility.

For Cervantes, as a fundamentally secular skeptic,
art is obviously questionable because it is understood
to be ultimately arbitrary, while nature is still more
problematic because it is so entrammeled with art, so
universally mediated by art, shaped by art's peculiar
habits of vision, that it becomes difficult to know
what, if anything, nature in and of itself may be. From
this point on, cultural creativity would proceed more
and more through a recapitulative critique of its own
past, and a major line of fiction would be avowedly
duplicitous, making the paradox of its magically real
duplicity one of its principal subjects. In these respects, Cervantes does not merely anticipate a later
mode of imagination but fully realizes its possibilities;
subsequent writers would only explore from different
angles the imaginative potentialities of a kind of fiction that he authoritatively conceived.

[In Alter's work there are numerous allusions to Cervantes' influence on particular writers, including
Sterne, Diderot, Faulkner, Proust, Virginia Woolf, Nabokov, Barth, Beckett, and Borges. For additional

comments by Alter on the nature of Cervantes' contributions to the novel, see item 274.]

9. Bailey, John. "Don Quixote: A Tercentenary Lecture."
    The Continuity of Letters, pp. 139-167. Oxford: The
    Clarendon Press, 1923.

    The language of the *Quijote* is easy, liberal, and at
    times ungrammatical. Cervantes, unlike Montaigne and
    others, writes for everyone, and his masterpiece, like
    Alice in Wonderland, appeals to all age groups for dif-
    ferent reasons. The *Quijote* begins the novel of ordi-
    nary life, the first imaginative treatment of ordinary
    life in prose as apart from drama and on a considerable
    scale. It presents a true picture of human nature, its
    weaknesses, its folly, its courage, its beauty, its wis-
    dom, its serious faith and inward glee. At times the
    Quijote shows the vanity of vanities, but there are mo-
    ments when the book fills us with a sense of the fine-
    ness of the quality of man's nature, a sense of life as
    a thing infinitely interesting and delightful, and not
    without some glimpses of the divine.
    Cervantes appeals to old age, whereas Shakespeare ap-
    peals to a younger reader. The Spaniard lacks the Eng-
    lish poet's depths and heights and is not as versatile.
    Cervantes is more orthodox in his religion than Shake-
    speare. The author of the *Quijote* was more like Sir
    Walter Scott in temperament and method. Both loved life,
    adventure, oddity, humor, goodness; both were fighters
    and patriots. Neither was interested in adventures of
    the spirit. Both sought the middle way, that of good
    sense, kindliness, and orthodoxy. Both took life, in
    the main, as they found it. Neither was a rebel, and
    neither was interested in pure speculation. Neither
    Cervantes nor Scott sought perfection of style like
    Flaubert or Henry James; neither sought the delicate
    and unerring felicity of Jane Austen. Both Scott and
    Cervantes broke rules and wrote carelessly; both were
    exuberant, moving like a great river, and like a great
    river sometimes overflowing its banks and out of its
    very exuberance producing lifeless floods and flat
    marshes. Both liked to mystify the reader, using fic-
    titious historians, a device which leads to humor. Yet
    Scott produced many characters, none of whom was great,
    while the Spaniard created two superb figures, the
    Knight and the Squire.

10. Blasco Ibáñez, Vicente. "La novela moderna." *Discursos
    literarios*, pp. 185-200. Valencia: Prometeo, 1966.

[Conferencia pronunciada en el teatro Odeón de Buenos
Aires en el año 1909.]

[The reason that Cervantes is eternal, states Blasco
Ibáñez, is that he found for his work, in a moment of
exaltation, the true representative type of humanity,
for in each of us there are two tendencies: high sentiments and perverse instincts; and Cervantes showed the
struggle between these two instincts before Pascal.]

11. Blasco Ibáñez, Vicente. "Cervantes." *Discursos litera-
     rios*, pp. 201-229. Valencia: Prometeo, 1966. [Con-
     ferencia pronunciada en el teatro Odeón de Buenos
     Aires en el año 1909.]

     [Blasco Ibáñez criticizes the false *cervantófilos*
     who have sought to show Cervantes to be all and to know
     all, instead of regarding him as what he was, a great
     novelist, which is enough for his glory. The reason
     for the continued importance of Shakespeare and Cervan-
     tes, states Blasco Ibáñez, is that they, and only they,
     were in contact with the people; both painted life in-
     tensely and created figures who passed to humanity; and
     Cervantes was closer to the people than Shakespeare,
     since Cervantes wrote in a genre better known to the
     public.]

12. Booth, Wayne C. "The Self-Conscious Narrator in Comic
     Fiction Before *Tristram Shandy*." *PMLA* 67 (March 1952):
     163-185.

     [Booth concludes that the *Quijote* is really the first
     important novel using the self-conscious narrator. The
     critic finds that prior to Fielding the self-conscious
     narrator is rare in fiction: Jonathan Swift's *A Tale of
     a Tub*; Scarron's *Le roman bourgeois*; Congreve's *Incog-
     nita*; Marivaux's *Le paysan parvenu* and *Pharsamon*. Booth
     states that Fielding goes far beyond Cervantes in the
     use of the self-conscious narrator device in *Joseph
     Andrews* and *Tom Jones*, and that Fielding's *Charlotte
     Summers* is dominated by a persistently intruding nar-
     rator.]

13. Castro, Américo. "Españolidad y europeización del
     Quijote." Prólogo a la edición de *Don Quijote*, pp.
     v-lix. Mexico: Porrúa, 1960. [English version: "An
     Introduction to the *Quijote*," in *An Idea of History:
     Selected Essays of Américo Castro*, pp. 77-139. Edited
     by Stephen Gilman and Edmund L. King. With an

Introduction by Roy Harvey Pearce. Columbus, Ohio:
Ohio State University, 1977.]

[Castro notes the influence of the *Quijote* on Stendhal's
figure Julien Sorel in *Le rouge et le noir* (the effect
of literature on life). The critic suggests a similar
influence on Flaubert, Dostoevski, Galdós, Dickens, and
Ricardo Güiraldes (*Don Segundo Sombra*). The major portion of this prolog deals with the problem of existence
(of fulfilling oneself) as reflected in Cervantes' masterpiece. Also discussed is the *loco-cuerdo* theme used
in the *Quijote* and by later writers. Another major item
discussed here is the semitic influence on Spanish literature, and the tendency of semitic literature to picture both the inner and the outer man. The problem of
the "New Christians" in Spain is dealt with at length.
In various items summarized in Volume One of this
bibliography (items 62-74, pp. 74-84) Américo Castro
expresses an opinion as to the reasons for the importance of the *Quijote*. His major emphasis has been on
the fact that Cervantes' characters seem real, they pur-
sue their own goals, take cognizance of themselves, they
project themselves in all directions. The *Quijote* is
unique, the critic finds, because it reveals the inter-
dependence, the interreality, of the extrapersonal world
and of the process of its becoming incorporated into
the life of a person. Cervantes' characters, Castro observes, succeed in constructing their existence as their
own; they let their presence be known as individuals who
are unfolding before us in a state of being and becoming.
Earlier in his career Castro had felt that Cervantes'
joining the world of fantasy with the everyday world was
the step that led to the modern novel. The critic, in
his 1925 *Pensamiento de Cervantes*, also noted the theme
of "perspectivism" in the *Quijote*, which Castro found
to be an important motif. Later, in "Incarnation in
Don Quixote" and in other works, Castro found that the
true innovation of Cervantes' masterpiece lay in es-
tablishing as true that which is authentically inter-
laced with vital experience, not that which lies behind
oscillating appearances.]

14. Ellis, Havelock. "Don Quixote." *The Soul of Spain*,
    pp. 222-243. Boston: Houghton Mifflin Company, 1937.
    [First published in 1908, London: Archibald Constable
    & Company.]

    [This item was summarized in Volume One of this bib-
    liography (item 99, p. 100). Ellis considers the major

contribution of Cervantes to lie in the mingling of the
chivalresque with the picaresque, creating something altogether original, an instrument that is capable of
touching life at every point and presenting the serious
and the gay, the ideal and the real.]

15. Entwistle, William J. *Cervantes*. Oxford: Clarendon
    Press, 1940. Pp. 192.

    [This item is summarized at length in Volume One of
    this bibliography (item 100, pp. 100-102). Entwistle
    finds the worth of the *Quijote* to lie not in its plot or
    its narration, but in the revelation of the inner man.
    This, Entwistle finds, is the essential step from the
    medieval romance to the modern novel.]

16. Ghiano, Juan Carlos. *Cervantes novelista*. Buenos
    Aires: Ediciones Centurión, 1948. Pp. 97.

    [The critic states that Cervantes takes a position
    above his characters; he plays with them in order to
    depict them in their maximum humanity, a technique re-
    newed in the twentieth century by Pirandello, Kafka, and
    Joyce, each with his own procedures. Ghiano indicates
    that Cervantes' great contribution to the novel was the
    fact that he was conscious of his literary innovation,
    the creation of a new narrative reality resolved in the
    critical attitude of the author.]

17. Green, Otis H. "Lope and Cervantes: Peripeteia and
    Resolution." *The Literary Mind of Medieval and Ren-
    aissance Spain*, pp. 201-208; 252. Lexington, Ken-
    tucky: The University Press of Kentucky, 1970.

    [The critic finds that Lope's figures do not change
    while Cervantes' Don and his companions do. However,
    Green observes, both writers bring their characters
    back to a final perception of unchanging truth, of per-
    fectly "reliable" reality. Cervantes' literary tech-
    nique is dynamic, the critic concludes, and this is why
    Europe could not escape Spanish influence; it is because
    of its infinite flexibility that the *Quijote* belongs to
    the literature of all times and all nations.]

18. Gutiérrez-Noriega, Carlos. "La personalidad y el carác-
    ter en la obra de Cervantes." *Revista de Neuro-
    psiquiatría* 10 (1947):516-541.

    [This item is summarized in Volume One of this bibliog-
    raphy (item 138, pp. 128-129). The critic finds that

Cervantes' great contribution to literature was his creation of complex characters in whom there are conflicts between reason and belief, between blind obedience to principles and free will.]

19. Krutch, Joseph Wood. "Miguel de Cervantes." *Five Masters: A Study in the Mutations of the Novel*, pp. 63-105. New York: Cape & Smith, 1931.

   [This item is summarized at length in Volume One of this bibliography (item 167, pp. 149-150). Krutch states that Cervantes advanced the art of story-telling more than anyone else in literary history, because he sets forth the chief intellectual problems of his day and paints the realistic details of everyday life with unapproached fidelity. However, Krutch adds, Cervantes' main contribution to literature is three-dimensional fiction: his power to suggest the emotional and intellectual complexity of any series of events is the very essence of the art of the modern novel.]

20. Lebois, André. "La révolte des personnages: De Cervantès et Calderon à Raymond Schwab." *Littérature Comparée* 23 (1949):482-506.

   [Lebois concludes that Cervantes was the first to create the character who talks of himself as a character, who claims for himself an existence both real and literary, and who affirms his right not to be treated indifferently by the author. Thus, the critic finds, Cervantes is the forerunner of Pirandello in the presentation of autonomous characters. The use by Calderón of autonomous figures in *El gran teatro del mundo* is observed. Lebois further points out the appearance of such figures in works by later writers, including Pirandello, Unamuno, Schwab, Grau, and Capek. The critic suggests the influence of Schopenhauer, Kierkegaard, and Bergson on more recent users of the autonomous-character device.]

21. Levin, Harry. "The Example of Cervantes." In *Contexts of Criticism*, pp. 79-96. Cambridge, Mass.: Harvard University Press, 1957. [Reprinted in *Cervantes: A Collection of Critical Essays*, pp. 34-48. Edited by Lowry Nelson, Jr. Englewood Cliffs, N.J.: Prentice-Hall, Inc., 1969.]

   [This article is summarized in more detail in Volume One of this bibliography (item 171, pp. 152-153). Levin points out Cervantes' use of the theme of the effect

of fiction on the human mind, and states that this
device was the one way for fiction to attain the impres-
sion of truth. The critic also concludes that Cervantes,
in effect, created a new literary form by criticizing the
old form. The central idea of the *Quijote*, Levin finds,
was the single pattern of art embarrassed by nature.

Levin suggests the influence of the Ginés de Pasamonte
episode on Gide's *The Counterfeiters* and on Thomas Mann's
Confessions of Felix Krull.

The use in the *Quijote* of the fictitious narrator device, Levin implies, may have been of influence on Sir
Walter Scott, Stendhal, and Manzoni. The general anti-
romantic tone of Cervantes' masterpiece, the critic indicates, was of influence on Charles Sorel's *Anti-roman,
ou le berger extravagant*, on Fielding's novels such as
Joseph Andrews and *Tom Jones*, and on Jane Austen's *Northanger Abbey*. Levin also notes the use of quixotic figures
by Flaubert (Mme Bovary) and by Dostoevski (Prince Myshkin).]

22.   Levin, Harry. "The Quixotic Principle: Cervantes and
      Other Novelists." In *The Interpretation of Narrative:
      Theory and Practice*, pp. 45-66. Edited by Morton W.
      Bloomfield. Cambridge, Mass.: Harvard University
      Press, 1970. [Translated into Spanish as "Cervantes,
      el quijotismo y la posteridad," in *Suma Cervantina*,
      pp. 377-396. Edited by J.B. Avalle-Arce and E.C. Riley.
      London: Tamesis Books Limited, 1973.]

      [This work is summarized in Volume Two of this bibliog-
      raphy (item 179, page 123). The critic states:] What
      should concern us is not so much the direct line of Cer-
      vantes' impact on later writers but the basic process
      which he discovered and its wider employment, which I
      shall call the quixotic principle: the tragicomic irony
      of the conflict between real life and the romantic imagi-
      nation, or the rivalry between the real world and the
      representation that we make of it for ourselves. It
      would be a mistake to believe that the quixotic principle
      is a negative one simply because it operates through dis-
      illusionment. Rather, it is a register of development,
      an index of maturation. The *Quijote*, as Georg Lukács
      stated in 1916 (*Die Theorie des Romans*), is the crucial
      link in the chain of narrative extending from the ancient
      epic to the modern *Bildungsroman*, wherein the subjectivity
      of the individual develops into an ironic overview of
      life. [Levin's article contains a detailed analysis of
      numerous writers who have applied the quixotic principle,

as well as a general history of the novelistic adaptations and imitations of Cervantes' novel.]

23. Salinas, Pedro. "Lo que le debemos a Don Quijote."
    Revista Nacional de Cultura Moderna, no. 10 (1947),
    pp. 97-109. [See also "Cervantes" in Salinas' *Ensayos
    de literatura hispánica*, pp. 77-147. Madrid: Aguilar,
    1958. For an abbreviated English text see "Don Quixote
    and the Novel." *The Nation*, 20 December 1947, pp.
    682-683.]

    [The ideas of Salinas were summarized in Volume Two of
    this bibliography (items 287 and 288, pp. 189-191). He
    states:] What do we owe to the *Quijote* today? First, a
    new conception of the novel, the "summa" novel, a novel
    that brings together all the aspirations of man, all of
    man's thoughts, into a majestic and proud body. The
    author not only unites the picaresque, the sentimental,
    and the chivalresque, but does so in such a way as to
    produce a work of wider vision that includes many points-
    of-view. Cervantes also produces a social novel, the
    story of the infinite possibilities in man's relationship
    with his society. The *Quijote* also is a symbolical
    novel, a novel of transcendental reality that goes beyond
    the events, the plot, and the characters. The *Quijote*,
    in its dual-hero in one, gives us a vision of human na-
    ture which includes the best and the worst. Cervantes
    presents us with a work in which the hero seeks to find
    a balance with others and with himself, a characteristic
    of the novel of today. Finally, we owe to the *Quijote* a
    work in which we are invited at every turn to exercise
    our freedom in deciding who is right and who is wrong,
    who is sane and who is insane.

24. Shroder, Maurice Z. "The Novel as a Genre." In *The
    Theory of the Novel*, pp. 13-29. Edited by Philip Ste-
    vick. New York: The Free Press, 1967. [Reprinted
    from *The Massachusetts Review* 9 (1963):291-308.]

    [This item is summarized in some detail in Volume One
    of this bibliography (item 285, pp. 236-238). Shroder
    finds that the theme that has dominated the novel from
    Don Quijote onward is the passage from a state of inno-
    cence to a state of experience, from that ignorance which
    is bliss to a mature recognition of the actual way of
    the world. The modern novel, Shroder finds, deals with
    the distinction between reality and appearances, a theme
    developed in Cervantes' masterpiece.]

25. Spitzer, Leo. "On the Significance of *Don Quijote*."
     Modern Language Notes 77 (1962):113-129. [Also found
     in *Cervantes: A Collection of Critical Essays*, pp. 82-
     97. Edited by Lowry Nelson, Jr. Englewood Cliffs,
     N.J.: Prentice-Hall, Inc., 1969.]

     [This item is summarized at some length in Volume One
     (item 290, pp. 241-242) of our bibliography. Spitzer
     finds that behind Cervantes' perspectivism there is or-
     der. Later writers, states the critic, do not stop at
     proclaiming the inanity of the world; they go so far as
     to doubt the existence of any universal order and, when
     imitating Cervantes' perspectivism (Gide, Proust, Conrad,
     Joyce, Virginia Woolf, Pirandello) they fail to sense the
     unity behind perspectivism--so that, in their hands,
     sometimes the personality of the author himself is al-
     lowed to disintegrate. Spitzer also notes the influence
     of Cervantes on Flaubert and others in the use of the
     theme of outworn literature. The critic regards Cervan-
     tes as the creator of the modern critical novel which
     expanded in the nineteenth century to a criticism not
     only of prior literature but of whole civilizations.
     Yet, Spitzer adds, Cervantes balanced the critical with
     the beauty of the fabulous; he did not create an anti-
     novel in its pure form.]

26. Vianna Moog, Clodomir. *Heróis da decadência: Petrônio,
     Cervantes, Machado de Assis*. 2nd edition. Rio de
     Janeiro, 1964. Pp. 143. [First edition, 1939.]

     [This work contains a brief preface and an introduction
     on the subject of humor and its various forms. Renan,
     Dickens, and Cervantes are described as mystic humorists.
     Vianna Moog believes that humor is a late historical de-
     velopment, and that there was no true humor in the clas-
     sic and medieval epochs. Cervantes is discussed under
     the heading of the decadence of the Middle Ages, the de-
     cline of the institution of chivalry. The critic finds
     that Cervantes' contribution to humor was the presenta-
     tion of the conflict between idealism and reality. Cer-
     vantes' humor, states Vianna Moog, has infinite subjecti-
     vism, containing pity and self-mortification.]

27. Willis, Raymond S. "Sancho Panza: Prototype for the
     Modern Novel." *Hispanic Review* 37 (April 1969):207-227.

     Sancho Panza is more "modern" than Don Quijote. The
     Knight becomes insane and generates his own faith, while
     Sancho has only a second-hand faith, like the novelistic

figures of today: creatures who are prey to doubt, discouragement, and vacillation. The Squire blunderingly stands on the side of faith, while at the same time he unconsciously defines the equivocal nature of human truth with his ludicrous word "basi-helmet." That is, he must see that the basin is a basin, yet believe it is a helmet, if, logically, he is to be able to keep the harness. In a sense, Cervantes, through Sancho, bequeathed to every modern novelist his central theme and preoccupation: the plight of modern man, the man of human dimensions, who is a stranger to himself, an exile in his own land, an alien to his own times, trying to forge an authentic existence within these impossible circumstances. [This item is summarized in Volume One of this bibliography (item 318, p. 264).]

28. Wouk, Herman. "You, Me, and the Novel." *Saturday Review*, 29 June 1974, pp. 8-13.

The novel that you and I know, that living authors of fiction try to write, first takes shape in *Don Quijote*, as an attack on non-realistic literature. Cervantes offered the reader the real world and showed it to be more amusing, more diverting, more entertaining than fables. That was the first thing that he did: to move the narrative art from the world of Amadís de Gaula into everyday reality.

Secondly, Cervantes moved the art away from high life and the beautiful people to all life and to all people.

It should be noted that the author of the *Quijote* had a go at the theatre, a crowd-pleasing medium. But Cervantes, like other novelists, failed as a playwright. Instead, he went on to devise a new form, big enough and loose enough to give reign to his creative force, and created a stage as big as all of Spain. His third contribution, thus, is that he broke out from the rigid, conventional form of crowd pleasing, the theatre, into a freer, broader form retaining the popular charm of dramaturgy.

[Wouk notes the influence of the *Quijote* on such writers as Walter Scott and Charles Dickens. The critic also traces the novel forward to our times, noting the tendency away from amusement toward challenge and protest, to the presentation of a world coming apart, which tendency Wouk traces back to the later novels of Dickens.]

The Critical Reception of the *Quijote*

29. Efron, Arthur. "Satire Denied: A Critical History of
    English and American Don *Quijote* Criticism." Ph.D.
    dissertation, University of Washington, 1964. Pp. 557.
    [Extensively revised and published as *Don Quixote and
    the Dulcineated World*. Austin, Texas: University of
    Texas Press, 1971. Pp. x + 203.]

    [This item was summarized in Volume One of this bibliog-
    raphy (item 96, pp. 98-99). Efron traces the various
    English and American interpretations of the *Quijote* and
    finds them lacking. The critic regards Cervantes' master-
    piece as a deep satire of idealism and of Western values.
    A lengthy bibliography is included.]

30. Icaza, Francisco A. de. *El "Quijote" durante tres siglos*.
    Madrid: Renacimiento, 1918. Pp. 229.

    [Icaza's work was summarized in Volume One of this
    bibliography (item 157, pp. 140-141). While this item
    contains few corroborating footnotes, it constitutes an
    excellent outline of attitudes toward the *Quijote* over
    the centuries. The first chapter examines the views of
    Cervantes' contemporaries. Chapters II through X study
    the reception of Cervantes' masterpiece in England,
    France, Germany, Italy, Portugal, Spanish America, Spain,
    the United States, and Russia. Chapter XI examines the
    attitudes toward the *Quijote* in the early twentieth
    century.]

31. Meier, Harri. "Zur Entwicklung der europäiochen Quijote-
    Deutung." *Romanische Forschungen* 54 (1940):227-264.

    [This item was summarized at length in Volume One of
    this bibliography (item 195, pp. 169-171). It discusses
    not only the English and French views of the *Quijote* but
    deals with the various threads of German interpretation
    in the eighteenth, nineteenth, and twentieth centuries.]

32. Meregalli, Franco. "Profilo storico della critica cervan-
    tina nel settecento," Stratto da *Rappresentazione ar-
    tistica e rappresentazione scientifica nel "Secolo dei
    Lumi."* Firenze: Sansoni, 1971, pp. 187-210. [Sum-
    marized by Alberto Sánchez in *Anales Cervantinos* 13-14
    (1974-1975):196-197. The original could not be ob-
    tained.]

    [Meregalli presents a general summary of eighteenth-
    century European criticism of Cervantes' works, and
    points out editions of Cervantes' masterpiece in various

languages. The reception of the *Quijote* in England and Germany is dealt with in certain detail.]

33. ´ Meregalli, Franco. "Cervantes nella critica romantica tedesca (Stato degli studi)," Stratto da *Annali della Facoltà di Lingue e Letterature Stranieri di ca' Foscari, Università degli Studi di Venezia, Paideia* 11, 2 (1972):381-395. [Summarized by Alberto Sánchez in *Anales Cervantinos* 13-14 (1974-1975):197-198. The original could not be obtained.]

[This article is a continuation of the previous item ("Profilo storico ..."). The critic notes two currents of *Quijote* criticism in the eighteenth century: (1) the neoclassical (largely French) view that Cervantes' novel was a funny book, an attack on madness in the name of reason; (2) the English view, continued by the Germans, which emphasizes the humanity of quixotic madness and regards the *Quijote* as a book of friendly irony toward something in all of us.]

34. Petriconi, H. "Kritik und Interpretation des *Quijote*." *Die Neueren Sprachen* 34 (1926):329-342.

[This article was summarized in Volume One of this bibliography (item 234, p. 198). It deals basically with the changes in the philosophical interpretation of Cervantes' masterpiece, rather than with its influence on writers of fiction. The sympathetic interpretation of the *Quijote* by Samuel Johnson is discussed to a certain degree.]

35. Predmore, Richard L. "La apoteosis de *Don Quijote*." *Revista de Filología Hispánica* 1 (1939):262-264.

[Predmore notes that Turgenev ("Hamlet y Don Quijote," 1860) regarded the Don as a Christ-like figure, and that Enrique Rodó continued this tendency in his "El Cristo a la jineta" (1906). Unamuno, the critic states, also found a divine element in Cervantes' hero, and Rubén Darío's "Letanías de Nuestro Señor Don Quijote" is an additional example of the tendency to deify the Knight of La Mancha. This item is summarized in Volume One of this bibliography (item 236, p. 199).]

36. Quilter, Daniel Edward. "The Image of the *Quijote* in the Seventeenth Century." Ph.D. dissertation, University of Illinois, 1962. Pp. vii + 327.

[This item is summarized in Volume One of this bibliography (item 241, pp. 202-203). Part I of this thesis deals with critical interpretations of the *Quijote* in

Spain, and also with the general reception of that novel
by readers. In the latter portion of this first part is
an examination of the Spanish dramatic and nondramatic
interpretations of Cervantes' masterpiece. Two plays by
Guillén de Castro are particularly studied, as well as
Quevedo's poem *El testamento de Don Quijote* and two
stories by Salas Barbadillo. Quilter finds that the influence of the *Quijote* on nondramatic literature is significantly less than that on the theatre. Part II of
Quilter's thesis is concerned with the reception of Cervantes' masterpiece outside of Spain. Chapters VI through
VIII discuss the *Quijote* in France, England, and other
European countries. "Appendix C" is an alphabetical list
of imitations of the *Quijote* in seventeenth-century
Spain.]

37. Real de la Riva, César. "Historia de la crítica e in-
     terpretación de la obra de Cervantes." *Revista de
     Filología Española* 32 (1948):107-150.

     [This item was summarized in Volume One of this bib-
     liography (item 243, pp. 204-205). Real de la Riva traces
     the Spanish and non-Spanish interpretations of Cervantes'
     works (especially of the *Quijote*) from the seventeenth
     century to the date of his article. Particular attention
     is devoted to English and German attitudes toward Cer-
     vantes' masterpiece.]

38. Rodríguez, Antonio. "*El Quijote* visto por grandes escri-
     tores." *Biblioteca enciclopédica popular*, 2ª época,
     núm. 179 (1947):1-93.

     [Rodríguez presents essays by Menéndez y Pelayo ("Cul-
     tura literaria de Miguel de Cervantes y elaboración del
     Quijote"), by Miguel de Unamuno (Chapters II, XII, XIII,
     and LXXIV of *Vida de Don Quijote y Sancho*), by Ramiro de
     Maeztu (Chapters IV and V of *Don Quijote o el amor*), by
     Ivan Turgenev ("Hamlet y Don Quijote"), by Salvador de
     Madariaga (excerpts from the chapter "El verdadero Don
     Quijote" in *Guía del lector del Quijote*), and by Thomas
     Mann (an excerpt from "A bordo con Don Quijote"). Also,
     brief remarks about the *Quijote* by other well-known
     writers are given, including Dostoevski, Goethe, Heine,
     Schelling, Schopenhauer, Tieck, and Ortega y Gasset.]

39. Schevill, Rudolph. "Three Centuries of *Don Quixote*."
     University of California Chronicle 15 (1913):181-206.

[Schevill briefly notes the changes that have taken place in the critical interpretation of the *Quijote*. The critic finds that in present times Cervantes' novel is esteemed because of its sympathetic interpretation of human nature, its comprehensive picture of the life of men and of society. Schevill discusses Cervantes' times in some detail, and examines the circumstances surrounding the composition of Cervantes' novel: the background of books of chivalry, pastoral tales, and picaresque novels. Cervantes' main contribution to literature, the critic finds, was that he remoulded existing literature into a different form "and by a happy combination created something novel, yet of a popular stamp."
Schevill finds a general absence of plan in the 1605 *Quijote* and a lack of polish, at times, in the style. The critic discusses Cervantes' humor at length, noting its general lack of malice.]

The Influence of the *Quijote* on the Later Novel

40. Adams, Robert M. "Two Lines from Cervantes." *Strains of Discord: Studies in Literary Openness*, pp. 73-104. Ithaca, N.Y.: Cornell University Press, 1958.

[Adams notes a "Cervantes tradition" among later writers and compares and contrasts in some detail the *Quijote*, Flaubert's *Madame Bovary*, and Stendhal's *Le rouge et le noir*. Other writers such as André Gide and Aldous Huxley are briefly discussed.]

41. Avalle-Arce, Juan Bautista. "Don Quijote, o la vida como obra de arte." *Cuadernos Hispanoamericanos*, núm. 242 (February 1970):247-280.

[This item was summarized at some length in Volume One of this bibliography (item 16, pp. 38-39). Avalle-Arce concludes that in the penance episode Don Quijote commits the first gratuitous act in literature when he imitates Amadís. This, the critic finds, leads later to Dostoevski's Raskolnikov, who explores the gratuitous act, and to Gide's Wluiki and Camus' Meursault, who commit senseless murders.]

42. Borbón, La Infanta María de la Paz. *Buscando las huellas de Don Quijote*. Freiburg in Breisgau: B. Herder, 1905. Pp. 96.

[This work is the Infanta's contribution to the 300th
anniversary of the publication of the *Quijote*. She mentions her first reading of Cervantes' masterpiece as a
child in Switzerland, and states that she received a
copy of the 1859 Gorchs edition (with illustrations by
Doré) as a wedding gift. The principal matter discussed
in the Infanta's work is the various editions of the
Quijote (largely non-Spanish editions). From time to
time, observations of critics are noted, as is the influence of Cervantes' masterpiece on later literature,
especially on the theatre. María de la Paz Borbón points
out (pp. 20-21) a poem by Frenzel in 1860 in which Shakespeare and Cervantes are contrasted. At pp. 22-23, a
similar contrast by Tolstoi is mentioned.]

43. Campos, Jorge. *Cervantes y el Quijote*. Madrid: Edicio-
     nes "La Ballesta," 1959. Pp. 170.

     [Chapter Nine of this work is concerned with the gene-
     ral influence of the *Quijote* on world literature and on
     such writers as Gogol, Melville, Swift, Daudet, Fielding,
     and Mark Twain. Movie adaptations of Cervantes' master-
     piece are briefly discussed.]

44. Clavería, Carlos. "Les mythes et les thèmes espagnols
     dans la littérature universelle." *Cahiers d'Histoire
     Mondiale* 6 (1961):969-989.

     [The influence of the *Quijote* in eighteenth-century
     England is examined, as is the interpretation of that
     work by German Romanticists. The critic finds that
     Goethe's *Wilhelm Meister* is similar in form and theme to
     Cervantes' novel. The influence of the *Quijote* on Flau-
     bert, Gogol, and Dostoevski is briefly noted.]

45. Conner, John Joseph. "The Quixotic Novel from the Point
     of View of the Narrative." Ph.D. dissertation, The
     University of Florida, 1977. Pp. 267. [Based on the
     summary found in *Dissertation Abstracts International*,
     Vol. 38A, no. 11 (May 1978):6700-6701.]

     [Conner studies the narrative system of several novels
     which he defines as quixotic: *Moby Dick* (Melville);
     Madame Bovary (Flaubert); *Middlemarch* (George Eliot); and
     The Great Gatsby (F. Scott Fitzgerald). The critic
     states:] The narratives of the later quixotic novels
     seem to be linked to each other and to the *Quijote* by
     their connection to an abstract substratum, a narrative
     system which is too complex to be fully described but

which can be identified. Certain narrative elements
found in the narrative system of the *Quijote* reappear in
each of the later novels. These "mobile fragments" take
different configurations in each of the novels, but by
studying these configurations we are able to compare the
novels and perceive how narrative structure engenders
meaning in the five novels.

46. Durán, Manuel. *Cervantes*. New York: Twayne Publishers,
    Inc., 1974. Pp. 189.

    [In Chapter IX, "Cervantes Across the Centuries: A
    Summation" (pp. 172-179), the critic presents a general
    discussion of the influence of the *Quijote*. Durán ob-
    serves that English novelists of the eighteenth century
    drew upon two aspects of the *Quijote*, the social satire
    and the psychological insights, and concludes that the
    English novel is born under the influence of Cervantes.
    The critic finds this to be logical, since the Age of En-
    lightenment was also the Age of Satire, and Cervantes
    offered an excellent example of satire in the novel.
    The use of the *Quijote* by Smollett, Sterne, and Fielding
    is noted. The reception of Cervantes' masterpiece by
    German Romanticists and by Italian and Russian writers
    is discussed. Durán briefly points out the influence of
    the *Quijote* on Alphonse Daudet's *Tartarin de Tarascon*,
    Dickens' *Pickwick Papers*, Dostoevski's *The Idiot*,
    Flaubert's *Madame Bovary*, Herman Melville's *Moby Dick*,
    and Mark Twain's *Huckleberry Finn*.]

47. Farinelli, Arturo. "España y su literatura en el extran-
    jero a través de los siglos." *La Lectura; revista de
    ciencias y artes* 1 (October 1901):523-542; 1 (December
    1901):834-849. [Also in Farinelli's *Ensayos y discur-
    sos de crítica literaria hispano-europea*. Vol. 1, pp.
    45-108. Rome: Fratelli Treves, 1925. See also Fari-
    nelli's *Divagaciones hispánicas*. Vol. 1, pp. 11-51.
    Barcelona: Bosch, 1936.]

    [The critic states that at least six English plays of
    seventeenth-century England were based on *The Curious Im-
    pertinent*. The influence of the *Quijote* on such eigh-
    teenth-century English novelists as Fielding and Smollett
    is briefly noted. Farinelli finds that various German
    writers, from Gerstenberg, Lessing, Wieland, and Herder,
    from Goethe, Jean Paul Friedrich Richter, Gottfried Kel-
    ler, and Paul Heyse, all owe part of their education to
    the *Quijote*. The critic concludes that the Cervantes
    cult even reached the point of idolatry in England and

Germany. (Pages 844-849 contain a basic bibliography on
the influence of the *Quijote* on world literature).]

48. Fürst, Rudolf. "Don Quijote=Spuren in der Weltliteratur."
     Allgemeine Zeitung, Beilage 61 (16 March 1898), pp. 3-8.

     [Fürst traces the use of the theme of madness due to
     excess reading of non-realistic literature, from the
     Quijote to Goethe's *Triumph der Empfindsamkeit*, 1778.
     The works of Charles Sorel (*Le berger extravagant*),
     Pierre Marivaux (*Pharsamon*), Jacques Cazotte (*La belle
     par accident*), Charlotte Lennox (*The Female Quixote*),
     Wieland (*Don Sylvio von Rosalva*), Johann Musäus (*Grandi-
     son der Zweite*), and Johann Gottwerth Müller (*Siegfried
     von Lindenberg*) are briefly discussed. Fürst observes
     that the heroes remain uncured in the *Quijote* (until
     deathbed) and in Goethe's play, but are brought back to
     reality in the intervening works.]

49. Hazard, Paul. "La fortuna de Don Quijote en la litera-
     tura europea." *Boletín del Instituto de las Españas*
     (superseded by *Revista Hispánica Moderna*), no. 11
     (1934), pp. 65-67.

     [Hazard discusses the initial popularity of the *Qui-
     jote* and its spread to the rest of Europe and to the New
     World. The critic observes a decline in popularity of
     the *Quijote* after the middle of the seventeenth century,
     and attributes this decline to the new dominance of
     French culture. The beginnings of the pessimistic inter-
     pretation of Cervantes' novel are pointed out briefly:
     the *Quijote* becomes an attack on the chivalresque spirit
     and nobility of heart, qualities that had made Spain
     great. Hazard describes the triumph of the *Quijote* in
     England at the end of the seventeenth and beginning of
     the eighteenth century, and finds that the English re-
     garded the story as humorous, not burlesque. The critic
     briefly notes the influence of the *Quijote* on the humor
     of Fielding's *Tom Jones*. The spread of the *Quijote*
     through French translations and abbreviated editions is
     pointed out. Hazard observes the conversion of the *Qui-
     jote* into a serious book by the German Romanticists, and
     asserts that this group held the story to be a work full
     of symbols and loaded with philosophy; it became a sad
     book, a metaphysical book, an idea spread by Sismondi in
     his *L'histoire des littératures du midi de l'Europe*.
         The critic briefly alludes to scholarly and erudite
     studies of the *Quijote* and of Cervantes in the nineteenth
     century, and mentions the increase in children's editions

of Cervantes' novel. The twentieth-century interpretation of the *Quijote* by Américo Castro (*El pensamiento de
Cervantes*, 1925) is examined: the tendency to regard it
as a compendium of knowledge and ideas left by the Renaissance, and as a book of personal psychology. Hazard concludes that the fact that the interpretation of the *Quijote* is still changing is an indication of its greatness.]

50. Hazard, Paul. *Don Quichotte de Cervantès; Étude et
analyse.* Paris: Editions Mellottée, 1949. Pp. 378.
[First published in 1931, Paris: Mellottée.]

[Paul Hazard's well-known work was summarized briefly
in Volume One of this bibliography (item 149, p. 136).
The sixth and final part of this work ("Au cours des
siècles") is a general discussion of the editions, translations, adaptations, and critical interpretations of
the *Quijote*. Note is made of the theatrical adaptations
of the *Quijote* in England by Beaumont and Fletcher, its
use by Samuel Butler in his *Hudibras*, and its influence
on eighteenth-century English novelists such as Fielding,
Sterne, and Smollett. The effect of the *Quijote* on
French writers and dramatists is observed: Sorel, Marivaux, Guérin de Bouscal; and on Russian writers such as
Gogol, Turgenev, and Dostoevski. The varying interpretations of the *Quijote* over the centuries are outlined:
the comic interpretation, the humorous interpretation,
the pessimistic interpretation, and the several symbolical approaches.

Appendix I (pp. 363-364) briefly notes French translations of Cervantes' masterpiece. Appendix II (pp. 364-
365) presents basic bibliographical material on the *Quijote* and its interpretation. Appendix III (pp. 366-369)
is a bibliographical aid in the study of the fortune of
the *Quijote* at the hands of critics and adaptors.]

51. Matthews, Brander. "Cervantes, Zola, Kipling & Co."
Aspects of Fiction and Other Ventures in Criticism,
pp. 236-255. 3rd ed. enlarged. New York: Charles
Scribner's Sons, 1902. [First published in 1896, New
York: Harper & Brothers.]

[Matthews briefly discusses the influence of the figure
Don Quijote on such characters as Fielding's Parson
Adams, Goldsmith's Dr. Primrose, Dickens' Mr. Pickwick,
Irving's "Knickerbocker," Twain's Tom Sawyer, Scott's
Antiquary, and Daudet's Tartarin de Tarascon.]

52. Mitchell, Jack. "Concepts of Reality in Cervantes' *Don
     Quixote*, Flaubert's *Madame Bovary*, Dostoevsky's *The
     Idiot*, and Barth's *The Sot-Weed Factor*." Ph.D. disser-
     tation, University of Redlands, 1971. Pp. vi + 156.

     Cervantes initiates the novelistic study of the nature
     of reality as the difficult relation between the knower
     and the known. He finds that the imagination operates to
     control the way one organizes his experiences. The au-
     thor of the *Quijote* appears to have doubts about the re-
     lation between experiences and the supporting reality,
     and he sees the gamelike quality of human existence.
     Nevertheless, Cervantes is basically committed to dualis-
     tic Christianity, good and evil. Flaubert and Dostoevski
     are not playful but make decisive choices within the tra-
     ditional dualism. They are not so concerned with the sub-
     tleties of the problem of reality as they are with de-
     ciding on solutions to it. John Barth looks upon the
     statement of moral, epistemological, and theological
     problems in dualistic terms as unsatisfactory and obso-
     lete. He solves the problem proposed by Cervantes by
     destroying it. Barth avoids the serious solution-oriented
     acceptance of dualistic thought-patterns which character-
     ize *Madame Bovary* and *The Idiot* and picks up the Cervan-
     tean comic sense, developing the perspectivism of the
     Quijote into a non-dualistic and relativistic concept of
     reality in *The Sot-Weed Factor*. [Mitchell notes, from
     time to time, the use by these later writers of Cervan-
     tine devices. For example, the critic points out Barth's
     use of interpolated episodes to illustrate a particular
     idea about reality.]

53. Outumuro, María de las Mercedes. "Sentido y perspectiva
     del personaje autónomo." *Cuadernos Hispanoamericanos*
     72 (October 1967):158-177.

     [Outumuro discusses Cervantes' freeing of his charac-
     ters in Part II of the *Quijote*, and points out that they
     even discuss Part I, a work in which they themselves par-
     ticipate. The result, states the critic, is that the
     Knight and Squire seem true, the only ones responsible
     for their destiny; and the author, like any historian,
     is reduced to telling of their lives and adventures.
     Outumuro notes the use of the autonomous character tech-
     nique by Galdós, Unamuno, Gide, Cerretani, and Gómez Bas.]

54. Palacín Iglesias, Gregorio B. *El Quijote en la literatura
     universal*. Madrid: Leira, 1965. Pp. 70.

[This item is summarized in Volume One of this bibliography (item 236, p. 193). It is a very general study of the influence of the *Quijote* on world literature. The first chapter sets forth opinions on the *Quijote* by famous critics; Chapter II discusses the diffusion of Cervantes' masterpiece; Chapter III examines the influence of the *Quijote* on European writers; the fourth chapter briefly studies the use of Cervantes' masterpiece by North American writers; in the final short chapter Palacín praises the *Quijote* as a book of inspiration.]

55. Parker, J.H. "Influencia del *Quijote* en el extranjero." *Revista Universidad de San Carlos* 7 (1947):57-73.

[Parker's essay is divided into four brief parts: translations, illustrations, adaptations, and criticism. Under translations Parker particularly notes Shelton's English version of Part I of *Don Quijote* in 1612, and of Part II in 1620. Oudin's French version of Part I in 1614, and Rosset's French translation of Part II, are commented upon. Parker also points out Franciosini's Italian translation in 1622, the Dutch version of 1657 by Bos, the Russian translation by Osipov in 1769, and the Danish version of 1776 by Biehl. The critic gives particular attention to Ludwig Tieck's German translation, Filleau de Saint-Martin's French version (in which the ending is modified), and Motteux's English rendering of 1700.
Under illustrations of the *Quijote* Parker mentions the drawings found in the second English edition of 1617 and the twenty-five sketches by Coypel in the eighteenth century. As regards adaptations, Parker gives attention to the 1609 French version of the Marcela episode, Sorel's *Le berger extravagant*, and Butler's *Hudibras*. Other works probably influenced by the *Quijote*, Parker states, are Swift's *Tale of a Tub*, Fielding's *Joseph Andrews*, Marivaux's *Pharsamon*, Smollett's *Sir Launcelot Greaves*, and Daudet's *Tartarin de Tarascon*.
The criticism of the *Quijote* by Englishmen is briefly discussed, beginning with Motteux in 1700, continuing through Bowle, 1781, and up to Fitzmaurice-Kelly in the twentieth century. Among the French critics, Parker reserves particular praise for Sismondi, Sainte-Beuve, Morel-Fatio, and Foulché-Delbosc. A number of German critics are noted, such as Schelling, Bouterwek, Tieck, and Heine. Farinelli, Mele, and Cantù, among the Italians, and Turgenev among the Russians, are noted with interest; and the North Americans Ticknor, Prescott, and

Schevill are especially commended for their contributions
to the study of Cervantes and his works.]

* Rius y de Llosellas, Leopoldo. *Bibliografía crítica de
   las obras de Miguel de Cervantes Saavedra.* Madrid:
   M. Murillo, 1895-1905. 3 vols. Cited above as item 4.

   [These three excellent volumes contain a discussion of
   the editions of Cervantes' works and the critical comments about them. Volume II, Chapters IV through VI,
   lists and describes imitations of Cervantes' works.
   Chapter IV is concerned with the *Quijote.*]

56. Robert, Marthe. "Toujours Don Quichotte." *Sur le
   papier*, pp. 7-44. Paris: B. Grasset, 1967.

   Don Quijote is the prototype of the theologian of literature who believes not only in the communicative power
   of the written truth but subordinates all to the accom-
   plishment of his mission. The novel is in effect quixotic to the extent that the hero believes that writing has
   an indefinable, yet certain, relationship to reality, to
   such an extent that he is capable of saying and doing
   something outside the paper to which he is consigned.
   And having this gift, it is his right and duty to stir,
   teach, and agitate life, and thereby change it. All
   novels strictly speaking have the Don's sublime innocence, and all novelists make (at least implicitly) the
   art of writing an act of mystically efficient faith. It
   is not by chance that the Quijote figures multiply in the
   nineteenth century, when the novel feels itself the most
   adapted genre for reflecting the course of things and of
   correcting them: Balzac, Stendhal, George Sand, Zola,
   Maupassant, Oscar Wilde, Gogol, Tolstoy, Kafka. [From
   pages 24-25.]

             Theatrical, Poetic, and Cinematographic
                 Interpretations of the *Quijote*

57. Babinger, Georg. "Die Wanderungen und Wandelungen der
   Novelle von Cervantes *El curioso impertinente* mit
   spezieller Untersuchung von Brosses *Le curieux impertinent.*" *Romanische Forschungen* 31 (1912):486-549.

   Guillén de Castro's play *El curioso impertinente*
   (published in 1618) is the first play truly based on

Cervantes' novel. Later Spanish adaptations of this
novela were written by A. López de Ayala and Antonio Hurtado, Enrique Cisneros, and José Echegaray. In France,
N. de Brosse, in 1645, produced a theatrical adaptation
of Cervantes' tale, and Destouches, in 1711, did the
same. Destouches' play was put into Italian in 1754,
and in 1756 an *opera buffa* was produced entitled *Il
curioso del suo propio danno*. In England several seventeenth-century plays are based on *El curioso impertinente*:
Philip Massinger's *The Second Maiden's Tragedy*, 1611;
Nathan Field's *Amends for Ladies*, 1618; and Thomas
Southerne's *The Disappointment or the Mother in Fashion*,
1684. Massinger's *The Fatal Dowry*, 1632, though it contains the words "curious impertinent," is not based on
Cervantes' story, nor is *The Coxcomb*, 1612, by Beaumont
and Fletcher. In Germany one finds a 1630 play entitled
Tragödie vom unzeitigen Fürwitz.
[Part II of Babinger's essay is a detailed comparison
of Brosse's play with Cervantes' intercalated story.]

58. Coe, Ada M. "Cervantes Miscellany." *Hispania* 30 (August
    1947):341-345.

    [Mrs. Coe presents a list of various adaptations of the
    Quijote, including cartoons and comics, not noted in
    other bibliographies.]

59. Diego, Gerardo. "Cervantes y la música." *Anales Cer-
    vantinos* 1 (1951):5-40.

    [The latter portion of Gerardo Diego's article deals
    with musical adaptations of the *Quijote*. Numerous musi-
    cal versions of the *Quijote* are discussed, from *Le ballet
    de D. Quichot, dansé par Sautenir*, 1614, to de Falla's
    El retablo de Maese Pedro. This latter work is dealt
    with in some detail.]

60. Espinós [Moltó], Víctor. "Las realizaciones musicales
    del *Quijote*. Ensayo biográfico crítico." *Revista de
    la Biblioteca, Archivo y Museo del Ayuntamiento de
    Madrid* 10 (1933):34-62.

    [Espinós lists the various musical adaptations of the
    Quijote which had been gathered by the Ayuntamiento,
    from Thomas d'Urfey and Henry Purcell's *The Comical His-
    tory of Don Quixote* (London, 1694), to J. Rivier's
    Ouverture pour un Don Quichotte (Paris, 1931). Each
    musical selection is commented upon.]

61. Espinós Moltó, Víctor. *El "Quijote" en la música.* Con
    prólogo de José María Pemán. Barcelona: Patronato del
    IV Centenario del Nacimiento de Cervantes, 1947. Pp.
    x + 166 + 4.

    [Espinós, in his introduction, begins with a general
    discussion of the influence of Spain on world music.
    Next, the critic turns his attention to the *Quijote*, ob-
    serving that all schools of music have paid tribute to
    Cervantes' masterpiece. Espinós' work contains eight
    chapters, the first seven dealing with the musical adap-
    tations of the *Quijote* in Spain, Portugal, France, Ger-
    many, Italy, England, and Switzerland, in that order.
    The final chapter deals with musical adaptations of the
    Quijote in other lands. Within each country the arrange-
    ment is chronological. A total of 186 adaptations are
    listed. Some are only briefly noted; others are dis-
    cussed in detail. In his conclusion Espinós points out
    the continuing enthusiasm for the *Quijote* and the Knight
    among musicians. Pages 129-166 contain illustrations of
    musical scores of *Quijote* adaptations, photographs of
    composers and singers, paintings of scenes, and other
    material. At the end of Espinós' work is a short bibliog-
    raphy and an index.]

62. Fernández Cuenca, Carlos. "Historia cinematográfica de
    Don Quijote de la Mancha." *Cuadernos de Literatura* 3
    (1948):161-212.

    [The critic traces the various movie versions of the
    Quijote from the Pathé Frères version of 1902 to the
    Spanish version of 1948. The length of each movie is
    given in meters, and various actors and directors are
    listed. The North American version of 1916 is described
    as a failure.]

63. García Blanco, M. "Algunas interpretaciones modernas
    del *Quijote.*" *Revista de Ideas Estéticas* 1 (1948):
    137-166.

    [García Blanco discusses various dramatic interpreta-
    tions of the figure Don Quijote, including Manuel de
    Falla's *Retablo de Maese Pedro*, A.V. Lunacharski's *Don
    Quijote libertado*, and Gaston Baty's *Dulcinea*. Azorin's
    Cervantes o la casa encantada and Benjamín Jarnés'
    Viviana y Merlín are examined in detail. García Blanco
    devotes some attention to G.W. Pabst's film of *Don
    Quijote*, which was produced in France and presented in
    Madrid in 1933.]

64. Haywood, Charles. "Musical Settings to Cervantes Texts." In *Cervantes Across the Centuries* ... *A Quadricentennial Volume Edited by Ángel Flores and M.J. Bernardete,* pp. 254-263. New York: Dryden Press, 1947. [1969 reprint, Gordian Press, pp. 264-273.]

   [Haywood lists operas, ballets, and orchestral compositions based on the *Quijote.* The same procedure is followed for the *Novelas ejemplares* and the *entremeses.* Operas based on Cervantes' life are also noted.]

65. Pérez Capo, Felipe. *El Quijote en el teatro. Repertorio cronológico de 290 producciones escénicas relacionadas con la inmortal obra de Cervantes. Ilustrado con notas y comentarios propios y ajenos.* Barcelona: Edit. Milla, 1947. Pp. 91.

   [This work contains four chapters, one for the productions of each century since the *Quijote.* Items 1-28 are adaptations of the *Quijote* in the seventeenth century; 29-110 are from the eighteenth; 111-225 from the nineteenth; 266-289 from the twentieth century. Pérez Capo freely admits that his work is not a complete catalog of dramatic adaptations of the *Quijote.* The entries run chronologically from *The Knight of the Burning Pestle* (Beaumont and Fletcher, 1611) to 1947 (item 288, a playlet called *Don Quijote en Barcelona,* produced by the critic himself). Thirteen illustrations of first pages, *portadas,* etc., are included. Pérez Capo comments upon various adaptations in reasonable detail, and on occasion presents excerpts.]

66. Sánchez-Castañer y Mena, Francisco, ed. *Homenaje a Cervantes.* 2 vols. Valencia: Mediterráneo, 1950.

   [The first volume, entitled *Corona poética cervantina,* consists of a short introduction by the editor, a prolog by Vicente Aleixandre, two hundred sixty-one short poems about Cervantes or his works, a "junco final" by Gerardo Diego, three short appendices, and three indices (subject matter, author, general). Volume II contains a short introduction by Sánchez-Castañer, six photographs, an index, and nineteen critical articles.]

67. Sedó Peris-Mencheta, Juan. *Ensayo de una bibliografía de miscelánea cervantina; comedias, historietas, novelas, poemas, zarzuelas, etc. inspiradas en Cervantes o en sus obras.* Barcelona: Impr. Escuela de la Caridad, 1947. Pp. xlvii + 241.

[In his "estudio preliminar" Sedó seeks to define
"Imitación Cervantina" and gives the term a broad interpretation: it includes continuations and works inspired
by a particular work by Cervantes. This latter category
is divided into five subcategories: (A) works with a
character taken from a Cervantine work; (B) works dealing
with an episode in Cervantes' life; (C) works similar in
thought and plot; (D) works with the same title; (E)
adaptations in verse.

Sedó states that the vast majority of the imitations
of the *Quijote* here listed are of a particular episode,
and that the episodes most often imitated are: the first
sally; the Cardenio episode; Don Quijote in the Sierra
Morena; the adventure of the galley slaves; the *Curioso
impertinente*; the Captive's tale; Camacho's wedding; the
ducal palace episode; and Sancho's government. Among the
imitations of the *Quijote* particularly praised by Sedó
is Gaston Baty's *Dulcinea*, 1942.

There are three parts to this *Ensayo*. Part I lists and
describes works written or printed, or which have been
noted in prior bibliographies; Part II lists works printed
but which are lacking in bibliographical information;
Part III contains works not published but listed in other
bibliographies (mostly theatrical works whose date of
printing or performance is not known). Part I is by far
the largest part, the last numbered item being number
1093. Parts II and III have forty-eight and eighty-one
items, respectively. In his *Apéndice* are found additions
to Parts I and II. Pages 177-181 present a bibliography
of works consulted; pages 183-241 contain a detailed index listing authors, works, publishers, editors, comediog-
raphers, printers, etc., referred to in the *Ensayo*.]

68. Valencia, Gerardo. "Aspectos teatrales del *Quijote*."
     Boletín de la Academia Colombiana 12 (1962):311-318.

[Valencia notes the spontaneous nature of the characters in the *Quijote*. He points out the adaptation of
these characters to the stage in the seventeenth century,
in such plays as *Los invencibles hechos de Don Quijote*,
1617. The critic states that not only was the autonomous
nature of the Don and the Squire noted by dramatists of
the early seventeenth century, but that various episodes
suggested themselves to many playwrights: the knighting
ceremony, the Cardenio episode, Camacho's wedding, the
Curious Impertinent, the Trifaldi episode. Verse adaptations of the *Quijote* are examined by the critic and
found to be unreal: e.g., *Las bodas de Camacho* by Meléndez

Valdés. Valencia concludes that the dialog, so rich in
the novel, loses its flavor when abbreviated and put into
verse. A 1947 play by Salvador Novo based on the *Quijote*
is discussed in some detail.]

II. *DON QUIJOTE* IN SPAIN

General

69. Cotarelo y Mori, Emilio. "Las imitaciones castellanas
del *Quijote*." *Estudios de historia literaria de España*," Vol. 1, pp. 71-100. Madrid: Imp. de "La Revista
Española," 1901. [Discurso leído ante la Real Academia Española en la recepción del autor el día 27 de
Mayo de 1900.]

Spanish imitators of the *Quijote* draw upon the aspect
of least value in that novel, namely the satirical.
Toward the middle of the eighteenth century the objects
of satire were, first, bad preachers, later the introduction of new industry and feverish invention, then re-
volutionary ideas, later politics, still later the results of modern philosophy. Padre Francisco José de
Isla's *Fray Gerundio* criticizes bad preaching. In spite
of its good style Padre Isla's novel cannot be compared
to Cervantes' masterpiece. *Vida y empresas del ingeniosísimo caballero Don Quijote de la Manchuela*, by D.
Cristóbal de Azarena (pseud.), satirizes the educational
system of the times. Alonso Ribero y Larrea's *Historia
de D. Pelayo Infanzón de la Vega* mocks the mania for
hidalguía; Arias de León's *Historia del valeroso D.
Rodríguez de Peñadura* attacks the liberals of the day;
and Juan Francisco Siñeriz' *El Quijote del siglo XVIII*
criticizes eighteenth-century philosophy. [Numerous
other imitations of the *Quijote* are noted and briefly
discussed, including A.J. de Salas Barbadillo's *El
Caballero puntual* and Juan Montalvo's *Capítulos que se
le olvidaron a Cervantes*.]

70. Herrero-García, Miguel. "Cervantes." *Estimaciones
literarias del siglo XVII*, pp. 353-420. Madrid: Editorial Voluntad, 1930.

[This item was summarized in Volume One of this bibliography (item 151, pp. 137-138). Part of this chapter is devoted to a number of adaptations of the *Quijote*, particularly Spanish adaptations.]

71. LaGrone, Gregory Gough. *The Imitations of "Don Quixote" in the Spanish Drama*. Philadelphia: University of Pennsylvania, 1937. Pp. vii + 145. [Publication of the *Series in Romance Languages and Literatures*, no. 27.]

[After discussing the various theories as to the date and authorship of the *Entremés de los romances*, LaGrone continues:] Another farce, *Entremés de los invencibles hechos de Don Quixote de la Mancha*, was published by Francisco de Ávila in 1617. In 1618, the playwright Guillén de Castro published two plays based on episodes in the *Quijote*. Both were probably written about 1610 and thus may well be the first imitations of Cervantes' masterpiece. One is based on the *Curioso impertinente*. The other is an adaptation of the Cardenio episode. Don Quijote and his Squire have relatively small roles in both plays. Calderón wrote a now lost play based on the *Quijote* which was presented in 1637. [Other seventeenth-century plays based on Cervantes' novel are discussed, such as *Don Gil de la Mancha* and a play purportedly by Juan de Matos *et al*. This latter work is described by LaGrone as "not a great play, but an interesting one." LaGrone concludes:] A development in the interpretation of *Don Quijote* may be traced in its imitations, which usually parallel the official criticism. The Don Quijote (or his progeny) of the seventeenth-century plays is as crazy as crazy can be; yet he is a sprightly and sometimes amusing fellow. The Don Quijotes of the eighteenth century are more superficial and grotesque than the earlier ones, no doubt because they are less influenced by the model. Nineteenth-century plays based on the *Quijote* are unoriginal. Don Quijote is admired, but the copies are poor. The twentieth century again brings exact dramatizations, with improved technique; and these works are the best.

Seventeenth-Century Spain

72. Caus, Francisco A. "Ecos cervantinos en la obra de Salas Barbadillo." *Anales Cervantinos* 13-14 (1974-1975): 165-168.

[Caus points out Salas Barbadillo's use of monomaniac
figures to express wisdom, such as the character Ceñudo
in *El necio bien afortunado*. The presence of a poor
hidalgo figure, Paladio, in *La estafeta del dios Momo* is
noted. The critic finds nothing quixotic about the
character Juan de Toledo in *El caballero puntual*.]

73. Durán, Manuel. "El *Quijote* de Avellaneda." In *Suma
    Cervantina*, pp. 357-376. Edited by J.B. Avalle-Arce
    and E.C. Riley. London: Tamesis, 1973.

    [Durán briefly discusses the custom of plagiarism in
    Cervantes' times, as well as the practice of an author's
    continuing the work of another. A detailed summary of
    the plot of the false *Quijote* is presented, and the
    style of Avellaneda's work is compared and contrasted
    with the style in Cervantes' novel. Durán also sum-
    marizes prior criticism of the false *Quijote*. The cri-
    tic regards Avellaneda as the harbinger of the long win-
    ter that was to paralyze the novel of Spain for many
    years to come.]

74. Gilman, Stephen. *Cervantes y Avellaneda, estudio de una
    imitación*. Prólogo de Américo Castro. Mexico: Colegio
    de México, 1951. Pp. 182. [Publicaciones de la *Nueva
    Revista de Filología Hispánica*, II. Traducción del
    original inédito por Margit Frenk Alatorre.]

    [This work contains a preface, five chapters, and an
    appendix. Gilman concludes that the author of the false
    Quijote was probably a Dominican priest and was clearly
    a man with a highly moralistic outlook. To Gilman, the
    author of the spurious *Quijote* opposed Cervantes' setting
    up of an autonomous human level in his novel. To Ave-
    llaneda, the critic states, Cervantes' *Quijote* was a
    picaresque novel without the ascetic-moralizing element.
    The styles of Cervantes and Avellaneda are contrasted,
    as are the differences in the characterization of the
    hero. In Cervantes' story, Gilman finds, the Don has an
    aberration of the will; in Avellaneda's version, an aber-
    ration of the intelligence. The two Sanchos are also
    contrasted. The absence of love in the false *Quijote* is
    observed, as is the lack of true dialog. Gilman notes
    the preference of French and Spanish Neoclassicists for
    Avellaneda's version on the grounds that it was, to them,
    more natural. The critic points out that in the spurious
    Quijote the figures stay the same to a large extent,
    except that the Squire becomes more simpleminded and the
    Knight more grotesque. Gilman compares Avellaneda to

naturalistic writers and finds that both have a pessimistic vision of the world and of the individual.
   In the appendix the critic notes the similarities between Avellaneda's *Quijote* and Cervantes' Part II, and
concludes that Avellaneda was the plagiarist, not Cervantes, thus disagreeing with such critics as Menéndez
Pidal (summarized in Volume One of this bibliography,
item 196, pp. 171-172).]

75. Hammond, John H. "References to Cervantes in the Works
    of Francisco Santos." *Library Chronicle of the Uni-
    versity of Texas* 3 (1948):100-102.

   Francisco Santos, a moralist and *costumbrista* novelist
of the latter half of the seventeenth century, indicates
by various references that he was well familiar with the
works of Cervantes. Also, Santos deals with the *loco-
cuerdo* theme in *Periquillo el de las Gallineras* and in
El sastre del Campillo, an idea found both in the *Quijote* and in *El licenciado Vidriera*. While some of Santos' references to Cervantes appear to be uncomplimen-
tary, the former was an admirer of the author of the
Quijote, as is revealed in *El arca de Noé*. The references to the *Quijote* which seem derogatory are concerned
with an abstract quality, false pride, rather than with
the literary merits of that work.

76. Navarro González, Alberto. *El Quijote español del siglo
    XVII*. Madrid: Ediciones Rialp, 1964. Pp. 410.

   [Part One of this work, "El Quijote de Cervantes
crítico y escritor," discusses what defects and good
characteristics Cervantes sought to give to his hero.
The critic describes the Don's madness: belief, the de-
formation of reality, and the transfiguration of reality.
   In Part Two Navarro deals with seventeenth-century
interpretations of Cervantes' masterpiece. The view that
Spaniards of that age, and the author himself, did not
grasp the full reach of the *Quijote* is studied in some
detail. Navarro concludes that there was a select Spanish minority who saw the Knight's good points (for
example, Juan de Robles and Félix Nieto de Silva).
   Part Three of this work compares and contrasts Don
Quijote and the Cid.]

77. Sánchez, Alberto. "Reminiscencias cervantinas en el
    teatro de Calderón." *Anales Cervantinos* 6 (1957):262-
    270.

Cervantes was the first to use the *ovillejo* verse
form. Three poems in this meter are found in Chapter
XXVII, Part I of the *Quijote* and four in *La ilustre
fregona*. Calderón follows Cervantes, using the *ovillejo*
in *La fiera, el rayo y la piedra*, and in *Tu prójimo como
a ti*. Calderón alludes to the *Quijote* in several plays,
and even wrote a now lost *comedia* based on Cervantes'
masterpiece. In addition, Calderón adopts the use of
the theater-within-a-theater device in his *El gran teatro del mundo*, a technique employed by Cervantes in *El
retablo de las maravillas*. Although the figure Don Mendo
in Calderón's *El alcalde de Zalamea* is somewhat similar
to Don Quijote, it is more likely that Mendo was based
on the poor knight in *Lazarillo*.

Eighteenth-Century Spain

78. Cotarelo y Mori, Emilio. "Otro imitador de Cervantes en
    el siglo XVIII." *Estudios de historia literaria de
    España*. Vol. 1, pp. 53-69. Madrid: Imp. de "La Re-
    vista Española," 1901. [Essay dated 21 February 1899.]

    There are two types of imitations of the *Quijote*:
    (1) those which use the same principal characters; and
    (2) those in which the "intención y procedimiento" are
    similar to that of Cervantes' novel. This second group
    satirizes a particular thing and concentrates its in-
    terest on a particular caricaturesque figure: *Hudibras*,
    by Samuel Butler; *Sir Launcelot Greaves*, by Smollett;
    Don Sylvio von Rosalva by Wieland. *El tío Mamuco*, 1789,
    satirizes the reforms in Spain under Carlos III, espe-
    cially those undertaken by Floridablanca to introduce new
    industry. The error of all these imitators was to as-
    sume that the merit of the *Quijote* lay exclusively in
    its satire against books of chivalry.

79. Pollin, Alice M. "*Don Quijote* en las obras del P. An-
    tonio Eximeno." *PMLA* 74 (December 1959):568-575.

    The eighteenth-century musicologist, philosopher, and
    author Antonio Eximeno was exiled from Spain in 1767,
    along with other Jesuits. He returned to Spain from
    Rome in 1798, but was back in Rome in 1802. In 1806 his
    Apologia de Cervantes was published. Eximeno was a
    great admirer of Cervantes and resented his detractors,

such as Vicente de los Ríos, who sought to point out
numerous "errors" in Cervantes' works. A particular
point about which Eximeno disagreed with prior critics
concerned the epoch with which the *Quijote* dealt. To
some, Cervantes' novel dealt with an ancient era; to
Vicente de los Ríos, Cervantes was describing his own
epoch. Eximeno disagreed with both views, concluding
that the *Quijote* dealt with an imaginary time.

There is a vague likeness between Don Quijote and
Eximeno's character Agapito Quitóles in *Don Lazarillo
Vizcardi*, and both Cervantes and Eximeno discuss the
contemporary theatre in their works. Both have a puppet-
show episode. But Eximeno's novel is didactic, while
the *Quijote* is poetic, and there is no true analogy between Don Agapito Quitóles and the Knight of La Mancha.

80. Ramírez-Araujo, Alejandro. "El cervantismo de Cadalso."
     Romanic Review 43 (December 1952):256-265.

There are similarities between the eighteenth-century
writer Cadalso's passages of literary criticism and
those of Cervantes. But more important than this is the
fact that both authors show moderation in jokes; both
have an aversion to insult. José Cadalso's smile, like
that of Cervantes, may denote sadness and bitterness,
but never revenge. Cervantes and Cadalso spent many
years in Andalucía, and this section of Spain appears to
have exerted great influence on both of them.

                    Nineteenth-Century Spain

General

81. Balanzat, Luisa. "Don Quijote y el capitán Ribot."
     Boletín del Instituto de Estudios Asturianos 7 (1953):
     597-600.

[Balanzat compares and contrasts the hero of Cervantes'
masterpiece with the hero of Armando Palacio Valdés' *La
alegría del capitán Ribot*. The critic believes that
neither novel would be well received if written today,
because of the lack of obscenity in both stories. The
idealism and sexual abstinence of the Knight and the
Captain are noted and briefly discussed.]

82. Boring, Phyllis Z. "Some Reflections on Clarín's *Doña
     Berta*." *Romance Notes* 11 (Winter 1969):322-325.

[Boring concedes that the French influence on "Clarín" (Leopoldo Alas) is heavy, and that *Doña Berta* has a definite relationship to Flaubert's *Madame Bovary* and Guy de Maupassant's *Une vie*. However, the critic states that the influence of Cervantes' *Quijote* was equally great on Clarín, and that the author of the *Quijote* exerted a powerful effect on the two French writers. Boring observes that Clarín's Berta has the following quixotic qualities: she reads romantic stories to excess; she is anachronistic and grotesque, and is ridiculed because of these characteristics; she cannot live without her illusions and dies; in spite of her faults she is a very sympathetic character. At the end of her article Boring concludes that both Cervantes and Clarín wrote "poetic" novels in that each took the characteristics of the contemporary literature of harsh reality and mellowed them with touches of poetry and idealism.]

83. Howell, Stanley E. "Does Bréton's *Marcela* Stem from *Quijote*?" *Modern Language Notes* 53 (March 1938):195-196.

The heroine of Manuel Bréton de los Herreros' play *Marcela, o ¿cuál de los tres?*, 1831, has several similarities to the Marcela in Cervantes' *Quijote*, Part I. Both state that they are rich and beautiful. Each explains her refusal to marry, and each lives with a kindly uncle who suggests that she marry but does not insist upon it. Both Marcelas make a speech to their suitors, but in neither case is their common sense argument appreciated. Each is called a scourge to mankind: "cruel, desdeñosa, ingrata." All in all, it seems quite possible that Bréton's play was suggested by the Marcela episode in the *Quijote*.

84. Jackson, Robert M. "'Cervantismo' in the Creative Process of Clarín's *La Regenta*." *Modern Language Notes* 84 (March 1969):208-227.

[Jackson concludes that there is a direct influence of Cervantes on Leopoldo Alas ("Clarín"), as well as an indirect influence through Flaubert's *Madame Bovary* and through the works of Pérez Galdós and Eça de Queiroz. The critic finds that literature influences the conduct of virtually all of the characters in *La Regenta*, 1884-1885, and that each character's literary preference is described in detail by Clarín. In addition, Jackson asserts, all the figures of the town of Vetusta form an imaginary self-conception based on their readings. Both

the comic as well as the tragic side of this quixotic
process is shown, states Jackson. The critic is careful
to note both the similarities and differences between
the two writers. On the whole, the critic finds that
Cervantes frees his characters, believing that reality
is to be found in their experience, while Clarín wishes
to remain in full control of his figures in order to
study them from every angle.

The critic also discusses the Cervantic perspectivism
in *La Regenta*, pointing out various "pareceres." Particular attention is given to Ana Ozores: her actions are
interpreted by various characters from their individual
perspectives. *La Regenta*, Jackson concludes, would have
been impossible without the *Quijote* and without certain
nineteenth-century novels equally influenced by Cervantes'
masterpiece.]

85.   Lott, Robert E.   "*Pepita Jiménez* and *Don Quixote*: A
      Structural Comparison." *Hispania* 45 (September 1962):
      395-401.

In formal structure *Pepita Jiménez* is very different
from *Don Quijote*. Cervantes' novel is primarily based
on the Knight-Squire antithesis of idealism versus materialism, illusion versus reality, learning versus common sense. In Valera's novel there is no Sancho, and
the contrast between illusion and reality is primarily
psychological, usually occurring within the mind of the
protagonist Luis. *Don Quijote* is episodic with many sub-
plots. It has interwoven leitmotifs and themes almost
infinitely amplified or modified, suggesting the complexity of life itself. Each part of Cervantes' novel has a
focal setting: the main inn (Part I) and the ducal palace
(Part II). The structure of Valera's story is dramatic;
space and setting are unimportant to the plot. There are
other differences in style and tone between these two
novels. Cervantes' irony is more constructive than that
of Valera, who is the more anti-establishment of the two.
Cervantes' characters are more complex than those of
Valera. In the end, Cervantes' hero renounces his illusions, whereas Luis moves from one illusion to another.

Yet *Pepita Jiménez* is much closer to the *Quijote* than
these differences would indicate. What Valera learned
from Cervantes was the use of parody and irony and how
to represent reality as it appears in the quixotic mind
of a protagonist. Valera's hero Luis, a candidate for
priesthood, is, however, handled in a restrained and
sophisticated style. The author sought to picture a

self-deceiver, not a monomaniac like the Knight. The major common purposes of Cervantes and Valera may be reduced to those of parody and the treatment of the reality problem. In both novels literature is most important, and both protagonists are profoundly affected by their readings: the Knight by books of chivalry and Luis by mystic works.

86. Molina, G. "Un nuevo imitador de Cervantes, desconocido." *Bibliografía Española* 15 (1915):14.

[Molina refers to the work *Historia verdadera de César Nonato, el avieso: Caballero manchego de Relance*, written under the pseudonym Alonso Vargas Machuca, c. 1830. The critic concludes that the allegedly true author (stated in a note in the *portada* to be the Canon of Madrid, "el Sr. Vega") is not the real author. Molina suggests instead several Spanish émigrés of the 1820's. The critic also states that the alleged publisher ("La Oficina Tipográfica Alcuzcuziana" in Tangiers) never existed, and suggests London or Paris as the likely place of publication. Commenting on the content of the novel, Molina finds that it was written "con el pensamiento puesto en el Hidalgo Machego," and states that the novel is an imitation of the *Quijote* not listed in prior bibliographies.]

87. Tamayo, Juan Antonio. "Una obra cervantina de Bécquer." *Anales Cervantinos* 1 (1951):295-324.

La venta encantada by Bécquer and Luis García Luna, 1859, is based on the Fernando-Dorotea, Cardenio-Luscinda episode in Part I of the *Quijote*. The Cardenio theme had been adapted to the theatre on several occasions prior to *La venta encantada*: for example, by Guillén de Castro in 1610, by an anonymous playwright in 1750, and by Ventura de la Vega in 1832. Although *La venta encantada* is somewhat similar to Ventura de la Vega's play, Bécquer and García Luna probably did not know of that *comedia*. However, they were quite cognizant of the 1750 play (*El Alcides de la Mancha y famoso Don Quijote*) and may have drawn on it for details. The structure of *La venta encantada* generally follows the *Quijote*, but a great deal is omitted, and the last act of the *comedia* is almost entirely invented by Bécquer and García Luna.

88. Thompson, Clifford R., Jr. "Cervantine Motifs in the Short Stories of Leopoldo Alas." *Revista de Estudios Hispánicos* 10 (1976):391-403.

[The critic compares the techniques used by Leopoldo
Alas ("Clarín") and by Cervantes to confront the ideal
with the real by juxtaposing two contrasting literary
traditions. Particular attention is devoted to the following works by Alas: "Doctor Sutilis"; "Un documento";
"Doña Berta"; "La imperfecta casada"; and "La fantasía
de un delegado de Hacienda."]

89. Zúñiga, Ángel. "El cervantismo de Juan Valera." *ABC*
    (Madrid), 19 October 1954, p. 19. [Based on a summary
    by Alberto Sánchez in *Anales Cervantinos* 4 (1954), p.
    395. The original could not be obtained.]

    [Zúñiga notes two lectures by Valera at the Real Aca-
    demia Española dealing with the *Quijote*. Valera, the
    critic states, found the unity in Cervantes' novel to
    lie in its thought, not in its action, and also observed
    that Cervantes was very Spanish because of his sense of
    the ridiculous and familiarity with failure. Valera also
    stated that Cervantes crucified his hero with ridicule,
    but, Valera hoped, the spirit of the Knight would be
    resurrected in the better Spaniards.]

Pérez Galdós

90. Ayala, Francisco. "Los narradores en las novelas de
    Torquemada (Homenaje a Casalduero)." *Cuadernos His-
    panoamericanos*, nos. 250-252 (1970-1971), pp. 374-381.

    [Ayala notes Galdós' remark in *Napoleón en Chamartín*
    that the *Quijote* was "la matriz de todas las novelas del
    mundo." One characteristic of the modern (or Cervantine)
    novel, states the critic, is that it has diverse perspec-
    tives, from which there arises a certain and sought-after
    ambiguity, an imitation of what life itself offers. The
    modern novel, Ayala continues, is no longer a simple,
    direct relation between teller and listener, and the in-
    terest is no longer in the facts told but in the charac-
    ters, who tend to acquire autonomy even in the outside-
    the-book world. Ayala notes Galdós' use of certain Cer-
    vantine techniques to create this impression of autonomy:
    (1) using characters who existed in a prior work of fic-
    tion, a technique which Galdós acquired from Balzac but
    which is essentially a Cervantine device; (2) inviting
    the reader to enter the world of fiction; (3) the use of
    the author both as an omniscient writer and as a charac-
    ter inside the novel; (4) the joking use of the fictitious

author technique. Ayala concludes that the multiple
perspectives in Galdós' mature works greatly enrich the
illusion of reality.]

91.   Azorín [Martínez Ruiz, José]. "Cervantes y Galdós."
      Obras completas. Vol. 9, pp. 223-224. Madrid: Agui-
      lar, 1963. [From *Con permiso de los cervantistas*,
      Madrid: Biblioteca Nueva, 1948.]

      The human personality is not definitively sanctioned
      until the end of the eighteenth century. Cervantes' Don is
      a case of excess development of personality and is treated
      comically. Galdós, living in an age when the personality
      has been freed, creates parallels to the Knight, but his
      quixotic figures lose all comicness. The ascetic figure
      Guillermo Bruno in *Amor y Ciencia* is a slave to scienti-
      fic research, and the character Nazario Nazarín (*Nazarín*)
      is a religious ascetic who carries out sublime works of
      charity.

92.   Casalduero, Joaquín. *Vida y obra de Galdós (1843-1920).*
      Tercera edición ampliada. Madrid: Gredos, 1970. Pp.
      294.

      [Casalduero (p. 7) states that Dickens, Balzac, Zola,
      and especially Cervantes make up the literary background
      of Pérez Galdós. Cervantes, the critic continues, be-
      sides transmitting to Galdós the ironic form for captur-
      ing a character or planting a problem, or conceiving a
      conflict, guides Galdós in the complex of the crystalli-
      zation of Spanish culture. Casalduero also notes (pp.
      70-71) that while both writers deal with the conflict be-
      tween reality and imagination, Cervantes treats the prob-
      lem metaphysically, Galdós, sociologically.
      The novels *Nazarín* and *Halma*, Casalduero finds, are
      particularly influenced by the *Quijote*: not only does
      Nazarín find himself in situations identical to those of
      the Don, but more importantly the spirit of Galdós' two
      novels is the same as that of Cervantes' masterpiece.
      Discussing the relative influence of various writers on
      Galdós, the critic concludes (p. 182) that Cervantes
      allowed Galdós to contemplate Spanish reality and to
      create the grotesque outline of many of his characters.
      One of the works in which Galdós most competes with
      Cervantes in *Carlos VI en la Rápita*, states Casal-
      duero (p. 257): here Galdós plays with Cervantes' senten-
      ces, manages with identical mastery the grouping of the
      characters and the rhythm of the action, and shows the
      same joy in the invention of characters.]

93. Correa, Gustavo. "Tradición mística y cervantismo en
    las novelas de Galdós, 1890-97." *Hispania* 53 (Decem-
    ber 1970):842-851.

    It is evident that the heroism of Don Quijote finds a
    common source with the heroism of the mystic soul, both
    being nourished by a nutritious sap of deep inwardness.
    Basically, the heroic quixotic drive is turned outward
    toward famous deeds, while the mystic drive is directed
    inward toward the interior of the conscience and rests
    upon acts which propose the extinction of the person and
    imply, for that very reason, the absence of all fame.
    But the mystic drive carries with it an overflowing of
    inner forces which end by exercising their action on the
    environment and on other persons. The projection of the
    mystic in Galdós carries the form of an exercise of
    Christian charity. In this way, the *misadventures* of
    Nazarín correspond to the *adventures* of Don Quijote, the
    madness of the Don to the *sanity* of Nazarín, and the two
    can never be reconciled. On the contrary, the disappear-
    ance of the Don's madness and his return to reason mean
    for the Knight the disintegration of his real being,
    which leads to his subsequent death. With Nazarín, his
    madness is more apparent than real and is resolved in
    the highest form of sanity, or sainthood. In the *Qui-*
    jote the hero invents his lady-love and sustains himself
    by the power of his invention. His personality begins to
    crumble when he is assailed by doubts regarding her exis-
    tence. On the other hand, Galdós' character Ángel loves
    and exalts his beloved Leré more and more as he comes to
    know her inner being.
    Both Cervantes and Galdós present characters who seem
    independent of their creators. No doubt the Don imposed
    himself on Cervantes by the power of a coherent internal
    personality and with an independence that is emphasized
    by his multiplicity of perspectives; Galdós' heroes em-
    phasize their individuality and autonomy in a similar
    game of perspectives and of coherent internal action.
    The novel *Halma* puts into relief (like Part II of the
    Quijote) numerous angles of vision which end by accen-
    tuating the illusion of the real existence of the
    characters.

94. Durand, Frank. "The Reality of Illusion: *La desheredada*."
    Modern Language Notes 89 (March 1974):191-201.

    [The critic points out strong parallels between Pérez
    Galdós' *La desheredada* and the *Quijote*: the name of Gal-
    dós' "canónigo" is Quijano-Quijana, who is from La Mancha;

a letter from the "canónigo" to Isidora parodies Don Quijote's advice to Sancho on how to govern. By these bla-
tant imitations, states Durand, Galdós achieves a certain
depth in his play with reality. Galdós, Durand concludes
(pp. 195-196), shows not only the disparity between the
protagonist's illusions and the world she inhabits but
also follows Cervantes' technique of playing with the
question of what is "reality." Furthermore, continues
Durand, by intentionally creating a caricature of Cervantes' work, Galdós accentuates the realistic depiction
of the life he is so interested in portraying. In his final
sentence the critic states: "The Cervantine influence in
La desheredada, an influence which appeared early in his
work and which he develops more and more in succeeding
novels, not only adds dimension to scenes of reality and
imagination, fiction and history, but also provides Galdós with the proper ironic framework for his commentary
on Spain."]

95. Falconieri, John V. "Un capítulo de Galdós que no se le
     olvidó a Cervantes." *Revista de Estudios Hispánicos*
     6 (1972):145-151.

     [Falconieri compares the duo Don Quijote-Sancho Panza
     to Pepe Rey-Tio Licurgo in *Doña Perfecta* in its presen-
     tation of two views of reality as affected by the force
     of prejudices, opinions, and concepts. Chapter II of
     Galdós' novel ("Un viaje por el corazón de España") is
     the subject of special analysis. The critic notes that
     Pepe Rey is meditative, intellectual, well-read, proud;
     Tío Licurgo is humble, rustic, astute, and even imitates
     Sancho's style of speech. Licurgo's warning to Pepe Rey
     not to intervene in *aventuras* is compared to similar
     warnings by Sancho to his master.]

96. Gillespie, Gerald. "Reality and Fiction in the Novels of
     Galdós." *Anales Galdosianos* 1 (1966):11-31.

     It was through the Cervantine tendency to transcend
     his own subject that Galdós achieved genuine universality
     and renewed the mission of the Spanish novel. Galdós
     tirelessly ascended from the wry irony of naturalistic
     truth to indulgent meditation, progressing along a path-
     way analogous to that of his great predecessor from Part
     I to Part II of the *Quijote*. The question of truth
     and illusion has been standard in the European novel
     since the *Quijote*. What distinguishes Galdós' treatment
     of the "real" from that of Balzac and Stendhal is its
     Cervantine consciousness. For Galdós "fiction" and

"reality" are not dichotomous, but interacting, aspects
of human existence. What provides cohesion to Galdós'
works is no particular doctrine that sunders fact and
fancy, but the Cervantine interplay of various "fictions"
and "realities."
The region of La Mancha remains throughout Galdós'
novels a Spanish hinterland which is the breeding ground
for deluded souls and extravagant idealists. To under-
score his thematic adaptation of Cervantes, Galdós
divides Isidora's story (*La desheredada*) into two parts,
the first of which ends with the humorously mad letter
from her uncle the canon, Quijano-Quijana, on his deathbed. Isidora's madness is an inversion of the Knight's
idealism; she does not ennoble anything; when her illusion is destroyed she dies, but in vileness, not in
dignity.
Galdós' reworking of Cervantine themes raises questions about man's reality and freedom long before Unamuno. Cervantes directly, and not the Romantics, taught
Galdós about subjectivity. His tendency to shift the
"point of view" is evident in his earlier novels. Basically, the Galdosian method of narration comprises several
points of view; the author's "reality" is multidimensional,
in keeping with his Cervantine heritage.

97. Green, Otis H. "Two Deaths: Don Quijote and Marianela."
     Anales Galdosianos, no. 2 (1967), pp. 131-133.

     [The critic describes the circumstances in which Gal-
     dós' heroine dies from despair in the novel *Marianela*,
     1878. Her beloved, Pablo Penáguilas, regains his sight
     and, occing Marianela for the first time, rejects her.
     Otis Green next discusses the death scene in the *Quijote*,
     1615, stating that the readers of that day clearly ac-
     cepted the idea that melancholy could produce death. The
     medical theories of Cervantes' time regarding melancholy
     are discussed at length.
     The critic finds the parallel between the *Quijote* and
     Marianela not in the deaths of the central figures but
     in the relationship between the lament of Sancho and the
     lament of Florentina and Golfín. Green concludes that
     Galdós wanted the perceptive reader to see the parallels
     between the deaths of the two protagonists: the death-
     dealing melancholy, the efforts used to stave off the
     death of the central figures, the questions, the pro-
     tests, the final resignation.]

98. Herman, Jack Chalmers. *Don Quijote and the Novels of
     Pérez Galdós*. Ada, Oklahoma: East Central Oklahoma

State College, 1955. Pp. 68. [This work is based on
the author's Ph.D. dissertation, University of Kansas,
1950.]

Galdós greatly admired *Don Quijote* and even had his
characters express their admiration for Cervantes' hero.
Such words as *quijotil*, *quijotismo*, *quijotada*, *quijo-
tería*, and *quijotesco* appear with relative frequency in
Galdós' works and are used in several different senses.
Occasionally such words refer to haughtiness or immodera-
tion, but at times they refer to a reforming zeal or to
a desire to help the afflicted. These two great Spanish
writers have similarities in their literary technique.
Both love proverbs and both make use of unusual pairs of
characters. A number of Galdós' figures, like several of
Cervantes' characters, are obsessed. The problem of the
general good versus minute particulars is a problem dealt
with by both Cervantes and his successor, and each describes situations where lies are accepted by society as
truths.

99. Herman, J. Chalmers. "Galdós' Expressed Appreciation
     for *Don Quijote*." *Modern Language Journal* 36 (1952):
     31-34.

In 1872, Galdós devoted almost an entire article to
the praise of Cervantes in the April 15th edition of the
Illustración de Madrid. The only Cervantine work referred to in this article is the *Quijote*. Galdós echoes
his praise of Cervantes' masterpiece in several novels.
From *La fontana de oro*, 1867-1868, to *El caballero encantado*, 1909, Galdós puts praise for the *Quijote* in the
mouths of his characters. Never does he make a derogatory reference to Cervantes' novel.

100. Herman, J. Chalmers. "Quotations and Locutions from *Don
     Quijote* in Galdós' Novels." *Hispania* 36 (May 1953):
     177-181.

From his first published novel, *La fontana de oro*, to
his very last, *La razón de la sinrazón*, there is instance
after instance of Galdós' citing and paraphrasing Cervantes' original text. Galdós appears to have retained
significant and interesting phrases from the *Quijote*
and made them part of his own vocabulary. [Numerous
examples of Galdós' use of Cervantes' locutions are set
forth.]

101. Latorre, Mariano. "Cervantes y Galdós." *Atenea* 24
     (October 1947):11-40.

Neither Cervantes nor Galdós could get away from the
Spanish masses. However, Cervantes devotes more attention to the aristocracy than does Galdós, who is more
concerned with the middle class. Galdós' sense of humor
is less tragic than that of Cervantes. Yet both writers
have a strange predeliction for the tragic aspects of
life. Both writers also have an abundance of madmen,
men with illusions. Galdós is more combative, less
smiling than Cervantes. The latter becomes resigned to
life smiling; the former attacks and teaches. Cervantes
was a writer of great syntheses. His elaboration was
methodical, careful, prolonged. Galdós, on the other
hand, was an improviser, an intriguing creator of types
and of novelistic fables.

102.   Montesinos, José F. *Galdós*. 3 vols. Madrid: Castalia,
       1968-1973.

[All three volumes of Montesinos' work contain passages
discussing the influence of Cervantes on Galdós. Particular attention should be given to Volume I, pp. xvii-
xx; Volume II, pp. xi-xix; and Volume III, pp. 342-343.
These pages examine the influence of the *Quijote* on
Galdós during the various epochs of his literary produc-
tion.]

103.   Nimetz, Michael. *Humor in Galdós: A Study in the
       "Novelas contemporáneas."* New Haven and London:
       Yale University Press, 1968. Pp. vii + 227.

[At pages 119-120 Nimetz insists that Galdós made use
of Don Quijote's advice to Sancho in *La desheredada*.
The critic finds that this is only one of countless Cervantine echoes heard throughout Galdós' works. The employment of the fictitious author device in *Nazarín* is
said to have been taken from the *Quijote*, as is the use
by Galdós of an already fictionalized character in
Nazarín and *Halma*.]

104.   Obaid, Antonio Hadad. "El *Quijote* en los *Episodios
       Nacionales* de Pérez Galdós." Ph.D. dissertation,
       University of Minnesota, 1953. Pp. 330.

[Obaid examines forty-six volumes of Galdós' *Episodios*
and finds that no book receives as much praise from
Galdós as the *Quijote*. The critic further concludes
that no other work furnished Galdós more material for
his *Episodios*. In Chapter One of this thesis the
critic studies the quixotic characters in the *Episodios*

and finds fifty-one such figures. The second chapter
is concerned with Galdós' idea that Spain was a quixotic
country par excellence. Chapters Three and Four discuss
Galdosian characters based on Dulcinea and Sancho.
Chapter Five deals with La Mancha and Manchegan figures
in the *Episodios*. Obaid concludes that Galdós draws on
Cervantes' style, situations, adventures, locales, quotations, themes, and technique of composition. The
critic also finds that there are evident signs of Cervantine influences in at least forty-two of the forty-
six novels of the *Episodios*, and that Galdós utilized
material from no fewer than thirty-eight chapters of
the first part and forty-two chapters of the second
part of *Don Quijote*.]

105. Obaid, Antonio H. "Galdós y Cervantes." *Hispania* 41
     (September 1958):269-273.

     [Obaid presents excerpts from Galdós' works, showing
     that author's many references to Cervantes or his writ-
     ings. The critic is of the opinion that Cervantes was
     of far more influence on Galdós than was any other
     novelist. Many of Galdós' characters, Obaid observes,
     have read the *Quijote*, even if they have read little
     else, and all enjoyed it and found consolation in it.]

106. Obaid, Antonio H. "Sancho Panza en los *Episodios
     Nacionales* de Galdós." *Hispania* 42 (May 1959):199-204.

     There are no fewer than fifty-one quixotic figures in
     Galdós' *Episodios*, and when the author introduces such
     a character, it is always with a reference to Cervantes'
     immortal Knight. The Sancho Panza type is used by Gal-
     dós much more sparingly, but his characters Padre Sal-
     món, Padre Celelí, Bruno Carrasco, and José Milagro all
     have a certain resemblance to Cervantes' Squire.

107. Obaid, Antonio H. "La Mancha en los *Episodios Nacionales*
     de Galdós." *Hispania* 41 (March 1958):42-47.

     [Obaid states that one who analyzes the *Episodios* will
     soon discover that when Galdós introduces a person from
     La Mancha it is an almost certain sign that he is going
     to create in him a quixotic of Sancho-like character.
     The critic notes various Galdosian figures from La
     Mancha, including Santiago Fernández (called El Gran
     Capitán).]

108. Pedraz García, Margarita María. "La influencia del
     Quijote en la obra de Pérez Galdós." Ph.D.

dissertation, Universidad de Madrid, 1967. [As summarized in *Revista de la Universidad de Madrid* 16
(1967):38-39.]

[This thesis contains four chapters. The first deals
with the modern realistic novel and with the place
which Cervantes occupies within Spanish realism. The
second chapter describes the quixotic types found in
Galdós' works. The critic observes that in Galdós'
Episodios Nacionales the Quijote figures are heroic and
patriotic, while in Galdós' *Novelas* they are either mys-
tics or reformers. In Chapter Three Pedraz García
points out Galdós' various allusions to the *Quijote*.
The final chapter seeks to define the meaning of *quijotismo* as presented by Galdós: evasion of reality and
individualism. The critic concludes that Galdós does
not reject *quijotismo* but seeks to integrate it into
the Spanish personality.]

109. Pérez de Ayala, Ramón. "Cervantes y Galdós." *Lectura*
      20 (1920):67-68.

      Cervantes created the modern novel, and Galdós carried
      it to its highest level of perfection and maturity.
      Both elevated themselves above the false style of
      their times, breaking with affectation and creating a
      new language to express emotions. Both Cervantes and
      Galdós suffered; both knew people of all classes; each
      expressed the Spain of his times.

110. Rodríguez Chicharro, César. "La huella del *Quijote* en
      las novelas de Caldós." *La Palabra y el Hombre*, no.
      238 (1966), pp. 223-263.

      [The critic divides the influence of the *Quijote* on
      Galdós into two areas: (1) structural; and (2) linguis-
      tic. Under the first category Rodríguez notes that
      both writers comment on their sources and both speak
      of themselves through their characters. In addition,
      states Rodríguez, in the *Quijote* and in Galdós' works
      the characters allude in a second part to what was said
      of them in the first part. Both Cervantes and Galdós,
      the critic observes, present characters who comment on
      what they have read, and both novelists have writers as
      characters. Another similarity, Rodríguez finds, is
      that both authors use humorous chapter headings, and
      there is a certain similarity of topics of discussion,
      such as arms and letters.

Under linguistic similarities the critic points out
various matters, such as the use of allegorical names,
literary allusions, errors in names, and emblematic
phrases.]

111. Sackett, Theodore A. *Pérez Galdós, An Annotated Bibliog-
     raphy*. Albuquerque, N.M.: The University of New Mexico
     Press, 1968. Pp. xiv + 130.

     [In his index (at page 128) Sackett lists numerous
     item numbers which deal with the question of Cervantes'
     influence on Pérez Galdós.]

112. Sanín Cano, Baldomero. "Cervantes: un vínculo inmortal
     de dos pueblos." In *Cervantes en Colombia*, pp. 241-
     250. Edited by E. Caballero Calderón. Madrid: Patro-
     nato del IV Centenario de Cervantes, 1948.

     The influence of Cervantes on Spanish literature lay
     dormant until Pérez Galdós in the mid-nineteenth century.
     Ganivet, it is true, drew upon the author of the *Qui-
     jote*, but he could not mentally or physically sustain
     such a burden. Valera was affected by Cervantes, but
     his laughter degenerates at times into the cackle of a
     joking Andalusian. Ortega was a humoristic disciple
     of Cervantes, but Ortega's manner is much too solemn.

113. Smith, Paul C. "Cervantes and Galdós: The Duques and
     Ido del Sagrario." *Romance Notes* 8 (Autumn 1966):
     47-50.

     [Smith compares the twenty-six chapter episode at the
     palace of the Duke and Duchess with the scene involving
     Juanito, Jacinta, and the mad Ido del Sagrario in Gal-
     dós' *Fortunata y Jacinta*, 1886-1887. Both Juanito Santa
     Cruz and the *Duques* are shallow, are deliberately left
     undeveloped, and are implicitly condemned, Smith finds.
     Both, he continues, are cruel toward a madman whom they
     find entertaining, and whose mental aberration they ex-
     ploit for the sole purpose of amusement. Smith states
     that both episodes leave a bad taste in the reader's
     mouth. The critic points out, however, that neither
     author comments upon the evil behavior of the mockers.
     Nor, he continues, does either writer condemn a whole
     social class, merely idle, irresponsible types in the
     upper strata of society. Smith concludes that Galdós
     had the episode of the *Duques* in mind when he wrote the
     scene with Juanito, Jacinta, and Ido del Sagrario.]

114. Warshaw, J. "Galdós' Indebtedness to Cervantes." *His-
      pania* 16 (May 1933):127-142.

      All in all, Galdós owes more to Spanish writers than
      to non-Spanish writers, and his indebtedness to Cervan-
      tes is particularly heavy in several areas: (1) Galdós
      is inspired by Cervantes' character development; (2)
      the good-humored irony of Cervantes appeals to Galdós;
      (3) Galdós frequently presents obsessed or pathological
      characters; (4) he is so thoroughly steeped in Cervan-
      tes that a marked Cervantine savor emanates from nearly
      every one of his novels and from some of his dramas.
         There are many references in Galdós' works to Cervan-
      tes, sometimes fleeting and decorative; at other times
      the recollections of Cervantes are didactic or are ar-
      tistically purposeful and consciously imitative. There
      are many quixotic characters in Galdós' works: individu-
      alistic, radical, eccentric, or obsessed, quixotic mix-
      tures of extravagance and soberness, mysticism and
      lucidity, logic and nonsense. A few even resemble the
      Don physically.
         Like others of his times, Galdós saw Spain's problem
      as that of not being able to adjust herself to a world
      in motion. He thought that Spain must de-quixotize her-
      self. Yet Galdós did not condemn *quijotismo* as an un-
      mixed evil.

115. Woodbridge, Hensley C. *Benito Pérez Galdós: A Selec-
      tive Annotated Bibliography*. Metuchen, N.J.: Scare-
      crow Press, 1975. Pp. xi + 321. [See also Wood-
      bridge's earlier work "Benito Pérez Galdós: A Select-
      ed Annotated Bibliography," in *Hispania* 53 (Decem-
      ber 1970):899-971, esp. pp. 913-914.]

      [Under "General Sources" Woodbridge notes and sum-
      marizes (pp. 51-53) various works dealing with the
      overall influence of Cervantes on Galdós' total literary
      production. Critical books and articles noting a Cer-
      vantine influence on individual Galdosian novels or
      plays are also summarized (pp. 98-99; 117-118; 145; 153-
      154; 242; 262; 271).]

116. Zeidner, Betty Jean. "Cervantine Aspects of the Novel-
      istic Art of Benito Pérez Galdós." Ph.D. disserta-
      tion, University of California, Berkeley, 1957. Pp.
      v + 230.

      [The critic seeks to discover the influence of Cer-
      vantes on Galdós during the various epochs of the lat-

ter's career. This dissertation contains an introduction,
nine chapters, a conclusion, notes, and bibliography.
In Galdós' early writings, such as *La fontana de oro*,
Zeidner finds only superficial Cervantine influence,
largely in the form of isolated allusions. In the
second major phase the critic notes in Galdós' works
certain Cervantine techniques, such as numerical pre-
cision, age descriptions, proverbs (in *Doña Perfecta*,
1876), and the conflict of reality and imagination (in
La familia de León Roch, 1878). In this latter novel
Zeidner also sees the beginnings of Galdós' use of
unique characters.

The period of profound Cervantine assimilation (as
opposed to imitation), Zeidner concludes, is in Galdós'
series of *Novelas españolas contemporáneas*. The novel
La desheredada, 1881, is studied in some detail, especially as regards the reality-imagination conflict in
the mind of Isidora. In this same epoch, the critic
states, Galdós' characters become endowed with con-
trolled independence. A special chapter is devoted to
a later novel of this era, *Fortunata y Jacinta*, to many
the climax of Galdós' literary career. Here, states
Zeidner, Galdós becomes highly interested in the function of the novelist and the relationship between the
creator and his created work. The characters in *Fortunata y Jacinta*, the critic finds, lead "incited" lives,
like the characters of Cervantes. In other novels after *Fortunata*, such as *Nazarín*, 1895, Zeidner observes
the fullest assimilation of Cervantine character presentation. The structure of *Nazarín* is compared to that
of the *Quijote*: departure in search of adventures; journey and return home; the dominant theme of hope; the
hero a victim of the ridicule of a society which does
not understand him. Also, notes Zeidner, the reader of
Nazarín, like the reader of Cervantes' masterpiece,
must make up his own mind regarding the insanity of the
protagonist. The critic discusses the novel *Halma*, a
sequel to *Nazarín*, and points out that the characters,
like the Knight and Squire in the 1615 *Quijote*, become
aware of their existence in a literary work in circu-
lation.

In Galdós' last years of writing Zeidner sees no
major Cervantine influence. Galdós, she finds, becomes
fantastic and symbolistic in such works as *El caballero
encantado*, an imitation of a chivalry novel, the hero
of which symbolizes the degenerate youth of Spain seeking purification and regeneration. The major area of
Cervantine influence on this novel, Zeidner concludes,

lies in Galdós' feigned concern over historical accu-
racy and in his critical allusions to an alleged original manuscript.]

Marcelino Menéndez y Pelayo

117. Rubinos, José. "Cervantes y Menéndez y Pelayo: algunas
     semejanzas." *Boletín de la Academia Cubana de la
     Lengua* 6 (1975):5-12.

     Both Cervantes and Menéndez y Pelayo were extraordi-
     nary men; both were chivalresque geniuses. Cervantes
     and Menéndez y Pelayo have a smile of understanding
     toward the human soul; both avoid hurting others. The
     style of both men reveals a plain plasticity, and both
     write works which are completely Catholic.

118. Socorro, Manuel. *Menéndez Pelayo y Cervantes*. Las
     Palmas de Gran Canaria: Tip. Alzola, 1957. Pp. viii
     + 205.

     [This well-documented work contains a prolog and
     twenty-three short chapters. In his prolog the critic
     states that he has searched all of Menéndez Pelayo's
     critical studies (not merely those few dealing specific-
     ally with Cervantes) in order to discover Don Marcelino's
     ideas about the author of the *Quijote*. Socorro finds
     Menéndez Pelayo to be saturated with the spirit of Cer-
     vantes. For Don Marcelino, states the critic, litera-
     ture is divided into two epochs: pre-Cervantine and
     post-Cervantine. Socorro concludes that Menéndez Pe-
     layo's contribution to the true evaluation of Cervantes
     is "capitalísima."
     The twenty-three chapters of this study examine many
     aspects of Cervantes' life and writings, and on each
     point the views of Menéndez Pelayo are cited. Of par-
     ticular interest is Chapter XX, which discusses eigh-
     teenth-century criticism of Cervantes and his works in
     some detail. Chapters XXI and XXII are devoted to the
     reception of Cervantes' works in America and in Europe,
     respectively. The fact that Don Marcelino viewed Cer-
     vantes as a truly national writer is noted in the pro-
     log and, especially, in Chapter XVII. Socorro also de-
     votes attention to Menéndez Pelayo's views on Cervantes'
     lesser works, and to the false *Quijote*.]

The Generation of 1898

General

119. Descouzis, Paul Marcel. *Cervantes y la generación del 98; la cuarta salida de Don Quijote.* Madrid: Ediciones Iberoamericanas, 1970. Pp. 158. [See also Descouzis' earlier work: "Cervantes y la generación del 98," Ph.D. dissertation, University of Maryland, 1959. Pp. 175.]

[This work is summarized in some detail in Volume One of this bibliography (item 90, pp. 94-95). Descouzis discusses the interpretation of the *Quijote* by various writers at the turn of the century: Unamuno considered the Don endowed with a divine, inspirational madness which should be imitated by Spaniards, and Azorín (José Martínez Ruiz) praised the Knight's lofty moral values of truth and justice. However, Descouzis observes, Maeztu regarded the *Quijote* as a decadent and pessimistic book, and Valle-Inclán questioned the value of Cervantes' masterpiece as a force for the regeneration of Spain. Ganivet, the critic observes, did use the galley slave episode to illustrate the injustice of Spanish laws.]

120. García Morejón, Julio. "El *Quijote* y la generación de 1898." *Miscelánea Universitas* 2 (1956):7-27.

[The ideas of Ganivet, Unamuno, Maeztu, Ortega y Gasset, and "Azorín" on the *Quijote* are examined. All these writers, states the critic, are concerned with the problem of Spain and how to awaken her from her lethargy or *abulia*, and several of the Generation of 1898 erect the Knight as a standard bearer and redeemer of Spain. Unamuno is said to be the most feverish defender of the quixotic myth, though Ganivet was the first Spaniard to speak of the Don as a symbol of Spanish ideals. Maeztu, it is observed, regarded the *Quijote* as a decadent work written when Spain was exhausted. Azorín, states García Morejón, did not consider Cervantes an anti-idealist but merely opposed to vain and mad exaltation.]

121. Seda-Rodríguez, Gladys. "Unamuno, Critic of Cervantes." Ph.D. dissertation, Columbia University, 1968. Pp. 294.

[This item deals largely with the critical interpretation of the *Quijote*, and other Cervantine works, by
members of the Generation of 1898. However, attention
is devoted to the influence of Cervantes' *obras* on the
fiction of Spanish writers around the turn of the century. Seda-Rodríguez notes (pp. 215-220) Unamuno's
Cervantine fascination with autonomous characters, as
reflected in *Niebla* and *Amor y pedagogía*. The critic
finds (p. 220) that Alejandro Gómez in *Nada menos que
todo un hombre* is one of the most Cervantine of Unamuno's characters, being similar to the Curious Impertinent in that he puts his wife's virtue to the test and
destroys her and himself.

Attention is devoted to other fiction writers of the
Generation of 1898. The artistic re-creations of Cervantine episodes by Azorín are discussed (pp. 248 *et
seq.*): *La ruta de Don Quijote*, "El Caballero del Verde
Gabán"; and "Don Álvaro de Tarfe." Seda-Rodríguez also
states (p. 254) that Yuste, in Azorín's *La voluntad*, is
a quixotic type. The critic further notes that the
figure Víctor in *Cervantes o la casa encantada* converses
with a fictional Cervantes, raising the question of the
superiority of fictional characters over real characters.

The influence of Cervantes on Ganivet is dealt with
to a certain extent (pp. 261-262). Seda-Rodríguez finds
that the hero Pío Cid (*Los trabajos del infatigable Pío
Cid* and *La conquista del reino de Maya*) is perhaps the
most literal and direct translation of the quixotic
type in the novel of the Generation of 1898: Pío Cid
helps the needy; he sees beauty in the ugly and sordid;
his ideal is a society based on purity, love, and justice; he is aware of himself and the life that he is
creating (the essence of his quixotism).

Seda-Rodríguez notes (pp. 263-264) the use by Baroja
of quixotic men of action (e.g., Zalacaín). The critic,
however, devotes more attention to Ramón Pérez de
Ayala, especially to his *Belarmino y Apolonio*, regarded
by some as the *Don Quijote* of the modern novel, an
interplay of reality and ideality, presented from the
multiple view of the narrator and reflected in the
parallelism of the plot and the characters.

Seda-Rodríguez finds (p. 266) a contrast between the
mature serenity which is revealed in Cervantes' masterpiece and the feeling of anguish produced in those who
read the lives of the quixotic prototypes of the Generation of 1898.

In the final portion of her thesis Seda-Rodríguez
discusses the interpretation of the *Quijote* by post-

Generation of 1898 critics, including Ortega y Gasset,
Madariaga, and Américo Castro.]

"Azorín" (José Martínez Ruiz)

122. Balseiro, José A. "Azorín y Cervantes." *Modern Lan-
      guage Journal* 19 (April 1935):501-510.

      There are several similarities between Cervantes and
      Azorín (José Martínez Ruiz). Both disdain rhetoric and
      use a language different from that of their contemporar-
      ies. However, Cervantes uses simple language naturally,
      while Azorín's verbal simplicity is a carefully studied
      renovation. Another strange similarity between the two
      men is that both, at first, condemned a leading literary
      figure of their times: Cervantes criticized Lope's plays
      (Part I, *Don Quijote*), and Azorín condemned Valera for
      being too enamored with the elegant life. Both later
      retracted their previous charges.
      [Balseiro gives a general summary of Azorín's remarks
      about Cervantes and his works. He finds that for Azo-
      rín the *Quijote* was a book of realities. Balseiro ob-
      serves, also, that Azorín appears to praise *El Persiles*
      even more than he praises the *Quijote*.]

123. Catena, Elena. "Azorín, cervantista y cervantino."
      Anales Cervantinos 12 (1973):73-113.

      [Catena points out the admiration of the writers of
      the Generation of 1898 for Cervantes. Particular praise
      is given to Azorín, Unamuno, and Maeztu, none of whom
      were slavish imitators of Cervantes. Azorín, states
      Catena, was a dedicated student of Cervantes who found
      the earlier writer a living author, a "classic" author
      in the sense that we can see ourselves in his works.
      Attention is given to Azorín's *La ruta de Don Quijote*,
      and to his interest in the Quijote figure, in Sancho,
      in Diego de Miranda, and in Alvaro Tarfe. Catena ob-
      serves that Azorín, even prior to Américo Castro, saw
      that in the *Quijote* there lay an energetic attempt to
      express the reality of living, as a dynamic process, an-
      guished and always problematical. The critic comments
      upon the tendency of Azorín to follow Cervantes in mix-
      ing poetry and history, fantasy and reality.]

124. Cruz Rueda, Ángel. "El cervantismo de un cervantista."
      Cuadernos de Literatura 5 (1949):85-113.

[This work is a detailed summary of Azorín's writings
on Cervantes, from 1904. The critic concludes that
Azorín absorbed the essence of Cervantes' work but is,
nevertheless, an original writer.]

125. Sánchez, Alberto. *El cervantismo de Azorín.* Madrid:
      "Cervantes," 1975. Pp. 35. [Based on a summary by
      the author in *Anales Cervantinos* 12 (1973):244-245.
      The original could not be obtained.]

      [Sánchez examines Azorín's creative *cervantismo* in
      three epochs: (1) 1905; (2) 1916; (3) 1947. The critic
      points out Azorín's sympathy for Cervantes and his de-
      votion to his works, and notes that though Azorín
      placed the *Quijote* at the top of the pedestal, he did
      not disdain Cervantes' other works. Sánchez observes
      that Azorín does not follow the tendency of some to re-
      gard Cervantes and the *Quijote* as detached from each
      other.]

Miguel de Unamuno

126. Basdekis, Demetrios. "Cervantes in Unamuno: Toward a
      Clarification." *Romanic Review* 60 (October 1969):
      178-185.

      [Basdekis seeks to undo the notion that Unamuno did
      not admire Cervantes. Unamuno's apparent anti-Cervantes
      statements, the critic finds, should not be taken liter-
      ally, but should be regarded as Unamuno's attempt to
      move readers and critics away from myopic criticism of
      the *Quijote* (an emphasis on biographic minutiae and ar-
      bitrary detail) toward a confrontation with the novel
      itself. To Unamuno, Basdekis finds, *quijotismo* has em-
      bedded in it that ideal, open forum which allows the
      reader and the critic to unshackle themselves, to con-
      front author, literary work, and protagonist in an effort
      to "re-create," to give fresh, vital, new meaning to
      the work of an author long dead, and to collaborate in
      a genuine literary experience.
      Unamuno's *Vida de Don Quijote y Sancho*, Basdekis
      asserts, is his preparatory thrust toward the creation
      of a new novel, which will culminate in *Niebla*, where
      Unamuno assumes the role which he would attribute to
      Cervantes: he steps aside and allows his work, the
      reader, and the protagonist to confront one another
      and *him* in an elaborate and intense dialectic wherein

the reader-critic is unquestionably involved in and col-
laborates in an "in-process" novel. At the end of his
article Basdekis lists various favorable references by
Unamuno to Cervantes.]

127. King, Willard F. "Unamuno, Cervantes y *Niebla*." *Re-
     vista de Occidente* 16 (February 1967):219-231.

     [King discusses the influence of the *Quijote* on Una-
     muno's *Niebla*: Unamuno's hero, Augusto Pérez, like the
     Knight, has little pre-history; both heroes come alive
     only after they begin to idealize a beloved; both pro-
     tagonists die peacefully.

     Also discussed in this article is the influence of
     Cervantes' masterpiece on Unamuno's conception of the
     new novel, the *nivola*: (1) an undetermined plot that
     would develop spontaneously; (2) characters who would
     create themselves; (3) limited description of the set-
     ting; (4) an abundance of dialogs and monologs; (5) the
     use of tragicomedy, in that serious matters would be
     treated comically, and comic matters would be treated
     seriously.]

128. Unamuno, Miguel de. "Maese Pedro." *Obras completas*.
     Vol. 5, pp. 116-117. Edited by Manuel García Blanco.
     Madrid: Escelicer, 1968.

     [The editor notes that in 1928 Unamuno revealed to
     José Forns his intention to write a play about Maese
     Pedro. A double stage was to be used, Maese Pedro to
     be on a stage above that of the puppets. He was not,
     apparently, to have a merely passive function but would
     intervene in the roles of the puppets from time to time.
     No notes on this play have been located.]

129. Unamuno, Miguel de. "Don Quijote y Don Juan." *Obras
     completas*. Vol. 5, pp. 110-111, 185. Edited by
     Manuel García Blanco. Madrid: Escelicer, 1968.

     [In 1905, Unamuno revealed to Eduardo Marquina his
     intention to write a play about Don Quijote and Don
     Juan. On January 4, 1910, he reconfirmed this plan in
     a letter to Francisco Antón. It appears that in Una-
     muno's unfinished play Don Juan would be the suitor
     and perhaps seducer of Don Quijote's niece, and that at
     the end the Knight would defeat Don Juan. Unamuno's
     brief notes on this projected play are reproduced by
     the editor.]

130.   Unamuno, Miguel de. "La muerte de Sancho." *Obras com-*
       pletas. Vol. 5, pp. 107-108, 871. Edited by Manuel
       García Blanco. Madrid: Escelicer, 1968.

       [Unamuno's notes on a planned play about Sancho Panza
       state: "Tres actos. En el segundo una donosa burla, la
       venida de Amadís a buscarle de escudero, o la de Don
       Quijote. Se vuelve loco." A letter to Unamuno from
       Juan Barco, dated August 15, 1899, reveals that Barco
       was pleased with the idea of the play as a continuation
       of the career of Don Quijote. However, Barco suggested
       to Unamuno that the career of Sancho should be written
       first as a novel. In September, 1928, Unamuno mentioned
       the planned play of Sancho's life to José Forns while
       Azorín (José Martínez Ruiz) was present. Unamuno was
       concerned about the type of language to be used in the
       play, archaic or contemporary. Azorín urged that modern
       language be used. The editor suggests that the play
       would involve Sancho's quixotization, as Unamuno de-
       scribed it in 1905, in his *Vida de Don Quijote y
       Sancho*.]

                         Twentieth-Century Spain

131.   Ellis, Keith. "Cervantes and Ayala's *El Rapto*: The Art
       of Reworking a Story." *PMLA* 84 (January 1969):14-19.

       Francisco Ayala's *El rapto*, 1965, is clearly based on
       Chapter 51, Part I of the *Quijote*, even as to the name
       of the central figure, Vicente de la Roca. Ayala's
       Vicente returns from Germany and visits his Spanish
       village. Julita, daughter of a well-to-do family, runs
       off with Vicente. Ayala's treatment of the story dif-
       fers from that of Cervantes in several respects. Cer-
       vantes' narrator, Eugenio, tells the story of Vicente
       in the first person, keeping his own interest in the
       foreground. Ayala uses the third person and draws upon
       dialog in order to narrow his focus. Ayala also adds
       up-to-date empirical details to lend realism to the
       story. He further seeks to make Julita's remaining a
       virgin seem more verisimilar to the reader by exploring
       more deeply Vicente's personality.

132.   García Lorenzo, Luciano. "Jacinto Grau: *Las bodas de
       Camacho* y *El rey Candaules*." *Anales Cervantinos* 11
       (1972):217-272.

[García Lorenzo reprints two plays by Jacinto Grau:
Las bodas de Camacho, written in cooperation with Adriá
Gual (printed 1903), and *El rey Candaules*. In his introductory notes the critic observes that the first play
is based on Chapters 20 and 21 of Part II of the *Quijote* and finds that there is a relationship between the
play *El rey Candaules* and Cervantes' *Tale of the Curious
Impertinent*. García Lorenzo suggests that Herodotus'
tale of the voyeur king of Lydia may be the forerunner of
Cervantes' story of the husband who tempts his wife.
García Lorenzo finds that Cervantes' tale, in turn, influenced Grau's modern version of King Candaules.]

133. Martínez, Armando. "Reflejos cervantinos en el teatro
      de Alejandro Casona." Ph.D. dissertation, The Univer-
      sity of Alabama, 1972. Pp. iv + 270.

      [This work contains an introduction, four chapters,
and a conclusion. In his introduction, Martínez states
that both Cervantes and Casona mix fantasy and reality,
humor and poetry, in order to present human problems in
a non-bitter way. The critic further finds that both
writers show tolerance toward mankind and faith in man's
values, that both men reveal stoic serenity in facing
adversities and present an optimistic view of life,
and that both are moral writers without being moralizing.
      In the first chapter Martínez compares the lives of
Cervantes and Casona, and finds that both men lived in
critical times and had similar artistic and personality
affinities. The critic also notes here that both authors create realistic works as well as works that are
part fantastic and part real, and that both writers find
eternal values in common people. Martínez states that
both Cervantes and Casona are indefinite as to time and
space, that both inter-mix poetic elements in their
works, and that their heroes maintain a dignity in ad-
versity and serenely accept the collapse of their
worlds.
      In Chapter Two, the critic points out that there were
great differences in the worlds in which Cervantes and
Casona lived but that their artistic treatment of reality is similar. Three levels of "reality" are here discussed: (1) "realidades extraordinarias"; (2) "realidades corrientes o cotidianas"; (3) "realidades depri-
mentes." It is stated that in the works of both writers
the "realities" in (1) and (2) predominate over the de-
pressing realities.

Chapter Three studies the similarities in the attitude
of both authors toward humanity and their depiction of
human figures. Martínez emphasizes that Cervantes and
Casona are both compassionate and stress inner reform,
that their characters are contradictory, not stereotypes,
and that both reject the circumstantial (social class)
and look for that which is inherent in man.

The attitude of both writers toward nature is the
subject of Chapter Four. Both writers flee the city
and place their heroes in contact with nature, the critic observes. Martínez notes that although the landscape is different in the works of each author (Casona
was from the mountains of Asturias, Cervantes from the
arid central plains), both men have a love for the bu-
colic, both describe nature and climate well, and above
all each has an idealizing tendency in regard to nature.
Yet, the critic continues, in spite of the fact that
both Cervantes and Casona stress the spiritual well-
being that nature brings, the rationalistic tendencies
of each writer prevent him from making nature divine or
a cure for all evils.]

134.   Salgues Cargill, Maruxa. "Mito de Don Quijote y Sancho
        en *Belarmino y Apolonio*." *Insula* 24, núm. 274
        (September 1969):16.

[Salgues finds that two of Ramón Pérez de Ayala's
characters, the shoemakers Belarmino and Apolonio, are
partly an ingenious and original re-creation of Don
Quijote and Sancho. Salgues notes the following parallels between the *Quijote* and *Belarmino y Apolonio*,
1921: both novels have a didactic function; both are
full of social criticism; both have traditional Spanish
humor. Several similarities between the Knight and
Belarmino are observed: Belarmino represents the ridicule of philosophers as the Don is a parody of knights-
errant; each has a face that is described as "enjuto";
each speaks in a manner out of the ordinary; both are
avid readers; both are mocked by humanity; both have a
superiority complex; each has grave defeats; both have
been written about and are thus well known to their contemporaries; at the end each withdraws from the world
to die in his village.

Similarities between Sancho and Apolonio are pointed
out: both are ambitious for their children; each is on
familiar terms with a duchess who mocks him; Sancho
speaks in proverbs while Apolonio at times speaks in
verse; both fail, Sancho in his government and Apolonio
in his verse drama.]

135. Sánchez, Alberto. "Cervantes y Francisco Ayala: original
       refundición de un cuento narrado en *El Quijote*."
       Cuadernos Hispanoamericanos 66 (April 1966):133–139.

       Francisco Ayala's *El rapto* is based on the Vicente de
       la Roca episode in Part I, Chapter 51, of the 1605 *Qui-
       jote*. Both stories contain the same plot of a young
       man returning to his Spanish home town, eloping with a
       wealthy local girl and robbing her of all but her chas-
       tity. Even the name of the protagonist is the same.
       Both stories have a similar three-part structure: (1)
       an introduction; (2) the story itself; (3) an epilog.
       However, Cervantes' introductory material is bucolic
       while that of Ayala is sociological. Also, in the plot
       itself, Ayala furnishes more details about the environ-
       ment. The conclusions are also somewhat different: Cer-
       vantes' heroine Leandra is sent to a convent on her re-
       turn; Ayala's heroine Julita merely goes on a trip with
       her mother to get over her unpleasant experience with
       Vicente. Ayala's epilog brings out the character of
       the protagonist and seeks to clarify why he did not
       bother to seduce Julita.

III. *DON QUIJOTE* IN FRANCE

General
(*see also* Item 5)

136. Azorín [Martínez Ruiz, José]. "Don Quijote en Francia."
     Obras completas. Vol. 9, pp. 241-242. Madrid: Agui-
     lar, 1963. [From *Con permiso de los cervantistas*,
     Madrid: Biblioteca Nueva, 1948.]

     Quijotismo is the most universal concept which Spain
     has contributed to world literature. Diderot created
     his own Don Quijote, namely Jacques the fatalist. Dau-
     det created his version of the Knight, Tartarin.
     Jacques wanders through the world, from adventure to ad-
     venture, driven by fate; Tartarin is the victim and
     beneficiary of his own imagination. Flaubert has created
     Bouvard and Pécuchet, two quixotic figures who seek to
     know and understand all things. They suffer defeats of
     illusions, yet they acquire a new illusion after every
     defeat. Cervantes' *Quijote* is the apology for vital
     force; Flaubert's *Bouvard et Pécuchet* is the apology for
     comprehension.

*   Babinger, Georg. "Die Wanderungen und Wandelungen der
     Novelle von Cervantes *El curioso impertinente* mit
     spezieller Untersuchung von Brosses *Le curiex im-
     pertinent.*" *Romanische Forschungen* 31 (1912):486-
     549. Cited above as item 57.

     [In this article Babinger discusses in detail N. de
     Brosse's 1645 adaptation of *El curioso impertinente*.
     Another French version noted by the critic is that of
     Destouches in 1711.]

137. Bardon, Maurice. *"Don Quichotte" en France au XVII*[e] *et
      au XVIII*[e] *siècle, 1605-1815.* Paris: H. Champion,
      1931. Pp. 932.

      In 1608 the *Curioso impertinente* was translated into
      French, and in 1609 the Marcela-Grisóstomo episode and
      the speech on Arms and Letters. Oudin, in 1614, trans-
      lated Part I of the *Quijote*, and in 1618 Rosset rendered
      Part II into French. Cervantes' masterpiece was imita-
      ted by Sorel in *Le berger extravagant*, by Du Bail in *Le
      gascon extravagant*, and by Du Verdier in *Le chevalier
      hyponcondrique.* On the French stage the Cardenio epi-
      sode was adapted by Pichou in 1628, and three comedies
      by Guérin de Bouscal between 1638 and 1641 are based on
      the *Quijote.* During the French Classical period Cer-
      vantes' Sancho Panza had a possible influence on
      Molière's Sosie in *Amphitryon.*

      While critical references to the *Quijote* in the seven-
      teenth century are generally favorable, Chapelain did
      not consider it superior to *Lazarillo*, and Pierre Per-
      rault and P. Bouhours thought Cervantes' novel mediocre.
      In the eighteenth century Lesage considered Avellaneda's
      spurious *Quijote* superior to the original and criticized
      the *Curioso impertinente* for lack of verisimilitude.
      Voltaire, however, thought the *Quijote* the only book in
      Spanish that was worth reading, though the hero was a
      fool.

      While there were many references to *Don Quijote* by
      French critics prior to 1815, Bernadin de Saint-Pierre
      was practically the only writer to see its importance,
      and to believe that it was one of the world's great
      books. Cervantes and Rabelais, he concluded, caused a
      revolution in customs and ideas. Bernadin de Saint-
      Pierre, who viewed the *Quijote* as a book of combat, is
      a forerunner of the Romantic interpretation of that
      novel.

138. Brunetière, Ferdinand. "L'Influence de l'Espagne dans
      la littérature française." *Études critiques sur
      l'histoire de la littérature française.* Vol. 4, pp.
      51-71. Paris: Hachette et Cie, 1891.

      [Allusions to the *Quijote* are surprisingly rare in
      this short work and do not add to an understanding of
      the influence of Cervantes' masterpiece on French
      literature.]

139. Farinelli, Arturo. "España y Francia." *Ensayos y dis-
      cursos de crítica literaria hispano-europea.* Vol. 2,
      pp. 305-355. Rome: Fratelli Treves, 1925.

[The critic briefly notes (p. 330) the early translations of Cervantes' works in France.]

140. Hazard, Paul. "Ce que les lettres françaises doivent à
l'Espagne." *Revue de Littérature Comparée* 16 (1936):
5-22.

[Hazard only briefly touches upon the influence of
the *Quijote* on French literature. The critic does note
that the sentimental interpretation of the *Quijote* in
France did not arise until late. A very brief history
of the changes in the interpretation of the *Quijote* in
France is presented: first it was a book for laughter;
then a pessimistic book which condemned lofty ideals;
still later an idealistic book which defended liberty.]

141. Huszár, Guillaume. *L'Influence de l'Espagne sur le
théâtre français des XVIIIe & XIXe siècles.* Paris:
H. Champion, 1911. Pp. 190.

[At pages 47-48 the critic notes the general influence
of the *Quijote* on French literature. Huszár points out
the use by Marivaux of Cervantes' masterpiece in *Pharsamon, ou le Don Quichotte moderne* (p. 74). The influence of *La tía fingida* and *La gitanilla* on Victor Hugo
is suggested (pp. 140-141). Huszár finds possible
echoes of the *Quijote* in three plays by Rostand: *Les
Romanesques*, *La Princesse lointaine*, and *Cyrano de
Bergerac* (pp. 181-190).]

142. Neumann, Max-Hellmut. "Cervantes in Frankreich (1582-
1910)." *Revue Hispanique* 78 (1930):1-309.

[Neumann's essay contains eleven chapters and discusses French adaptations, translations, and criticism
of Cervantes' works in detail. The early *roman à clef*
approach to the *Quijote*, used by Segrais and Rapin, is
noted in Chapter III. The eighteenth-century view of
Marmorel and Bernadin de Saint-Pierre that Cervantes
was a humorous reformer of customs like Rabelais is
examined in Chapter VI. The clash between the optimistic and the pessimistic interpretation of the *Quijote*
is the subject of detailed study in Chapter X. Neumann
regards Bouterwek's history of Spanish literature,
1804, as having a profound effect on French criticism,
for prior to his work, Neumann concludes, critics in
France had regarded the *Quijote* as a mere satire on chivalric novels, a *roman à clef*, or a human comedy.
Bouterwek, he observes, introduced into French criticism
the idea that Cervantes' Knight was a striver after all

that was grand and noble. Auger's psychiatric study of
the *Quijote*, 1825, is also examined in Chapter X.]

143. Rogers, Paul Patrick. "Spanish Influence on the Litera-
      ture of France." *Hispania* 9 (October 1926):205-235.

      [The first portion of this article is a general dis-
      cussion of the French reception of Spanish literature.
      Rogers notes (p. 213) that the *Quijote* and the *Novelas
      ejemplares* were translated into French on various occa-
      sions. The latter, and larger, portion of this article
      is a "List of French authors whose works show the influ-
      ence of Spain," which list is arranged more or less chrono-
      logically. The following works are said to be influ-
      enced by the *Quijote*: *Curieux impertinent*, 1645, by N.
      de Brosse; *Les folies de Cardenio*, 1629, and *L'infidèle
      confident*, 1630, by Pichou; *Le berger extravagant*, 1627,
      by Charles Sorel; *Le gouvernement de Sanche Pansa*, 1624,
      and *Dom Quixote de la Manche*, 1638, by Guérin de Bous-
      cal; *Sancho Pança gouverneur*, 1712, by Florent Dancourt;
      Le curieux impertinent, 1710, by Philippe Destouches;
      Pharsamon, ou le Don Quichotte moderne, 1717, by Pierre
      Marivaux; and *Tartarin de Tarascon*, 1872, by Alphonse
      Daudet. Rogers suggests a partial influence of the *Qui-
      jote* on Jean Florian's *Gonzalve de Cordue*, 1782. The
      critic (pp. 234-235) includes a bibliography of works
      dealing with the influence of Spain on French litera-
      ture.]

144. Ropa, Denis L. "Cervantes y la literatura francesa."
      Anales de la Universidad de Santo Domingo 12 (1947):
      79-90.

      France was the first country to discover the merit of
      Cervantes' works, but what is his influence on French
      literature? Like Don Quijote, several of Corneille's
      heroes remain deaf and blind to earthly realities, de-
      livering themselves entirely to an imaginary cause;
      and Cervantes' praise of liberty is echoed by Rousseau,
      who is similar to the author of the *Quijote* in a number
      of ways. In addition, the bitter lesson of Cervantes'
      masterpiece, that a single, elderly man cannot correct
      the injustices of the world, is reflected in the works
      of Molière and La Fontaine. Finally, the Spaniard's
      idea that truth depends upon each individual's perspec-
      tive is reflected in Proust, Alain-Fournier, Gide, and
      Valéry.

Seventeenth-Century France

145. Adam, Antoine. *"Don Quichotte* en France au XVIIe
      siècle." *Lettres Françaises*, 18 August 1955, p. 9.

      [Adam points out that the *Quijote* was one of the
      most popular books in France in the seventeenth cen-
      tury. Various Frenchmen of that age who referred to it
      are mentioned: Voiture, Saint-Amant, Mme de Sévigné,
      Racine. It is observed, however, that Frenchmen in the
      early part of that century viewed Cervantes' novel as
      an amusing or comical work not basically different from
      Guzmán de Alfarache. Later in the seventeenth century,
      states Adam, French criticism becomes more penetrating:
      Mme d'Aulnoy praises the delicateness of Cervantes'
      language, and Saint-Évremond ranks Cervantes with Pe-
      tronius as a painter of characters and customs and a
      master of gay satire.]

146. Bidou, Henry. "Ce que nos aïeux ont pensé de *Don
      Quichotte."* *Annales: revue mensuelle de lettres
      françaises* 18 (15 March 1924):303-316.

      [Bidou notes the early popularity of the *Quijote* in
      France. Two plays based on the Cardenio episode are
      examined: Pichou's *Les folies de Cardenio*, 1629, and
      Guérin de Bouscal's *Dom Quixote de la Manche*, 1638.
      The critic also notes another play by Bouscal, *Le
      gouvernement de Sanche Pansa*, 1641. Several late
      seventeenth- and early eighteenth-century plays based
      on the *Quijote* are briefly examined, including Dufresny's
      Sancho Pança, 1694. Bidou observes that there was very
      little interest in the *Quijote* in France between 1641
      and 1694, which generally corresponds to the reign of
      Louis XIV.]

147. Crooks, Esther J. "Translations of Cervantes into
      French." In *Cervantes Across the Centuries ... A
      Quadricentennial Volume Edited by Ángel Flores and
      M.J. Benardete*, pp. 294-304. New York: The Dryden
      Press, 1947. [1969 reprint, Gordian Press, pp. 304-
      314.]

      In 1614, Oudin translates Part I of the *Quijote*, and
      in 1618 Rosset renders Part II into French. In 1615,
      Rosset and d'Audiguier introduce the *Novelas ejemplares*

to the French public. Sorel, in 1627, writes an imitation of the *Quijote*, *Le berger extravagant*, an attack
on the pastoral novel. Between 1660 and 1700 the French
public is indifferent toward Cervantes' works, but in
the eighteenth century he is read with interest. Under
Louis XV Cervantes declines in popularity but gains increased attention during the Pre-Romantic movement.

148.   Crooks, Esther J.   *The Influence of Cervantes in France
        in the Seventeenth Century.*   Baltimore: The Johns
        Hopkins Press; London: Oxford University Press, 1931.
        Pp. xi + 271.

        Most of the references by seventeenth-century French
        critics to Cervantes' works are favorable, though Sorel
        questioned the probability of the Duke and Duchess
        spending large sums of money just to make sport of Don
        Quijote. In the first half of the seventeenth century
        Cervantes' hero was regarded as a *miles gloriosus*,
        while in the second half of that century he was consi-
        dered brave. The first translation of a portion of the
        Quijote is Baudouin's rendition of the *Curious Imperti-
        nent* in 1608. In the following year Jean Richer pub-
        lished an arrangement of the Marcela-Grisóstomo episode.
        Charles Sorel's *Le berger extravagant*, 1627-1628, is an
        imitation of the *Quijote*. There the hero goes insane
        reading pastoral novels. In seventeenth-century France
        the *Quijote* was much more influential on the stage than
        in the novel. The hero, however, is misunderstood.
        Only his ludicrous side is seen.

149.   Davison, C.F.   "Cervantes, Voiture and the Spirit of
        Chivalry in France."   *Studi Francesi*, nuova serie,
        no. 52 (1974), pp. 82-86.

        [Davison examines the possible influence of Cervantes'
        writings on Vincent Voiture, 1597-1648. The critic con-
        cludes that it was the *Quijote*, not Cervantes' short
        story *El amante liberal*, which influenced the spirit of
        Voiture's unfinished novel *Alcidalis et Zélide*, namely
        in the mixture of admiration for chivalry and mockery
        of it. Also noted here are Voiture's imitations of Cer-
        vantes' style, and his allusions to the *Quijote* in his
        personal letters.]

150.   Huszár, Guillaume.   *Molière et l'Espagne.*   Paris: H.
        Champion, 1907. Pp. ix + 332.

[Huszár finds (p. 196) a similarity between Sancho
Panza and Molière's Sganarelle in the play *Dom Juan*,
and suggests (p. 223) the influence of Cervantes' Squire
on the figure Sosie in *Amphitryon*. The critic also observes (pp. 208, 242-243) the influence of the *Quijote*
on *Le misanthrope* and *Le bourgeois gentilhomme*.]

151. Kaplan, David. "The Lover's Test Theme in Cervantes
      and Madame de Lafayette." *French Review* 26 (February
      1953):285-290.

[Kaplan compares the "lover's test" theme in Cervantes'
Curioso impertinente with two *récits* in Madame Marie-
Madalaine de Lafayette's *Zayde, histoire espagnole*,
1670: the episode of "Alphonse et Bélasire" and that of
"Alamir, Prince de Tharse." The latter episode is said
to be particularly close to Cervantes' interpolated
novela. The critic concludes that the "lover's test"
theme in *El curioso impertinente* was probably of influence upon *Zayde*, and ultimately upon Madame de Lafayette's masterpiece, *La princesse de Clèves*. The princess, states Kaplan, is really Anselmo himself, the
curioso impertinente, wiser than he is in that she re-
fuses to attempt a test impossible of success, but
foolish since her wisdom leads directly to an unnatural
emotional immobility and finally to the annihilation of
her vital forces.]

152. Lanson, Gustave. "Études sur les rapports de la lit-
      térature française et de la littérature espagnole au
      XVIIe siècle (1600-1660)." *Revue d'Histoire Littér-
      aire de la France* 3 (1896):45-70.

[Part II of this article deals with the diffusion of
Spanish literature in France. At p. 53 the critic notes
the Rosset translation of the *Quijote* into French in
1618.]

153. Lanson, Gustave. "Études sur les rapports de la lit-
      térature française et de la littérature espagnole aux
      XVII° siècle." *Revue d'Histoire Littéraire de la
      France* 8 (1901):395-407.

[Lanson briefly notes allusions to the *Quijote* by the
seventeenth-century French poet and writer Sarasin in
his poems *Le mélancolique* and *Dulot vaincu*.]

154. Morley, S. Griswold. "Notes on Spanish Sources of
      Molière." *PMLA* 19 (1904):270-290.

Guérin de Bouscal drew heavily upon the *Quijote* in
writing *Le gouvernement de Sanche Pansa* and *La suite
de Don Quichotte*. This latter play, in turn, was of
particular influence on Molière's *Le bourgeois gentilhomme*.

155. Neuschäfer, Hans-Jörg. "Cervantes und die Tradition
der Ehebruchsgeschichte zur Wandlung der Tugendauf-
fassung." *Beiträge zur romanischen Philologie*,
Sonderheft (1967), pp. 52-60.

[This article deals with the origin and influence of
the *Curioso impertinente*. The critic finds that Cervantes gives a new twist to the adultery plot: his female
protagonist seeks to avoid adultery; she is not condemned to commit it. Cervantes, Neuschäfer continues,
examines the question whether true virtue is possible,
and to what extent it can resist the attack of passions.
The critic concludes that an earlier story by Marguerite de Navarra (*Heptameron* 26) is the principal ante-
cedent of Cervantes' famous tale. Neuschäfer finds a
definite influence of *El curioso impertinente* on Mme de
Lafayette's *La princesse de Clèves*, but suggests that
Cervantes' tale of *El celoso extremeño* may also have
been a partial source of Mme de Lafayette's story.]

156. Palmer, Melvin D. "Madame d'Aulnoy and Cervantes."
Romance Notes 11 (1970):595-598.

[Palmer states that Marie-Catherine Jumelle de Barne-
ville, Comtesse d'Aulnoy, admired Cervantes, and in one
of her stories, *Nouveau-gentilhomme bourgeois*, 1698,
used the *Quijote* as a model. The critic asserts that
the hero, Dandinardière, is at first a comic figure but
later incites pathos. Palmer concludes that Madame d'
Aulnoy understood the ambiguity of Cervantes' hero. The
critic also observes that the latter part of *Nouveau-
gentilhomme bourgeois* is a frame for a series of tales
which raise the fiction-reality question, a device used
by Cervantes in the *Quijote*.]

157. Smoot, Jean J. "Alceste: The Incomplete Don Quijote."
Romance Notes 12 (Autumn 1970):169-173.

Both Don Quijote and Alceste, of Molière's *Le misanthrope*, confuse their ideal with their ego. Both tend
to idealize the women of their dreams. Both men strive
to fit their ideals to their experience. They are severe
and argumentative. But Don Quijote acquires moderation;

he becomes more human as the story progresses. He grows
to love Sancho. Alceste, however, cannot accept the
friendship of Philinte; he cannot become reconciled to
the world and retreats into his desert. Alceste is incomplete; he represents disenchanted, cynical man. Unlike the Knight, he is not able to express man's nobler
nature as well. *Le misanthrope* ends in pessimism. The
hero is not willing to be crucified in order to change
the world. The *Quijote*, however, ends in optimism, because the hero is willing to suffer. To him, virtue is
worth pursuing in spite of, or even because of, the way
men live and act. The Don admits defeat and dies happy.

158. Terraguso, Antoinette Mahieu. "Reminiscências cervan-
     tinas na obra de Molière." *Estado de São Paolo,
     Suplemento Literario*, 30 December 1973, p. 6.

     [This article deals largely with the influence of the
     Quijote on Molière's plays, especially on the French-
     man's depiction of certain types of servants who are
     different from the rascally ones of the *Commedia dell'
     Arte*. Molière's servants, states Terraguso, are more
     complicated, like Sancho Panza, and are an amalgam of
     contrasting feelings. In the figure M. Jourdain (*Le
     bourgeois gentilhomme*), the critic states, Molière fuses
     the figures of Don Quixote and Sancho: Jourdain resembles
     Sancho physically and in his total ignorance but has
     certain quixotic characteristics (persistence). Terra-
     guso observes similarities between the last part of
     Molière's play and the episode of the Don at the palace
     of the Duke and Duchess.]

                    Eighteenth-Century France

159. Harland, Frances, and Beall, Chandler B. "Voltaire and
     Don Quijote: Supplementary Notes." *Modern Language
     Forum* 25 (1940):113-116.

     [Harland and Beall observe that in *La pucelle* Voltaire
     imitated the episode of the galley slaves. Also, a por-
     tion of Voltaire's *Des arts*, originally intended to be
     a part of *Essai sur les moeurs*, is reproduced, which
     excerpt criticizes the Marcela episode and other ma-
     terial in the *Quijote*. Voltaire, Harland and Beall
     conclude, believed that Cervantes' novel lacked a co-
     herent wholeness and that its adventures were not prop-
     erly tied together.]

160. Sarrailh, Jean. "Lesage, adaptateur d'Avellaneda."
     Bulletin Hispanique 66 (1964):359-362.

     [The critic briefly presents a description of the
     style and tone of Avellaneda's spurious *Quijote* of
     1614. Lesage's French translation of Avellaneda's
     novel, 1704-1716, is generally praised. Sarrailh points
     out the major change made by the translator: the Don is
     allowed to be killed off by the Santa Hermandad.]

161. Showalter, English, Jr. "Did Robert Challe Write a
     Sequel to *Don Quixote?*" *Romanic Review* 62 (1971):
     270-282.

     [In 1713, there appeared a six-volume French edition
     of the *Quijote* with a continuation purportedly by "Sieur
     Saint-Martin." In 1714, Challe claimed authorship of
     the second part of the continuation, Volume VI. Show-
     alter believes that Challe was the author of this con-
     tinuation, and that he probably composed it around 1702.
     The influence of the ideas in the *Quijote* on Challe's
     Les illustres françoises, 1713, is briefly discussed:
     ideas on such matters as marriage and the place of women
     in society.]

162. Showalter, English, Jr. "Robert Challe and *Don Quixote.*"
     French Review 45 (1972):1136-1144.

     For most of the seventeenth century, the French re-
     garded *Don Quijote* as a mere satire or burlesque. It
     could be reduced to a formula: take a pretentious and
     outmoded literary genre, use its conventions to relate
     trivial and vulgar events, and the result will be *Don
     Quijote*. The Classical Age seems to have had little
     sense of the Knight's dignity, not to mention Sancho's.
     [Showalter finds that the *Quijote* had no true admirers
     during the epoch of French Classicism, and that Cervan-
     tes' masterpiece was regarded merely as a book of in-
     genious satire, a collection of sayings and anecdotes.
     The critic lists the following works as mechanical imi-
     tations of the *Quijote* in France: Adrien Perdou de Sub-
     ligny's *Fausse Clélie*; Pierre Carlet de Marivaux's
     Pharsamon; Abbé Bordelon's *Monsieur Oufle*. Showalter
     notes that in each case the hero has read too many
     books. Also briefly noted as shallow imitations of the
     Quijote are Paul Scarron's *Le roman comique*, Antoine
     Furetière's *Le roman bourgeois*, and Bougeant's *Le
     voyage merveilleux du Prince Fan-Férédin*, 1735. Simi-
     larly, states Showalter, Robert Challe, in his

Continuation de l'histoire de l'admirable Don Quichotte,
1713, seldom captures the spirit of the original, although he did turn the Knight into a sort of seventeenth-
century French "honnête homme," which view represents a
new attitude toward the hero and toward the work. In
this continuation, Showalter finds, the hero is brave,
talks reasonably, behaves politely, and achieves beneficial results; Challe's Quijote figure is also a social critic and moralizer, typical of the era. At the
same time, the critic finds, this new interpretation of
the Don is not inconsistent with a profound new compre-
hension of the *Quijote*, much closer to the nineteenth-
century heroic interpretation and the twentieth-century
humanistic interpretation than to a seventeenth-century
burlesque reading.

The critic discusses the intellectual crisis during
the last years of Louis XIV's reign regarding the reliability of knowledge. One effect of this crisis, he observes, was that it became suddenly obvious that a narration told more about the narrator than about the facts
narrated. And, Showalter continues, novelists quickly
exploited this by putting the narrator into the novel,
and making his fallacies part of the story; thus *Don
Quijote*, the original masterpiece of narrative irony,
was rediscovered.

The influence of the *Quijote* on Challe's *Les illustres
françoises*, 1713, is examined in some detail: (1) personal disillusion stands for national disillusion; (2)
the characters are strangely unaware of the golden age
around them, and are dominated by the recent past; (3)
the figures behave in life as if they were in a romance, projecting their imaginative view of the reality
around them, until the inevitable disaster occurs; (4)
the most quixotic figure in the work, Des Frans, is
even referred to as the "chevalier de la triste figure";
(5) Des Frans' failure stems from a lack of self knowledge: too late does he learn that he loves a real
flesh-and-blood woman, not some ideal embodiment.

In his final paragraph Showalter concludes that
Challe, like Cervantes, appears to recommend resigna-
tion and the acceptance of whatever happiness life can
offer. Challe, the critic finds, learned from Cervantes
to temper his moral truth with human understanding, and
the Frenchman's work is animated by some of the same
sympathy for the idealistic and hopeful youths, and by
some of the same sadness and regret for the wisdom which
reality forces upon them.]

163. Wolf, Martin. "Avellanedas *Don Quijote*, sein Verhältnis
      zu Cervantes und seine Bearbeitung durch Lesage."
      Zeitschrift für vergleichende Litteraturgeschichte 17,
      neue folge (1909):1-70.

      [Wolf notes the lack of success of the false *Quijote*,
      pointing out that there were no further editions and
      practically no critical references to it in the seven-
      teenth century. Non-Spanish editions of the false *Qui-
      jote* are briefly discussed, and various theories as to
      the true identity of Avellaneda are presented. An out-
      line of the plot of the spurious *Quijote* is set forth.
      Wolf states that Avellaneda's work follows the general
      sense of Part I of the original, but that the protago-
      nists lose their freshness and are at times overdone.
      Evaluations of the false *Quijote* by various critics are
      summarized. Similarities between Avellaneda's *Quijote*
      and Cervantes' Part II are pointed out by Wolf, who in-
      dicates that Cervantes was the copier. The changes
      made by Lesage in Avellaneda's *Quijote* are listed and
      discussed. The critic notes that the Frenchman freely
      inserts extra short stories and even changes the ending,
      killing off the hero. Wolf observes Lesage's preference
      for the spurious *Quijote* over the original on the ground
      that it was, to him, more probable.]

                    Nineteenth-Century France

164. Alarcos Llorach, E. "La interpretación de *Bouvard et
      Pécuchet* de Flaubert y su quijotismo." *Cuadernos de
      Literatura* 4 (1948):139-176.

      Bouvard et Pécuchet, like the *Quijote*, is a grotesque
      tragedy. The two protagonists are quixotic in character
      and are comical only on the surface. But what is the
      real relationship between *Don Quijote* and *Bouvard et
      Pécuchet*? What does Flaubert owe to Cervantes? In
      both works two grown men depart from their dull routine
      and undertake enterprises which, objectively viewed,
      are beyond their powers and training; both pairs always
      end up bitterly deceived yet do not give up hope. At
      the end of both novels the protagonists seek a more in-
      timate outlet for their dreams: Bouvard and Pécuchet
      return to their old jobs to tell of their woes and dis-
      illusionment; Don Quijote and Sancho consider taking up
      the pastoral life to tell of their sufferings. Both
      the *Quijote* and *Bouvard et Pécuchet* were considered
      comical works by contemporary readers. Yet both are
      philosophical works in which the moral is that the ideal

should not wither away in spite of all the unpleasant-
ness involved in upholding it. In addition, both authors, instead of condemning their heroes, appear to
indict the masses for their failure to understand exaltation.

In spite of the above similarities between Flaubert
and Cervantes, these two writers are very different in
their techniques. Flaubert finds a novelistic theme,
and, thinking about it and around it, makes concentric
circles, deepening his original plan. From the beginning he knows where he is going. Cervantes, on the
other hand, finds a theme but does not lay seige to it
like the Frenchman. The Spaniard does not formulate a
plan but hurls himself through the first open breach
out into the unknown. He continues in this manner,
novel and theme being formulated at one and the same
time. Thus while Flaubert knows what he wants from the
beginning, Cervantes only suspects what he desires.

All in all, there is no proof that Flaubert consciously
imitated Cervantes' masterpiece. It is more true to say
that Flaubert was infected with the melancholy gaiety
of the *Quijote*, with its fusion of reality and illusion,
the realistic and the romantic. In essence, *quijotismo*
was already a part of Flaubert's personality, and *quijotismo* is thus reflected in *Bouvard et Pécuchet*.

165. Ames, Van Meter. *Aesthetics of the Novel*. Chicago:
The University of Chicago Press, 1928. Pp. ix + 221.

Among the first duties of the realist is the correc-
tion of romance, which has distorted vision and spoiled
the perspective of homely things. Cervantes' *Quijote*
showed how too much reading takes away common sense.
Yet, also, that same novel does justice to the beauty
of the ideals of chivalry. The hero can never become
a comic character because the ideals which he exaggerates
have been so wrought into the race that even absurd devotion to them stirs admiration.

[At pages 125-126 Ames compares and contrasts the Don
with Flaubert's Emma Bovary. While the brains of both
become addled from excessive reading, there is a difference, states Ames: romance inspires the Don to be gener-
ous and gentlemanly, to go abroad to the relief of the
weak and oppressed; Emma Bovary is not so inspired, but
withdraws within her tower whence she shall not even look
upon the outside world except as she may see it dreamily
reflected in her mirror.]

166. Baquero Goyanes, Mariano. "Cervantes, Balzac y la voz
del narrador." *Atlántida* 1 (1963):579-596.

[Baquero examines Balzac's use of the Quijote figure
in physical descriptions, and also observes his Cervantine technique of utilizing interpolated tales. The
employment by both writers of narrative economy is observed: they will refer to a trait (such as an accent
or a lisp) but will not belabor the point naturalistically. Baquero also finds that both Cervantes and Balzac are writers who will not renounce their presence in
a story. The critic concludes that Balzac, from his
reading of Cervantes and other writers, saw the possi-
bility of picturing an entire era of history.]

167.   Bardon, Maurice. "*Don Quichotte* et le roman réaliste
       français: Stendhal, Balzac, Flaubert." *Revue de Lit-
       térature Comparée* 16 (1936):63-81.

       [Bardon notes the references of Stendhal, Balzac, and
       Flaubert to the *Quijote* and devotes particular attention
       to Stendhal's *Chartreuse de Parme* and *Le rouge et le
       noir*, to Balzac's *Recherche de l'absolu* and *Cousin Pons*,
       and to Flaubert's *Madame Bovary* and *Bouvard et Pécuchet*.
       The untiring characters in the above novels are compared
       to Cervantes' Knight. The critic finds Emma Bovary, for
       example, to be "une sorte de Don Quichotte," who, like
       Bouvard and Pécuchet, strives to overcome the mediocre;
       and all are led to disaster just as the Don. *Don Qui-
       jote*, *Madame Bovary*, and *Bouvard et Pécuchet*, Bardon
       concludes, are all critiques of exaltation: *Don Quijote*
       in the realm of action, *Madame Bovary* in the realm of
       sentiment, and *Bouvard et Pécuchet* in the realm of
       knowledge.]

168.   Bardon, Maurice. "*Don Quichotte* en France. L'Interpré-
       tation romantique." *Les Lettres Romanes* 3 (1 November
       1949): 263-282; 4 (1 May 1950):95-117.

       [Bardon states that the French romantic interpretation
       of the *Quijote* is based on the works of Bouterwek and
       Sismondi, which spread the views of the German Romanti-
       cists. The critic examines the ideas of numerous French
       critics, from Victor Hugo (*William Shakespeare*, 1827) to
       Laurent Tailhade (*Un monde qui finit*, 1910), and con-
       cludes that virtually all French critics during that
       epoch proclaim the *Quijote* to be a bitter poem of dis-
       illusion.]

169.   Bertrand, J.-J.A. "Génesis de la concepción romántica
       de *Don Quijote* en Francia." *Anales Cervantinos* 3
       (1953):1-41.

       Sismondi's history of European literature, 1813,

spread the romantic views of Friedrich and August Wilhelm Schlegel in France. Though Sismondi's work contains errors, it is important for its conception of
literature as an expression of society. In 1836 and
1837 Viardot translated the *Quijote* into French, using
Clemencín's version as a basis. In his preface Viardot
states that *Don Quijote* started out as a satire on chivalric novels, but that Cervantes grew to like his figures and provided them with good qualities, giving wisdom to Don Quijote and common sense to Sancho.

Prósper Mérimée praises the pictures of customs in
the *Quijote*. He is amazed at the joy in that novel,
the joy of a man content to live in human society as it
is. Théophile Gautier viewed Don Quijote as chivalresque
exaltation, Sancho as anti-enthusiasm, and Dulcinea as
a joke directed at love. He thought also that Cervantes
was making fun of himself while making fun of his hero.
Sainte-Beuve concluded that Part II of the *Quijote* was
more premeditated than Part I, that those with cold
judgment prefer Part II, while those who are poetic and
imaginative tend to favor Part I. Sainte-Beuve, who did
not regard the *Quijote* as philosophical, warned the
reader against confusing his own ideas and reflexions
with those of Cervantes. Victor Hugo did not reflect on
the *Quijote* until his later years. In Chapter XIII of
William Shakespeare, he praises Cervantes' three gifts:
creation, invention, and imagination.

170. Bertrand, J.-J.A. "Génesis de la concepción romántica
      de *Don Quijote* en Francia. Segunda Parte." *Anales
      Cervantinos* 4 (1954):41-76.

      Stendhal concluded that Don Quijote and Sancho repre-
      sented a complete contrast, the idealist and the real-
      ist, and that the Sanchos in life always win out. Bal-
      zac, the most *quijotista* of the French Romanticists,
      was influenced by Cervantes, especially in character
      portrayal. Flaubert is an authentic disciple of the
      Spanish master. To Flaubert the important thing in the
      Quijote was its lack of artifice, its perpetual fusion
      of illusion and reality, and its inspiration. Chateau-
      briand at first thought *Don Quijote* was primarily a
      satire but later concluded that the hero was the noblest,
      the least mad, and the most lovable of men. Chateau-
      briand could not understand the cruel joy of that novel
      except through sad reflection.

171. Bertrand, J.-J.A. "Génesis y desarrollo de la concep-
      ción romántica de *Don Quijote* en Francia. Tercera
      Parte." *Anales Cervantinos* 5 (1955-1956):79-142.

Daudet, in the late nineteenth century, considered
the *Quijote* a contrast between enthusiasm and life,
between imagination and reality. L. Tailhade, a bitter
satirist, saw *Don Quijote* as an extremely pessimistic
work, the comic element being merely a mask. J. Péladan ("le Sar"), similarly, interpreted Cervantes' novel
as a Bible of pessimism, in which an enthusiastic ad-
venturer is defeated by fate.

172. Chaix-Ruy, J. "Cervantes, G. Flaubert et L. Pirandello."
      Anales Cervantinos 6 (1957):123-132.

Flaubert often praised Cervantes' characters for their
vividness. He referred to the fact that the Spaniard
fused illusion and reality in such a way as to make the
Quijote both comic and poetic. Flaubert also observed
that Cervantes left the reader with a vivid picture of
Spain, although the author never really described Spain
in words. Thus the Spaniard taught Flaubert that sug-
gestion was more powerful than minute description. Yet
Cervantes' influence on the Frenchman is more in sub-
stance than in technique. The Spaniard instilled in
Flaubert the theme of *ridicule triste* ... *attaché à la
grandeur.*
Pirandello, like Cervantes, saw his own heroic efforts
turned to naught, and in some of his works the Italian,
like the Spaniard, gets his revenge by showing what happens to the man who aspires to sainthood.

173. Durand, René L.F. *Balzac y Don Quijote.* Caracas:
      Dirección de Cultura Universitaria de la Universidad
      Central de Venezuela, 1950. Pp. 17.

[Durand finds that the life and works of Balzac contain many quixotic features and that he is the most
quixotic and Cervantine of all French writers: he knew
the *Quijote* well, like Flaubert, and in his novels there
are numerous allusions to Cervantes' masterpiece. Dur-
and observes that in his personal life Balzac often
could not distinguish between reality and illusion, and
that he carried on an idealistic love affair with Eveline Hanska, similar to the Don's love for Dulcinea.
Also, the critic continues, Balzac and many of his
characters, like Cervantes' hero, are monomaniacs guided
by a single passion.]

174. Girard, René. *Mensonge romantique et vérité romanesque.*
      Paris: B. Grasset, 1961. Pp. 312. [Translated into
      English as *Deceit, Desire and the Novel; Self and*

Other in Literary Structure. Baltimore: The Johns
Hopkins Press, 1965.]

[Girard discusses unhealthy ("triangular" or "meta-
physical") desire, such as that of Don Quijote whose
desires are based on ideas from the *Amadís*. This type
of desire is contrasted with healthy or spontaneous desire. The critic observes the tendency of Cervantes
constantly to contrast the normal with the exceptional,
which tendency is later used by writers such as Stendhal
and Flaubert. With Cervantes, the critic states, the
exception (Don Quijote) desires unhealthily, and the multitude desires healthily; with Stendhal the opposite is
true. But neither writer, Girard adds, is completely
consistent in this matter, for one character can embody
successively both ontological sickness and good health.
With Flaubert, the critic finds, there are no real oppo-
sitions, only grotesque antitheses, and the ideas of his
characters are even more devoid of significance than
those of Stendhal's *vaniteux*.

Proust and Dostoevski are also discussed and are compared and contrasted with Cervantes in regard to the
technique of contrasts. The varying devices used by
these authors in describing death and renunciation of
illusions are discussed in some detail.]

175. Hatzfeld, Helmut. *"Don Quijote* und *Madame Bovary."*
      Jahrbuch für Philologie 3 (1927):54-70; 116-131.
      [Spanish version *"Don Quijote* y *Madame Bovary,"* in
      Hatzfeld's *Don Quijote como obra de arte del lenguaje*,
      pp. 346-362. Madrid: C.S.I.C., 1966. See also Hatz-
      feld's *Estudios de literaturas románicas*, pp. 322-
      337. Barcelona: Planeta, 1972.]

What did Cervantes reveal to Flaubert? The same thing
that Velázquez revealed to the early Impressionists: a
modern conception of certain problems of form. What details in *Madame Bovary* are drawn from the *Quijote*?
There are six main areas where Flaubert follows Cervantes: (1) he uses a scene at an inn to create a picture
of the society of the times; (2) his heroine reads too
much, to the point of unhealthiness; (3) Flaubert uses
dialog to give an inner picture of a character; (4) he
will create a mood by the use of evil omens; (5) the
Frenchman uses a tumult scene to enhance reality; and
(6) he arranges his sentences to create suspense.

176. Jouglard, Madeleine. *"Don Quichotte* et la *Maison du
      berger."* *Revue de Littérature Comparée* 7 (1927):548-
      549.

[Jouglard compares Don Quijote's description of poetry
(as like a young woman of tender age and unsurpassed
beauty) with certain verses in Alfred Victor de Vigny's
Maison du berger, 1864.]

177. Levin, Harry. *The Gates of Horn, a Study of Five
     French Realists*. New York: Oxford University Press,
     1963. Pp. xii + 554.

     [The *Quijote*, as an anti-romantic work, is examined in
     detail. Levin (pp. 41-50) gives an overall summary of
     the use of Cervantine anti-romanticism by later writers.
     The influence of the *Quijote* on Stendhal (esp. p. 99)
     and on Flaubert (esp. pp. 248-251) is studied in some
     detail. The Knight is compared and contrasted with
     Flaubert's Emma Bovary.]

178. Lugli, Vittorio. "Flaubert e il *Don Chisciotte*." *Cul-
     tura* 15 (1927):401-407.

     [Lugli gathers together Flaubert's various allusions
     to Cervantes' masterpiece. The critic observes that
     Flaubert does not refer to any of Cervantes' minor works.
     Frequent references by Flaubert, in 1852 and 1853, to
     the *Quijote* are quoted, and attention is briefly given
     to the French author's often-cited remark about the
     lack of artifice and the perpetual fusion of reality
     and illusion in Cervantes' novel. Lugli notes certain
     similarities between the *Quijote* and *Madame Bovary*: both
     works deal with bookish madness and attack excess imagi-
     nation and false ideals. The critic, however, finds
     Flaubert's *Bovary* a pessimistic work full of selfish il
     lusions, the *Quijote* a novel of generous illusions.
     Lugli sees only vague echoes of the Knight-Squire duo
     in *Bouvard et Pécuchet*.]

179. Markovitch, Milan. "Alphons Dode i Servantes." *Venac*
     (Zagreb) 18, nos. 7-8 (1933):3-20.

     [Markovitch's short study frequently refers to the
     influence of the *Quijote* on Daudet, 1840-1897, and his
     Tartarin de Tarascon.]

180. Sarrailh, Jean. *Discours d'usage (Rentrée, novembre
     1934), prononcé par M. Jean Sarrailh, professeur à la
     Faculté des Lettres de Poitiers*. Alençon: Imp. Cor-
     bière & Jugain, [1935]. Pp. 22.

     [Sarrailh finds that Anatole France, 1844-1927, had
     no real connection with Spain. Nevertheless, the critic

continues, the French author was familiar with the *Quijote* and cites it with frequency. It appears, states
Sarrailh, that Anatole France read Cervantes' novel on
various occasions. At pages 10 to 14 the critic seeks
to find the influence of the Don Quijote figure on
several of France's characters: Evariste Gamelin; Paphnuce; Choulette; M. d'Astarac; l'abbé Coignard; Georges
de Blanchelande; M. Bergeret; le recteur Leterrier;
Sylvestre Bonnard; Sarriette; Jean Servien. Similarities
between Sancho Panza and several of France's characters
are also noted: Barbe (the mother of Jacques Tournebroche); Mme Gamelin; the squire Francoeur; Palémon.
Anatole France, states the critic, appreciated the discourses, the burlesque-epic scenes, and the spirit of
tolerance in the *Quijote*.]

181. Slavín, León. "Quijote y Tartarín." *El Nacional*, 11
      August 1940. [This item could not be obtained. It is
      summarized by Rafael Heliodoro Valle and Emilia Romero
      in *Bibliografía cervantina en la América española*
      (425), p. 248.]

      [Slavín states that Daudet was wrong to say that his
      hero Tartarin contained both the Knight and the Squire,
      for Tartarin is only a *fanfarrón*, empty, ridiculous,
      whereas the Don and Sancho utter wise statements and
      teach the reader effectively.]

182. Thibaudet, Albert. *Gustave Flaubert*. Paris: Galli-
      mard, 1935. Pp. 281. [First published in 1922, Paris:
      Plon-Nourrit et Cie.]

      [Thibaudet (pp. 79-114) compares *Don Quijote* and
      Madame Bovary. The critic notes Flaubert's love for
      Cervantes' masterpiece, its apparent absence of art,
      its fusion of illusion and reality. Thibaudet states
      that both authors described the society in which they
      lived, that both their works dealt with the disparity
      between reality and dreams, and described the sadness
      which follows ambition.]

183. Torner, Florentino M. "Cervantes y Flaubert." *El
      Nacional*, 29 April 1947. [This item could not be ob-
      tained. For a brief summary, see Rafael Heliodoro
      Valle and Emilia Romero, *Bibliografía cervantina en
      la América española* (425), p. 254.]

      [A general discussion of the influence of the *Quijote*
      on Flaubert. Torner states that the French author knew
      Cervantes' novel by heart.]

Twentieth-Century France

184. Bourne, Marjorie A. "Don Quijote on the Boards in
      France." *Revista de Estudios Hispánicos* 5 (1971):
      189-202.

      [Bourne analyzes a play by Ives Jamiaque, *Don Qui-
      chotte*, brought to the stage in Paris on February 12,
      1965, after premiering in Lyons. The setting, states
      the critic, is closely related to the surrealist thea-
      tre, the stage being divided into a number of sections
      on various levels, each with its own props. Bourne
      finds that Jamiaque goes beyond the imagination of Cer-
      vantes in various instances. The play is also said to
      be cynical at times. The critic concludes that the
      hero of the play loses stature and dignity and is essen-
      tially a figure of one dimension, a person completely
      at odds with his environment. Sancho, Bourne finds,
      is also changed in the play; he is sophisticated, self-
      analytical, and highly cynical. On the whole, Bourne
      finds that the Don Quijote of Jamiaque's play is held
      up to too much jocular ridicule.]

185. Hainsworth, Georges. "Cervantès en France. A propos
      de quelques publications récentes." *Bulletin His-
      panique* 34 (1932):128-144.

      [Hainsworth devotes several pages to a critical exami-
      nation of three works: (1) "Cervantes in Frankreich
      (1582-1910)," by Max-Hellmut Neumann (142); (2) *The
      Influence of Cervantes in France in the Seventeenth
      Century*, by Esther J. Crooks (148); and (3) *"Don
      Quichotte" en France au XVIIe et au XVIIIe siècle, 1615-
      1815*, by Maurice Bardon (137). The weaknesses and strong
      points of these three studies are set forth in detail.
      Hainsworth believes that more study should be given to
      how Cervantes influenced the spirit and form of the novel
      and short story, and is most doubtful whether the collec-
      tion of allusions to Cervantes is the best manner to
      accomplish this. However, the final part of Hainsworth's
      article consists of "détails supplémentaires pour la
      fortune de Cervantès en France," a list of twenty-nine
      items in which there are allusions to Cervantes' works.]

186. Pinilla, Norberto. "Cervantes y Baty." *Atenea* 85
      (1946):86-93.

[Pinilla summarizes and praises Gaston Baty's play *Dulcinea*, written in French and performed in 1938 in the Montparnasse Theatre in Paris. The critic concludes that this drama penetrates the essence of the *Quijote*. The play, states Pinilla, is divided into two parts, each part containing four *cuadros*. A central idea of the play, the critic finds, is that Dulcinea becomes infected by *quijotismo*. The weakness of the play, to Pinilla, is that the Knight, on his deathbed, denies the existence of Dulcinea, and dies before she appears before him. Also, the critic concludes, the work lacks dramatic cohesion in that Dulcinea disappears for a good while during the play, and her reappearance (transformed by the sorcery of love) is too late to achieve the proper effect.]

187. Reparaz-Ruiz, G. de. "Hispanism in France." *Bulletin of Spanish Studies* 23 (1946):187-192.

[This work deals with Hispanic studies in France during World War II. Little note is taken of the *Quijote*. The critic, however, points out, under work in progress, the translation of Cervantes' masterpiece by Bataillon.]

IV. *DON QUIJOTE* IN ITALY

General

188. Farinelli, Arturo. "Ispanesimo nel cinquecento: rinas-
cimento e decadenza." *Italia e Spagna*. Vol. 2, pp.
103-233. Torino: Fratelli Bocca, 1929.

[In the first chapter of this work ("Letteratura e
lingua ispanica nell'Italia rinascente") the critic
briefly notes (p. 135, fn. 1) the influence of the *Quijote* on Italian writing.]

189. Flaccomio, Rosario. *La fortuna del Don Quijote in
Italia nei secoli XVII e XVIII e il Don Chisciotti di
G. Meli*. Palermo: Santi Andó & Figli, [1928?]. Pp.
166.

The first Italian translation of Part I of the *Quijote*
is that of Lorenzo Franciosini in 1622. This work does
not attempt to translate the verse, and many changes are
made, especially in the matter of oaths, to avoid diffi-
culties with the authorities. In 1625, Franciosini
translates Part II of the *Quijote*, and here the poems
are rendered in Italian by Alessandro Adimari. With
Franciosini the Knight and the Squire are purely laugh-
able types. There was no other Italian translation of
Cervantes' novel until 1818, but a number of Spanish
editions were published in Italy. The first mention of
the *Don Quijote* in Italy was by Tassoni in his poem
Secchia rapita, written about 1615. The first notation
of the satirical function of Cervantes' novel was in
Giulio Cesare Capaccio's dialogs of the *Forastiero*,
published in 1634.

Another writer of the seventeenth century, Carlo de'
Dottori, mentioned Don Quijote in his poem *L'asino*,
which contains an episode similar to that of the braying

village. But this episode was also based on an historical fact, the quarrel between Padua and Vicenza recorded
by lo Scardeone in his *De claris mulieribus.*

Already in the seventeenth century there were Italian
plays which drew heavily on the *Quijote* or which contained the Knight as a character: that published by
Francesco Nicolini in 1680, and three plays by G. Gili
between 1687 and 1698. In the eighteenth century the
Quijote is dramatized by Zeno and Pariati. But more
important is G. Meli's poem, *Don Chisciotti e Sanciu,*
1787. This work is the only Italian adaptation of Cervantes' novel, in either century, in which the Knight
and the Squire are not wholly comic. All in all, the
Quijote was of no real influence in Italy until the end
of the eighteenth century.

190.   Fucilla, Joseph G. "Italian cervantiana." *Hispanic
       Review* 2 (July 1934):235-240.

       [Fucilla offers additions and corrections to Ford and
       Lansing's bibliography. Italian translations and adap-
       tations of Cervantes' works are listed, as well as cri-
       tical Cervantine studies by Italians.]

191.   Fucilla, Joseph G. "Bibliografía italiana de Cervantes
       (Suplemento a Ford and Lansing: *Cervantes: a Tenta-
       tive Bibliography*)." *Revista de Filología Española,*
       Anejo 59 (1953):50-62.

       [Fucilla, as the title of the article indicates, adds
       further supplementary material regarding translations of
       Cervantes' works in Italy and critical material by Ital-
       ian Cervantistas.]

192.   Meregalli, Franco. *Presenza della letteratura spagnola
       in Italia.* Firenze: Sansoni, 1974. Pp. 113. (Col.
       "Sansoni Scuola aperta," 49.) [Summarized by Alberto
       Sánchez in *Anales Cervantinos* 13-14 (1974-1975):198.
       The original could not be obtained.]

       [Meregalli presents a general synthesis of the influ-
       ence of Spanish literature upon Italy from the Middle
       Ages to the nineteenth century. Chapters VII and VIII
       are devoted to Cervantes. Italian translations of the
       Quijote and the *Novelas ejemplares* are noted. Refer-
       ences to the *Quijote* by such writers as Tassoni (*La
       secchia rapita,* 1610) and Carlo Dottori (*Asino,* 1652)
       are pointed out. The critic observes that the *opera
       bufa* of the eighteenth century uses certain aspects of

Cervantes' masterpiece. The interpretation of the *Quijote* by Giovanni Meli is discussed, and allusions to Cervantes' novel by Ugo Foscolo are noted.]

193. Popescu-Telega, Al. *Cervantes și Italia. Studiu de literaturà comparate.* Craiova: Ramuri, [1932]. Pp. 218. [This item could not be obtained. It is reviewed by Elisabeth Jossier in *Études Italiennes* 3 (1933):259-260, and by B. Sanvisenti in *Convivium* (Torino) 5 (1933):912-913. The summary below is based on materials found in these two reviews.]

[Popescu-Telega first examines the influence of Cervantes on Italy in the seventeenth and eighteenth centuries, and finds it to be quite small. The number of translations of Cervantes' works into Italian, states the critic, is very limited. Italian critics who have studied Cervantes are noted. The major part of Popescu-Telega's work deals with Cervantes' allusions to Italy and with the Italian influence of his works.]

194. Sedwick, B. Frank. "Don Quijote in Italian Opera." *Modern Language Journal* 40 (April 1956):202.

Several attempts have been made to put the figure Don Quijote on the Italian stage, but all have been short-lived. Some believe that this failure is due to the fact that the *Quijote* is a philosophical work with few lyrical qualities, and that opera is ill-disposed to treat the former and reluctant to omit the latter. This is perhaps true. The success of the philosophical Faust on the stage is due to the fact that operas which deal with him are limited to the love episode. One reason why the *Quijote* has failed in serious and comic opera is that it lacks a love affair. Another reason that the story of the Knight has not succeeded in opera is that people expect a comic interpretation of the hero.

Seventeenth-Century Italy

195. Croce, Benedetto. "Due illustrazioni al *Viaje del Parnaso* del Cervantes." In *Homenaje á Menéndez y Pelayo en el año vigésimo de su profesorado. Estudios de erudición española con un prólogo de D. Juan Valera.*

Vol. 1, pp. 161-193. Madrid: V. Suárez, 1899. [Also
in Croce's *Saggi sulla letteratura italiana del sei-
cento*, pp. 125-159. Bari: Laterza & Figli, 1911.]

[Croce notes that the *Quijote* was first translated
into Italian in 1622 by Franciosini. He observes that
the first mention of the *Quijote* in Italy, as far as he
knows, was by Alessandro Tassoni in *Secchia rapita*,
written in 1615 and published in 1622. The satirical
intent of Cervantes' masterpiece, Croce states, was
first pointed out in Italy by Giulio Cesare Capaccio in
his *Forastiero*, published 1634. (But see Mele, 198.)]

196. Croce, Benedetto. "Spanish Culture in Italy in the
      Seventeenth Century." *Hispania* 10 (December 1927):
      383-388.

      Spanish literature brought no new awakening in Italy.
      Reinvigorated Catholicism was nothing new, nor was
      medieval knight-errantry, which held on longer in Spain
      than elsewhere. By its very lack of originality of
      philosophic thought, or of a new concept of moral and
      religious life, Spanish poetry and art made a deep im-
      pression on Italian culture, in so far as they were full
      of popular freshness or were poetical masterpieces.
      The realism of the Spanish picaresque novel was also no
      new thing in the Italy of Boccaccio's continuers. In
      general, the so-called Spanish realism consisted merely
      of a special kind of humor. Hence *Don Quijote* was read
      with pleasure as a book which excited laughter, but its
      profound poetic significance was not comprehended. Nor
      did the *Quijote* even drive out chivalric novels in Italy,
      for they continued to exist, if not under the names
      Amadís and *Esplandián*, at least in the form of romances
      of love and adventure, like *Calloandro*. Only the senti-
      mental and bourgeois novel of English and French origin
      finally drove them out.

197. Croce, Benedetto. *Noterelle e appunti di storia civile
      e letteraria napoletana del seicento*. Napoli: Tip.
      Sanitaria, 1926, pp. 56-67.

      [Croce furnishes several obscure references to the
      Quijote by Italians of the seventeenth century.]

198. Mele, Eugenio. "Per la fortuna del Cervantes in Italia
      nel seicento." *Studi di Filología Moderna* 2 (1909):
      229-255.

There is disagreement as to the date of publication
of the first Italian version of Part I of *Don Quijote*,
but the correct date is 1622. The translator, Lorenzo
Franciosini, published Part II of the *Quijote* in Italian
in 1625. The first reference to the *Quijote* in Italy
was made by Alessandro Tassoni in his *Secchia rapita*,
written in 1615 and published in 1622. This same author
mentioned Cervantes' masterpiece on several other occasions. Benedetto Croce (195) is not correct in stating
that G.C. Capaccio, in 1634, was the first Italian to com-
ment on the satirical aspects of the *Quijote*, because
seven years earlier Adriano Banchieri had done so in
his *Trastulli della villa*. In 1680, a play by Marco
Morosini, *Don Chisciotte della Mancia*, was performed in
Venice. The music for this drama was composed by Carlo
Sajon. According to the literary historian Antonio
Bellori, the work of Morosini was puerile. In general,
the Italians of the seventeenth century regarded the
Quijote as purely a book of recreation, since it did
not conform to classical rules.

199. Mele, Eugenio. "Más sobre la fortuna de Cervantes en
Italia en el siglo XVII." *Revista de Filología Española* 6 (October–December 1919):364-374.

[Mele observes that B. Croce (195) noted an imitation
of the *Curioso impertinente* by Francesco Bracciolini in
1630. Mele reveals that F. Bracciolini crudely translated the *Curioso* on another occasion. Various seventeenth-century Italians who referred to the *Quijote*
are noted.]

200. Mele, Eugenio. "Nuevos datos sobre la fortuna de Cervantes en Italia en el siglo XVII." *Revista de Filología Española* 8 (July–September 1921):281-283.

[This article deals in part with Agostino Mascardi's
Discorsi morali, 1620, in which work (Discourse VIII)
that author noted Cervantes' satire against introduc-
tions which contained flowery, laudatory poems.]

201. Mele, Eugenio. "Nuevos datos sobre la fortuna de Cervantes en Italia en el siglo XVII." *Revista de Filología Española* 14 (April–June 1927):183-184.

[Mele discusses references to the *Quijote* by various
seventeenth-century Italians, including Valerio Fulvio
Savoiano in *Avisso di Parnaso*, 1618, and Nicola Villani
in *Ragionamento sopra la poesia giacosa*, 1634.]

Eighteenth-Century Italy

202. Garrone, Marco A. "Il *Don Chisciotte* siciliano e il *Don Chisciotte* spagnuolo." *Studi de Filología Moderna* 4 (1911):79-96.

[The critic compares the career of Cervantes with that of the Sicilian poet G. Meli. A detailed analysis is presented of Meli's *Don Chisciotti e Sanciu Panza*, 1770-1787, a narrative, heroic-comic poem of twelve cantos of ottava rima. Meli's poem is compared and contrasted with Cervantes' masterpiece.]

203. Nava, Ernesto. "Ancora l'Italia e Cervantes." *Il Marzocco*, no. 19 (21 May 1916), p. 3.

[Nava briefly comments on G. Meli's eighteenth-century mock-heroic poem about the Knight and the Squire.]

204. Rabizzani, Giovanni. "L'Italia e Cervantes." *Il Marzocco*, no. 18 (30 April 1916), p. 1.

[Rabizzani presents a general discussion of the influence of Italian culture on Cervantes and of Cervantes' influence on Italian literature. The critic takes note of a comic-epic poem in ottava rima by G. Meli in the eighteenth century, *Don Chisciotti e Sanciu Panza*. Translations into Italian of Cervantes' works are noted, and Cervantine studies by Italians are pointed out.]

Nineteenth-Century Italy

205. Fucilla, Joseph G. "Notes on the Vogue of Cervantes in Italy." *Hispanic Review* 8 (April 1940):161-165.

[Here Fucilla discusses a pageant held in Bassano del Grappa in Northern Italy on February 24, 1824 ("Il Matrimonio di Don Chisciotte della Mancia e di Donna Dulcinea"). Three documents concerning this pageant are presented.]

206. Fucilla, Joseph G. "A Travestied *Don Quijote*." *Hispania* 30 (August 1947):336-340.

In 1814, Nicola Limosino's seven-canto poem *Don Chisciotte della Mancia* was published. This adaptation

deals with the knighting ceremony (Canto I), the windmill adventure (Canto II), the blanket-tossing and
sheep-battle episodes (Canto III), the finding of Mambrino's helmet (Canto IV), the freeing of the galley
slaves (Canto V), and the Cardenio episode (Cantos VI
and VII). Limosino increases the buffoonish element by
divesting the Don of his idealism, by exaggerating Sancho's crassness, and by transforming most of the other
figures into caricatures. Dulcinea, for example, is
described as being extremely grotesque.

207. Getto, Giovanni. *"I promessi sposi,* i drammaturghi
    spagnoli e Cervantes." *Lettere Italiane* 22 (1970):
    425-499.

    [Getto states that Alessandro Manzoni probably read
    the *Quijote* for the first time in 1819. The critic
    notes that both Cervantes and Manzoni use the fictitious
    manuscript device, both often insert Latin phrases in
    their works, and both cause a book to be found at an
    inn. The library of Don Quijote is compared to the
    library of Don Ferrante.]

208. Girardi, Enzo Noè. "Manzoni e Cervantes." *Aevum*
    (Milano) 37 (1963):543-552.

    [Girardi seeks to show similarities between the works
    of Cervantes (the *Quijote* and the *Novelas ejemplares*)
    and Alessandro Manzoni's *I promessi sposi*. The critic
    concludes that Manzoni apparently read the *Quijote* in
    1819.]

209. Hatzfeld, Helmut. *"Don Quijote* e *I promessi sposi."*
    Estudios de literaturas románicas, pp. 297-321. Bar-
    celona: Edit. Planeta, 1972. [Also in Hatzfeld's *El
    "Quijote" como obra de arte del lenguaje,* pp. 321-346.
    Madrid: C.S.I.C., 1966.]

    [In footnote 3, page 297, the critic presents a brief
    bibliography on the question of the influence of Cer-
    vantes on Alessandro Manzoni's *I promessi sposi.* Hatz-
    feld agrees with those who find a distinct similarity in
    spirit between the two novelists, a certain catholic,
    interior attitude. Both, Hatzfeld concludes, are joy-
    ful, joking, and open-hearted, and both possess a
    superior ironic sense. Also, Hatzfeld continues, both
    Cervantes and Manzoni are tolerant of human weakness,
    are essentially realistic, and lack mysticism and asce-
    ticism. To compare the two writers in more detail the

critic divides his article into six short parts: (1) the
love problem; (2) the social problem; (3) the psycholo-
gical-moral problem; (4) the problem of popular language;
(5) the problem of classical beginning; (6) the problem
of humor. Hatzfeld notes the presentation of similar
ideas and the use of similar techniques in the *Quijote*
and in *I promessi sposi*: non-passionate love; social
mission with self-sacrifice; authentic characters; an
interest in moral problems; stylistic perfection which
includes the popular; an interest in eternal matters;
the avoidance of biting satire; and the use of indul-
gent irony.]

*   Icaza, Francisco A. de. *El "Quijote" durante tres
        siglos*. Madrid: Renacimiento, 1918. Pp. 229. Cited
        above as item 30.

        [Chapter Five (pp. 91-93) of this work discusses the
        possible influence of the *Quijote* on Manzoni's *I pro-
        messi sposi*. The critic is most skeptical of such in-
        fluence. Icaza strongly criticizes those critics who
        find Manzoni's novel to be superior to Cervantes'
        masterpiece.]

210.   Ovidio, Francesco d'. "Manzoni e Cervantes." *Opere
        complete*. Vol. 6 (*Studii Manzoniani*), pp. 73-90.
        Caserta: Casa Editrice Moderna, 1928. [Memoria letta
        alla R. Accademia di Scienze morali e politiche di
        Napoli, nella seduta dell' 8 Marzo 1885, ristampata
        nelle *Discussioni Manzoniane*.]

        [D'Ovidio points out similarities between the *Quijote*
        and Manzoni's *I promessi sposi*: the omission of the
        name of the place of action, a festive tone, the use of
        the fictitious manuscript device, a feigned modesty in
        the introductions, frequent episodes at inns, the inter-
        polation of material, both protagonists being mono-
        maniacs to one degree or another, the attention given
        to the libraries of Don Quijote and Don Ferrante. The
        critic much prefers the work of Manzoni, finding it to
        contain all of life, and considers the *Quijote* to be
        merely a satirical novel. D'Ovidio concludes that Man-
        zoni's humor is always fine and gentle but that Cervan-
        tes' humor is at times base. The critic also states
        that Cervantes' novel has a true protagonist while Man-
        zoni's work does not.]

211.   Puppo, Mario. "Foscolo e Don Chisciotte." *Anales
        Cervantinos* 9 (1961-1962):259-260.

Ugo Foscolo (died 1827) admired Don Quijote's capacity
for absolute passion and illusion, and considered the
Knight to be the incarnation of the tragic, heroic, and
idealistic side of his own personality. Foscolo's Dulcinea was Italy, which he loved with a quixotic passion.
At the end, the Italian writer, like the Knight, came
to see his own generosity as fruitless and his heroism
in behalf of his ideal as folly.

212. Rondani, Alberto. *Scritti Manzoniani a cura di Emilio
     Bertana*. Città di Castello: S. Lapi, 1915. Pp. xliii
     + 271.

     [In Chapters V, VI, and VII (pp. 99-152) of this work
     the critic contrasts the *Quijote* and Manzoni's *I pro-
     messi sposi*. Rondani does not see Cervantes' greatness
     and much prefers the work of the Italian writer. To
     the critic Cervantes' irony is derisive, while Manzoni's
     irony is charitable. Rondani finds the *Quijote* to be
     characterized by exaggeration, *I promessi sposi* by
     moderation. Cervantes' Squire is compared and con-
     trasted with Manzoni's Don Abbondio. Rondani also dis-
     cusses alleged similarities between Don Quijote and Don
     Ferrante but finds none.]

213. Sanvisenti, Bernardo. "Ariosto, Cervantes, Manzoni."
     Convivium 4 (1932):641-674.

     [Sanvisenti lists the various references in the *Qui-
     jote* to Ariosto's *Orlando furioso*: the allusion (at the
     second inn) to Agramonte's camp; Sansón's reference to
     Brunello; the use of material in *Orlando* for the *Curioso
     impertinente*. Sanvisenti concludes that Cervantes
     learned a great deal about technique from Ariosto and
     transmitted his own technique to Manzoni, thus furnish-
     ing a link between the two Italian writers.]

214. Torraca, Francesco. "Di alcune fonti dei *Promessi
     sposi*." *Scritti Critici*, pp. 487-583. Napoli: Fran-
     cesco Perrella, Editore, 1907.

     [The critic concludes that Manzoni's figure Don Fer-
     rante (*I promessi sposi*) is not based on Don Quijote.
     Torraca also sees little similarity between the libraries
     of the two Dons and does not believe that Manzoni drew
     upon the *Quijote* for the fictitious historian device.
     Other possible sources for *I promessi sposi* are dis-
     cussed, including several novels by Sir Walter Scott.]

Twentieth-Century Italy

215. Castro, Américo. "Cervantes y Pirandello." *Hacia Cer-
      vantes*, pp. 477–485. Madrid: Taurus, 1967. [First
      published in *La Nación*, 16 November 1924.]

      [The critic studies the use of self-aware characters
      in Cervantes' *Quijote*, Calderón's *El gran teatro del
      mundo*, Unamuno's *Niebla*, and Pirandello's *Sei personaggi
      in cerca d'autore*. Castro concludes that Cervantes
      initiated the use of the character who rebels against
      his creator.]

216. Chaix-Ruy, J. "Cervantès, Flaubert, Pirandello."
      Humanitas 12 (August–September 1958):611–618.

      [At the end of this article the critic briefly com-
      pares the author of the *Quijote* with Pirandello.]

217. Consiglio, Carlo. "Datos para una bibliografía italiana
      de Cervantes." *Revista Bibliográfica y Documental* 2
      (1948):107–118.

      [Consiglio seeks to supplement Leopoldo Rius' bibliog-
      raphy with a list of translations, versions, and adap-
      tations of Cervantes' works done in Italy during the
      first forty years of the twentieth century. Critical
      works by Italians are also listed. In his introductory
      remarks Consiglio praises the first Italian translation
      of the *Quijote* by Franciosini in 1622. Later revisions
      of this translation are noted. Consiglio briefly com-
      ments upon the poetic adaptations of the *Quijote* by
      Giovanni Meli, 1787, and by Emmanuele Nappi, Vincenzo
      Morena, and Raffaele Cappozzoli.]

218. Monner Sans, José María. "De Cervantes a Pirandello."
      La Prensa (Buenos Aires), 16 November 1947; *Diario de
      Yucatán*, 25 January 1948; *Diario de la Marina*, 8
      February 1948. [This item could not be obtained.
      For a summary see Rafael Heliodoro Valle and Emilia
      Romero, *Bibliografía cervantina en la América española*
      (425), p. 181.]

      [The critic believes that Pirandello's *Six Characters
      in Search of an Author* could have been inspired by Part
      II of the *Quijote*, where the protagonists become auton-
      omous figures who are aware of themselves as characters
      in a book.]

219. Monner Sans, José María. "Cervantes y el humorismo
     pirandeliano." *La Prensa* (Buenos Aires), 18 January
     1948. [This item could not be obtained. It is sum-
     marized in Rafael Heliodoro Valle and Emilia Romero,
     Bibliografía cervantina en la América española (425),
     p. 180.]

     [Monner Sans believes that there are possible influen-
     ces of the *Quijote* on Pirandello's *Six Characters in
     Search of an Author*. The critic finds Pirandello's
     work to be an attempt to show life as a sad *opéra
     bouffe*, a mixture of the tragic and comic.]

V.   *DON QUIJOTE* IN ENGLAND

General

220.   Armas y Cárdenas, José de. *Cervantes en la literatura*
       inglesa. Conferencia leída en el Ateneo de Madrid el
       día 8 de mayo de 1916. Madrid: Ateneo de Madrid
       (Imprenta Renacimiento), 1916. Pp. 38. [Also in
       Revista Cubana 22 (1947):52-74.]

       Between 1607 and 1623 there were various allusions to
       the *Quijote* by such English writers as George Wilkins
       and Ben Jonson. In 1611, there were three comedies
       based on the *Curioso impertinente*. In the eighteenth
       century Fielding, Sterne, and Smollett were all greatly
       influenced by the *Quijote*. In addition, Charlotte Len-
       nox, in 1752, and Richard Graves, in 1773, both wrote
       imitations of Cervantes' masterpiece.

221.   Becker, Gustav. *Die Aufnahme des Don Quijote in die*
       englische Litteratur (1605 bis c. 1770). Berlin:
       Carl Salewski, 1902. Pp. 32.

       Since chivalric novels were still popular in England
       after 1605, Cervantes' satire of them had little im-
       mediate effect on English tastes. Thomas Shelton's
       1612 translation of Part I of the *Quijote* has many
       errors. Peter Motteux's 1700 version is better, but,
       like Shelton's work, is overly influenced by cognates.
       Furthermore, Motteux does not vary his style to suit
       the character portrayed. Charles Jarvis' translation
       of 1742 is the truest up to that time, though on occa-
       sion it is too literal. Tobias Smollett's version of
       1755 suffers from the same defect, though that trans-
       lator is generally an excellent stylist. Charles Henry
       Wilmot, in 1774, plagiarizes Motteux though he often
       omits entire sentences.

[At page 25 et seq. Becker briefly examines English
criticism of the *Quijote*, noting the British tendency
to view Cervantes' novel as a satire against the Spanish people. He observes that some critics, like William Temple, Richard Steele, and Daniel Defoe, believed
that Cervantes destroyed Spain. Becker also comments
on the false *Quijote* and notes the various English
translations of that work.]

222. Burton, A.P. "Cervantes the Man Seen Through English
      Eyes in the Seventeenth and Eighteenth Centuries."
      Bulletin of Hispanic Studies 45 (1968):1-15.

[Burton analyzes the interaction between the knowledge
of Cervantes' life and the interpretation of the *Quijote*
in England. The critic finds that only in 1675 did information regarding Cervantes' life appear in England,
with the translation of Rapin's *Réflexions sur la poétique de Aristote*.... However, Burton adds, most of
the information found in this work was of dubious merit,
such as the idea that the *Quijote* was an attack on the
Spanish nobility in general and on Lerma in particular--
an idea repeated by later writers.
      Burton finds that in the early eighteenth century
Cervantes became regarded as an irresistible satirist
(and the *Quijote* as primarily a satire), though superior
to Rabelais because the Spaniard was more serious and
solemn.
      The critic discusses the appearance in 1738 of Mayáns'
biography and states that the biographer knew little of
Cervantes' life and went so far as to create the legend
that the author of the *Quijote* had been imprisoned in
La Mancha. Toward the middle of the eighteenth century,
Burton observes, the English became aware of Cervantes'
life as a prisoner in Algiers, and the author comes to
be regarded as a dashing figure; he was much admired by
Smollett and others, who regarded him as a perfect,
gentle knight. This admiration for Cervantes, the critic
notes, becomes extended to the figure Don Quijote, and
with Henry Brooke's *Fool of Quality*, 1766, the Knight
becomes a superior and suffering struggler for the
right, an idea repeated by various writers, including
Florian in his biography of Cervantes (English version,
1785).
      Thus, concludes Burton, Cervantes moved from a destroyer
of chivalry (early eighteenth-century English view) to a
model of chivalry (English view at the end of the
eighteenth century).]

223. Fitzmaurice-Kelly, James. *The Relations Between Span-*
      ish and English Literature. Liverpool: University
      Press, 1910. Pp. 32.

      [The critic mentions the *Cardenio*-Shakespeare problem,
      and notes the influence of Cervantes' masterpiece and
      of his *Novelas ejemplares* on John Fletcher's plays.
      Fitzmaurice-Kelly states that there are two opinions re-
      garding the influence of the *Quijote* on Fletcher's *The*
      Knight of the Burning Pestle.
      The critic sees little connection between the *Quijote*
      and Samuel Butler's *Hudibras*, but notes the influence
      of Cervantes on Fielding's *Joseph Andrews* and Smollett's
      The Adventures of Sir Launcelot Greaves. Various edi-
      tions of the *Quijote* are briefly commented upon, and
      Mrs. Charlotte Lennox's *Female Quixote* is noted in
      passing.]

224. Fitzmaurice-Kelly, James. "Dos palabras sobre las imi-
      taciones del *Quijote* en Inglaterra." In *Cervantes y*
      el Quijote, pp. 165-167. Edited by J.C. García López.
      Madrid: Tip. de La Revista de Archivos, Bibliot. y
      Museos, 1905.

      [Fitzmaurice-Kelly notes the early reception of the
      Quijote in England, mentioning the Shelton translation
      of 1612 and early allusions to Cervantes' novel. The
      use of material from the *Quijote* by various English
      playwrights is briefly pointed out. The critic dis-
      cusses the possible use by Shakespeare of the Cardenio
      episode in a lost play. Sámuel Butler's *Hudibras*,
      1663, is described as a crude imitation of Cervantes'
      masterpiece, especially since Cervantes loved his pro-
      tagonists while Butler hated Hudibras and his squire
      Ralpho. Fitzmaurice-Kelly states that Edward Ward's
      rhymed version of thirty-one chapters of the 1605 *Qui-*
      jote is so full of nonsense and obscenities that it
      ceases to be a translation of the original. The critic
      points out that D'Urfey's musical version of the *Qui-*
      jote, written with Henry Purcell, was so immoral that
      it caused an outcry by Jeremy Collier. John Arbuthnot's
      Don Bilioso de l'Estomac is described as an unworthy
      imitation of Cervantes' novel. Fitzmaurice-Kelly dis-
      agrees with those who find Swift to be kin to the author
      of the *Quijote* in temperament. Charlotte Lennox's *The*
      Female Quixote, Richard Graves' *Spiritual Quixote*, and
      William Combe's *Dr. Syntax* are criticized. However,
      the critic praises Fielding, Smollett, Sterne, Dickens,
      and Thackeray as true disciples of Cervantes and as
      founders of the modern realistic novel.]

225. Hannay, David. *The Later Renaissance.* New York: Burt
      Franklin, 1964. Pp. 381. [First published in 1898,
      London: W. Blackwood.]

      Is not Don Quijote the elder brother of Sir Roger de
      Coverley (Addison), of Matthew Bramble (Tobias Smollett),
      of Parson Adams (Henry Fielding), of Bradwardine (Sir
      Walter Scott), of Colonel Newcome (William Thackeray),
      and of Mr. Chucks (Frederick Marryat), the brave, gen-
      tle, not over-clever men we love all the more because
      we laugh at them tenderly? [From pp. 145-146.]

226. Hume, Martin. *Spanish Influence on English Literature.*
      London: Eveleigh Nash, 1905. Pp. xviii + 322.

      [Hume briefly notes (pp. 180-182) the influence of the
      Quijote on Samuel Butler's *Hudibras* and on Charles
      Dickens' *Pickwick Papers.* The critic also points out
      early references in England to tilting windmills: by
      George Wilkins in *The Miseries of Infant Marriage* and
      by Thomas Middleton in *Your Five Gallants.* References
      to the *Quijote* by Ben Jonson in *The Silent Woman* and
      The Alchymist are noted. Hume (p. 276) is of the opin-
      ion that John Fletcher burlesqued the *Quijote* in *The
      Knight of the Burning Pestle.* The influence of the
      Novelas ejemplares on English drama is briefly dis-
      cussed (pp. 276-277).]

227. Knowles, Edwin B. "Cervantes and English Literature."
      In *Cervantes Across the Centuries ... A Quadricenten-
      nial Volume Edited by Ángel Flores and M.J. Benardete,*
      pp. 267-293. New York: The Dryden Press, 1947. [1969
      reprint, Gordian Press, pp. 277-303. Spanish version
      "Cervantes en la literatura inglesa." *Realidad* 2
      (September-October 1947):268-297.]

      There are four relatively distinct English interpre-
      tations of the *Quijote*: (1) the seventeenth century saw
      it as only a farce; (2) the eighteenth century esteemed
      its serious satire; (3) the nineteenth century Romantic
      view deprecated the satire and comedy in order to exalt
      the deep spiritual implications of the work; and (4) the
      late nineteenth-century (and current) eclectic view
      finds that the *Quijote* is an eternal human classic of a
      richly complex nature. The popularity of the *Quijote*
      in England, contrary to general belief, had a slow
      growth. Cervantes' name is mentioned only five times
      prior to 1660. *Hudibras* by Samuel Butler, in 1663, and
      a trilogy of plays by D'Urfey, 1694-1696, are farcical

interpretations of the *Quijote*. In the first three-
fourths of the eighteenth century Cervantes acquires
many admirers, such as Samuel Johnson, who see his greatness. With Motteux the idea arises that Don Quijote
represents humanity, that there is a little of the
quixotic in all of us, and that we should pity the Don
rather than condemn him. Fielding saw Cervantes as a
great social-moral force, and *Joseph Andrews* has many
surface correspondences with *Don Quijote*, such as funny
chapter headings.

The influence of the *Quijote* in England followed three
general lines: (1) it blended with the picaresque traditions to stimulate long, peripatetic novels with in-
serted short stories; (2) it produced a kindly and elevated social and moral satire; and (3) Don Quijote became a model for lovable eccentrics.

In the Romantic Period new characteristics were dis-
covered in the *Quijote*. Byron and Lamb came to view
Cervantes' novel as a sad work, while E.G. Morrison
found that the Don was a Christ-like figure. In 1897,
Francis Thompson adopted the present view that *Don Quijote* is a many-faceted masterpiece.

228. Lathrop, Henry Burrowes. "In Praise of Cervantes." In
     Essays in Memory of Barrett Wendell by His Assistants,
     pp. 169-187. Edited by W.R. Castle, Jr., and Paul
     Kaufman. New York: Russell & Russell, 1967. [First
     published in 1926, Cambridge.]

     [Lathrop notes the influence of the *Quijote* on various
     English writers, particularly in the use of amiable but
     grotesque characters: Addison, Fielding, Goldsmith,
     Smollett, Sterne, Scott, Thackeray, Dickens.]

229. Lathrop, Henry Burrowes. *The Art of the Novelist*. Re-
     vised Edition. New York: Dodd, Mead and Company, 1927.
     Pp. ix + 337. [First published in 1919, New York:
     Dodd, Mead and Company.]

     [Lathrop (pp. 191-192) points out quixotic and beloved
     characters in English literature: Henry Fielding's Par-
     son Adams; Oliver Goldsmith's Vicar of Wakefield; Tobias
     Smollett's Matthew Bramble; Laurence Sterne's Uncle Toby;
     William Thackeray's Colonel Newcome; Sir Walter Scott's
     Bradwardine; and Charles Dickens' Mr. Pickwick.]

230. Peers, E. Allison. "Cervantes in England." *Bulletin
     of Hispanic Studies* 24 (1947):226-238. [Also in *Dub-
     lin Review*, no. 441 (Autumn 1947), pp. 20-27. See also

Peers' *Saint Teresa of Jesus, and Other Essays and
Addresses*, pp. 239-242. London: Faber and Faber, 1953.
Spanish version "Cervantes en Inglaterra." In *Homenaje
a Cervantes*. Vol. 2, pp. 267-286. Edited by Francisco
Sánchez-Castañer y Mena, Valencia: Mediterráneo, 1950.]

England gave a greater welcome to Cervantes than any
other nation. There the *Quijote* was received with immediate acclamation, which has not died to this day.
About 1607, Thomas Shelton prepared his translation of
Part I of the *Quijote* in forty days, according to his
own statement. This English version was not published
until 1612. It is full of loose paraphrasing and frequent lapses into overliteralness. Shelton is often
misled by Spanish words similar in appearance to English
words, though of different meaning: *sucesos, desmayarse,
admirar*. The 1620 English translation of Part II of the
Quijote is also by Shelton, in all probability.

Peter Motteux's English version of the *Quijote*, 1700-
1703, appeared in four small volumes. The style in this
translation is better than Shelton's, but Motteux tends
to put too much of himself into the work. He uses open
burlesque where Cervantes merely hints and suggests.
Edward Ward's 1711 "merry" English rendering of the *Quijote* into Hudibrastic verse (iambic tetrameters) is hor-
rible. Charles Jarvis is more faithful to the Spanish
text than previous English translators in his 1742 rendering of Cervantes' masterpiece, though the style is
undistinguished and pedestrian. Tobias Smollett's translation of 1755 is often coarse, but the style is the
best up to that time. In 1822 Lockhart revised the
Motteux version, correcting many of the errors. Lockhart, in his preface, reacts against the view that Cervantes was a superior kind of buffoon, and concludes
that we admire the Don even though we laugh at him.

In 1881, Duffield, a late-Romantic, translates the
Quijote. In another work in that same year (*Don Quijote, his Critics and Commentators*) Duffield comes to
the conclusion that Cervantes was a man seeking to bring
about a moral, social, political, and religious reformation in Spain. In 1885, John Ormsby produced a superior
English translation of the *Quijote* and came to the conclusion that Cervantes' novel was originally intended to
be a short story. Since that date Watts has produced a
translation, and Fitzmaurice-Kelly has edited several
reprints of prior editions.

231. Starkie, Walter Fitzwilliam. Introduction to *Glimpses
      of Don Quixote & La Mancha*, pp. ix-xix. Edited by
      Homer D. Crotty. Los Angeles: The Zamorano Club, 1963.

      Don Quijote is Cervantes' spiritual biography as well
      as the first modern novel. It is dual natured; part of
      it has its feet on the ground while part soars. The
      first biography of Cervantes was printed in England in
      1738. John Bowle, in 1781, undertook the first serious
      study of the *Quijote*, and at the end of the eighteenth
      century and the beginning of the nineteenth, English
      critics ceased to view Cervantes' novel as a gay, sati-
      rical book, and found it to be a tragedy.

232. Starkie, Walter Fitzwilliam. "Cervantes y la novela in-
      glesa." In *Homenaje a Cervantes*. Vol. 2, pp. 351-
      363. Edited by Francisco Sánchez-Castañer y Mena.
      Valencia: Mediterráneo, 1950. [English version "Miguel
      de Cervantes and the English Novel" in *Essays by
      Divers Hands* 34 (1966):159-179.]

      England was the first country to translate the *Quijote*,
      and an Englishman, Lord Carteret, was the first to com-
      mission a biography of Cervantes. It was an Englishman,
      too, who produced the earliest commented edition of the
      Quijote, John Bowle. There are, in the seventeenth cen-
      tury, references to Cervantes' masterpiece by Ben Jon-
      son, and imitations by Beaumont and Fletcher (*The Knight
      of the Burning Pestle*) and by Samuel Butler (*Hudibras*,
      1663-1668). However, the profound humor of Cervantes
      does not penetrate the English mind until late, for
      Gayton, in his commentaries on the *Quijote* in 1654, saw
      only the bitter and satirical side of the novel.
      The first profound interpretation or imitation of the
      Quijote is Fielding's *Joseph Andrews*, 1743. *Tom Jones*
      is also a Cervantine work. The *Quijote* had a definite,
      though indirect, influence on Laurence Sterne's *Tristram
      Shandy*; and Tobias Smollett, who also translated the
      Quijote, was affected by Cervantes' novel in his *Sir
      Launcelot Greaves*, 1762, and in other works. The struc-
      ture of Dickens' *Pickwick Papers* is based on the *Qui-
      jote*: Pickwick, a good-natured idealist, goes out into
      the world to have adventures. He finds the down-to-
      earth Weller, just as Cervantes' Knight finds Sancho.
      In addition, Dickens' work has excellent dialogs be-
      tween his leading characters, and, from time to time,
      interpolated short stories.

Lord Byron and Charles Lamb misinterpreted the *Qui-jote*, seeing only its sad side, and John Ruskin, after first praising the novel in 1843, concluded ten years later that it was to be condemned for mocking sacred principles. Coleridge, in 1836, concluded, however, that Cervantes did not intend to destroy chivalric novels, but merely sought to show that they should be read as novels, not as history. Late in the nineteenth century, George Meredith observed that though the heart may laugh at the Don, one still grieves for him.

233. Tave, Stuart M. *The Amiable Humorist. A Study in the Comic Theory and Criticism of the Eighteenth and Early Nineteenth Centuries*. Chicago and London, 1960. Pp. xi + 304.

[Tave's work consists of a preface and four parts, with a total of eleven chapters. Much attention is de-voted to the change in the concept of humor in England, from destructiveness to good-naturedness. The ideas of Sir Richard Steele, Sir William Temple, Corbyn Morris, and numerous others are presented. Of particular in-terest is the critic's tracing of the change in the in-terpretation of the Quijote figure in England from the seventeenth to the early nineteenth century: from the object of broad comedy, to a figure of mockery (or, at best, a symbol of wrongheadedness in general), to a noble symbol with Henry Fielding, to a champion of liberty with William Hazlitt in the early nineteenth century. The influence of the *Quijote* on the fiction of the seventeenth, eighteenth, and nineteenth centuries is examined in some detail, especially with regard to the creation of amiable, eccentric characters by such writers as Laurence Sterne, Henry Fielding, and Charles Dickens.]

234. Torner, Florentino M. "Don Quijote en Inglaterra." *El Nacional*, 27 March 1946. [This item could not be ob-tained. For a summary, see Rafael Heliodoro Valle and Emilia Romero, *Bibliografía cervantina en la América española* (425), pp. 254-255.]

[Torner discusses the general influence of the *Quijote* on English literature. The Shelton translation is noted, and its possible use by Shakespeare in the lost play *Cardenio* is mentioned. Edward Ward's verse rendering of the *Quijote* is pointed out, and there is a general dis-cussion of the influence of Cervantes' masterpiece on Fielding, Smollett, and Richard Graves.]

Seventeenth-Century England

235. Astrana Marín, Luis. "Cervantes y Shakespeare." *Lecturas Dominicales* (Bogotá), 24 June 1934. [This item could not be located. For a brief summary, see Rafael Heliodoro Valle and Emilia Romero, *Bibliografía cervantina en la América española* (425), pp. 21-22.]

   [Astrana Marín asks if Shakespeare was familiar with the *Quijote*, noting the lost play *Cardenio*, supposedly by Fletcher and Shakespeare, a play possibly based on the Cardenio episode in the 1605 *Quijote*. For additional works on the lost play *Cardenio* see Theobald, items 297-301.]

236. Ayala, Francisco. "Los dos amigos." *Revista de Occidente* 10 (1965):287-306. (Also in Ayala's *Los ensayos: teoría y crítica literaria*, pp. 695-714. Madrid: Aguilar, 1972.)

   [Ayala quotes Webster's dictionary as stating that the English expression "Lothario" for a seducer is taken from a figure in a play by Nicholas Rowe, *The Fair Penitent*, 1702, which, states the critic, is based on Cervantes' *Curioso impertinente*. The influence of that *novella* on other English plays is suggested: Massinger's (?) *The Fatal Dowry* and *The Second Maiden's Tragedy*; D'Avenant's *The Cruel Brother*; Aphra Behn's *The Amorous Prince*; T. Southerne's *The Disappointment*; and John Crowne's *The Married Beau*.]

237. Bahlsen, Leopold. "Spanische Quellen der dramatischen Litteratur, besonders Englands zu Shakespeares Zeit." *Zeitschrift für vergleichende Litteraturgeschichte* 6 (1893):151-159.

   [Bahlsen states (p. 155) that *The Knight of the Burning Pestle* (Beaumont and Fletcher) was undoubtedly influenced by the *Quijote*. The influence of Cervantes' *Novelas ejemplares* on English plays is dealt with in some detail.]

238. Bawcutt, N.W. "*Don Quixote*, Part I, and *The Duchess of Malfi*." *Modern Language Review* 66 (1971):488-491.

   [Bawcutt notes F.M. Todd's (263) previous article on a supposed borrowing by John Webster from the *Quijote*. Todd asserted that the pyramid image used in a speech

by Bosola in *The Duchess of Malfi* was taken from the
1615 *Quijote*, chapter 6. Bawcutt, however, asserts that
Webster's play was performed prior to the 1615 *Quijote*
and that the play was *not* revised prior to publication
in 1623. Instead, the critic finds it more likely that
Webster drew upon a pyramid image used in the 1605 *Quijote*, chapter 7. Bawcutt also points out other possible
sources of borrowings by Webster from the 1605 *Quijote*:
(1) the discussion of the power of potions in the galley-
slave episode; (2) the use of the expression "create no
new world, nor custom" found in Dorotea's bedroom speech
to Fernando, Pt. I, chapter 28. The critic also compares the entry of Fernando into Dorotea's chamber to
the entry of Ferdinand into the Duchess's bedroom. Bawcutt concludes that Webster probably used Shelton's 1612
translation of the *Quijote*, not the original Spanish
version.]

239. Becker, Gustav. "Die erste englische Don Quijotiade."
      *Archiv für das Studium der neueren Sprachen und
      Literaturen* 122 (1909):310-322; 123 (1909):298-304.

[Becker asserts that Robert Anton's small work *Moriomachia*, 1613, was the first English humoristic novel and
that it was undoubtedly based on the *Quijote*. Anton's
work, states Becker, is directed against fairy tales.
After giving a detailed summary of *Moriomachia* and comparing certain episodes therein to episodes in the *Quijote*, the critic concludes that Anton was not a very
skillful writer. The latter portion of this article is
a re-edited version of the 1613 *Moriomachia*.

In the continuation of this article Becker points out
a 1595 work by Henry Robarts called *Pheander, the Mayden
Knight*. Various editions of this work are discussed,
and a detailed summary of the plot is given. The critic
concludes that this fairy tale could well have inspired
the satirical work of Robert Anton.]

240. Bond, R. Warwick. "On Six Plays in *Beaumont and Flet-
      cher, 1679*." *The Review of English Studies* 11 (July
      1935):257-275.

[Bond, at p. 260, indicates strongly that Sancho Panza
was of influence on the figure Castruccio in *The Double
Marriage*. At pp. 274-275 the critic concludes that the
figure Don Quijote was drawn upon in depicting Chatillion in *The Noble Gentleman*. In this same play, Bond
finds, the influence of the delusions of Marine on the
simple Jaques is very much like the effect of the
Knight's madness on Sancho.]

241. Bradford, Gamaliel, Jr. *"The History of Cardenio by
     Mr. Fletcher and Shakespeare."* Modern Language Notes
     25 (1910):51-56.

     In 1727, Lewis Theobald produced a play entitled
     Double Falsehood, or the Distressed Lovers and professed
     to have drawn on earlier manuscripts. Theobald's play
     has as its ultimate source the Cardenio episode in *Don
     Quijote*. Was Theobald really in possession of certain
     manuscripts, as he asserted? Yes, and this play was
     written in part by Fletcher. Does Shakespeare have any
     connection with Theobald's play? There are some traces
     of Shakespeare's later rugged, vigorous period in
     Double Falsehood, and it is possible that he wrote Acts
     I and II and the first portion of Act III. The latter
     portion of this play, however, appears to have been orig-
     inally composed by Fletcher, for it contains several
     characteristics of his style. [For additional works on
     the lost play *Cardenio* see Theobald, items 297-301.]

242. Entwistle, William J. *"Un Quijote inglés."* In *Miguel
     de Cervantes Saavedra. Homenaje de Ínsula en el
     cuarto centenario de su nacimiento 1547-1947*, pp. 79-
     85. Madrid: Ínsula, 1947.

     [Entwistle summarizes in some detail the plot of *The
     Knight of the Burning Pestle* by Beaumont and Fletcher,
     1613. The critic describes this play as their best and
     as one of the most original of the times. Entwistle ob-
     serves, however, that this play was rejected by the
     audiences.]

243. Fitzmaurice-Kelly, James. Introduction to the First
     Part of *The History of Don Quixote of the Mancha*.
     Vol. 1, pp. xlvi-li. Translated from the Spanish of
     Miguel de Cervantes by Thomas Shelton annis 1612,
     1620. London: David Nutt, 1896.

     [The critic believes that Fletcher used the Shelton
     translation of the *Quijote* in writing *The Knight of the
     Burning Pestle*. Fitzmaurice-Kelly also discusses the
     question of the lost play *Cardenio* and concludes that it
     is not rash to assume that Shakespeare found the mate-
     rial for that play in Shelton's 1612 translation.]

244. Fitzmaurice-Kelly, James. *"Cervantes in England."*
     Proceedings of the British Academy (1905-1906), pp.
     11-29. [Address read January 25, 1905.]

     [Fitzmaurice-Kelly examines the early popularity of
     the *Quijote*, its reception in England, its influence on

playwrights such as John Fletcher and Nathan Field. English translations of the *Quijote* are also noted, and
English criticism of Cervantes' masterpiece is briefly
examined.]

245. Fitzmaurice-Kelly, James. "Cervantes and Shakespeare."
      Proceedings of the British Academy (1915-1916), pp.
      297-317.

      [The critic states that Cervantes never heard of
      Shakespeare, but that it is not impossible that Shake-
      speare had heard of Cervantes. It is conceivable, Fitz-
      maurice-Kelly asserts, that Shakespeare read Shelton's
      1612 translation of Part I of the *Quijote*. The question
      of the lost play *Cardenio* is discussed but no conclusion
      is reached. Sancho Panza is compared to Falstaff, and
      the Knight is contrasted with Hamlet. Fitzmaurice-
      Kelly points out similarities and differences in the
      thought and style of Shakespeare and Cervantes. The
      critic notes (p. 300) that both writers refer to drama
      as being a mirror held up to nature.]

246. Freehafer, John. "*Cardenio*, by Shakespeare and Fletcher."
      PMLA 84 (May 1969):501-513.

      [The question of the authorship of the lost play *Car-
      denio*, listed by Humphrey Moseley in 1653 as written by
      "Mr. Fletcher & Shakespeare," is examined here in de-
      tail. Prior works on the subject are noted. Freehafer
      accepts what has become the general view: that Shake-
      speare wrote the first part of the lost play, and
      Fletcher the last. The critic regards Theobald's
      Double Falsehood as probably a "heavily cut version of
      Cardenio" and accepts as true Theobald's assertions re-
      garding the existence of several manuscripts of the
      play. Freehafer also concludes: that *Cardenio* was based
      on the 1612 Shelton translation of the *Quijote*; that *Car-
      denio* was cut and perhaps modified during the Restora-
      tion period and then altered by Theobald; that Theo-
      bald's lack of forthrightness in dealing with the author-
      ship of the play resulted from his obligation to support
      his patron's erroneous belief that the original play was
      wholly by Shakespeare and from Theobald's desire to pro-
      tect his reputation as a Shakespeare scholar. For addi-
      tional works on the lost play *Cardenio* see Theobald,
      items 297-301.]

247. Gale, Steven H. "The Relationship between Beaumont's
      The Knight of the Burning Pestle and Cervantes' *Don
      Quijote*." *Anales Cervantinos* 11 (1972):87-96.

[Gale notes that the first ten allusions to the *Qui-jote* in England are found in the seventeenth-century drama. Various similarities between Beaumont's play *The Knight of the Burning Pestle*, 1607 or later, and the *Quijote* are noted: (1) spoofing of knight-errantry in general; (2) the loss of money by a lover in the forest; (3) freeing prisoners; (4) a barber's basin; (5) the name of the barber, Nick (Nicolás); (6) inns mistaken for castles. The critic concludes that the *Quijote* did influence the plot and atmosphere of Beaumont's play but doubts if the English dramatist knew of Cervantes' novel firsthand.]

248. Hobbs, Edna Earle. "Spanish Influence on the Plays of Beaumont and Fletcher." Ph.D. dissertation, Florida State University, 1963. Pp. 242.

[Hobbs examines some fifty-two plays by Beaumont, Fletcher, and their collaborators, principally Massinger. The critic points out the possible influence of the main plot of the *Quijote* on *The Knight of the Burning Pestle* and of *The Tale of the Curious Impertinent* on *The Coxcomb*. The influence of Cervantes' *Novelas ejemplares* and the *Persiles* on English drama is also noted. This dissertation contains a lengthy bibliography. Appendix B, pp. 238 *et seq.*, lists the various plays studied and notes their possible sources. In the main body of this work references to the *Quijote* are found throughout, especially at pp. 15-16, 25-26, 28-30, 128-131, 162-166, and in the Conclusion. Hobbs divides her thesis into various parts: theme, plot, language, and character, and examines the sources of the plays of Beaumont and Fletcher in these several aspects. The critic finds that prior investigation of the Spanish influence on English drama has neglected the area of language and character.]

249. Knowles, Edwin B., Jr. *Four Articles on Don Quixote in England*. New York: New York University, 1941. Pp. 12.

[The genesis of these four articles is an unpublished dissertation at New York University in 1938 ("The Vogue of *Don Quixote* in England from 1605 to 1660"). The first article was read before the English Section of the Modern Language Association in December, 1938; the second selection is based on an article in *Philological Quarterly* 20 (October 1941):573-586; the third article is from *Hispanic Review* 9 (April 1941):252-265; and the final selection is from *Hispania* 23 (May 1940):103-115.]

   Don Quijote was not an immediate success in England,
and it is correct to state that the influence of Spanish
literature on England has been greatly exaggerated.
Beaumont's *Knight of the Burning Pestle*, 1610, is not a
direct imitation of *Don Quijote*. However, *The Second
Maiden's Tragedy* (Massinger, *et al.*, 1611) is based on
The Tale of the Curious Impertinent, as is Nathan
Field's *Amends for Ladies*, c. 1611. *Cardenio*, a lost
play attributed both to Shakespeare and to Fletcher,
was performed on May 20, 1613, and may have been based
on the Cardenio episode (*D.Q.* I). Fletcher's and Massinger's *The Double Marriage* is, vaguely, an adaptation
of the Barataria episode in Part II of the *Quijote*,
while Fletcher's *The Pilgrim*, 1621, is only remotely
kin to the *Quijote*.
   The first English adaptation based on the main plot
of Cervantes' masterpiece is D'Avenant's *The Cruel
Brother*, but it is only vaguely similar to the *Quijote*.
Altogether there are only nine imitations of the *Quijote*
in England prior to 1660. This is not impressive,
since the French drew upon Cervantes' novel to a much
larger extent. Prior to 1660, there were only three
English editions of Part I of the *Quijote*, while in
France there were fourteen during this same period.
Therefore, it is preposterous to say that England led
Europe in the popular reception of the *Quijote*. In ad-
dition, in England there were few serious allusions to
Don Quijote prior to 1660; in France there were many.
Edmund Gayton's *Pleasant Notes Upon Don Quixot*, 1654,
is not a serious study and indicates that the English
of the seventeenth century were blind to the finer
points of Cervantes' masterpiece.

250.   Koeppel, E. "Don Quixote, Sancho Panza und Dulcinea in
       der englischen Litteratur bis zur Restauration (1660)."
       *Archiv für das Studium der neueren Sprachen und
       Literaturen* 101 (1898):87-98.

       [Koeppel points out a reference to knights-errant (a
       possible allusion to Don Quijote) in *The Knight of the
       Burning Pestle* (Beaumont and Fletcher, c. 1610-1611).
       Commenting on the Squire, the critic observes that San-
       cho does not have a worthy successor on the English
       stage, but notes that in *The Double Marriage* (Fletcher
       and Massinger) there is a scene that is possibly based
       on the Pedro Recio episode during Sancho's government.
       In *The Cruel Brother*, Koeppel continues, one finds a
       Don Quijote-Sancho Panza type pair, Lothario and Borachio.

Koeppel points out that there are various allusions to
Dulcinea in seventeenth-century English literature, and
furnishes citations to works by such writers as Robert
Burton, Ben Jonson, and Thomas May. A 1615 ballet about
Dulcinea is also noted.]

251. Koeppel, Emil. *Quellen-Studien zu den Dramen Ben Jon-
son's, John Marston's und Beaumont's und Fletcher's.*
Erlangen und Leipzig: A. Deichertsche Verlagsbuchh.
Nachf. (Georg Böhme), 1895. Pp. viii + 158.
[*Münchner Beiträge zur romanischen und englischen
Philologie* 11 (1897).]

[The critic discusses (pp. 41-44) the influence of the
Quijote on *The Knight of the Burning Pestle* (Beaumont
and Fletcher). Also examined (pp. 54-55) is the possible
influence of the *Curioso impertinente* on *The Coxcomb*,
attributed to Beaumont, Fletcher, and others. Koeppel
contends (p. 82) that Fletcher and Massinger made use of
the Sancho Panza figure in their play *The Double Marriage*, where the comic figure Castruccio receives treatment similar to that received by Sancho while governor
(*D.Q.* II, 47). The critic also contends (p. 103) that
Fletcher utilized the Barber's tale of the man who
thought he was Neptune (*D.Q.* II, ch. 1) in writing *The
Pilgrim* (Act III, sc. 7). Koeppel, however, doubts
(pp. 105-106) that Fletcher and Massinger made use of
the Barataria episode in *The Prophetess*, where the
clown Geta becomes a judge. (This theory was suggested
by Moriz Rapp in 1862, in his *Studien über das englische
Theater*, p. 75.)]

252. Koeppel, Emil. *Quellen-Studien zu den Dramen George
Chapman's, Philip Massinger's und John Ford's.* Strassburg i.E.: Karl J. Trübner, 1897. Pp. 229. [*Quellen
und Forschungen zur Sprach- und Culturgeschichte der
germanischen Völker* 82 (1897).]

[Koeppel asserts (p. 95) that the reference to the
Duchess's drainage tubes (*D.Q.* II, ch. 48) had an influence on a scene in *The Duke of Milan* (Philip Massinger). The critic also finds (p. 99) a trace of the
cautivo episode in Massinger's *The Renegado*.]

253. Maxwell, Baldwin. *Studies in Beaumont, Fletcher, and
Massinger.* New York: Octagon Books, Inc., 1966. Pp.
vii + 238. [First published in 1939, Chapel Hill, The
University of North Carolina Press.]

[The critic (pp. 147-148) discusses the authorship of
the play *The Noble Gentleman* and indicates that there
is an influence of the *Quijote* on that drama. Maxwell
(pp. 273-275) also suggests Cervantes' masterpiece as
the source of *The Knight of the Burning Pestle*. At
pages 56 and 177-178 the authorship and the sources of
the lost play *The History of Cardenio* are briefly
examined.]

254.   Murch, Herbert S. "*The Knight of the Burning Pestle*,
       by Beaumont and Fletcher." *Yale Studies in English*
       33 (1908). Pp. 442.

       [Murch's work is a revised version of his Ph.D. dis-
       sertation in English at Yale University, an edition of
       The Knight of the Burning Pestle, with notes, glossary,
       bibliography, along with a 114-page introduction deal-
       ing with the possible sources of the play. He concludes
       that the *Quijote* was *not* a source of this work by Beau-
       mont and Fletcher, for, in his opinion, Cervantes' mas-
       terpiece had not appeared in English when the play was
       written, and the playwrights knew no Spanish. Murch
       concludes that the origins of *The Knight of the Burning
       Pestle* are to be found in French and Spanish romances
       such as the *Amadís*.]

255.   Orgill, Douglas Harold. "The Influence of Cervantes on
       the Plays of John Fletcher." Ph.D. dissertation, Uni-
       versity of Southern California, 1960. Pp. iv + 300.

       [Chapter IV of this thesis discusses the influence of
       the *Quijote* on the plays of Fletcher and his collabora-
       tors. Six plays attributed to Fletcher, at least in
       part, are examined in detail: (1) *The Coxcomb*, 1608-
       1610; (2) *The Double Marriage*, 1620-1621; (3) *The His-
       tory of Cardenio* (lost), c. 1613; (4) *The Knight of the
       Burning Pestle*, 1607-1610; (5) *The Pilgrim*, 1621-1622;
       and (6) *The Prophetess*, 1622. Orgill finds "some
       striking parallels" between Cervantes' short story *El
       curioso impertinente* and *The Coxcomb* and concludes that
       Fletcher used that tale as one of his sources. *The
       Double Marriage*, Act V (dealing with the kingly dis-
       appointments of Castruccio) seems, states Orgill, to be
       suggested by the frustrations of Sancho during his
       government in Part II of the *Quijote*. There is no
       doubt, he concludes, that Fletcher used the scene of
       Sancho's banquet. *The History of Cardenio* is discussed
       at length, and the critic notes that there is no extant
       copy of this play. The theory that Theobald's *The*

Double Falsehood, 1727, is a revision of the lost play
is examined. Orgill concludes in favor of this theory
and further finds that the Cardenio episode in Part I
of the *Quijote* is the origin of both the lost play as
well as that of Theobald. (For additional works on the
lost play *Cardenio* see items 297-301.)

The Knight of the Burning Pestle is next discussed,
and the critic concludes that it is incorrect to state
that the *Quijote* was of little or no influence on that
play. Numerous similarities between the *Quijote* and
The Knight of the Burning Pestle are pointed out. *The
Pilgrim*, Orgill finds, is based in part on Lope de Vega's
El peregrino en su patria but also contains a scene from
Chapter I, Part II of the *Quijote* (the lawyer who thought
he was Neptune). The role of Geta in *The Prophetess* is
compared and contrasted with that of Sancho in the Barataria episode. Orgill states as follows: "If Fletcher
fashioned the role of Geta after that of Sancho the
governor, he did so with great freedom, making many al-
terations of his own, and producing a role inferior to
Sancho's."

In his conclusion Orgill finds that Fletcher often
drew on Cervantes' plots and situations that contained
suspense, intrigue, and surprise, but that the Englishman did not seek ideas, characters, or dialog. The use
of devices such as disguises and mistaken identities by
Fletcher and Cervantes is contrasted. Orgill concludes
that, all in all, Fletcher seldom improved Cervantes'
characters; instead he consistently diminished their
importance.]

256.   Peery, William. *"The Curious Impertinent* in *Amends for
       Ladies."* *Hispanic Review* 14 (October 1946):344-353.

Gerard Langbaine, in 1691, stated in his *An Account
of the English Dramatick Poets* that the plot of the
Curioso impertinente was used in Nathan Field's *Amends
for Ladies*, and later scholars have echoed this obser-
vation. Rosenbach (258) concluded that Field was
heavily indebted to Cervantes' interpolated *novela* not
only for the plot but for the dialog as well, and
Knowles (249) asserted that Field borrowed the idea of
the tempting husband either from the *Curioso* or from
The Second Maiden's Tragedy (anon., 1611). These con-
clusions are not correct. It should be noted that
since Field's *Amends for Ladies* (published in 1618) was
probably acted in 1611, a year before Shelton's English
manuscript, it is quite likely that he merely heard of

the story of the *Curioso* by way of mouth. This is true
in spite of the fact that several passages in *Amends*
are similar to those in the *Curioso*. One should also
note that the wife-tempting episode makes up only a
small portion of Field's play.

257.   Randall, Dale B.J. *The Golden Tapestry: A Critical
       Survey of Non-Chivalric Spanish Fiction in English
       Translation (1543-1657)*. Durham, N.C.: Duke Univer-
       sity Press, 1963. Pp. viii + 262.

       [The first influence of the *Quijote* on English writing,
       states Randall, was on the drama. Several plays are
       cited as being affected by Cervantes' novel: *The Knight
       of the Burning Pestle* (c. 1608); *The Second Maiden's
       Tragedy* (1611); *Amends for Ladies* (c. 1611); *The Double
       Marriage* (c. 1620); *The Cruel Brother* (1630); *The Tri-
       umph of Peace* (1634); *The History of Don-quixot* (an-
       nounced in 1651, 1658, and 1661); *The Disappointment*
       (1681); *The Married Beau* (1694); and *The Comical History
       of Don Quixote* (1694-1696). Of another work, Robert
       Anton's humorous novel *Moriomachia*, 1613, the critic
       states that it may fairly be called the first English
       successor of the *Quijote*. Edmund Gayton's *Pleasant
       Notes upon Don Quixot*, 1654, is criticized as a purely
       farcical interpretation of Cervantes' masterpiece.
       Randall points out that John Phillips, in 1687, produced
       a burlesque *Don Quijote*.]

258.   Rosenbach, Abraham S. Wolf. "*The Curious-Impertinent*
       in English Dramatic Literature Before Shelton's Trans-
       lation of *Don Quixote*." *Modern Language Notes* 17
       (June 1902):357-367.

       With the possible exception of *The Knight of the
       Burning Pestle*, the play *The Second Maiden's Tragedy*
       (attributed to several playwrights, including Shake-
       speare) is the first English drama that was indebted to
       Cervantes. This play, performed on October 31, 1611,
       deals with a husband who, like Cervantes' curious Ansel-
       mo, puts his wife to a test of her virtue. The English
       play closely parallels the *Curious Impertinent* in other
       respects, including the dialogs. If the author of *The
       Second Maiden's Tragedy* did not read Spanish, he may
       have read the French version of *El curioso impertinente*,
       1608, by Baudouin, or he may have had access to Shel-
       ton's manuscript (not published until 1612).
       Nathan Field's play *Amends for Ladies*, published 1618,
       is culled, at least in its subplot, from the *Quijote*;

but Beaumont's and Fletcher's *The Coxcomb* is not, in
spite of the opinion of other critics. *The Knight of
the Burning Pestle* (Beaumont and Fletcher) was not published until 1613, but according to William Burne it
predates Shelton's translation of Part I of the *Quijote*
by more than a year.

259. Russell, P.E. "English Seventeenth-Century Interpreta-
      tions of Spanish Literature." *Atlante* 1 (1953):65-77.

[Very little is found in this article on the influence
of the *Quijote* on English writers. Russell takes note
of Shelton's translation of Cervantes' masterpiece and
points out the general popularity of that work, and of
the *Novelas ejemplares*, in England. The critic concludes that the *Quijote* did not destroy the popularity
of chivalresque novels in England.]

260. Schevill, Rudolph. "On the Influence of Spanish Litera-
      ture upon English in the Early 17th Century." *Roman-
      ische Forschungen* 20 (1907):604-634.

[Schevill generally discounts the influence of Spanish
literature on English writing. Speaking of the *Quijote*
the critic, pp. 611-612, finds that too much is inferred
from the fact that the Knight is casually mentioned in
plays only a few years after the publication of the *Quijote* in Spanish. This influence could have been by word
of mouth, states Schevill, not from a familiarity with
the novel itself. Allusions to windmills twice in 1608,
he continues, do not prove that Spanish literature was
fast in getting to England. The critic discusses the
influence of the *Quijote* on Ben Jonson and concludes
that Jonson probably did not read the *Quijote* in Spanish
but more likely had access to Shelton's manuscript of
an English translation. All in all, Schevill finds that
Ben Jonson's knowledge of the *Quijote* was not deep.
   Schevill also concludes that the *Quijote* did not influence *The Knight of the Burning Pestle* of Beaumont and
Fletcher, since, to the critic, the whole play is singu-
larly unlike anything in Cervantes' novel. The fact
that Ralph, the hero of the play, mistakes inns for
castles and pays for his lodging with thanks, not money
(as well as the allusion to a copper basin in Ralph's
adventure with the giant Barbaroso) is not, to Schevill,
sufficient evidence of a direct influence of the *Quijote*
on *The Knight of the Burning Pestle*.]

261.   Siles Artés, José. "La influencia de *Don Quijote* en
       Hudibras." *Filología Moderna* 5 (1965):185-192.

       [Siles Artés states that the principal idea which
       Samuel Butler takes from the *Quijote* is that of a
       knight-errant who goes out to reform the world. The
       critic points out other similarities between *Hudibras*
       and Cervantes' novel: allusions to self-flogging,
       harangues, beatings by supposed beings from the other
       world, allusions to knight-errantry, and the use of a
       squire. The widow in Butler's poem, states Siles
       Artés, is, like Dulcinea, an inspiration to the hero.
       The critic observes, however, that the central figures
       in both works are quite different: the Don is a madman
       while Hudibras is a religious fanatic; the servants
       Sancho and Ralpho are also different, the former being
       a contrast to his master, the latter being a fanatic,
       hypocrite, and cynic like Hudibras.]

262.   Thomas, H. "Shakespeare and Spain." In *Homenaje of-
       recido a Menéndez Pidal.* Vol. 1, pp. 225-253.
       Madrid: Hernando, 1925.

       [Thomas points out certain similarities between Cer-
       vantes and Shakespeare: both state that the purpose of
       the theatre is to hold a faithful mirror up to nature
       (*Hamlet*, II, ii, 24 and *D.Q.* II, ch. 12); the similar
       thoughts of Falstaff and Sancho (*Henry IV*, Part II, V,
       i, 24 and *D.Q.* II, ch. 10). Thomas also compares the
       sudden elevation of Sly to the nobility to Sancho's re-
       ceiving a governorship (*D.Q.* II). The critic com-
       pares a scene with Petruchio and his horse (*Taming of
       the Shrew*) to Don Quijote and Rocinante, and finds that
       Falstaff's threat to toss Pistol in a blanket (*Henry IV*,
       Part II, II, iv, 222-223) is reminiscent of Sancho's
       tossing in Part I of the *Quijote*. Thomas (p. 241) notes
       the lost play *History of Cardenio* (purportedly by
       Shakespeare and conceivably based on material in Part I
       of the *Quijote*) but takes no position in regard to the
       authorship or source of that play.]

263.   Todd, F.M. "Webster and Cervantes." *Modern Language
       Review* 51 (July 1956):321-323.

       In Chapter VI, Part II of the *Quijote*, the Knight
       uses the pyramid as an image in describing the structure
       of medieval chivalry. John Webster, in his play *The
       Duchess of Malfi*, uses this same figure of speech, draw-
       ing on Cervantes' work (probably in the original or in

the French version of 1618). On two occasions Webster
alludes to windmills. [In regard to the pyramid image,
see item 238.]

264. Underhill, John Garrett. *Spanish Literature in the
      England of the Tudors*. New York: The Macmillan Com-
      pany, 1899. Pp. x + 438.

      [The period covered by this work ends with the death
      of Elizabeth I in 1603, prior to the influence of the
      Quijote. However, the later influence of Cervantes'
      works on Beaumont and Fletcher is pointed out.]

265. Wann, Louis. "The Oriental in Elizabethan Drama."
      Modern Philology 12 (1914-1915):423-447.

      [Wann's study is limited to the oriental matter in
      English plays between 1558 and 1642. He states that
      Massinger's *The Renegado* was influenced by Part I of
      the *Quijote* and by *Los baños de Argel*.]

266. Wilson, Edward M. "Cervantes and English Literature of
      the Seventeenth Century." *Bulletin Hispanique* 50
      (1948):27-52.

      Edmund Gayton's *Pleasant Notes upon Don Quixot*, 1654,
      is almost entirely facetious, being full of coarse jokes
      and brutal humor. It is a burlesque commentary on what
      Gayton thought was a burlesque novel. He often seeks
      to be funny when commenting upon a non-humorous passage
      of the *Quijote*.
      Several playwrights in seventeenth-century England
      adapted the *Quijote*, or parts of it, to the stage. Most
      critics believe that *The Knight of the Burning Pestle*
      (Beaumont and Fletcher) is based on the *Quijote*. Leon-
      hardt reached this conclusion in 1885, but Murch (254)
      is of the opposite opinion.
      Samuel Butler, though he read the *Quijote* carefully,
      saw no more in it than Gayton. In his *Hudibras* he
      makes his central characters stand for classes of people
      he does not like: Presbyterians, in the form of Hudi-
      bras, and Independents, in the form of Ralpho, who is
      modeled after Sancho. There are numerous similarities
      between *Hudibras* and *Don Quijote*. Tricks are played on
      Ralpho's mount similar to those played on Rocinante and
      Rucio in Barcelona. Hudibras attacks processions; he is
      cudgelled by devils as Don Quijote is mistreated in the
      bedroom scene with Doña Rodríguez. In addition, Hudi-
      bras' advice to Ralpho is reminiscent of the Knight's

consejos to Sancho. Other similarities are the dis-
cussions on the spoils of war, on procuring, and on the
duties of a knight-errant. The general mock-heroic tone
is the same in both works.

267. Wilson, Edward M. "Edmund Gayton on Don Quixote, Andrés,
      and Juan Haldudo." *Comparative Literature* 2 (Winter
      1950):64-72.

      In his *Pleasant Notes upon Don Quixot*, 1654, Gayton
shows no sympathy for Cervantes or for the Knight. Gayton is diffuse, obscure, insensitive, pornographic, and
sadistic. He saw nothing admirable about the Don or
the Squire. Some of Gayton's observations are valid,
however. He saw Cardenio as the personification of
cowardice, as Madariaga was to do in his *Guía del lector del Quijote* in 1926. Also Gayton viewed the Knight
as boastful, as A.A. Parker does in "*Don Quijote* and
the Relativity of Truth" in 1947.

      Most modern critics believe that we should feel pity
for Andrés, especially after the second cruel flogging
he receives at the hands of Juan Haldudo. Américo Castro asserts that this episode shows Don Quijote's moral
error (*Pensamiento de Cervantes*, p. 119) but also concludes that we should be sympathetic to the wretched
young Andrés. Gayton, however, views the boy as a
criminal who deserves flogging.

      In 1711 Ned Ward published a coarse and inferior ver-
sion of the *Quijote* in Hudibrastic verse. Ward reached
the same conclusion as Gayton in regard to Andrés.

                      Eighteenth-Century England

General

268. Close, Anthony. "Don Quixote as a Burlesque Hero: A
      Reconstructed Eighteenth-Century View." *Forum for
      Modern Language Studies* 10 (1974):365-378.

      [This article does not, to any great extent, deal
directly with the influence of the *Quijote* on eighteenth-
century novelists. However, the interpretation of the
Quijote by such writers as Fielding is given attention.
Close considers Cervantes' masterpiece a comic epic and
the hero, in some essential respects, a burlesque hero.]

269.   Cross, Wilbur L. *The Development of the English Novel.*
       New York: The Macmillan Company, 1935. Pp. ix + 329.
       (First published in 1899.)

       [Cross (pp. 9–10) finds that Fielding, Goldsmith,
       Sterne, Thackeray, and in a lesser degree Smollett,
       Scott, Dickens, and Bulwer, were influenced by Cervan-
       tes, with the result that they created characters re-
       minding one of Don Quijote, and that among these charac-
       ters are Parson Adams, Uncle Toby, Jonathan Oldbuck, and
       Colonel Newcome. The critic (pp. 52–53) considers
       Fielding to be too much influenced by Cervantes' charac-
       ter portrayal. Trusting to Cervantes, states Cross,
       Fielding seemed to think that there is some causal con-
       nection between nobility and grotesque manners. Thus,
       in making exceptional and quixotic characters like these
       representative of the better side of human nature,
       Fielding lent to his portrait of eighteenth-century man-
       ners a want of symmetry and harmony. The influence of
       the *Quijote* on Smollett and Sterne is briefly noted
       (pp. 63, 70).]

270.   Niehus, Edward Lee. "The Nature and Development of the
       Quixote Figure in the Eighteenth-Century English
       Novel." Ph.D. dissertation, University of Minnesota,
       1971. Pp. 255.

       [Niehus traces the variations in the interpretation
       of the Quijote figure and attempts to show "trends in
       the degree of manner of realizing the various satiric,
       comic, and sentimental potentialities of the figure."
       Chapter One deals with seventeenth-century, non-
       novelistic interpretations, such as Samuel Butler's
       Hudibras. Chapter Two is concerned with Swift's satir-
       ical attitude toward Quijotism in *Tale of a Tub* and in
       Gulliver's Travels. The third chapter discusses the
       more sympathetic attitude of Fielding and the increasing
       tolerance of individuality. Chapter Four deals with the
       numerous quixotic characters of Tobias Smollett, ranging
       from satiric butts to romantic heroes. The following
       chapter discusses Laurence Sterne who, states Niehus,
       realizes not only the satiric and comic potential of
       the Quijote figure, but its sentimental and tragic quali-
       ties as well. The final chapter surveys a variety of
       minor quixotic characters in the works of Oliver Gold-
       smith, Henry Mackenzie, Charlotte Lennox, and Richard
       Graves, some of whom viewed the Don as sentimental and
       romantic, while others saw him as an object of ridicule.]

271. Patterson, Malcolm Howie. "Early English Novels Imita-
     ting *Don Quijote.*" Ph.D. dissertation, University of
     Oklahoma, 1975. Pp. iv + 206.

     In the eighteenth and early nineteenth centuries there
     are at least ten English novels which imitate the *Qui-
     jote*: *The Female Quixote* by Charlotte Lennox; *Joseph
     Andrews* by Henry Fielding; *Sir Launcelot Greaves* by
     Tobias Smollett; *The Spiritual Quixote* by Richard Graves;
     the anonymous *Philosophical Quixote*; *Sir George Warring-
     ton* by Jane Purbeck; *The Infernal Quixote* by Charles
     Lucas; *The Political Quixote* by George Buxton; the
     anonymous *The Amicable Quixote*; and *Sancho, or, the
     Proverbialist* by John William Cunningham.
     These English writers had various purposes in pattern-
     ing their novels after Cervantes' masterpiece. For
     example, Charlotte Lennox attacked the foolish litera-
     ture of her time; five of the writers (Purbeck, Graves,
     Lucas, Buxton, and the anonymous author of *The Philo-
     sophical Quixote*) used characters of different degrees
     of infamy to defame movements of their day. Most saw
     Don Quijote's vision as worthless, foolish, and selfish.
     The value of *Don Quijote* to the eighteenth century was
     not its serious message, and Cervantes' masterpiece was
     not used to promote change, but to prevent it.

272. Small, Miriam Rossiter. *Charlotte Ramsay Lennox, an
     Eighteenth-Century Lady of Letters.* New Haven: Yale
     University Press, 1935. Pp. iv + 268. [*Yale Studies
     in English Literature*, Vol. 85 (1935); as reprinted
     in 1969 by Archon Books, Hamden, Conn.]

     [The critic, in Chapter III (pp. 64-117), summarizes
     in detail the plot of Mrs. Lennox's *The Female Quixote*,
     1752, a story of the overly romantic Arabella. The
     fact that the authoress draws upon the language of Cer-
     vantes' *Quijote* is noted. Under the category of imita-
     tions of characters various English works influenced by
     the *Quijote* are discussed, including *Joseph Andrews*,
     Tristram Shandy, *Humphry Clinker*, and *Tom Jones*. Under
     imitations of title and plot, Small notes Fielding's
     Don Quixote in England and Smollett's *The History of
     Sir Launcelot Greaves*, which are discussed at length.
     Under the heading of superficial imitations the critic
     mentions several lost works and Richard Graves' *The
     Spiritual Don Quixote; or the Summer's Ramble of Geoffry
     Wildgoose* (c. 1773); *The Amicable Quixote* (anon.,
     1788); Mrs. Lennox's (or Jane Purbeck's) *The History of
     Sir George Warrington, or the Political Quixote*, 1797;

Charles Lucas' *The Infernal Quixote, A Tale of the Day*,
1801; George Buxton's *The Political Quixote, or, The
Adventures of the Renowned Don Blackibo, Dwarfino, and
his Trusty "Squire," Seditonio*, 1820. Two works by
Americans are also discussed: Tabitha Tenney's *Female
Quixotism*, c. 1808; and H.H. Brackenridge's *Modern
Chivalry*, 1792-1815.]

273. Staves, Susan. "Don Quixote in Eighteenth-Century England." *Comparative Literature* 24 (1972):193-215.

[Staves asserts that there are three stages of the
Quijote figure in England: (1) the buffoon, the madman
of the farce; (2) the still ridiculous, still a buffoon
figure who is strangely noble, even saintly; (3) the
idealistic and noble hero. Staves notes the exploita-
tion of the Quijote figure for burlesque, satire, or
humor in: Charlotte Lennox's *The Female Quixote*, 1752;
Jane Austen's *Northanger Abbey* (the figure Catherine
Mooreland, a reader of Gothic novels); Richard Graves'
The Spiritual Quixote, 1773 (the figure Geoffry Wildgoose); Charles Lucas' *The Infernal Quixote*, 1800 (the
figure Mariander); Sterne's *Tristram Shandy*, which has
several quixotic figures; Smollett's *Sir Launcelot
Greaves*. Staves points out the use of a Quijote figure
in Mrs. Charlotte Smith's romantic novels: *Desmond*,
1792; *The Banished Man*, 1794; *The Old Manor House*, 1793;
and *The Young Philosopher*, 1798. Staves also notes the
use by Sir Walter Scott of a literary Quijote figure in
Waverley, not to destroy romance but to create it.]

Henry Fielding

274. Alter, Robert. *Fielding and the Nature of the Novel*.
Cambridge, Mass.: Harvard University Press, 1968. Pp.
x + 211.

[Alter finds several similarities between Fielding
and Cervantes. At pages 40-41 the critic notes the
ironic distance of both writers, a device necessary to
avoid overwhelming the reader with contemporary details.

The critic (pp. 76-77) states that from the *Quijote*
on, novels tend to be about people trying to play roles,
that the Don attempted to create for himself a role
from literature because he was no one in particular and
wanted desperately to become someone. The same is true,

Alter continues, of a whole line of heroes of novels--
Julien Sorel, Rastignac, Emma Bovary, Dorothea Brooke,
Raskolnikov, Kafka's K., Leopold Bloom--all, whether
pathetically or boldly, in search of an identity through
playing a role. The critic finds a similar tendency in
the works of recent American novelists as different as
Saul Bellow, John Barth, Bernard Malamud, and Walker
Percy, who have created protagonists who, unsure of who
they are or what they can become, try on roles like
clothing.

Another innovation of the *Quijote*, states Alter (pp.
101-102), is the way Cervantes continually imposes pat-
terns on the stuff of reality, playing with the ambiguous status of his book as art-or-reality. Indeed, the
critic continues, it could be argued that the real subject of the novel is the stubborn ambiguity of the relationship between literary creation and reality.

The use of interpolated episodes by Cervantes and
Fielding is discussed (p. 108). The employment of such
material, states Alter, is another reflection of the
novelist's awareness of the novel as a made thing. The
style of such material, he observes, tends to be formal,
with none of the animated inventiveness of the main narrator; by contrast, the surrounding narrative is made
to seem both livelier and more likelike than it other-
wise would. The tendency of both Fielding and Cervantes
to interrupt these interpolated interruptions is observed, a device designed, states Alter, to heighten
the contrast between the interpolation and the main
plot.

Summing up the history of the novel (pp. 181-182) the
critic states:] The history of the novel is a dialectic
between consciousness and things, between personality
and the world of unyielding objects that impinges upon
it. There is no dialectic of this sort in the older
narrative forms because they generally reflect a sense
of organic connection between man and the things with
which he lives. Since the Renaissance, however, the
sense, or perhaps dream, of organic connection between
man and things has been ruptured. The novel begins at
the turn of the seventeenth century when a would-be
hero's imagination tries to resist the unredeemed neu-
trality, the sodden gayness, of the alien things that
surround him: his heroism consists in his brave, pathetic, noble, and, of course, mad attempt to force the indifferent things of his world into consonance with his
own heroic ideals. The explicit pattern of the *Quijote*
was repeated in many novels, but even where it was not,

a kind of tense interplay between people and things
persisted.
[Cervantes, to Alter (p. 78), was a man no longer certain of what nature really was, and his ability to
translate this profoundest of uncertainties into fiction
is a measure of the undying greatness of his novel.]

275. Bosdorf, Erich. *Entstehungsgeschichte von Fieldings
      "Joseph Andrews."* Weimar: R. Wagner Sohn, 1908. Pp.
      vi + 82.

      [Bosdorf's work contains a foreword and six chapters.
      The critic discusses the realistic features of Fielding's
      novel and his attack on Richardson and idealistic fic-
      tion. Chapter V deals specifically with the influence
      of the *Quijote* on *Joseph Andrews*. A brief summary is
      given of the opinions of prior critics regarding the
      meaning of the phrase used by Fielding with respect to
      his novel: "Written in imitation of the manner of Cer-
      vantes, author of *Don Quixote*." Bosdorf pictures the
      Knight as essentially a realistic figure in spite of his
      madness. The critic also compares Parson Adams with the
      Don, and Joseph Andrews with Sancho, and further notes
      the use by Fielding of several scenes from the *Quijote*.]

276. Brooks, Douglas. "The Interpolated Tales in *Joseph
      Andrews* Again." *Modern Philology* 65 (1967-1968):208-
      213.

      [The critic discusses the structure of the "Tale of
      the Curious Impertinent" with its interruptions and its
      parallels with material outside the interpolated tale.
      Brooks finds that Fielding surpasses Cervantes in the
      comic irony of using thematic parallels between material
      inside and outside the inner story. Particular atten-
      tion is devoted here to "The Unfortunate Jilt" and "The
      History of Two Friends," interpolated tales in *Joseph
      Andrews*.]

277. Buck, Gerhard. "'Written in Imitation of the Manner of
      Cervantes.'" *Germanisch-Romanische Monatsschrift* 29
      (1941):53-61.

      The subtitle to Fielding's *Joseph Andrews* states that
      the story is "Written in Imitation of the Manner of Cer-
      vantes." This statement has often been commented upon
      by critics. There are actually three points in the dis-
      cussion of the Cervantes-Fielding relationship: (1)
      Fielding's attitude toward Richardson and Cibber, which

is similar to Cervantes' attitude toward books of chivalry; (2) Bosdorf's (275) idea of the epic nature of
Joseph Andrews and *Don Quijote*; (3) Hazlitt's view on
the similarity between the Knight and Parson Adams.

It is true that Fielding satirizes the affectation of
Richardson as Cervantes satirizes the absurdities of
chivalresque novels. Fielding also allows his characters to bring a literary standard into daily reality.
But here the parallel between Joseph and the Don ends,
as does the use of parody, for with Fielding this parody
is limited to the first few chapters. Thus the debt of
Fielding to Cervantes is not to be found in the area of
parody of prior literature.

Fielding, in his *Coffee-House Politician*, 1730, indicates his acceptance of the eighteenth-century view that
the *Quijote* was a didactic study of excess, and that
good-heartedness should be moderate. However, Parson
Adams, like the Don, has certain traits which make him
lovable. In reality, the Parson is a recurring, autonomous figure of the knight-errant type, though he is
not a direct imitation of the Knight.

Fielding stated in the *Foreword* to *Joseph Andrews*
that he wished to write a comic prose epic, with extended
and comprehensive action, containing a large circle of
incidents and introducing a great variety of characters.
He saw the validity of the comic epic in its breadth,
yet resorts to stock figures in *Joseph Andrews*. Hence
he does not here find the right way between individuality
and universality in his characters. In a true sense
Fielding does not write "in Imitation of the Manner of
Cervantes" until *Tom Jones*, where a true character, not
a type, is presented in depth.

278.   Coburn, William Leon. "In Imitation of the Manner of
       Cervantes: *Don Quixote* and *Joseph Andrews*." Ph.D.
       dissertation, University of California, Davis, 1969.
       Pp. iv + 187.

       [This work consists of a preface and three chapters.
       As the author states in his preface, the purpose of this
       thesis is to examine the influence of Cervantes on
       Fielding's first novel, *Joseph Andrews*, and to ascertain
       Fielding's deviations from the narrative and structural
       techniques found in the *Quijote*. Coburn's first chapter
       discusses the reception of the *Quijote* in England and
       concludes that its influence was not significant prior
       to 1660. Great attention is devoted to the change in
       the conception of humor with Anthony Ashley Cooper,

third Earl of Shaftesbury, and with other English writers
such as Fielding and Steele. The effect of this change
on the gradual reinterpretation of the *Quijote* and its
protagonist is examined.

The second chapter discusses the use by Cervantes and
Fielding of an all-important narrator who constantly
keeps the reader aware of his craftsmanship.

The final chapter, "The Narrator and the Structure,"
begins with a discussion of the differences between the
two novelists. Fielding's principal object of satire,
states Coburn, is society at large (knavish people;
fashions; institutions) while Cervantes' satirical object is chivalric novels. The most important distinction between the two writers, Coburn asserts, is that
Fielding does not create a fictional author as the pri-
mary source of the account, at least not one with a
name. But there are marked parallels between the two
men, the critic adds, for both are concerned about the
tendency of romance to deceive readers by presenting
(as facts) actions and characters that never existed,
could never exist, and ought never to exist; both
writers oppose excess involvement with the characters of
the story. Coburn notes the concern of both Cervantes
and Fielding with the "literature-versus-life" theme,
and examines the tendency of both writers to use this
theme to control the reader's attitude. The critic also
observes the employment by both novelists of a merci-
ful narrator to establish the reliability of the
account.

Under "structural influences" Coburn notes that Part
I of the *Quijote* and the novel *Joseph Andrews* are divided
into four parts. The lack of logic behind the ending of
chapters in both stories is discussed, and the use by
both novelists of interpolated tales, reprises, and thematic progression is studied in some detail.]

279. Driskell, Leon V. "Interpolated Tales in *Joseph Andrews*
     and *Don Quixote*: The Dramatic Method as Instruction."
     South Atlantic Bulletin 33 (May 1968):5-8.

     [The critic concludes that in Cervantes' novel, even
     more than in Fielding's work, the interpolated tales
     depend for their meaning on recognition of their dramatic
     function, for it is vital to the plot that certain
     characters hear certain stories, either fully or par-
     tially. Driskell notes that both Cervantes and Fielding
     had a common apprenticeship as playwrights and both ex-
     celled in what is known as tragicomedy. The critic
     finds that both are essentially dramatic writers.

Comparing the general outlook of *Joseph Andrews* with
that of the *Quijote*, Driskell finds that for all the
hilarity of both novels, they show us a somber world in
which pleasure frequently derives from mischief, if not
from downright evil; that the Parson and Joseph reach
their goal not because of their goodness but in spite of
it; that Don Quijote suffers because of his idealism,
not in spite of it.]

280. Elistratova, A.A. "H. Fielding y el *Quijote*." In
      Servantes i vsemirnaia literatura, pp. 117-140. Edited
      by N. Balashof, A. Mijailof, and I. Terterian. Moscow:
      Nauka, 1969.

      [The critic notes the early English translation of the
      Quijote by Shelton, in 1612, during Cervantes' lifetime.
      Elistratova also points out the influence of Cervantes'
      masterpiece on English playwrights such as Beaumont and
      Fletcher, and on Samuel Butler's satirical poem *Hudibras*.
      Attention is devoted to Henry Fielding's play *Don Qui-
      xote in England*, 1734, and the use of themes and situa-
      tions from the *Quijote* in *Tom Jones* and *Joseph Andrews*
      is discussed. The remarks of Defoe, Addison, and Steele
      about the *Quijote* are recorded. The critic briefly men-
      tions Charlotte Lennox's *The Female Quixote*.]

281. Goldberg, Homer. "The Interpolated Stories in *Joseph
      Andrews* or 'The History of the World in General'
      Satirically Revised." *Modern Philology* 63 (1965-1966):
      295-310.

      [Goldberg presents a detailed discussion of the in-
      fluence of Eugenio's tale and the "Tale of the Curious
      Impertinent" on Fielding's inserted tales of "The Un-
      fortunate Jilt" and "The History of Two Friends." The
      influence of the episode of Diego Miranda (El Caballero
      del Verde Gabán) on the episode of Mr. Wilson is also
      examined. The critic concludes that Fielding is satiri-
      cally imitating Cervantes' stories.]

282. Goldberg, Homer. *The Art of "Joseph Andrews."* Chicago
      and London: The University of Chicago Press, 1969.
      Pp. xii + 292.

      [This work is a detailed study of the influence of
      Cervantes, Scarron, Lesage, and Marivaux on the style of
      Joseph Andrews. Goldberg points out the early dramatic
      adaptation of Cervantes' novel by Fielding (*Don Quixote
      in England*) and asserts that here Fielding saw more than

the comic-burlesque elements of Cervantes' Knight.
Goldberg concludes, after a long summary of the plot of
the *Quijote*, that Fielding was aware of the progressive
enhancing of the character of the Don. The critic observes the quixotic features of Parson Adams but is
careful to note the differences between the parson and
Don Quijote: Adams does not transform reality; he merely
misjudges character. Goldberg studies Fielding's con-
struction of comic action and notes the similarity of his
style to that of Cervantes. The use of the inflation
technique (hyperbolic description of trivia) by both
novelists is observed. The critic compares Fielding's
technique of protracting comic episodes beyond their
climax with analogous devices used by Cervantes, and
points out similarities in their stylistic humor (descriptions of characters; affectation of naive unaware-
ness of a figure's psychology; ironic mode; satiric
commentary on life).

Also found in this work are observations on Fielding's
use of the Eugenio and Grisóstomo episodes and of *The
Curious Impertinent*. Goldberg finds that certain of
Fielding's interpolated tales are comic adaptations of
Cervantes' material.]

283.   Greene, J. Lee. "Fielding's Gypsy Episode and Sancho
        Panza's Governorship." *South Atlantic Bulletin* 39
        (May 1974):117-121.

[Greene notes the general influence of Cervantes on
Henry Fielding, especially on *Joseph Andrews*. In regard to the episode of the gypsies in *Tom Jones* Greene
finds that this episode, like that of Sancho's government, presents an ideal political, civil, and social
system. The gypsy king, the critic observes, is, like
Sancho, an ideal ruler who avoids pomp and dresses
plainly. More important, states Greene, is the inci-
dent which occasions justice in both episodes: an
attempted rape, and the shame of the woman. Shame, it
is pointed out, is the ultimate punishment in Fielding's
utopian society, and this is specifically stated by
Fielding; it is only implied in the *Quijote*.

Greene asks if these two episodes are attacks on specific rulers (Philip II or George II). While the critic
finds this to be open to doubt he concludes that there
can be no question that a general condemnation of the
political and social situation is pervasive in both
novels and may well culminate in these episodes.

Greene also concludes that both of these episodes are
ironic comments on the differences between appearances
and reality, and that the reader must look beneath surface appearances to see the true worth and frailty of
characters and systems; in both episodes the reader must
re-examine his first evaluation of characters.]

284.   Johnson, Maurice. "The Art of Comic Romance: *Joseph
        Andrews.*" *Fielding's Art of Fiction: Eleven Essays on
        Shamela, Joseph Andrews, and Amelia*, pp. 47-60.
        Philadelphia: University of Pennsylvania Press, 1969.

"Good" comic romance expresses a particular concept
of reality by means of a challenging contrast, thus
creating a world in which fiction seems truth: distorted
reflections of the literary burlesque become, in the
light of day, convincing images true to human nature.
"Good" comic romance, I mean to say, can achieve the
illusion of reality by the display and rejection of
"bad" serious romance.
        Reading the most durable of all works of prose fic-
tion, *Don Quijote*, we are first involved in burlesque,
sharing Cervantes' critical amusement at preposterous
chivalric romance, laughing at archaic, rhetorical style;
and then as we watch, the mad burlesque is wonderfully
metamorphosed into "good" comic romance.
        [Johnson notes several often-observed similarities
between the *Quijote* and *Joseph Andrews*: (1) chapter
headings; (2) symbolic, interpolated tales; (3) adventures on the road; (4) contrast of real and illusory
evils; (5) similarity between the Knight and Parson
Adams. The critic adds:] But, it seems to me, Fielding's announcement in his subtitle--"Written in Imitation of the Manner of Cervantes, Author of *Don Quixote*"
--may also be taken as a clue to the general structure
of *Joseph Andrews*. As in *Don Quijote*, a *burlesca* movement introduces themes that are, in a series of variations, elevated to "good" comic style.

285.   Kayser, Wolfgang. "Origen y crisis de a novela moderna."
        Cultura Literaria, no. 47 (1955), pp. 5-47. [Trans-
        lated from the German by Aurelio Fuentes Rojo; based
        on *Entstehung und Krise des modernen Romans*. Stutt-
        gart: J.B. Metzler, 1955.]

[Kayser seeks to establish the true influence of the
Quijote on Fielding's *Joseph Andrews* and concludes that
it is more a question of authorial outlook than the use
of a contrasting pair of heroes. In particular, the

critic finds that Cervantes (and Fielding following him)
sympathized with his hero, despite surface indications
to the contrary; hence both are *humorous*, as opposed to
comic writers.]

286. Mack, Maynard. *"Joseph Andrews* and *Pamela."* In *Field-
ing: A Collection of Critical Essays*, pp. 52-58.
Edited by Ronald Paulson. Englewood Cliffs, N.J.:
Prentice-Hall, Inc., 1962. [From the Introduction to
Joseph Andrews, New York: Holt, Rinehart and Winston,
Inc., 1948, pp. ii-xxiv.]

Fielding's attack on Richardson's *Pamela* is similar to
Cervantes' parody of chivalric novels. The serious danger in romancing, Cervantes seems to have felt, lay in
diverting moral idealism into tilts with sensational or
merely apparent evils--giants who were only windmills--
when all about real evil walks unchallenged in homelier
shapes. Don Quijote, the crackbrained hero, collides
with the real world, which gives rise to rich ambiguous
comedy. Partly the comedy is from the discomfiture of
the Knight as the real world breaks about his ears, but
partly, in the background, it is from the discomfiture
of the world as it finds it cannot break his spirit.
Fielding's treatment of Parson Adams is based on this.
Both Adams and the Don are naive and idealistic; both
are thwarted. But there is one difference. While we
fall in love with Cervantes' Knight, we could not choose
his world; Adam's world we might.

287. Parker, A.A. "Fielding and the Structure of *Don Quixote." Bulletin of Hispanic Studies* 33 (1956):1-16.

[This item is summarized in more detail in Volume One
of this bibliography (item 231, pp. 196-197). It deals
to a large extent with the structure of the *Quijote* and
how Cervantes progresses from one motif to a closely related motif. Parker notes, and disagrees with, Fielding's assertion in 1752 that the *Quijote* was loose and
unconnected. The rambling structure of Cervantes' masterpiece is compared to Fielding's early novel *Joseph
Andrews*. The English author, states Parker, later
changed his structural technique, making *Tom Jones* co-
herent and well planned; he no longer appreciated the
style of *Don Quijote*.]

288. Penner, Allen Richard. "Fielding and Cervantes: The
Contribution of *Don Quixote* to *Joseph Andrews* and *Tom
Jones."* Ph.D. dissertation, University of Colorado,
1965. Pp. 222.

Cervantes and Fielding were aware that they were writing in the wake of a long tradition of popular, extravagant prose romances. Both writers sought not to fall
into the main error of those romances: the failure of
credibility. Both these novelists viewed the prose romance as an opportunity to display a variety of human
types, and both writers were convinced that their stories
served a moral and beneficial end. Cervantes and Fielding also recommended satirical treatment of universal
failings but deplored the use of vicious, personal
satire.

The extravagance of both the Don and Parson Adams
(*Joseph Andrews*) arises from their goodness of heart.
Both heroes have a sense of independent self-worth, and
it is this independence of spirit that in part gives
Adams and the Knight their heroic quality, and it is
this, too, that makes them men of basically good sense.
It should be noted that Parson Adams also has certain
attributes of Sancho Panza. Both are superstitious;
both are married to women who often remind them of their
responsibilities.

Tom Jones and *Don Quijote* are works of the authors'
later years. Both writers establish in the opening
pages an attitude toward their readers that puts the
author at the reader's disposal, instead of *vice versa*.
Both Fielding and Cervantes discuss the problem of details, and both believe that characterization is the key
to probability: the hero should be admirable but within
the realm of believability. Both authors adopt a "prej-
udicial" attitude toward their protagonists, and this
adds credibility to both stories. Tom Jones, like the
Knight, has a chivalric attitude toward women combined
with an extravagant, amorous nature. But Fielding presents in normal terms what Cervantes had humorously
exaggerated. Tom's delusions about women can be attributed to youth; with the Don there can be no reasonable
explanation. The figure Partridge is introduced into
Fielding's masterpiece as a companion to Tom. Partridge
is a Sancho type, though he is different in many ways
from Cervantes' Squire. Fielding's servant is pedantic
and vain. However, both Sancho and Partridge are great
eaters; they weary easily and complain of physical dis-
comfort.

Actually, Fielding subordinated his own creative personality to Cervantes only once, in the early play *Don
Quixote in England*. In *Joseph Andrews* and *Tom Jones*
Fielding ceased to imitate any author; but the influence
of the Spanish novelist remained a pervasive, if trans-
muted, force.

289. Penner, A.R. "Fielding's Adaptation of Cervantes'
     Knight and Squire: The Character of Joseph." *Revue de
     Littérature Comparée* 41 (October–December 1967):508–
     514.

     Joseph Andrews does, in a sense, play the role of
     Sancho to his quixotic master Adams, for while Joseph
     recognizes Adams' superiority in literary matters, he
     also realizes that his master is ignorant in the ways
     of the world. But Joseph has some quixotic character-
     istics himself. For example, he is humorously chaste
     and is rebuked for his preoccupation with chastity by
     Lady Booby, just as the Don is rebuked by Altisidora.
     But whereas Cervantes carries amorous madness to an
     absurdity, Fielding naturalizes it and makes it more
     normal. He adopts the "manner" of Cervantes, but cre-
     ates a tone that is more indulgently romantic and never
     caustically satirical. Joseph changes from a set piece
     for burlesquing false virtue to a semi-naturalized Qui-
     jote who feverishly supplicates his model of chastity
     and pledges eternal devotion to his love, to become at
     last the archetype of the good-natured hero to emerge
     again in *Tom Jones*.

290. Pérez de Ayala, Ramón. "Fielding, eslabón entre Cer-
     vantes y Dickens." *La Prensa* (Buenos Aires), 18 July
     1944. [This item could not be obtained.]

     [Rafael Heliodoro Valle and Emilia Romero list this
     item, without comment, in *Bibliografía cervantina en la
     América española* (425), Mexico: Imp. Universitaria,
     1950, p. 204. It is also cited by Raymond L. Grismer,
     Cervantes: A Bibliography, vol. 2, p. 170. It appears
     likely that this article was re-edited and included in
     one of the items in *Principios y finales de la novela*,
     several of which items are summarized herein. See items
     316-318.]

291. Pérez de Ayala, Ramón. "Fielding y su *Joseph Andrews*."
     ABC (Madrid), 18 May 1956. [Re-edited by the author
     and published in *Principios y finales de la novela*.
     Madrid: Taurus, 1958, pp. 17-20. The 1956 article was
     reviewed by Alberto Sánchez in *Anales Cervantinos* 5
     (1955-1956):384.]

     [Pérez de Ayala finds that both the *Quijote* and Field-
     ing's *Joseph Andrews* have a similar genesis, perhaps an
     unconscious desire to correct a popular yet ridiculous
     genre of literature (chivalresque romances or sentimen-
     tal novels). However, both authors, the critic adds,

fell in love with their creations. Pérez de Ayala points
out that Parson Adams is a quixotic figure, and notes
other influences of Cervantes on the English author:
Fielding drew upon Cervantes' masterpiece for episodes,
dialogs, dramatic-burlesque peripeteia, descriptions,
interpolated episodes, and even for chapter-openings of
a mythological-ironical nature. Many of Fielding's adventures, the critic observes, also take place at inns.]

292. Pons, Émile. "Fielding, Swift et Cervantes. (De *Don
      Quixote in England* à *Joseph Andrews*)." *Studia Neo-
      philologica* 15 (1942-1943):305-333.

      [Pons discusses several works by Fielding: *Joseph
      Andrews*, *Don Quixote in England*, and *The Life of Jona-
      than Wild*. The *Quijote* is compared and contrasted in
      some detail with *Joseph Andrews*, and the quixotic fea-
      tures of Fielding's Parson Adams are noted.]

293. Spilka, Mark. "Comic Resolution in Fielding's *Joseph
      Andrews*." In *Fielding: A Collection of Critical
      Essays*, pp. 59-68. Edited by Ronald Paulson. Engle-
      wood Cliffs, N.J.: Prentice-Hall, 1962.

      [The critic compares Fielding's Parson Adams to Don
      Quijote, finding that both have a bizarre outer appear-
      ance yet maintain an inner dignity. Spilka concludes
      that Fielding drew on Cervantes in creating lovable yet
      ridiculous characters with whom Fielding identified.]

294. Unamuno y Jugo, Miguel de. "Glosa a un pasaje del cer-
      vantino Fielding." *Obras completas*. Vol. 7, pp. 1229-
      1231. Edited by Manuel García Blanco. Madrid: Esce-
      licer, 1969. [Published in *El Sol* (Madrid), 16 De-
      cember 1917. Found in *Quijotismo y cervantismo*.]

      [Unamuno concludes that Fielding was the greatest
      English *cervantista*, not because of research into Cer-
      vantes' life and works but because he followed in Cer-
      vantes' footsteps as a novelist. Attention is called
      to a passage in Chapter I, Book III, of *Joseph Andrews*
      where Fielding discusses historical truth and states
      that the deeds of Don Quijote are more historically
      true than ordinary history because they apply to all
      times, not just to one epoch.]

Tobias Smollett

295. Auburn, C. "Smollett et Cervantes." *Études Anglaises*
    15 (1962):122-129.

    [Auburn points out that the *Quijote* enjoyed a second
    popularity in England between 1742 and 1759. The influ-
    ence of Cervantes' masterpiece on such novels as *Joseph
    Andrews*, *Tom Jones*, *Roderick Random*, and *Tristram Shandy*
    is briefly noted. The critic examines Smollett's trans-
    lation of the *Quijote* and contrasts Cervantes' serene
    style with the dramatic style used by Smollett.]

296. Mays, Jack Thurston. "The Use of Quixote Figures and
    Allusions to *Don Quixote* in the Novels of Tobias Smol-
    lett." Ph.D. dissertation, Ball State University,
    1973. Pp. vi + 170.

    [This work contains a preface and seven chapters. The
    purpose of this thesis is to identify Smollett's use of
    Quijote figures and allusions in his five novels:
    Roderick Random, *Peregrine Pickle*, *Ferdinand Count Fa-
    thom*, *Sir Launcelot Greaves*, and *Humphry Clinker*. Mays
    finds that in all of Smollett's novels the major adven-
    tures are marked by the appearance of a Quijote figure
    who is unable to distinguish between illusion and reality.
    Moreover, the critic continues, in the first three no-
    vels the changes in the fortunes of the protagonists are
    signalled by an allusion to the *Quijote*.
    Mays states that none of the figures are complete Qui-
    jotes; most are comical, some are satirical, and at least
    one (Renaldo Melville in *Ferdinand Count Fathom*) is ro-
    mantic. However, he concludes, each resembles the
    Knight sufficiently to warrant identifying him or her
    as a Quijote figure.
    Attention is devoted to Smollett's translation of the
    Quijote, 1755, which was begun as early as 1748. Also,
    the influence of Cervantes' masterpiece on other English
    writers of the eighteenth century is discussed, especi-
    ally the influence on Fielding and Sterne. A chapter is
    devoted to each of Smollett's novels; and its Quijote
    figures and allusions to the *Quijote* are studied and
    analyzed in detail to show their function in each of
    the novels.]

Lewis Theobald (See also 241, 246, 255)

297. Frazier, Harriet C. *A Babble of Ancestral Voices.*
      Shakespeare, Cervantes, and Theobald. The Hague:
      Mouton, 1974. Pp. 161. (*Studies in English Litera-*
      ture.) [This work is based on a Ph.D. dissertation
      at Wayne State University entitled "Shakespeare, Cer-
      vantes, and Theobald: An Investigation into the
      Cardenio-Double Falsehood Problem," 1967. Pp. v +
      261.]

      [This book contains an introduction and seven chap-
      ters. The lost play *Cardenio*, attributed to Shakespeare,
      and the various entries referring to it are examined.
      The critic is skeptical as to the accuracy of these en-
      tries. A brief history of Shakespeare research is gi-
      ven, along with a discussion of the trends in the attri-
      bution of doubtful works to him.
      Frazier disagrees with the present tendency to attri-
      bute *The Double Falsehood* to Shakespeare. She con-
      cludes that Theobald, who published that play in 1728,
      was the true author. She further finds that similari-
      ties in style between *The Double Falsehood* and Shake-
      speare's plays (especially *Hamlet*) are attributable to
      Theobald's great familiarity with Shakespeare, acquired
      through editing his works.
      In Chapter Five, the critic examines adaptations of
      the Cardenio material prior to *The Double Falsehood* for
      their influence on Theobald's play: Pichou's *Les folies*
      de Cardenio; Mrs. Behn's *The Amorous Prince*; D'Urfey's
      Comical History of Don Quixote.
      Frazier concludes that Theobald deliberately and
      falsely attributed *The Double Falsehood* to Shakespeare
      out of a desire for the profit to be gained from using
      the popularity of Shakespeare and Cervantes in eighteenth-
      century England, and also out of a desire to show Shake-
      speare's possible familiarity with the Cardenio material
      in the *Quijote*.]

298. Frazier, Harriet C. "Theobald's *The Double Falsehood*:
      A Revision of Shakespeare's *Cardenio*?" *Comparative*
      Drama 1 (Fall 1967):219-233.

      [This item is similar to the prior entry. A great
      deal of the emphasis here, however, is on Lewis Theobald's
      1741 play *The Happy Captive*, based on the *cautivo* epi-
      sode in Part One of the *Quijote*. Frazier concludes that
      the existence of this play casts serious doubts on the

arguments of any critic who proposes an author of *The Double Falsehood* other than Lewis Theobald. The critic presents a lengthy discussion of the changes made by Theobald in his adaptation of the Cardenio and the captive captain episodes of the *Quijote.*]

299. Graham, Walter. "The *Cardenio-Double Falsehood* Problem." *Modern Philology* 14 (1916-1917):269-280, 568.

[Graham concludes: (1) that the immediate source of *Double Falsehood* (published by Lewis Theobald in 1728) was Shelton's translation of *Don Quijote*; (2) that the style of *Double Falsehood*, especially the second part, is quite different from the style of Theobald's acknowledged works; (3) that there are unmistakable evidences of two separate styles in *Double Falsehood*; and (4) that these distinct styles show a general similarity to the double style in *Two Noble Kinsmen* and *Henry VIII*, which are now recognized as belonging to Shakespeare and Fletcher jointly.]

300. Muir, Kenneth. "Cardenio." *Études Anglaises* 11 (1958): 202-209. [See also *Shakespeare as Collaborator* (Chap. 8: "*Cardenio,*" pp. 148-160). London: Methuen & Co., Ltd, 1960.]

[Muir states the facts known about the lost play *Cardenio*, attributed to Fletcher and Shakespeare by Humphrey Moseley in 1653. (The play was performed by the King's Men in 1613.) Lewis Theobald's play *Double Falsehood* (performed in 1727 and published in 1728) is discussed in some detail. Both *Cardenio* and *Double Falsehood*, states Muir, are based on the "Cardenio" episode in Part One of the *Quijote*. The plot of *Double Falsehood* is outlined, and Theobald's assertion that the play was by Shakespeare or perhaps Fletcher is discussed. Muir believes that Theobald did indeed revise an earlier manuscript but can reach no definite conclusion as to the original authorship of *Double Falsehood*.]

301. Schevill, Rudolph. "Theobald's *Double Falsehood?*" *Modern Philology* 9 (1911-1912):269-285.

Theobald's *Double Falsehood* was first performed on December 13, 1727, and was published the following year. This play is merely an imitation of Samuel Croaxall's *Adventures on the Black Mountains*, not published until 1729. Croaxall's work, in turn, is a revamping of the Cardenio episode in the *Quijote*. In essence,

Croaxall's story was "newly translated" out of Shelton's
English version of Cervantes' novel.   Does Theobald's
Double Falsehood follow the changes made in Croaxall's
Adventures on the Black Mountains?   Yes!   Theobald's
assertions about the manuscripts in his possession are
not correct, and *Double Falsehood* is thus not based on
a lost play by Shakespeare or Fletcher called *History
of Cardenio*.

John Bowle

302.   Cox, Ralph Merritt.   "The Rev. John Bowle: First Editor
       of *Don Quixote*."   Ph.D. dissertation, University of
       Wisconsin, 1967.   Pp. iv + 241 + 157 + 167.   [Re-
       edited and published without Bowle's "Anotaciones," as
       *The Rev. John Bowle: The Genesis of Cervantean Criti-
       cism*.   Chapel Hill, N.C.: The University of North
       Carolina Press, 1971.   Pp. 123.   (*North Carolina
       Studies in the Romance Languages and Literatures*, no.
       99.)]

       [Cox's dissertation contains seven chapters.   The
       first chapter is a detailed discussion of Bowle's life.
       The second chapter is of special interest for it con-
       tains a rather lengthy discussion of seventeenth- and
       eighteenth-century criticism of the *Quijote* in Spain,
       France, and England.   Particular attention is devoted
       to Charles de Saint-Évremond, Jean Baptiste d'Argens,
       Jacques Henri de Saint-Pierre, John Locke, and Samuel
       Johnson.   Saint-Évremond, states Cox, is the first real
       admirer of Cervantes and *Don Quijote*.   The third chapter
       compares Bowle's early manuscript to his final Spanish
       version of the *Quijote*, 1781.
           In Chapter IV, "The Editor's Concept of *Don Quixote*,"
       Cox points out how Bowle praises the style of that novel
       and how he saw the Knight as a transcendent figure.
       Here, states Cox, we have a faint glimpse of the Don as
       a kind of spiritual figure: thus, with Bowle, the Knight
       "very hesitantly has begun to become a symbol of the
       last bulwark against the enemies of all men's visions
       and hopes" (p. 142).
           In Chapter VI Cox finds that Bowle tends to put Cer-
       vantes on a pedestal, to make him too much of a scholar
       and a pedant.   With Bowle, Cox states, there is no hint
       that the author is tired, weak, and resigned; he is
       viewed as robust and fearless, a man of wit, charm, and
       wisdom, a man who spent much time in a library.   This,

Cox finds, is an interpretation of rural eighteenth-
century England: John Bowle makes Cervantes that good-
natured, benign, *honnête homme* representative of his own
country. Bowle, Cox concludes, more than any other
critic, brought about this interpretation of Cervantes.
Chapter VII compares and contrasts Bowle's ideas with
those of later critics, especially Sismondi, Bouterwek,
Clemencín, Pellicer, and Navarrete.
Cox attaches two lengthy appendices which contain
Bowle's "anotaciones" to the 1605 and the 1615 *Don
Quijote.*]

303. Cox, Ralph Merritt. "The Rev. John Bowle: the First
      Editor of *Don Quixote.*" *Studies in Philology* 67
      (January 1970):103-115.

      In 1781 Bowle published a three-volume Spanish edition
      of the *Quijote*, one volume of which edition contained
      copious notes and indexes. This work went through two
      editions in the above year, one at Salisbury and the
      other both at Salisbury and at London. Bowle shows a
      profound knowledge of Spanish customs, and many commen-
      tators draw on his work without citing their source.
      After the publication of his *Quijote* edition Bowle be-
      came highly sensitive to criticism and engaged in a
      bitter polemic with one G. Baretti who had commented un-
      favorably on Bowle's work. Baretti felt that the *Qui-
      jote* needed little or no comment in order to be
      appreciated.

Laurence Sterne

304. Booth, Wayne C. *The Rhetoric of Fiction.* Chicago and
      London: The University of Chicago Press, 1975. Pp.
      xviii + 455. [First edition 1961.]

      In the *Quijote*, as in Sterne's *Tristram Shandy* later,
      there are various comments and "intrusions" by a narra-
      tor. These actions of intrusion interrupt the comic ac-
      tion, but the two actions are really interdependent.
      The intrusions seem, like the great comic actions of
      Don Quijote and Tom Jones, to rise above any satirical
      intent, to exist ultimately as something to be enjoyed
      in its own right: the satire is for the sake of the
      comic enjoyment, and not the other way round.

305. Stedmond, John M. *The Comic Art of Laurence Sterne.*
      Convention and Innovation in "Tristram Shandy" and "A

Sentimental Journey." Toronto: University of Toronto
Press, 1967. Pp. 178.

[Stedmond notes a number of similarities between the
works of Sterne and Cervantes: (1) both use a digressive
technique; (2) Sterne, like Cervantes and other earlier
writers, is a "facetious rhetorician"; (3) both are fond
of proverbs; (4) Sterne follows Cervantes' skeptical and
critical attitude toward language, and has a perspecti-
vistic regard for names; (5) like Cervantes and Fielding,
Sterne inserts long stories in his novels; (6) Sterne
uses the split personality device (Rabelais' Panurge and
Pantagruel, Cervantes' Don Quijote and Sancho Panza).
The critic finds Uncle Toby (*Tristram Shandy*) to be
the most Cervantic of Sterne's characters--a figure of
fun who is presented sympathetically. Yorick (*A Sentimental Journey*), too, is said to be a descendant of Don
Quijote, though not as innocent as Uncle Toby. Stedmond
notices a difference in the sense of humor of Sterne
and Cervantes: Cervantes, like Rabelais, distances himself and is objective; Sterne projects his humoristic
self into the novel.]

306.   Stout, Gardner D., Jr. "Some Borrowings in Sterne from
       Rabelais and Cervantes." *English Language Notes* 3
       (December 1965):111-118.

       Tristram Shandy's remark that "great wits jump" may
       well be based on an observation by Sancho, and Yorick's
       statement that La Rochefoucauld's words deserve to be
       written in gold could have been drawn from a remark by
       the Squire's secretary at Barataria. Sterne's descrip-
       tion of the attacks of his critics contains phrases
       quite similar to those in Cervantes' description of the
       students' duel.

307.   Stout, Gardner D., Jr., ed. *A Sentimental Journey
       Through France and Italy by Mr. Yorick.* Berkeley and
       Los Angeles: University of California Press, 1967.
       Pp. xvii + 377.

       [Stout finds Yorick to be a Cervantic hero, mocked by
       the author for being led into ludicrous extravagances by
       the hypersensitivity of his heart. Yorick's benevolent
       impulses are the counterpart of Don Quijote's chivalric
       ideals, the critic observes, and as a result Sterne's
       hero "posts into quixotic dilemmas which dramatize the
       comic frustrations of sentimental knight-errantry."

Stout's index lists various allusions, or possible allusions, by Sterne in *A Sentimental Journey* to Cervantes' *Quijote*: a need for money and shirts; Sancho's lament on leaving home; the Squire's lament over losing his ass; Mambrino's helmet; Sancho's wife becoming a queen; a burlesque coat-of-arms; the missing manuscript device; the expression "Knight of the Woeful Countenance."]

308. Vaughan, C.E. "Sterne and the Novel of His Times." In *The Cambridge History of English Literature*. Vol. 10: *The Age of Johnson*, pp. 51-74. Edited by Sir A.W. Ward and A.R. Waller. New York: G.P. Putnam's Sons; Cambridge, England: University Press, 1913.

Sterne made no attempt to conceal his indebtedness to Cervantes, and Uncle Toby and Corporal Trim are variations of Don Quijote and Sancho Panza. But the differences between Sterne's characters and Cervantes' are stronger than the resemblances. Cervantes' master and servant have universal significance to the most casual reader: sense versus spirit, idealism versus materialism. This is not so deep in Sterne's work. There is also another difference. Cervantes is so sure of his knight-hero that he is not afraid to cover him with every outward mark of ridicule. Sterne, however, puts forth all his art to make us forget the futility of the craze which he has imagined for Uncle Toby.
There are moments, it must be confessed, when the ridiculousness in the *Quijote* is pushed further than we are willing to endure. In such moments it is clear that the satirist has got the better of the creative artist; and it is not on the hero, but on the author, that our resentment is, instinctively, apt to fall. Our admiration is proof against all that Cervantes himself can do to undermine it. Could the intrinsic nobility of his conception be more decisively driven home? Put either Uncle Toby or Walter Shandy to the same test, and who shall say that either of them would come through.

Other Writers

309. Gendre, Jean. "Une source d'inspiration pour Farquhar: *Don Quixote*." *Caliban* 6 (1969):29-32.

Without discounting the influence of Wycherley on George Farquhar, 1677-1707, the latter in writing the

play *Love and a Bottle* probably received part of his influence directly from Cervantes' *Quijote*. Farquhar knew
Motteux (who published the *Quijote* in English in 1700)
and cooperated with him in the farce *The Stage Coach*,
1704. It is true that *Love and a Bottle* was produced
two years prior to the publication of Motteux's translation, but this does not mean that Farquhar was unfamil-
iar with the material with which Motteux was busy.

The exclamation in Act I, scene I, of *Love and a Bottle* ("What, knight-errants in this country?") seems
taken from the *Quijote*. Furthermore, the secondary plot
of Farquhar's play is quite similar to Cervantes' interpolated story of the *Curious Impertinent*, although the
author of the *Quijote* presents the subject tragically
while Farquhar treats it comically.

There is also a kinship in atmosphere between the
Quijote and Farquhar's play *The Beaux' Stratagem*, 1707.
The English playwright even has the character Archer
say: "We are like to have as many adventures in our inn
as Don Quijote had in his."

310.   Hayes, Elizabeth Gentry. "Charlotte Ramsay Lennox: *The
        Female Quixote; or The Adventures of Arabella*.
        Edited with an Introduction and Notes, Two Volumes in
        One." Ph.D. dissertation, Stanford University, 1964.
        Pp. 577. [Based on the summary found in *Dissertation
        Abstracts International*, Vol. 25A, no. 4, p. 2489.]

        [Hayes' thesis contains an introduction in five parts,
        a bibliographical list of imitations of Cervantes' *Qui-
        jote* in English literature (1605-1810), a selected
        bibliography, an authoritative index, extensive notes,
        and two appendices. The critic points out that Mrs.
        Lennox's *Female Quixote* was first published in England
        on March 13, 1752, that it went through eight English
        editions, and was also translated into French, German,
        and Spanish. Hayes further observes that this novel
        was highly esteemed by prominent writers and critics.
        The Female Quixote, she concludes, is a key work in an
        important literary tradition, and that to read this
        novel is to learn more about how the neo-classic mind
        interpreted the *Quijote*. The critic states that during
        the investigation of the literary background of the
        Female Quixote several previously unidentified *Quijote*
        imitations came to light, suggesting that the influence
        of Cervantes' masterpiece on English literature of the
        Restoration was not only greater than has been suspected
        but of a slightly different nature. (For additional
        material on Charlotte Ramsay Lennox see item 272.)]

311. Navarro González, Alberto. *Robinson y Don Quijote*.
     Madrid: Ateneo, 1962. Pp. 57.

     [This work contains four chapters and a conclusion
     and records a speech by the critic at the Universidad
     Hispanoamericana de la Rábida in Seville on September 5,
     1961. Navarro González does *not* expressly discuss the
     literary influence of the *Quijote* on Daniel Defoe's
     Robinson Crusoe, but compares and contrasts the two
     literary myths. He examines the religious attitude of
     both heroes, their attitude toward nature and toward
     their fellow man.]

312. Rosenheim, Edward W., Jr. *Swift and the Satirist's Art*.
     Drawings by Rainey Bennett. Chicago and London: The
     University Press, 1963. Pp. ix + 243.

     Certainly other satirists than Swift have made much
     use of characters, "spokesmen" or otherwise, who are
     persistently deluded or obsessed or wicked and who can,
     in short, be regularly relied upon to be entirely "wrong"
     in their response to an actuality which is only the mir-
     ror of their own illusions. Don Quijote, of course, has
     his virtues, but we are all quite aware of the outlines
     of an unalterable quixotic world; the same thing is
     true, I think, of the great comic "types" of Jonson and
     Molière, and of such figures as Pangloss or Micawber.
     The destructive play of reality against their comprehen-
     sive illusions is supplied, so to speak, by the author,
     either through characters who display, in some form or
     other, a Sancho-like practicality, or through the au-
     thor's own narrative or discursive insistence upon true
     matter of fact. [From pp. 146-147.]

313. Singleton, Mack. "Cervantes, John Locke, and Dr. John-
     son." In *Studia Hispanica in Honorem R. Lapesa*. Vol.
     1, pp. 531-547. Edited by Eugenio de Bustos, *et al.*
     Madrid: Edit. Gredos, 1972.

     [Singleton presents lengthy quotations from English
     writers regarding the *Quijote*: John Locke, Samuel John-
     son, Alexander Pope. On the whole, the critic finds
     that eighteenth-century English criticism is acute at
     times, but not deep, and does not deal with the essen-
     tial meaning of the *Quijote*. Furthermore, eighteenth-
     century England is blamed by Singleton for leading the
     way toward the hysterical trend in the eighteenth and
     nineteenth centuries in which there arises a deification
     of the Knight. The critic cautions the reader against
     ignoring the Don's faults (pride and lack of prudence)

and being so carried away by the Knight's attractive-
ness as to convert good into evil, evil into good.]

Nineteenth-Century England

Charles Dickens

314. Ashbee, H.S. "*Don Quixote* and *Pickwick.*" *Revue His-
      panique* 6 (1899):307-310.

      Cervantes' *Quijote* and Dickens' *Pickwick Papers* have
numerous striking similarities. Both works were written
with a purpose and both inaugurate a new departure in
fiction. In the *Quijote* the ridicule was aimed at ted-
ious, prolix romances of chivalry with their impossible
adventures; in *Pickwick* the humor, spirit, and bouyancy
rendered unpalatable for the future the dull ladies and
gentlemen and chaste but insipid maidens in whose doings
prior readers had delighted.
      Both works lack a plot, properly so called; both con-
sist of a series of adventures, frequently incongruous
and independent of each other, but strung together with
such consummate skill that they follow on quite natural-
ly. Both stories contain tales foreign to the main plot.
The chief personages in both novels grow and develop as
the author proceeds. The Don starts as a lunatic and
ends as a philosopher; Pickwick begins as a foolish old
gentleman but becomes a man of sterling common sense,
though retaining his simplicity and kindliness. Both
the Knight and Pickwick are philanthropists in their respective ways; their efforts, generally misplaced, to
right wrongs or to benefit their fellow creatures pro-
duce the awkward quandaries in which they constantly
find themselves.
      Both the Don and Pickwick, shortly after starting on
their adventures, are furnished with a follower, a man
of common sense, wit, and a love for creature comforts.
Both servants see through their master's follies but
each loves and respects his master all the same, serving
him faithfully. Both servants are given to loquacity,
storytelling, and proverbs.
      Cervantes and Dickens are more successful in portray-
ing members of the middle and lower classes. Both the
Quijote and *Pickwick* were immediately popular, something
unusual for books destined to live for a long time, and
both books were imitated by contemporaries.

If Cervantes had never lived, Dickens' genius would
nevertheless have shown through, though it would have
appeared in a different form.

315. Gale, Steven H. "Cervantes' Influence on Dickens, with
Comparative Emphasis on *Don Quijote* and *Pickwick
Papers*." *Anales Cervantinos* 12 (1973):135-156.

[Gale states that since the publication of an article
in the *Edinburgh Review* in 1838, most scholars have
assumed the influence of the *Quijote* on *Pickwick Papers*.
The critic presents a brief history of English interpretations of Cervantes' novel, from jestbook to tragedy,
and lists Dickens' allusions to the *Quijote*, beginning
with the preface to the third edition of *Oliver Twist*.

The motives of both novelists are examined, and the
critic concludes that each wanted to expose the present
to itself. Similarities in technique in the *Quijote*
and in *Pickwick Papers* are pointed out: both works are
written in the third person singular; chapter headings
are similar; neither novel has a plot, as such, only the
unity of a wandering "hero"; both novels belong to the
picaresque tradition, but are *not* picaresque stories;
both works are more universal than national; both novels
are relatively moral and clean.

Gale next notes the similarities between the Knight
and Pickwick, and between Sancho and Weller, and summarizes prior studies on this question. Both the Don
and Pickwick, states Gale, are full of sympathy for
others; both are in their late middle years, are without
money worries and without family ties. The critic observes the similarity in function of Sancho and Weller:
to place the visionary attitude in the perspective of
the rational, and the rational in the perspective of the
visionary.

Other similarities between the two novels are pointed
out: neither Sancho nor Weller appears in the early chapters; both stories have interpolated tales and episodes
which reinforce an essential aspect of morality; there
are poetry passages in both novels as well as exchanges
of letters; descriptive passages are at times similar;
humor is important in both works; and maxims are frequent
in both stories.

Gale also observes dissimilarities between the *Quijote*
and *Pickwick Papers*; the Knight is lean while Pickwick
is chubby; Pickwick is not insane, merely naive; Weller
lacks Sancho's gullibility; Dickens' leading figures do
not grow like one another; Pickwick does not have the Don's

depth of character; *Pickwick Papers* lacks the violence
of the *Quijote*; Cervantes seems more bitter toward the
clergy than Dickens; Cervantes is more critical of wom-
en; the ending of the two stories is quite different
(the Knight dies, while Pickwick and the others live
happily ever after); form is more important in the *Quijote* than in *Pickwick*.]

316.   Pérez de Ayala, Ramón. "La lente quijotesca y la visión
       del mundo en Dickens." *La Prensa* (Buenos Aires),
       27 June 1943, and in *ABC* (Madrid), 4 December 1955.
       [Re-edited by the author and published in *Principios y
       finales de la novela*, pp. 49-53. Madrid: Taurus,
       1958. The 1955 article was reviewed by Alberto Sán-
       chez in *Anales Cervantinos* 5 (1955-1956):383.]

       [Pérez de Ayala finds that Charles Dickens' father,
       John, was a quixotic figure who influenced his son.
       Mr. Pickwick is said to be based on Dickens' father, as
       is Mr. Micawber of *David Copperfield*. The important
       thing, states the critic, is that the angle of quixotic
       vision regarding the world, so persistent in all of
       Dickens' works, was received from his father, and that
       Charles Dickens, still quite young, saw this same angle
       of vision in Cervantes.]

317.   Pérez de Ayala, Ramón. "Cervantes en Dickens." *ABC*
       (Madrid), 3 May 1956. [Re-edited by the author and
       published in *Principios y finales de la novela*, pp.
       63-65. Madrid: Taurus, 1958. The 1956 article was
       summarized by Alberto Sánchez in *Anales Cervantinos* 5
       (1955-1956):383 384.]

       [Pérez de Ayala concludes that Cervantes influenced
       Dickens through Fielding, and that there was also a
       direct influence of the *Quijote* on Dickens through Smol-
       lett's translation of Cervantes' masterpiece. The cri-
       tic also finds that the *Quijote*, *Joseph Andrews*, and
       Pickwick Papers all had a similar genesis--satires on
       existing literature.
       Pérez de Ayala points out that all three writers
       place themselves inside their leading characters, al-
       most from the start, and reveal the inner nobility of
       their heroes, not merely their outer, comic side. Other
       similarities of Cervantes, Fielding, and Dickens are
       pointed out: all three humanize and universalize their
       central figures; all three wrote peripatetic novels with
       hectic and humorous adventures; all three employed in-
       terpolated episodes; both Pickwick and Parson Adams are

Quijote figures. Ayala notes the absence of a true Sancho Panza figure in *Joseph Andrews* but finds Weller of
Pickwick Papers to be a true descendant of the Squire.]

318. Pérez de Ayala, Ramón. "La experiencia humana en Dickens." *ABC* (Madrid), 11 December 1955. [Re-edited by
the author and published in *Principios y finales de
la novela*, pp. 55-58. Madrid: Taurus, 1958. The 1955
article was reviewed by Alberto Sánchez in *Anales
Cervantinos* 5 (1955-1956):383.]

[Pérez de Ayala finds Fielding to be a spiritual son
of Cervantes and notes that both the *Quijote* and *Joseph
Andrews* began as satires on popular novels of the respective times (the chivalresque novel or the sentimental
novels of Richardson). Nevertheless, the critic adds,
both works end as great novels. The critic also believes that Fielding's *Tom Jones* was inspired by the
Quijote. The novels of Fielding and Smollett, both
disciples of Cervantes, were of great influence on Dickens, Ayala states, and Smollett's translation of the
Quijote was well known to Dickens.]

319. Roopnaraine, Rupert. "Reflexive Techniques in *The
Pickwick Papers*." Ph.D. dissertation, Cornell University, 1972. Pp. ix + 208.

[The true subject of *The Pickwick Papers*, states
Roopnaraine, is the very composition of *Pickwick Papers*;
it is a work that is concerned with the nature and
status of fictionality; and Dickens' novel aligns itself,
however gingerly, with the tradition of the reflexive,
parodic novel that begins with *Don Quijote*, and includes such works as *Tristram Shandy*, *Les Faux-Monnayeurs*, *Die Blechtrommel*, and more discreetly *The Brothers Karamazov* and *L'Étranger*. We find in *Pickwick
Papers*, states the critic, that modern tendency of the
novel towards its own self-destruction, a tendency which
is very much in the fore in the works of Gide, Joyce,
Svevo, and Robbe-Grillet, and which is pursued with a
manic implacability in the novels of Beckett. The chief
instrument of this self-destruction, Roopnaraine finds,
is reflexivity, that process by which the novel turns
upon itself.
    In Chapter Two the critic deals specifically with the
relationship between the *Quijote* and *Pickwick Papers*,
and examines the opinions of prior critics on this question in some detail. Roopnaraine finds that the true
relationship between these two works is that they both

house, at their innermost core, a reflexive concern with
the nature and status of their own fictionality. In
Pickwick Papers, the critic states, Dickens makes creative play with several of Cervantes' key ideas: (1) the
wiles of the fictitious historian; (2) the problematic
relationship of language to reality; (3) the Aristotel-
ian dispute over the moral status of certain kinds of
"history."]

320. Wagner, Horst. "Zur Frage der Erzähleinschübe in *Don
      Quijote* und in den *Pickwick Papers.*" *Arcadia* 9 (1974):
      1-22.

      [Wagner lists the interpolated episodes in the *Qui-
      jote* and in Dickens' *Pickwick Papers* and divides this
      material into two classes: (1) long, lofty, serious epi-
      sodes about people of the upper classes; (2) short
      moralistic insertions. The critic discusses the atti-
      tude of both writers toward their interpolations
      (favorable in both cases) and presents a brief summary
      of the critical acceptance of the intercalated matter.
      Wagner finds that the interpolations serve different
      purposes, the longer, lofty ones having the function of
      contrast to the comic, realistic style of the main plot,
      and the shorter ones having a moralistic or exemplary
      function. Cervantes, he observes, uses the long, lofty
      insertions in Part I, where the contrast with the
      picaresque atmosphere of the main plot is aesthetically
      needed. Since Part II of the *Quijote* is not picaresque
      to Wagner, and the contrast between reality and litera-
      ture is more subtle, he believes that such lofty, ser-
      ious insertions would have been out of place in that
      part of the story. In Dickens, Wagner continues, there
      is no strong switch from one type of insertion to ano-
      ther. Both writers wrestled with the problem of inter-
      polations, Wagner concludes, and Dickens sought to solve
      it thematically, Cervantes by technically interweaving
      such matter.]

321. Welsh, Alexander. "Waverley, Pickwick, and Don Quixote."
      Nineteenth-Century Fiction 22 (1967-1968):19-30.

      Dickens' contemporaries, such as Washington Irving and
      Dostoevski, noticed similarities between *Pickwick Papers*
      and the *Quijote*, and John Forster, in his *The Life of
      Charles Dickens*, 1872-1874, referred to Sam Weller and
      Mr. Pickwick as the "Sancho and the Quixote of Londoners."
      Like Cervantes, Dickens began with a tried formula
      and ended with a figure that transcended both the formula

and his added invention. He sent his elderly hero on a
random or near-random journey, interpolated short stories, and introduced a squire for his knight-errant just
in time to keep the whole enterprise from flagging.
More remarkable, he reproduced the uncanny process by
which a hero who begins as an object of ridicule is
transformed into an object of love. The result is a
hero and a fiction that are as different from the rest
of Dickens' creations as the *Quijote* is from Cervantes'
romances. Both heroes, too, it should be observed,
apologize for their careers at the end.

Appropriately, in a refined work of quixotism, Sam
Weller enters the story at a more sophisticated level
than Sancho Panza at the beginning of the *Quijote*.
Sancho's characteristic utterance, the proverb, even-
tually bridges the gap between his earthy origins and
the culture of the Don; Sam Weller's characteristic
utterance, the cockneyism, returns the cultured common-
place back to earth.

Ruskin, in 1870, believed that Dickens was as little
understood as Cervantes, and almost as mischievous. He
felt the *Quijote* to be a deadly work, in that it accused
all true chivalry of madness. The same can be said of
Pickwick, and in the hero's retirement at the end one
can sense Dickens cautiously withdrawing his commitment
to his first great creation.

Sir Walter Scott

322. McDonald, W.U., Jr. "Scott's Conception of *Don Quixote*."
      Midwest Review 1 (1959):37-42.

Sir Walter Scott regarded the *Quijote* as something
more than mere satire. He also realized that the romance and the novel were different, the former dealing
with marvellous events, the latter dealing with ordinary events and the modern state of society. Why does
Scott apply the term "romance" to the *Quijote*? Because
he believed that the romance kept pace with society; it
became a picture of manners. To Scott the romance
could contain "real" as well as marvellous events. He
regarded the *Quijote* and the *Amadís* as a reflection of
actual life.

Scott apparently regarded the novel as a comprehensive
work of art with an unmistakable foundation in reality,
a kind of comic romance that combined the marvellous,
the humorous, and the realistic. Scott's views on

Don Quijote put him in a middle position between the
earlier extreme attitude which regarded it as satire
or pure farce and the views of some of his contemporaries, who regarded Cervantes' novel as basically tragic.

323. Wolfe, Clara Snell. "Evidences of Scott's Indebtedness
      to Spanish Literature." *Romanic Review* 23 (1932):
      301-311.

      [Wolfe notes that Scott's library at Abbotsford con-
      tained seven editions of the *Quijote*, and that the
      British author himself planned an edition of Cervantes'
      novel. The critic also observes that there are more
      than one hundred references to the *Quijote* in Scott's
      Waverley novels, and that these references occur not
      only among his writings on literary criticism, but in
      the midst of his composition of romantic fiction, in
      his work on political and educational reform, among his
      familiar letters, and even in his diary, where he is
      setting down his most intimate personal feelings. Wolfe
      notes Scott's fondness for Sancho and his sayings. The
      Englishman's allusions to episodes in the *Quijote* are
      pointed out: Maese Pedro's puppet show, Montesinos'
      cave, Altisidora's journey to the gates of hell.
      Wolfe finds it strange that it never seemed to occur
      to Scott that the shafts of Cervantes' ridicule were
      directed at the same sort of chivalresque material that
      formed the basis of Scott's own romantic writing. Also
      strange to Wolfe is the fact that Scott, on several oc-
      casions, compared himself to Cervantes as a writer. The
      critic reaches no definite conclusion as to whether or
      not Scott's admiration for Cervantes was more potent at
      one time than another, though it is observed that refer-
      ences to the *Quijote* decline after *Redgauntlet* in 1824.]

Lewis Carroll (Charles Dodgson)

324. Boynton, Mary Fuertes. "An Oxford Don Quixote."
      Hispania 47 (December 1964):738-750.

      There are many similarities between *Don Quijote* and
      Charles Dodgson's (Lewis Carroll's) *Alice in Wonderland*
      and *Through the Looking Glass*: the descent by Alice into
      Wonderland is similar to the Knight's descent into the
      cave of Montesinos and Sancho's fall into a steep pit;
      the banquet in honor of Queen Alice is very much like
      Sancho's meal during his governorship; one episode

between Alice and the Red Queen is similar to Don Quijote's losing count of the goats in Sancho's tale. The
humor of Dodgson and of Cervantes is, at times, similar,
though the Englishman is subtle and delicate, while the
Spaniard can be painful and slapstick. Both authors
enjoy puns. Both use the device of interpolated stories.
More important, however, is the fact that the same leading questions are found in both Dodgson's and Cervantes'
novels. The personal identity question is found in the
Montesinos' cave adventure as well as in Dodgson's uni-
corn and caterpillar episodes. The question of what is
"real" is a dominant feature both of the *Quijote* and of
Lewis Carroll's novels of Alice. However, there would
appear to be no direct influence of Cervantes on the
works of Dodgson.

325. Hinz, John. "Alice Meets the Don." *South Atlantic
     Quarterly* 52 (April 1953):253-266.

Both Alice and the Don awake in a hostile world full
of enchantments. The theme of madness underlies both
works. In the *Quijote* the world is, or appears to be,
sane, the hero mad. In *Alice in Wonderland* the world
seems deranged, the central character sane. But is it
actually the Don who is mad, the world that is sane?
And isn't there something quite mad in Alice's sweet
reasonableness? Alice's seeming sanity and Don Quijote's
seeming madness alienate them from the "real" world.
Both stories end in the same fashion: with the end of
the dream. Both accelerate to a close. Both burst suddenly out of their dream world. Don Quijote dies; that
trusting Alice of the dream world surely disappears for-
ever. The greatest similarity, however, between *Don
Quijote* and *Alice in Wonderland* is their common arrangement of elements: comic, tragic, and heroic. Both works
are complex beneath the surface. They have that strange
quality shared by only a select few books such as *Gulliver's Travels*, that of being readable on several levels
at the same time and without confusion. They resemble
a series of boxes nesting one within the other, each
progressively more difficult to open and yielding a
more valuable favor. And, as in any great work of art,
the innermost can never quite be reached. At the first
level each story is a child's tale, full of delightful
nonsense. The next level is perhaps a satire (*Alice*
about growing up, the *Quijote* about chivalric romance).
The next inner level is, for the *Quijote*, a commentary
on Spain; for *Alice* a picture of Oxford. The germ of

both works is the author himself, for these two stories
are autobiographical in a special sense.

Other Writers

326. Kent, W.H. "The Tercentenary of *Don Quixote*." *The
      Dublin Review* 136 (January-April 1905):375-388.

      The *Quijote* is not a cynical satire on the spirit of
      chivalry nor is it a purely humorous fiction. It is
      part tragic, and the Don is a sublime and pathetic fig-
      ure. Plainly as we see the absurdity of his mistakes,
      we are none the less kept in full sympathy with his
      generous aspirations, and we are filled with pity for
      him in his tragic failures. In the whole range of
      literature we shall scarcely meet with a character in
      whom the two elements of humor and pathos are so subtly
      blended as they are in the Knight of the Doleful Coun-
      tenance.
      [Kent briefly compares the Don to William Thackeray's
      Colonel Thomas Newcome (*The Newcomes*), 1853-1855.]

327. McDonald, W.U., Jr. "Hazlitt's Use of *Don Quixote* Al-
      lusions." *Romance Notes* 2 (Fall 1960):27-30.

      William Hazlitt must be placed high on the list of
      Quijote enthusiasts of the early nineteenth century.
      His various allusions to Cervantes' masterpiece denote
      the pervasive influence of that work. Besides testify-
      ing to Hazlitt's fondness for the *Quijote*, the allu-
      sions contribute to the pungency and figurativeness of
      his prose, primarily as members of similes. Most often
      a *Quijote* allusion forms one part of a figure of speech
      involving a comparison of character or situation in
      Cervantes' novel with something unexpected outside it.

328. McDonald, W.U., Jr. "Inglis' Rambles: A Romantic Tri-
      bute to *Don Quixote*." *Comparative Literature* 12
      (1960):33-41.

      Henry David Inglis' *Rambles in the Footsteps of Don
      Quixote* appeared in 1837. It was based on two of the
      author's prior works, *Spain in 1830* and "Recent Rambles
      in the Footsteps of Don Quixote," 1831. It was the
      first extensive English comment on Cervantes' novel in
      fifty years, since the work of John Bowle, in 1781. In-
      glis' marriage of a travel book on Spain with a commen-
      tary on *Don Quijote* is not the first of its kind. In

1775 Richard Twiss published such a work, entitled
Travels Through Spain and Portugal in 1772 and 1773, as
did William Dalrymple two years later in his *Travels
Through Spain and Portugal in 1774*. Henry Swinburne,
in 1779, also commented upon the *Quijote* in *Travels
Through Spain in the Years 1775 and 1776*. In 1781, John
Talbot Dillon, in *Letters from an English Traveller in
Spain in 1778*, reflected on Cervantes' masterpiece from
time to time. Except for rare brief mention, the *Qui-
jote* then disappeared from travel literature until after
the Peninsula War. Incidental allusions to the *Quijote*
in travel books by John Milford, in 1815, and Michael J.
Quin, in 1823, were followed by the return in force of
the reminiscence-reality-reverence theme in Arthur
Brooke's *Sketches in Spain and Morocco*, and Inglis'
Spain in 1830 and in the 1831 magazine version of
Rambles.

In his *Rambles* Inglis introduces characters out of
the picaresque novel and the *Quijote*. His fictional
traveling companion, the barber Lázaro, is a quixotic
figure who praises the Knight's perfection. While the
fictional author appears to view the *Quijote* as a funny
book, Lázaro defends it as a serious and a perfect work.
The author concludes that Cervantes was accurate in depicting the daily life in Spain.

329. O'Donovan, Michael [O'Connor, Frank]. *The Mirror and
the Roadway*, pp. 8, 18. New York: Alfred A. Knopf,
1956.

[O'Donovan states that the temper of the true novelist
is always reacting against romanticism in fiction. He
further concludes that Jane Austen, in *Northanger Abbey*,
is only reacting to Gothic romance as Cervantes did to
medieval romance, and with similar results: the thing
against which they react disappears, and with it disappears the very reason for the reaction.]

330. Sarmiento, Edward. "Wordsworth and Don Quijote."
Bulletin of Hispanic Studies 38 (1961):113-119.

In *The Prelude*, Book V, lines 50 to 165, Wordsworth
tells of how he fell asleep while reading by the side of
the sea. He has a dream, and in that dream there appears
an uncouth figure, who is part Bedouin and part Don Quijote. He carries a lance, a stone, and a shell. The
lance is from Cervantes' text; the stone and the shell
represent the pure intellect and the poet's intuition,
respectively. The Knight-Arab claims to be saving these

symbols from the destruction about to be inflicted by
the sea. The dreamer longs to learn from the grotesque
Arab-Knight, but the latter, who cannot help him, rides
away on his camel.

One should note that Wordsworth's Arab-Quijote figure
is sterile just as Cervantes' Don was barren. He fights
to no avail; he helps no one. Wordsworth neatly symbolizes this impotence by having the Bedouin's lance at
rest. It is the Knight's weapon, but it is impotent
against the kind of attack which he is about to experience. What Wordsworth's mounted figure is attempting
to do is to find an area in the world (and in life,
therefore) in which to preserve the perfection of the
mind and the radiance of poetic intuition, symbolized
by the stone and the shell.

Wordsworth is, in effect, telling us that Cervantes'
Don is crazed, ineffective, powerless to help (in a
word, on the wrong track), yet also, that there is, in
part at least, some true idealism behind his mistaken
quest. The desire to preserve the stone and shell is
doomed to fail, but Wordsworth feels this desire to be
his own. The romances of chivalry which the Don reads
have the same entrancing effect on him as Shakespeare
and Milton on Wordsworth.

Neither Cervantes nor Wordsworth solves the deeper
problem of the spirit. For Cervantes, fame is a snare and
a selfish, impure source of motivation; the whole appa-
ratus of chivalry is an outworn vessel for the ideal it
once expressed. For Wordsworth, humanity has the works
of man's mind but no guarantee of their permanence.
Both authors, however, inculcate faith in the mind,
particularly in the imagination.

Twentieth-Century England

331. Azorín [Martínez Ruiz, José]. "Don Alonso Quijano en
      Londres." *Obras completas.* Vol. 4, pp. 91-95.
      Madrid: Aguilar, 1961. [From *Fantasías y Devaneos*,
      1920; written in 1904.]

      [Azorín refers to an article in the London *Daily
      Chronicle* dated January 20, (1904?) which described a
      gathering of *cervantistas* at the Hotel Metropole. The
      Spanish ambassador, the Duque de Mandas, addressed the
      group, and stated that the *Quijote* destroyed chivalresque

fantasies in Spain but did not leave the Spanish people
without elevated idealism and noble aspirations for progress. The actor Irving spoke and revealed that he had
acted in an adaptation of the *Quijote* that was a failure.
Irving disagreed with the idea that Cervantes' masterpiece could not be adapted to the stage.]

332. Busi, Frederick A. *"Waiting for Godot*: A Modern *Don
      Quixote.*" *Hispania* 57 (December 1974):876-885.

      [Busi compares Cervantes' *Quijote* with Samuel Beckett's
      Waiting for Godot, 1954, and finds that the characters
      in both works are hard pressed to draw objective connec-
      tions between what they experience and what they wish to
      experience; Vladimir, in Beckett's play, like the Knight,
      seeks to overcome earthly limitations, to discover a
      source of fruitfulness and creativity, but to no avail.
      The major figures in both works, Busi continues, are
      clowns, with a common background in the *commedia dell'
      arte*. Both writers use similar techniques, the critic
      reveals: indicative names for characters, a contrasting
      pair of irreconcilable figures (Don Quijote-Sancho,
      Vladimir-Estragon), and the confusion-of-words device.
      Busi finds several veiled allusions to Cervantes' novel
      in Beckett's play: mysterious thrashings (Sancho and
      Estragon), ingratitude of freed slaves, the concern over
      eating (Sancho and Estragon). Other similarities which
      Busi notes are: the importance of encounters with pas-
      sersby, the reflection of self as seen in other charac-
      ters, the play-within-a-play device to reinforce and
      give depth to a central idea (the complex relationship
      of reality and illusion).]

333. Pérez Firmat, Gustavo. *"Don Quixote in Heart of Dark-
      ness*: Two Notes." *Comparative Literature Studies* 12
      (December 1972):374-383.

      [The critic finds that the *Quijote* had a profound
      effect on Joseph Conrad's *Heart of Darkness*. Pérez
      points out the use by both authors of a discovered manu-
      script with marginal comments which contradict the main
      text. Also, the critic notes a striking similarity be-
      tween the Knight and Conrad's Kurtz: both have a para-
      doxical madness; both are orators; both are conspired
      against by their associates; both are frustrated ideal-
      ists who face reality only on their deathbeds; both have
      delusions of grandeur; Kurtz relates to explorers as
      the Don relates to knights-errant; both represent the
      decadence of an allegedly glorious past, a past that

has been fictionalized. Pérez also finds a strong similarity between Dulcinea and Kurtz's ideal figure, the
Intended, both of whom represent love and illusion, and
neither of whom has an independent existence. Allusions
to the *Quijote* by Conrad in various works are pointed
out. Previous critics who have alluded to a possible
Cervantean influence on Joseph Conrad are briefly noted.]

334. Sánchez Escribano, Federico. "El *Quijote* ante la agonía
     de un inglés." *Anales Cervantinos* 7 (1958):283-284.

     George Gissing remarked in *The Private Papers of Henry
     Ryecroft*, 1903, that he (speaking through Ryecroft)
     wanted to give up the mere pursuit of knowledge and read
     the *Quijote* again before he died. Gissing saw that the
     Quijote was neither comic nor defeatist, that it, in-
     stead, was "satisfying" and "abiding."

335. Trilling, Lionel. "Manners, Morals, and the Novel."
     *The Liberal Imagination: Essays on Literature and
     Society*, pp. 205-222. New York: The Viking Press,
     1951. [Read at the Conference on the Heritage of the
     English-Speaking Peoples and Their Responsibilities,
     Kenyon College, Sept., 1947, and first published in
     the *Kenyon Review* 10 (Winter 1948):11-27.]

     Cervantes sets for the novel the problem of reality:
     the shifting and conflict of social classes becomes the
     field of the problem of knowledge, of how we know and
     of how reliable our knowledge is, which at that very
     moment of history is vexing the philosophers and scien-
     tists. And the poverty of the Don suggests that the
     novel is born with the appearance of money as a social
     element, money, the great solvent of the solid fabric of
     the old society, the great generator of illusion. Or,
     which is to say the same thing, the novel is born in re-
     sponse to snobbery.
     [Trilling discusses E.M. Forster's *The Longest Journey*
     and Henry James' *The Princess Casamassima* noting the
     addiction to strong "reality" in both novels, and the
     replacement of direct human feeling by abstraction.
     These two works, states Trilling, descend from the *Qui-
     jote*: in these two modern stories the young protago-
     nists come into life with large, preconceived ideas and
     are knocked about as a consequence; both Forster's and
     James' novels are concerned with the problem of appear-
     ance and reality and present the conflict between social
     classes and differences in manners.]

VI. *DON QUIJOTE* IN GERMANY.

General

336. Bergel, Lienhard. "Cervantes in Germany." In *Cervantes
      Across the Centuries* ... *A Quadricentennial Volume
      Edited by Angel Flores and M.J. Benardete*, pp. 305-342.
      New York: Dryden Press, 1947. [1969 reprint, Gordian
      Press, pp. 315-352.]

      Generally speaking, prior to the nineteenth-century
      Romanticists the *Quijote* was regarded as a satire, an
      attack on the fantastic. Wieland adopted this general
      view. However, J.K. Wezel conceived the hero to be tra-
      gic, thus foreshadowing the romantic approach. Also
      prior to the Romanticists, Bodmer considered the *Quijote*
      to be less a satire than a representation of complicated
      states. Schiller, who drew upon the episode of Roque
      Guinart for his *Die Räuber*, conceived of Don Quijote as
      a man who misconceived his abilities and his powers, a
      man who had too much energy and who was bound to collide
      with other forces. Thus to Schiller he is heroic, not
      ridiculous. Among the Romanticists, Schelling viewed
      Don Quijote as a mythical saga-struggle between the real
      and the ideal, a struggle to restore harmony between
      them. A.W. von Schlegel viewed the Knight as a representa-
      tive of the poetry of chivalry and Sancho as a symbol of
      mere prose. Friedrich von Schlegel regarded *Don Quijote* as
      a product of romantic wit, a desire for irresponsible
      playing. He saw Cervantes' art as a delectable inter-
      twining of episodes. Ludwig Tieck viewed Don Quijote
      as deserving both laughter and veneration. Tieck also
      saw a relationship between the *Curious Impertinent* and
      the main plot of the *Quijote*, for it showed, to him, the
      folly of the main hero from a different angle--both the
      Curious Impertinent and Don Quijote sought to hold the
      invisible in their hands, to possess what can be enjoyed
      only through faith; and both failed.

Later Romanticists turn extremely pessimistic. Grillparzer (influenced by Byron) and the young Nietzsche conclude that the *Quijote* is a bitter book in which all that
is inspiring appears to be nonsensical. Heinrich Heine's
remarks in the introduction to the 1837 German edition
of the *Quijote* are at times vague, but he appears to view
the *Quijote* as a satire on all enthusiasm and as a bitter
self-irony. Karl Immermann considers *Don Quijote* a
parody of customs, not just of chivalric novels. Leo
Spitzer regards the author of the *Quijote* as, first and
foremost, a Catholic poet, and not a hypocrite as Américo Castro asserted. Ludwig Pfandl views Cervantes as
a fighter against the "Proletarisierung" of ideals. To
Pfandl, Cervantes was forced to criticize his hero in
order to entertain his readers. Thomas Mann is basically
a Romantic who views Cervantes as a writer who was not
conscious of his art. To Florens Christian Rang the
novel is an attack on the Counter Reformation. Joseph
Bickermann, in 1929, finds the Don to be a utopian reformer, a skillful rationalizer, and not a dreamer. To
Max Kommerell Don Quijote is a man who over-reaches himself through *hubris*; his disillusionment at death destroys his excessive pride and prepares him for Divine
Grace. Georg von Lukács, 1920, concludes that the *Quijote* is related to the progressive disintegration of
transcendental Christianity, and that the hero is the
prototype of modern subjectivism, an idealist in a hostile world.

337. Berger, Tjard W. *Don Quixote in Deutschland und sein
      Einfluss auf den deutschen Roman (1613-1800).* In-
      augural-Dissertation zur Erlangung der Doktorwürde der
      hohen philosophischen Fakultät der Ruprecht-Karls-
      Universität zu Heidelberg. Heidelberg: Universitäts-
      Buchdruckerei von J. Hörning, 1908. Pp. 103.

      [Berger's dissertation is divided into three parts and
      contains a total of fourteen chapters. Part I deals
      with the *Quijote* in Germany up to 1700. Here the critic
      points out that the *Curioso impertinente* was translated
      into German in 1617. He also discusses Pahsch Bastel's
      partial *Quijote* translation. The first German to note
      the satirical intent of Cervantes' masterpiece, states
      Berger, was Daniel Morhof in 1682.
      Part II traces the reception of the *Quijote* between
      1700 and 1750. Operettas based on Cervantes' novel are
      pointed out, as are minor eighteenth-century transla-
      tions. More importantly, Berger discusses in some

detail the influence of British writers, such as Steele
and Addison, on German critics, such as Bodmer, and
notes the interpretation of the *Quijote* by Lessing.
Another matter dealt with at length in this part is the
struggle between Richardson and Fielding (idealism versus realism) in the European novel. The final portion
of Part II discusses the influence of Fielding and Cervantes in late eighteenth-century Germany.

Part III of this thesis begins with a lengthy analysis
of three imitations of the *Quijote*: (1) Wieland's *Don
Sylvio von Rosalva*; (2) Musaeus' *Grandison II*; and (3)
J.G. Müller's *Siegfried von Lindenberg*. Other imitators
of the *Quijote* are also noted: J.G. Schulz, Leonhard
Meister, A. von Göchhausen. In Chapter XII Berger notes
the use of Cervantine motifs by German writers, e.g.,
robbers, mistaken identities, brawls, description of the
lower classes, interpolated stories. In Chapter XIII
Bertuch and his translation of the *Quijote*, 1775, are
dealt with at length. The final chapter of this dissertation deals with the German evaluation of the *Quijote*
after Lessing.]

338. Brüggemann, Werner. *Cervantes und die Figur des Don
Quijote in Kunstanschauung und Dichtung der deutschen
Romantik*. Münster, Westfalen: Aschendorff, 1958.
Pp. 380.

[In this well-documented work significant attention
is devoted to pre-Romantic criticism as a background to
the nineteenth-century interpretations of *Don Quijote*.
The reception of Cervantes' masterpiece in England and
France, as well as in Germany, is studied in some detail.
A comparison of the style of Cervantes and Goethe is
presented, and the *Quijote* and *Wilhelm Meisters Lehr-
jahre* are contrasted at length. The stylistic influence
of Cervantes on Tieck's *Franz Sternbald* and on other romantic works is also discussed. Particular attention is
devoted to the interpretations of the *Quijote* by Friedrich von Schlegel, A.W. von Schlegel, and Ludwig Tieck; and
Brüggemann analyzes portions of the *Quijote* in light of
the various romanticist theories on the unity and irony
found in Cervantes' novel.

The critic studies the pessimistic interpretation of
the *Quijote* from Juan Maruján in 1750, an interpretation
later followed by Byron and Grillparzer. Hegel's view
that Don Quijote was a man out of step with his times is
discussed, and Heine's often contradictory statements
about the *Quijote* are examined. Brüggemann also notes

the view of the *Jungdeutschen* that Cervantes' Knight is
a champion against oppression. The eighteenth-century
critic Mayáns is also discussed, and Brüggemann concludes that Mayáns is a forerunner of Romanticism because of his tendency to search for symbolism in the
Quijote.· The views of Spanish Romanticists and Symbolists are pointed out: Benjumea regarded Cervantes' novel
as an attack on the Inquisition, and B. Pallol treated
the work as a satire on the Holy Scriptures. Brüggemann
also examines the opinions of more recent Spanish critics, such as Unamuno, Ortega, and Maeztu. While Brüggemann would give the *Quijote* an almost religious meaning
(a study of a man insane in God), he is most skeptical
about the more degenerate romantic-symbolistic interpretations of the *Quijote*. He concedes, however, that the
early Romanticists made a great contribution to the re-
vitalization of Cervantes' novel.]

339. Dorer, Edmond. *Cervantes und seine Werke nach deutschen
      Urtheilen mit einem Anhange: Die Cervantes-Biblio-
      graphie*. Leipzig: Wilhelm Friedrich, 1881. Pp. vi +
      126 + 31 + 20.

      [This pre-1894 item contains lengthy excerpts from re-
      marks on Cervantes and his works by such German critics
      as Bodmer, Herder, Bouterwek, Goethe, Schelling, Hegel,
      Schopenhauer, Carl Gustav Carus, Tieck, A.W. von
      Schlegel, Friedrich von Schlegel, Eichendorff, Jean Paul
      Friedrich Richter, and Heinrich Heine. The appendices
      deal with such matters as translations, imitations, and
      adaptations of Cervantes' works. A general bibliography
      is included.]

340. Farinelli, Arturo. "Spanien und die spanische Littera-
      tur im Lichte der deutschen Kritik und Poesie." *Zeit-
      schrift für vergleichende Litteraturgeschichte* 5
      (1892):135-206, 276-332; 8 (1895):318-407.

      [Farinelli points out allusions to the *Quijote* by
      Gotthard Heidegger, in 1698, and by Postel, in 1724, and
      notes a German translation of Cervantes' masterpiece by
      an unknown Swiss. An opera by Heinrich Hinsch, 1690,
      and another by Joh. Samuel Müller, 1722, are said to be
      based on the *Quijote*, as is a play by Koenig, in 1727.
        The fact that Bodmer found the Knight to be a symboli-
      cal person is observed (p. 280). On the whole, Farinelli
      concludes that the *Quijote* was not of great influence in
      Germany prior to the mid-eighteenth century. The critic
      observes the comments of Lessing on the *Quijote*, and

discusses adaptations of Cervantes' novel by Wieland
(*Don Sylvio von Rosalva*, 1764), by Musäus (*Grandison
der Zweite*, 1760), and by Schiebeler (a dramatic poem,
"Basilio und Quiteria"). Various translations of the
Quijote are mentioned, and that of Ludwig Tieck is
particularly praised. Farinelli briefly notes the influence of the Roque Guinart episode on Schiller's *Die
Räuber*, and sets forth the favorable comments on Cervantes' novel by Herder, Böttiger, and Bertuch.]

341. Hämel, Adalbert. "The Spanish Movement in Germany."
    Modern Language Journal 12 (1928):261-271.

[Hämel states that Ludwig Tieck's German translation
of the *Quijote* caused that work to become one of the
"folk books" of the German people. The critic notes his
own critical edition of the *Quijote*, the first critical
edition to be published in Germany.]

342. Hoffmeister, Gerhart. *Spanien und Deutschland.*
    *Geschichte und Dokumentation der literarischen Bezie-
    hungen.* Berlin: Erich Schmidt Verlag, 1976. Pp. 208.

[Hoffmeister discusses (pp. 77-78) the early reception
of the *Quijote* in Germany, and mentions the appearance
in 1613 of Don Quijote as a figure in the festivities
held on the occasion of the marriage of Friedrich V of
the Palatinate. Also, the critic notes the use of a
Quijote figure in Opitz's German translation of a continuation (by Mouchemberg) of John Barclay's *Argenis*.
Early translations of Cervantes' masterpiece are also
pointed out, and a bibliography on this subject is
furnished (pp. 83-84).
   Hoffmeister devotes attention to eighteenth-century
German views of the *Quijote*. Note is taken of Bertuch's
1775 German translation, which, Hoffmeister finds (pp.
88-89), made Cervantes known to the whole German people.
The critic also sets forth (pp. 94-95) the views of Herder, who regarded the *Quijote* as a work which expressed
the way of thinking of the Spanish people. Eighteenth-
century German adaptations of the *Quijote* are briefly
discussed at pp. 95-96: W.E. Neugebauer's *Der teutsche
Don Quichotte*, 1753; Musäus' *Grandison der Zweite*, 1760-
1762; J.G. Müller's *Siegfried von Lindenberg*; J.K. Wezel's
Tobias Knaut; and Chr. M. Wieland's *Don Sylvio von Rosalva*.
   Hoffmeister notes the views of Goethe (p. 106) and
Schiller (pp. 111-112) regarding the *Quijote*, and points
out Schiller's use of the Roque Guinart episode in *Die*

Räuber. The views of such Romanticists as Friedrich von
Schlegel, Schelling, Heine, and Jean Paul Friedrich
Richter are briefly summarized (pp. 124-128). Hoffmeister takes note of the Tieck and Soltau translations of
the *Quijote* (p. 127). The critic finds a certain influence of Cervantes on Immermann's *Münchhausen*, 1838,
and on the works of Eichendorff and Novalis (p. 128).
Throughout this work is found abundant bibliographical information.]

343.   Hübner, E. "Spanien im Lichte der Weltliteratur."
       Deutsche Rundschau 96 (1897):363-385.

       [The influence of the *Quijote* is not discussed. Hüb-
       ner does mention (pp. 373-374) the numerous translations
       of the works of Calderón, Lope de Vega, and Cervantes
       during the German Romantic epoch.]

344.   Neumann, Max-Hellmut. "Cervantes in Deutschland." *Die
       neueren Sprachen* 25 (1917):147-162; 193-213.

       Bodmer was the founder of *Don Quijote* criticism in
       Germany in 1741. He realized the universality of the
       Knight, that each person is partly quixotic. Friedrich
       von Schlegel, in 1797, concluded that the *Quijote* was a
       tragic work, and A.W. Schlegel adopted a poetry (Don
       Quijote) versus prose (Sancho Panza) interpretation of
       Cervantes' novel. He also defended the 1615 *Quijote*
       against those, including Goethe, who attacked it. Tieck
       was profoundly influenced by the *Quijote*. Unlike
       Friedrich von Schlegel, Tieck did not generally view Cer-
       vantes' masterpiece as pessimiotic. Schelling regarded
       the *Quijote* as an international work, in spite of its
       elements of local color. He even considered the two
       central characters as mythological figures. [Neumann
       devotes great attention to the conflict between the
       optimistic and the pessimistic interpretation of the
       Quijote. Heine is regarded as the highpoint of pessimism
       in his *Reisebilder*, 1831. Neumann, however, does not
       consider Cervantes a pessimist but a resigned Christian
       mystic. Throughout his essay Neumann examines German
       translations and adaptations of the *Quijote* in some
       detail.]

345.   Overmans, Jakob. "Hamlet, Don Quijote, Deutschland."
       Stimmen der Zeit 46 (1916):38-46.

       [Overmans presents a general study of the German in-
       terpretation of the figures Hamlet and Don Quijote. The

critic finds that there has been no real political interpretation of the Quijote figure in Germany, and that
Cervantes' hero has not become a German figure like Hamlet. A poem to Don Quijote by Friedrich von Sallet is
presented. Opinions about the Knight by numerous German writers are briefly set forth.]

346. Schwering, Julius. *Literarische Beziehungen zwischen
      Spanien und Deutschland*. Münster: Schöningh, 1902.
      Pp. 92.

      [This item was summarized in our bibliography on the
      Novelas ejemplares, 1968, as item 534. It discusses in
      some detail the *Curioso impertinente* in German litera-
      ture.]

347. Schwering, Julius. "Cervantes' *Don Quijote* und der
      Kampf gegen den Roman in Deutschland." *Euphorion* 29
      (1928):497-503.

      In seventeenth-century German versions of the *Quijote*
      the author's explanatory introduction was omitted. For
      that reason the readers and critics in that country did
      not realize that Cervantes' novel was a satire against
      novels of chivalry. Not until Pierre Daniel Huet's
      widely circulated *Traité de l'origine des Romans*, 1671,
      did the anti-chivalresque aspect of the *Quijote* come to
      light in Germany. Hence Cervantes did not really in-
      fluence the seventeenth-century struggle in Germany
      against the chivalric novel; by the time that the pur-
      pose of his novel was understood, books of chivalry had
      already lost their popularity. [But see item 348.] In
      the very late seventeenth century, certain German com-
      mentators such as Christian Thomasius did begin to note
      the satire in Cervantes' masterpiece. In the eighteenth
      century the *Quijote* becomes very popular. Bodmer and
      Gottsched praise it. Wieland's *Don Sylvio von Rosalva*,
      a satire against false sentimentality, is heavily in-
      fluenced by the *Quijote*, and Friedrich Schiller draws
      upon it in writing his drama *Die Räuber*.

348. Tiemann, Hermann. *Das spanische Schrifttum in Deutsch-
      land von der Renaissance zur Romantik*. Hamburg:
      Ibero-Amerikanisches Institut, 1936. Pp. 226; reprint
      ed., Hildesheim-New York: Georg Olms Verlag, 1971.

      [The reception of Cervantes' masterpiece in Germany
      up to 1648 is briefly discussed, and Bertuch's transla-
      tion of the *Quijote* in 1775-1777 is noted. Tiemann

disagrees (pp. 88–89) with Schwering (item 347), who finds
that in the Baroque era German readers did not understand the satirical intention of the *Quijote*. The critic points out that the German translator of Cervantes'
masterpiece, in 1648, referred to that novel as a "Narr-
werck" (burlesque work).]

349. Van Maelsaeke, D. "The Paradox of Humor: A Comparative
      Study of *Don Quixote*." *Theoria* 28 (1967):24–42.

      [The critic examines the opinions of numerous German
      critics and creative writers regarding the *Quijote*: Wie-
      land, Bodmer, Herder, Goethe, the Schlegel brothers,
      Tieck, Jean Paul Friedrich Richter, and Heinrich Heine.]

                      Seventeenth-Century Germany

350. Barton, Erika Regina Seiberlich. "Die spanische Litera-
      tur in Deutschland im Zeitalter des Barock. Ein For-
      schungsbericht." Ph.D. dissertation, University of
      Nebraska, 1972. Pp. 286. [Based on a summary found
      in *Dissertation Abstracts International*, 33/07A, pp.
      3573–3574. The original thesis could not be obtained
      in time for a summary to be prepared.]

      [Barton points out the lack of agreement as to the
      part that Spain played in the development of German
      baroque culture. Prior works on this subject are
      examined. Attention is devoted to the picaresque genre
      and to the question of the relationship of Crimmels-
      hausen to Spanish literature. Barton states that the
      influence of Cervantes was small in seventeenth-century
      Germany. Pastoral literature is examined, as is the
      role of the Latin language as an intermediary between
      Spanish and German literature. The final chapter of
      Dr. Barton's thesis studies the contribution of Spain in
      the areas of religious-didactic works, the drama, and
      poetry. An evaluation of bibliographical contributions
      is found at the end of this work.]

351. Dimler, G. Richard. "Alienation in *Don Quixote* and
      Simplicius Simplicissimus." *Thought* 49 (1974):72–80.

      [Dimler states that there seems to be no direct in-
      fluence of the *Quijote* on Hans Jakob Cristoffel von
      Grimmelshausen's *Der abenteuerliche Simplicissimus*,
      1669, and finds that Cervantes' masterpiece does not
      seem to be directly influential in seventeenth-century

Germany. Nevertheless, the critic notes the following
similarities between the *Quijote* and *Simplicissimus*:
(1) both heroes are out of kilter with their environment; (2) both face new realities; (3) both figures experience loneliness and alienation in a new and meaning-
less world, a world "breaking-up"; (4) the feeling of
alienation from society, from self, and from God is
brought out by the same motifs in both works, namely the
fool-motif, the mask-motif, and the *nosce teipsum* theme.]

352. Schneider, Adam. *Spaniens Anteil an der deutschen Litteratur des 16. und 17. Jahrhunderts.* Strassburg i.
E.: Schlesier und Schweikhardt, 1898. Pp. xix + 347.

[An anonymous 1617 German translation of the *Curious
Impertinent* is noted (p. 222). The critic devotes attention (pp. 222-231) to the partial translation of the
1605 *Quijote* by "Pahsch Bastel von der Sohle." Chapter
8 of the 1669 edition of this translation is compared
with the French text of Oudin and with the Spanish text,
1885, Madrid. Schneider states (p. 223) that there were
two editions of Pahsch Bastel's partial translation
prior to 1669, namely a 1621 and a 1648 edition. (The
existence of an edition prior to 1648 has been seriously
questioned. For a bibliography on the question of the
earliest German edition of the *Quijote*, see Hoffmeister
(342), pp. 83-84.)]

353. Schnelle, Kurt. "Zur Wirkungsgeschichte der Literatur
des Siglo de Oro in der deutschen Frühaufklärung."
Beiträge zur romanischen Philologie, Sonderheft
(1967), pp. 137-147.

[Schnelle discusses the ideas of Christian Thomasius
about education and literature and his comments on fiction, revealed in his works toward the end of the seventeenth century. Thomasius, the critic observes, classi-
fied novels into four types, the *Quijote* being discussed
in the fourth group as satire which showed the folly and
vice of man and awakened the reader to virtue.]

354. Schweitzer, Christoph Eugen. "Spanien in der deutschen
Literatur des 17. Jahrhunderts." Ph.D. dissertation,
Yale University, 1954. Pp. 250. [As summarized in
Dissertation Abstracts International, 28/01A, pp.
203-204. The original could not be obtained in time
for a summary.]

[Schweitzer notes the unpopularity of Spaniards in
seventeenth-century Germany, because of the participation

of Spain in the Thirty Years War. The critic concludes
that *Lazarillo*, the *Quijote*, and the works of Spanish
moralists were preferred by Germans to other Spanish
works.]

355. Schweitzer, Christoph E. "Harsdörffer and *Don Quixote*."
     Philological Quarterly 37 (1958):87-94.

     Harsdörffer speaks favorably of the *Quijote* in his
     Gesprächspiele, 1647, although here, as elsewhere, he
     places great emphasis on the poems in Cervantes' novel
     and on matters of pure form. Unlike critics of the En-
     lightenment, such as Christian Thomasius, in 1689,
     Harsdörffer is no moralist. He should be placed between
     the end of the popularity of the chivalry novel and the
     beginning of the Enlightenment with its emphasis on
     moralistic interpretations, and should be viewed as a
     significant feature in the seventeenth-century recep-
     tion of the *Quijote* in Germany.

356. Steiner, Arpad. "Zum Thema des *Don Quijote* in Deutsch-
     land im 17. Jahrhundert." *Archiv für das Studium der
     neueren Sprachen und Literaturen* 58 (1930):101-104.

     [Steiner discusses Mouchemberg's 1626 continuation of
     John Barclay's *Argenis*, 1621, and the translation of
     both the original and the continuation into German by
     Martin Opitz in 1631. Mouchemberg's continuation,
     Steiner notes, contains an elderly Spaniard who resem-
     bles Don Quijote not only physically but in speech and
     manner. Steiner concludes that the first reflection of
     the Quijote figure in the German language is thus due
     to Opitz.]

357. Weydt, Günther. "Don Quijote Teutsch: Studien zur Her-
     kunft des simplicianischen Jupiter." *Euphorion* 51
     (1957):250-270.

     [Weydt studies the sources of the "Jupiter episode"
     in Grimmelshausen's *Simplicissimus*. Previous opinions
     are noted. The critic raises the question of the pos-
     sible influence of the *Quijote* on Grimmelshausen, and
     finds that this influence may well have come through
     Sorel, Harsdörffer, and others. The question of a di-
     rect influence of the Spaniard is left open. A diagram
     of the possible sources of the "Jupiter episode" is
     found on page 270.]

Eighteenth-Century Germany

358. Kurth, Lieselotte E. "W.E.N. - *Der teutsche Don Qui-*
      chotte oder die Begebenheiten des Marggraf von Bella-
      monte." *Deutsche Schillergesellschaft* 9 (1965):106-
      130.

      [Kurth examines Carl Gottfried Meyer's little-known
      humorous work *Der teutsche Don Quichotte*, 1753, pur-
      portedly by one Wilhelm Ehrenfeld Neugebauer (pseudonym)
      and allegedly based on a supposed French original.
      Pages 110-113 contain a plot summary of this story, a
      satire on young people overly influenced by French no-
      vels. Kurth finds that Meyer's story, not Wieland's
      Don Sylvio von Rosalva, 1764, introduced into German
      literature Cervantes' technique of the personal, inter-
      vening author.]

359. Tropsch, Stephan. "Wielands *Don Sylvio* und Cervantes'
      Don Quijote." *Euphorion* 4 (1899):32-61.

      [Tropsch points out allusions to the *Quijote* in Wie-
      land's correspondence and in *Don Sylvio von Rosalva*.
      In some detail the critic lists and discusses similari-
      ties between *Don Quijote* and *Don Sylvio*: (1) Cervantes
      attacks books of chivalry; Wieland attacks *Feenmärchen*;
      (2) both heroes have a squire; (3) both heroes believe
      that they are pursued by evil enchanters; (4) both au-
      thors use humorous chapter headings, with subjective ob-
      servations mixed with long sentences. Tropsch also
      notes other similarities between *Don Quijote* and *Don
      Sylvio*: both stories occurred "not long ago"; both
      heroes are idealistic, good-hearted, gullible, and
      brave; both are well-read; both judge with reason but
      act insanely when their fixation is upon them; both have
      lady-loves; the squires in the two novels are akin; both
      heroes have a priest and a barber as friends; various
      minor characters are alike, and there is a similarity be-
      tween various adventures, such as the salamander adven-
      ture of Don Sylvio and Don Quijote's windmill and basin-
      helmet episodes; both Dons have kindred dream adventures.
      Under stylistic similarities the critic states that
      both Cervantes and Wieland mix themselves into their
      stories; both are above their protagonists, yet they
      love them; both writers claim to be mere translators of
      their stories and both comment on the so-called "his-
      torical" versions.

In his conclusion Tropsch sums up the similarities
between *Don Quijote* and *Don Sylvio* but asserts that Wieland probably did not have the *Quijote* before him as he
wrote, since there are no long, detailed passages with
similar wording.]

360. Vordtriede, Werner. "Wilhelm Heinse's Share in the
     German Interest in Spanish Literature." *Journal of
     English and Germanic Philology* 48 (1949):88-96.

     [The critic states that prior authorities have over-
     looked the contributions of Wilhelm Heinse, 1749-1803,
     to the understanding of Spanish literature in Germany.
     Vordtriede points out that Heinse at first regarded
     the *Quijote* as a book of educational castigation of mis-
     guided enthusiasm and an exposition of sound rationalism
     in the figure Sancho Panza. Later, the critic states,
     Heinse saw the *Quijote* as a national book, long before
     Herder and the Romanticists, and also came to appreciate
     the necessity of the various episodes of Cervantes'
     masterpiece. Heinse, Vordtriede observes, in his later
     writings regarded the Knight as the hero, not Sancho,
     and concluded that the Don was not really a fool, al-
     though he was mocked by the author.]

Nineteenth-Century Germany

361. Azorín [Martínez Ruiz, José]. "Heine y Cervantes."
     Obras completas. Vol. 2, pp. 955-959. Madrid: Agui-
     lar, 1959. [From *Los valores literarios*, Madrid:
     Renacimiento, 1913.]

     Heinrich Heine's observations on the *Quijote* in the
     introduction to the 1837 German edition are among the
     most beautiful, basic, and perceptive that have ever
     been written. In Heine's pages are found many of the
     most important points of view which have been adopted in
     modern times regarding Cervantes' novel. The German
     author was repelled by the way the masses treated the
     Knight, but even more repelled by the way in which the
     upper classes dealt with him. At first, Heine believed
     that the ridiculousness of the *Quijote* derived from the
     hero's wish to introduce into contemporary life a past
     that had disappeared once and for all. Later, the Ger-
     man realized the bitterness of seeking to introduce the
     future too soon.

Cervantes, said Heine, was a man of deep intuition who
penetrated into the depths of his characters, and in the
Quijote got rid of artificial idealism. Yet, like all
great writers, Heine continued, Cervantes substituted
an idealism based on reality. Cervantes, the German
asserted, created the modern novel by introducing into
a book of chivalry the faithful description of the lower
classes, the life of the people. Heine also compared
Cervantes and Goethe, noting that both used an easy
prose colored with a sweet, innocent, and elevated irony.
Heine further observed that both had the same short-
coming—prolixity.

362. Bertrand, J.-J.A. *Cervantès et le romantisme allemand.*
      Paris: Félix Alcan, 1914. Pp. viii + 635.

The pre-Romantic Humboldt thought of the *Quijote* as a
picture of Spanish customs and types, and Herder viewed
Cervantes as a spokesman for his age. Friedrich von Schlegel appears to be the first to discover the romantic aspects of Cervantes' works. *Don Quijote*, to Friedrich von
Schlegel, was not comic, but serious, even tragic. To
him the unity of the *Quijote* was not in its dry logic
but in its mixture of the poetic and the prosaic. The
Quijote, stated Schlegel, has the same harmony as a
musical composition, or a tableau. It is both subjective and objective. August Wilhelm von Schlegel concluded
that Don Quijote symbolized poetry (idealism) and that
Sancho represented prose (reality). Both Friedrich and
A.W. von Schlegel concluded that Cervantes was a conscious
artist. Schelling considered the *Quijote* an example of
created mythology. In Part I of the *Quijote*, Schelling
stated, the ideal is treated naturalistically; in Part
II the ideal is mystified, the world with which the hero
struggles becomes ideal. The defeat of the hero, Schelling concluded, is only apparent.

Goethe, in 1819, had certain reservations about the
Quijote and thought that Cervantes only wrote Part II
to spite Avellaneda. The true interest in the story
dies, stated Goethe, when the hero ceases to be a fool
and merely becomes mystified. Schleiermacher, discussing the difference between the novel (*Roman*) and the
novella, concluded that *Don Quijote* was more like a *novella* than a novel, because, though the two central figures
stand out, incidents, not character portrayal, dominate
the story. Ludwig Tieck observed that Don Quijote incites our enthusiasm as well as our laughter. He is

absurd to us, Tieck stated, because his means are absurd, not his ideals. Heinrich Heine, in 1837, conceived of Cervantes as a strong, bighearted man, who
was profoundly Catholic. Cervantes, he stated, created
the modern novel by mingling the popular with the noble,
the noble being the dominant element. Eichendorff, in
1851, concluded that Cervantes was a modern humorist,
humor being the natural reaction of a still wholesome
mind against the times.

[Bertrand finds the greatest value in the romantic,
symbolistic interpretation of the *Quijote*, though he
himself is skeptical about the novel's symbolism. To
Bertrand, Cervantes' novel is primarily a book that expresses the soul of the author with its basic contradic-
tion, its double nature, part folly and part wisdom.]

363. Bertrand, J.-J.A. *Cervantes en el país de Fausto*.
      Madrid: Ediciones Cultura Hispánica, 1950. Pp. 230.

      [This item is a re-editing and translation into Span-
      ish of Bertrand's *Cervantès et le romantisme allemand*.
      The translation is by José Perdomo García.]

364. Bertrand, J.-J.A. "Encuentros de Schiller con España."
      Clavileño 6 (1955):38-42.

      [Bertrand notes Schiller's adaptation of the Roque
      Guinart episode of the *Quijote* in his *Die Räuber*.]

365. Bickermann, Joseph. *Don Quijote y Fausto, los héroes
      y las obras*. Barcelona: Araluce, 1932. Pp. xxix +
      422. [First published as *Don Quijote und Faust, die
      Helden und die Werke*. Berlin: A. Collignon, 1929.]

      [This item was summarized at some length in Volume One
      of this bibliography (item 38, pp. 54-55). Bickermann
      does not appear to imply that the Quijote figure in-
      spired Goethe's protagonist. The two heroes are merely
      compared and contrasted, and the critic finds that both
      men are inactive until late in life, both recognize their
      excess at the end, both want to achieve everything yet
      accomplish nothing, both yearn to return to the human
      fold, both are heroes not because of their deeds but be-
      cause they find themselves, and their renunciation is
      the cause of their greatness.]

366. Farinelli, Arturo. "Guillaume de Humboldt et l'Espagne."
      Revue Hispanique 5 (1898):1-250.

[Farinelli points out allusions to the *Quijote* by
such writers as Dorothea von Schlegel and Wieland. On
the whole, the critic believes that the *Quijote* had more
effect on German novelists than did Richardson, Rousseau,
and Voltaire. The influence of Cervantes' masterpiece
on Jean Paul Friedrich Richter and on Kotzebue is briefly discussed. An operetta by Soden is said to have been
based on the *Quijote*. In his *Appendice* ("Goethe et
l'Espagne: esquisse") Farinelli points out Goethe's use
of one of Sancho's proverbs and also Goethe's allusions
to the *Quijote*. The critic states that various contemporaries of Goethe (including Heine and Grillparzer)
noted a similarity between *Wilhelm Meister* and the
Quijote.]

367. Huebener, Theodore. "Goethe and Cervantes." *Hispania*
33 (May 1950):113-115.

Goethe seems to have read the *Quijote* in Bertuch's
translation of 1777. On several occasions the author of
Faust stated his admiration for Cervantes and his works.
The influence of the Spaniard is obvious in some of
Goethe's short prose selections, and in longer ones,
such as *Die Wahlverwandtschaften* and *Wilhelm Meister*.
As Heinrich Heine stated in 1837, Goethe resembles Cervantes even in the details of his style, in his use of
an agreeable prose tinged with the sweetest and most
harmless irony, and in his digressiveness.

368. Lussky, Alfred Edwin. *Tieck's Romantic Irony, with*
Special Emphasis upon the Influence of Cervantes,
Sterne, and Goethe. Chapel Hill: University of North
Carolina Press, 1932. Pp. viii + 274.

Cervantes used a number of destructive ironic techniques that were followed by Tieck. The Spaniard insists that his story is true, and that he will not
stray from the truth; he interrupts his novel to have
his characters make ironic remarks about the author, and
even makes himself a character in the book; Cervantes
also criticizes his own work, calling it a dry story,
and stating that parts of it are unnecessary or out of
place (*El curioso impertinente*). Other ironic recourses
used by both authors are: calling their narration a
mere piece of literary composition; referring to previous or subsequent chapters; stating that the work itself is a printed book rather than a frank and naive
narrative. Tieck also follows Cervantes' technique of

making sport of the readers, whom Cervantes refers to,
through Sansón, as an infinite number of fools.

369. Lussky, Alfred Edwin. "Cervantes and Tieck's Idealism."
     PMLA 43 (December 1928):1082-1097.

     About 1795, Tieck detected a deeper meaning in the
     Quijote and began to identify with the Knight. Cervan-
     tes' novel became to Tieck a work of spontaneous, roman-
     tic idealism, the only book in which poetry and joking,
     fantasy and real life, are raised to the level of a work
     of art. The effect of the *Quijote* on this German writer
     was: (1) to cause him to have a love for the absolute
     and the divine; (2) to increase his love of woman; (3)
     to create in him a love of great achievements; and (4)
     to cause him to have a transcendent love for ideal art
     and poetic imagination.
          Tieck particularly valued Cervantes' form of romantic
     irony, his deliberate destruction of an illusion in
     order to show the superiority of the author's ideal
     over his actual creation. In the case of both Tieck
     and Cervantes the irony concerns itself first with the
     reader, then with the environment of the author and the
     contemptible literature of the day, and finally with
     the author himself and his art.

370. Mirabent, F. "Sobre un aspecto del cervantismo alemán."
     Revista de Ideas Estéticas 10 (1952):115-139.

     [This article deals largely with humor and irony.
     The critic finds that Jean Paul Friedrich Richter was
     the German writer who penetrated most deeply into Cer-
     vantes' humor. Jean Paul, states the critic, considered
     Cervantes a man ingeniously balanced between realism and
     idealism.]

371. Pérez de Ayala, Ramón. "Don Quijote en el extrajero."
     In *El Ateneo de Madrid en el III centenario de la
     publicación de El ingenioso hidalgo Don Quijote de la
     Mancha*, pp. 361-378. Madrid: El Ateneo de Madrid
     (Impr. Bernardo Rodríguez), 1905.

     [Pérez de Ayala studies various theories as to why
     the *Quijote* is a humorous work. Heinrich Heine's love
     for Cervantes' masterpiece is noted in some detail. The
     critic concludes that only the suffering, wandering
     Heine, a true younger brother of the Knight, could have
     captured the soul of Don Quijote.]

372. Petriconi, Hellmuth. "Roland, Don Quijote und Simson."
     Romanistisches Jahrbuch 12 (1961):209-228.

     Heinrich Heine understood Don Quijote's death. He
     saw that prophesying the end of the heroic world was
     characteristic of the poetry of all peoples. But Heine,
     on reading of Don Quijote's death, did not think of
     Achilles' or Siegfried's death, but that of one of his
     own characters, Simson, who died in a duel defending the
     belief in God. Simson and Don Quijote, to Heine, were
     epic figures of the Gilgamesh type.

373. Rausse, Hubert. "Cervantes und Friedrich Halm. Eine
     Erinnerung an das 300 jährige Jubiläum der novelas
     ejemplares." *Jahrbuch der Grillparzer-Gesellschaft*
     24 (1913):278-285.

     [Rausse finds an influence of Cervantes' *Curioso im-
     pertinente* on Friedrich Halm's short story *Das Haus an
     der Veronabrücke* and on his proposed play *Freund und
     Frau*. The critic also states that there was an influence
     of the *Quijote* on Heinrich Heine's contrasting figures
     Gumpelino and Hyazinth.]

374. Struyk, John. "The Role of the Narrator in the Novels
     of Jean Paul Friedrich Richter." Ph.D. dissertation,
     University of Waterloo (Canada), 1976. [Based on the
     summary found in *Dissertation Abstracts International*,
     vol. 37A, no. 10, pp. 6479-6480.]

     [Struyk points out the different opinions regarding
     the merits of Jean Paul's use of the intrusive narrator
     technique. The critic finds that this device is an old
     recourse used by Cervantes and Sterne. Cervantes,
     states Struyk, by using a narrator dependent upon a fic-
     tional Arabic writer as well as upon a fictional trans-
     lator, can obtain objectivity. The critic examines
     several works by Richter which employ the device of a
     fictional narrator: *Die unsichtbare Loge*, *Hesperus*,
     Titan, *Der Komet*, and *Schulmeisterlein Wutz*.]

375. Vordtriede, Werner. "The Trial of the Books in Goethe
     and Cervantes." *Modern Language Notes* 62 (May 1947):
     339-340.

     In his *Der Triumph der Empfindsamkeit* Goethe borrows
     from Cervantes' trial-of-the-books episode (Part I,
     Chap. VI, *DQ*). In Goethe's play the sentimental hero
     Oronaro cherishes a doll (a life-size image of his

beloved) more than he cherishes the beloved herself.
As it happens, the doll is stuffed with sentimental
books, including Goethe's own *Werther*. As Cervantes
criticizes his own prior pastoral work, the *Galatea*,
Goethe likewise pokes fun at his own earlier sentimental
novel. One book after the other is examined, discussed,
and condemned by the examiner. King Andrason, who has
the function of the curate in *Don Quijote*, is, like the
priest, surrounded by women who advise him of the
hero's amorous affliction.

376. Wagner, José. "Don Quijote en Alemania." *La Crónica*,
     9 October 1947. [Based on a summary by Rafael Helio-
     doro Valle and Emilia Romero, *Bibliografía cervantina
     en la América española* (425), p. 310. The original
     could not be located.]

     [Wagner states that Germany began the appreciation of
     the *Quijote* and cites the interest of Tieck, Goethe,
     Heine, Nietzsche, and Schopenhauer in Cervantes' master-
     piece.]

377. Zeydel, Edwin H. *Ludwig Tieck, The German Romanticist:
     A Critical Study with a Preface to the Second Edition
     by the Author.* Hildesheim and New York: George Olms Ver-
     lag, 1971. Pp. xvi + 406. [First published in 1935,
     Princeton, N.J.: Princeton University Press for the
     University of Cincinnati.]

     [While there are allusions to Cervantes and his works
     throughout this volume, most of the critic's observa-
     tions regarding the *Quijote* are found in Chapter VII
     (esp. pp. 114 116). Zeydel notes Tieck's interest in
     Cervantes' masterpiece as a boy. Also pointed out by
     the critic is the tendency of the German Romanticists
     to raise Cervantes to a high pinnacle and to read Roman-
     ticist theories into his writings.
     Attention is devoted to Ludwig Tieck's interpretation
     of the Quijote figure as a martyr of knighthood, and
     note is taken of Grillparzer's opposing view: "What Cer-
     vantes, with an artist's wisdom, merely suggests in the
     background--the noble nature and lucid moments of his
     hero--, Tieck would like to bring into the foreground."
     Tieck, states Zeydel, thought Cervantes hid a secret
     meaning in his novel, a defense of the noblest qualities
     of chivalry and knighthood, an apology for what was
     best in the idealism of the Middle Ages. The critic
     also briefly discusses the relative merits of Ludwig
     Tieck's translation of the *Quijote*, 1799-1801, and of
     the rival version of Soltau, 1800.]

Twentieth-Century Germany

378. Bertrand, J.-J.A. "Renacimiento del cervantismo alemán."
      Anales Cervantinos 9 (1961-1962):143-167.

      [The critic examines Spanish and German editions of
      the *Quijote* that were published in Germany since 1914.
      Bertrand also discusses numerous recent studies of Cer-
      vantes' masterpiece, including those of Kommerell, Mann,
      Schwering, Meier, Auerbach, and Weinrich. The works of
      Rüegg, Schürr, and Brüggemann are commented upon in de-
      tail. Recent adaptations of the *Quijote* are briefly
      noted. In his *Anejo* Bertrand compares and contrasts
      Schiller's Karl Moor with Cervantes' robber Roque
      Guinart.]

379. Greene, Thomas. "Lawrence and the Quixotic Hero."
      Sewanee Review 59 (Autumn 1951):559-573.

      The most striking twentieth-century interpretation of
      the myth of Don Quijote is Kafka's *The Castle*. Kafka's
      hero, K., in his attempt to establish contact with the
      castle, encounters the same futility which D.H. Lawrence
      and Don Quijote encountered. Reward and punishment in
      the universe of Kafka and Cervantes alike are uncertain
      and whimsical; it is a universe which runs by irrational
      and unpredictable laws. The seen and the unseen, the
      known and the unknown, are always in an unbalanced pro-
      portion, in unstable equilibrium. Each book has the
      atmosphere of comedy, to be sure, but it is a comedy as
      uneasy and mystifying as the stories of Lewis Carroll.

380. Keele, Alan Frank. *Paul Schallück and the Post-War
      German Don Quixote: A Case-History Prolegomenon to
      the Literature of the Federal Republic*. Bern: Herbert
      Lang, 1976. Pp. vii + 134. (*Utah Studies in Litera-
      ture and Linguistics*, no. 5.) [Keele's work is based
      in part on his Ph.D. dissertation at Princeton Univer-
      sity, 1971: "*Don Quixote in Köln*: An Introduction to
      the Life and Works of Paul Schallück." *Dissertation
      Abstracts International*, 33A, no. 1 (July 1972), p. 315.]

      [Keele does not discuss in detail the influence of
      Cervantes on Schallück. However, the critic's summary
      (p. 12) of the plot of Schallück's *Don Quichotte in Köln*
      reveals that influence: Anton Schmitz, a cultural editor
      for a radio and television station, decides after seven
      years to go out into the world and practice his ideals,
      not merely to talk about them. He is accompanied by his
      unwilling friend Peter Scheel. To accentuate the

pan-mythical nature of the heroes, states Keele, the
author has the pair appear now as Christ and Peter, now
as Tünnes and Schäl of Köln folklore, and now as Don
Quijote and Sancho Panza.]

381. Perniola, Mario. "Metaletteratura e alienazione dell'
      arte in Cervantes e Kafka." *Revista di Estetica* 16
      (1971):83-92.

      [Perniola observes that the basic separation between
      reality and imagination, life and literature, stands at
      the basis both of the *Quijote* and of Kafka's *The Castle*,
      but that in Kafka's work there is a singular modifica-
      tion: the enchantment does not arise from literature,
      but from reality.]

382. Robert, Marthe. *L'Ancien et le nouveau. De Don Qui-
      chotte à Kafka*. Paris: Payot, 1967. Pp. 320. [First
      published in 1963, Paris: Grasset.]

      [This item was summarized in Volume Two of this bibliog-
      raphy (item 269, pp. 178-179). A certain portion of
      Robert's work discusses Cervantes' concern over the func-
      tion of literature in real life. Robert also compares
      and contrasts the treatment of this question by Kafka
      and Cervantes, as well as their varying approaches to
      the question of imagination and reality.]

383. Selig, Karl-Ludwig. "Cervantes y Kafka." *Anales Cer-
      vantinos* 5 (1955-1956):265-266.

      [Selig notes Kafka's "Die Wahrheit über Sancho Pansa,"
      found in *Beschreibung eines Kampfes*. Here Kafka states
      that Sancho dreamed up and named Don Quijote, and then
      followed him enthusiastically.]

384. Urzidil, Johannes. "Cervantes und Kafka." *Hochland*
      63 (1971):333-347.

      [Urzidil points out Kafka's aphorism, "Die Wahrheit
      über Sancho Pansa," in which the Squire becomes the
      driving force in the story, the Knight merely being
      Sancho's daemon. Also noted is Kafka's fragmentary out-
      line of a continuation of the *Quijote*, in which the hero
      was to visit southern France and northern Italy. The
      major part of this article, however, deals with the am-
      bivalence of various authors toward their own works and
      discusses the creative process itself. From time to
      time, parallels are drawn between Cervantes and Kafka:
      both deal with metamorphoses; both place the fantastic

and the realistic side by side.   Urzidil draws a comparison between Grisóstomo's desire to have his literary
works destroyed and a similar desire on the part of
Kafka.   The use of deep irony by Cervantes and Kafka is
examined in some detail.]

VII. *DON QUIJOTE* IN RUSSIA

General
(*See also* Item 5)

385. Balashof, N., Mijailof, A., and Terterian, I., eds.
"Cervantes en ruso. Bibliografía de la obra y crítica
literaria, 1958-1967." *Servantes i vsemirnaia literatura*, pp. 278-285. Moscow: Nauka, 1969.

[These pages furnish a basic bibliography for a study
of the recent influence of Cervantes on Russian literature and the interpretation of Cervantes' works by Russian critics.]

386. Belza, S.E. "El *Quijote* en la poesía rusa." In *Servan-
tes i vsemirnaia literatura*, pp. 214-238. Edited by
N. Balashof, A. Mijailof, and I. Terterian. Moscow:
Nauka, 1969.

[Belza collects allusions to the *Quijote* by numerous
Russian poets of the nineteenth and twentieth centuries,
including N.M. Karamzin, A.H. Radushev, D.P. Minaev,
and G. Gal.]

387. "Cervantes en la URSS." *Cultura Soviética*, October
1947, pp. 17-21.

Pushkin was the first to popularize Cervantes' works
in Russia, and Belinski considered Shakespeare and
Cervantes to be the founders of the modern art of writing, a synthesis of the richness of romantic art and
the plasticity of the classic. Cervantes was already
famous in Russia prior to the Soviet regime, but he becomes even more popular in the new epoch, his works being adapted both to opera and ballet. This increased
popularity is due in part to the arrival of many Spaniards in Russia after the fall of the Republic.

[Excerpts from the opinions of several Russians are set
forth: Belinski, Gogol, Dostoevski, Gorki, Lozinski,
and Lunacharski.]

388. Chtein, A. *"Don Quichotte* en Union Soviétique."
      Europe, nos. 121-122 (January-February 1956), pp.
      47-50.

      Prior to the Soviet revolution there were only three
      complete Russian translations of the *Quijote*, and only
      one (Watson's) was based on the Spanish text. Since
      1917 there have been fifty editions of Cervantes' mas-
      terpiece in Russia, and it has been translated into the
      various languages spoken in that country. In 1932, B.
      Krjevski and A. Smirnow published the first Soviet
      translation, and in 1951, N. Lioubimov completed a new
      Russian version. [Chtein notes Russian criticism of
      the *Quijote* during the Soviet regime. He asks why the
      Quijote is popular in Russia and concludes that it is
      because the Russians view the Don as a progressive who
      is struggling against feudalism.]

389. Derjavin, Const. "La crítica cervantina en Rusia."
      Real Academia de la Historia 94 (1929):215-238.

      The first Russian edition of the *Quijote* was published
      by Osipov in 1769, and reprinted in 1791. In 1804-1805,
      V. Joukovski published a new translation. Since 1812
      about thirty Russian editions, more or less complete,
      have been published, plus a more considerable number of
      abbreviated editions. The first original Russian criti-
      cism of the Quijote is Turgenev's article of 1860,
      "Hamlet y Don Quijote," which concludes that the Don
      and the doubting Dane symbolize the two basic human
      types, the idealist and the egoistic skeptic. Turgenev
      belongs to that group of critics who view the Don as
      tragic. In 1862, A. Lvov disputed Turgenev's oversim-
      plification of human types. Lvov, unlike Turgenev, con-
      cluded that the Knight was actually insane, that the
      sane philosophical discussions belonged to Cervantes,
      not to his hero. Whereas Turgenev viewed Sancho as a
      popular type who becomes infected with idealism, Lvov
      considered the Squire to be basically a picaresque fig-
      ure. Furthermore, while Turgenev concluded that Cer-
      vantes was a progressive Humanist, Lvov found him to be
      a reactionary.
         In 1866, V. Karelin in *Donquijotismo y demonismo*
      follows Turgenev's view that Cervantes was a progressive.
      This critic also finds a parallel between the Knight and

Milton's hero in *Paradise Lost*--their spirit of fanati-
cal abnegation. Karelin is the first to define *quijotismo* as a psychological fact not only in individuals
but in society as well, in certain moments of political
life. According to Karelin, the Don's sad madness re-
sulted from the poisonous atmosphere in which he lived.
In 1885, N. Storojenko concluded that the *Quijote* was
purely an attack on chivalry novels, and that the Don
was not truly a stoic but an egoist. In 1889, D. Merej-
kovsky saw the Knight as a forerunner of Rousseau in his
love of nature and contempt for civilization. Merejkov-
sky is the first Russian critic to study Sancho in detail, concluding that he is a ridiculous Mephistopheles
at the side of Faust.
     In 1901, L. Shepelevich concluded that the *Quijote*
was not truly a parody of books of chivalry but a work
that should be viewed in the light of Ariosto, Boiardo,
and the picaresque novel. Shepelevich praised Cervantes' ability to harmonize poetic and philosophical elements in his novel.
     P. Kogan, 1897, analyzed the social sources of the
Don Quijote type, finding the Knight to be the representative of the lower nobility of the sixteenth century,
the symbol of feudalism in conflict with a changing
Spain.
     In 1922, V. Shklovsky initiates a study of the form
and structure of the *Quijote*, concluding that Cervantes
did not originally intend for his hero to be part sane.
However, the author came to realize that the Don had become the mouthpiece for his (Cervantes') own ideas.

390. Derzhavin, K.N. *Servantes; zhizn' i tvorchestvo.* Mos-
      cow: Gos. izd-vo Khudozh. lit-ry, 1958. Pp. 740.

      [This work contains ten chapters dealing with Cervan-
      tes' life, his works, and their acceptance by critics
      and writers of fiction. Chapters V and VIII deal with
      the composition of the *Quijote*. Chapter X (pp. 576-678)
      is concerned with the acceptance of Cervantes' works
      within and outside Spain. Particular attention is de-
      voted to Russian editions, adaptations, and critical
      comments. Derzhavin furnishes a lengthy index of works
      cited (pp. 693-741). This item is summarized and criti-
      cized favorably by Alberto Sánchez in *Anales Cervantinos*
      10 (1971):257.]

391. Plaskacz, Bohdan. "Les rapports littéraires entre la
      Russie et les pays hispaniques." *Études Eslaves et
      Est-Européennes* 14 (1969):103-112.

[Plaskacz asserts that Turgenev appears to be the
first Russian writer to be familiar with Spanish literature in the original. His essay *Hamlet and Don Quijote*,
1860, is studied. Turgenev's conception of the Quijote
figure, states Plaskacz, is revealed in his novels, especially in *Nakanune (On the Eve)*, 1860. The critic
further finds that it is impossible to understand the
figure Insarov in that novel without first comprehend-
ing Turgenev's idealistic conception of Don Quijote.]

392. Pujals, Esteban. "Proyección de Cervantes en la litera-
     tura rusa." *Revista Nacional de Educación* (Madrid)
     21 (1951):22-37.

Belinski, c. 1840, was the first Russian critic to
evaluate the *Quijote* in his critique of V.A. Sollogul's
Tarantas. Pushkin and Gogol also reflected on Cervantes' masterpiece. While some believe that Pushkin's
figure Tatiana in *Eugene Onegin* was influenced by Cervantes' Knight, this does not appear to be correct.
However, Pushkin did draw on the *Quijote* in his *Poor
Knight*. In his *Dead Souls* Gogol undoubtedly was influenced by Cervantes' novel, for the Russian's work is
a picture of Russia just as the *Quijote* is a picture of
Spain. In addition, the figure Chichikov has certain
quixotic traits.

In 1860, Turgenev presented his famous essay, *Hamlet
y Don Quijote*, and viewed the figure of the Knight as a
man who has faith in something eternal. Karelin is the
first to define *quijotismo* not as a purely individual
trait but as something characteristic of certain racial
groups in particular moments of political life. Avseen-
ko, 1877, and Storozhenko, 1885, examine the purely
literary aspects of the *Quijote*, the latter critic discounting the various philosophical interpretations of
Cervantes' masterpiece.

Dostoevski is similar to Cervantes in a number of
ways. Both suffered a great deal in life. However,
Dostoevski lacks the Spaniard's sincerity, and the
Spaniard lacks Dostoevski's mysticism. Both are, nevertheless, sympathetic towards man's sufferings. In his
Diary, 1873-1881, Dostoevski discusses the generosity of
the Knight of La Mancha and praises the simplicity and
greatness of his soul. The Russian viewed Cervantes as
a bitterly ironic writer. The figure of the Don appears
to have influenced the character presentation of Devuchkin of *Poor Folk* and of Myshkin in *The Idiot*.

Merezhkovski, in his essay "Cervantes," 1889, examined the *Quijote* and concluded that it was a satire on intellectual activity and that the Don was a figure that ridiculed the deficiencies of medieval culture: its blind faith and over-imitative tendencies, which replaced originality and independent thought.

Marxist critics seek to analyze the economic structure of Spain through Cervantes' works and attempt to deduce the resulting psychology of the people. Lunacharski, in his *History of Western European Literature*, 1924, concluded that Cervantes buried feudalism in an extraordinary way: he regretted the loss of the beautiful qualities of that by-gone age. P.I. Novitski views the *Quijote* as an attack on the aristocracy, as a revelation of the historical limitations and internal contradictions of the times. Derjavin (*Servantes i Don Kikhot*, 1933) seeks to clarify the causes of the internal discord in Spain in Cervantes' era. To Derjavin the *Quijote* is a perfect picture of the decadence of the Spain of the Felipes and its social dislocations and misery, which Spain sought to overcome by means of bureaucratic despotism and religious fanaticism. To Derjavin, also, the paradox of the external grandeur and internal misery of Spain explains the madness of Cervantes' Knight.

Also to be noted are Lunacharski's play *Don Quijote libertado*, 1922, which uses Cervantine material to illustrate aspects of the Russian social revolution, and Chulkov's play *Don Quijote*, 1935, which is anti-aristocratic in tone and centers around the episode in the palace of the *Duques*. The play emphasizes the contrast between the pitiless conduct of the nobility and the dreams of human brotherhood held by the dignified Knight.

393. Schubart, Walter. *Russia and Western Man*. Translated by Amethé von Zeppelin. New York: Frederick Ungar Publishing Co., 1950. Pp. 300. [Original title *Europa und die Seele des Ostens*, Luzern: Vita Nova Verlag, 1938.]

[In Chapter XX the author compares the Spanish and Russian peoples, finding that both have strong oriental tendencies, and that both came in contact with Promethean (Western) culture without being absorbed by it. Schubart further notes that both countries were occupied by foreign, pagan powers (Spain by the Moors, Russia by the Tartars) and that both broke away toward the

end of the fifteenth century. The tendency of both
Russia and Spain to be receptacles of irrational forces
is observed, as is the tendency of both peoples toward
anarchy.

Spaniards, the critic states, are inspired by the
sole reality of God and the dreamlike quality of the
world, and the Spanish epic of *Don Quijote* was a product
of the same dream world as *The Idiot*, which is the most
Russian in character of all Dostoevski's novels. The
Knight and Myshkin, Schubart continues, are both characters whose roots lie in another world; they have lost
all sense of reality and cannot find their way back to
the real world; the one is a buffoon, The Knight of the
Rueful Countenance, whose follies are committed out of
the purest motives; the other is a helpless crank who
makes General Yepantshin's daughters giggle; both are
the antithesis of the successful Northern type of
humanity.]

394. Siler Salinas, Jorge. "Don Quijote en Rusia: De Dosto-
       yevski al cine actual." *Estudios de Comunismo,
       Revista Trimestral* 10 (April-June 1961):8-15.

       Dostoevski's interpretation of the *Quijote* is quite
       different from the Communist viewpoint. The Russian
       author viewed the Knight as essentially a Christian hero.
       Dostoevski's own figure Myshkin is a form of Quijote
       figure, a Christ-like figure, and Radomski is much like
       Cervantes' scoffing figure Sansón Carrasco. The Russian
       film interpretation is the culmination of a long-standing
       Communist viewpoint that regarded Cervantes' masterpiece
       as a reflection of the socio-economic conditions of the
       times, as a book of highest ideals written during the
       worst period of repression in Spain's history. In the
       film, the Don is a lover of liberty, but Sancho is the
       true hero. Most of the action is concentrated at the
       palace of the Duke and Duchess. The chaplain becomes a
       symbol for the Inquisition; Sancho symbolizes the pro-
       letariat; the Knight becomes a saint yearning for and
       predicting a future age of justice.

395. Soler Godes, E. "Cervantes en Rusia." *ABC* (Madrid) 21
       April 1957, pp. 49, 53. [Based on a summary by Alberto
       Sánchez in *Anales Cervantinos* 6 (1957), p. 362. The
       original could not be obtained.]

       [Soler Godes observes that the first Russian transla-
       tion of the *Quijote* was not done until well into the
       eighteenth century, and that this version was an

incomplete one based on a French translation. However,
the critic adds, this Russian translation did inspire
an *opera bufa* by Floridor (Filadar?), *Sancho Panza,
gobernador de la ínsula Barataria.* The first complete
Russian translation of the *Quijote*, Soler Godes continues, was done in 1886, and was based on Spanish as
well as French texts. The early twentieth-century Russian *Quijote* translations of Watson and Basinin are
noted. Soler Godes points out the influence of Cervantes' masterpiece on Gogol's *Dead Souls.* An exhibition
of Cervantes' works by the Lenin Library in Moscow is
discussed.]

396. Turkevich, Ludmilla Buketoff. *Cervantes in Russia.*
      Princeton, N.J.: Princeton University Press, 1950.
      Pp. xv + 255.

      [This work is divided into four parts. The first
      deals with the Pre-Pushkin and Pushkin eras (1763-1850);
      the second with the Age of Realism (1850-1880); the
      third with the era 1880-1903; and the final part with
      the years 1903-1940 ("The Marxists and the Soviet").
      In each chapter the critic studies in detail the trans-
      lations, adaptations, and criticism of Cervantes' works
      during the particular epoch. In Chapter One special
      attention is devoted to the influence of the *Quijote*
      on Pushkin's novel *Eugene Onegin* and his ballad *A Poor
      Knight.* The use by Gogol of Cervantine characterization
      in *Dead Souls* is studied. In the second chapter of her
      work the critic devotes her attention to Dostoevski's
      debt to, and interpretation of, the *Quijote*, especially
      in *Poor Folk*, *The Double*, and *The Idiot.*
      The portions of this work dealing with Russian criti-
      cism of the *Quijote* are most helpful. V. Belinski, in
      1837, found Cervantes' Knight the noblest of men, in
      spite of his comical attributes. Turgenev's philosophi-
      cal essay "Hamlet and Don Quixote" is studied at length,
      as is V. Karelin's "Don Quixotism and Demonism," where
      quixotism is defined as a psychological trait peculiar
      not only to individuals but to social groups at certain
      moments in their political life. Also studied are the
      thoughts of Avseyenko, 1877, who stressed the esthetic,
      as opposed to the ethical, value of the *Quijote*; he em-
      phasized the realism, not the symbolism, of the Knight
      and Squire. The critic N.I. Storozhenko's "The Philo-
      sophy of Don Quixote" is noted, which essay found the
      Knight to be a man out of step with his times. Symbolist
      critics at the end of the nineteenth century are also

examined (for example, Merezhkovski). Of particular
interest is Turkevich's analysis in Chapter IV of com-
munistic and formalistic criticism in Russia. The
Communist P.S. Kogan's "The Tragedy of Idealism,"
1895, is discussed, and it is noted that Kogan sympathized with the Knight but found him more dangerous
than beneficial to the world; P.I. Novitski, another
Communist critic, viewed the *Quijote* as a novel that
struggled against aristocratic culture. Turkevich
states that the Formalist School of Russian critics rejects all extra-literary elements and concludes that
Don Quijote is only an interplay of devices for making
reality seem strange. Shklovski, for example, concludes, in 1921, that Cervantes sensed the effective-
ness of a contrast between foolishness and wisdom, and
proceeded to exploit this duality for his artistic aims,
making Don Quijote a thread on which are strung speeches
on fame, linguistics, arms and letters, speeches for
which the actual motivations are but slight. Shklovski
also discusses the interpolated stories, their types,
and how they are linked. In 1928, P.N. Medvedev of the
Marxist school seeks to refute Shklovski, asserting
that the unity of the *Quijote* is *not* the result of external devices. To Medvedev the hero is the thematic
element as well as the unifying element of the story.

Adaptations of the *Quijote* are noted throughout this
work, from the performance in Moscow in 1785 of the
Italian Filidar's ballet *Sancho Panza* to A.V. Lunacharski's *The Liberated Don Quixote*, 1922, a play used to
depict the social revolution. Several other plays of
the 1920's and 1930's are pointed out.]

397. Turkevich, Ludmilla Buketoff. "Cervantes in Russia."
      In *Cervantes Across the Centuries* ... *A Quadricenten-
      nial Volume Edited by Ángel Flores and M.J. Benardete*,
      pp. 343-371. New York: The Dryden Press, 1947. [1969
      reprint, Gordian Press, pp. 353-381.]

      [This item is a comparatively short forerunner of the
      previous item, containing three parts. The first por-
      tion deals with Russian translations of Cervantes' works
      from the eighteenth to the twentieth century. Part Two
      discusses the literary influence of Cervantes on such
      novelists as Pushkin, Gogol, Turgenev, and Dostoevski,
      and notes the Cervantine influence on certain Russian
      dramatists, such as Lunacharski. The final part of this
      article is concerned with Russian criticism of Cervan-
      tes' works, especially the *Quijote*, since the 1840's.]

398. Turkevich, Ludmilla Buketoff. *Spanish Literature in*
      Russia and in the Soviet Union. Metuchen, N.J.: The
      Scarecrow Press, Inc., 1967. Pp. xi + 273.

      [Pages 32 through 132 (items 209-772) of this excel-
      lent bibliography deal with Cervantes and his works.
      Russian translations of the *Quijote* are listed and
      briefly discussed (items 219-287), as are Russian edi-
      tions of interpolated episodes in the *Quijote* (items
      288-293). A section is devoted to *Don Quijote* on the
      Russian stage and in Russian films (items 294-344). In
      a later section is found critical material concerning
      Cervantes' and his works (items 546-667 dealing with
      the *Quijote*). Also included are the following sections:
      "Foreign Press on Cervantes and Russia" (items 697-733);
      "Cervantes or His Heroes in Belles-Lettres" (items 734-
      745); "Poetry Dedicated to Cervantes and the Image of
      Don Quixote" (items 746-768). In general, the material
      is arranged chronologically under each heading.]

                       Nineteenth-Century Russia

399. Ferrer, Olga Prjevalinsky. "*Las almas muertas* de Gógol
      y *Don Quijote*." *Cuadernos de Literatura* 8 (1950):
      201-214.

      Gogol was most interested in Spain and appears to have
      visited that country in June and July of 1837. He often
      told anecdotes about Spain to his Russian friends, some
      of whom did not believe that he had actually been there.
      In several of his works Gogol refers to Cervantes. For
      example, in *Dead Souls* the Russian describes the charac-
      ter Koskarov as a modern Don Quijote.
         Pushkin advised Gogol to read the *Quijote* and to write
      a novel in its manner. Presumably Pushkin meant a
      long, peripatetic story based on Gogol's travels. The
      work was to be *Dead Souls*. Like the *Quijote*, Gogol's
      novel has a multitude of characters. There is a great
      deal of traveling about; there are many picturesque en-
      counters with unexpected outcomes. The hero of Gogol's
      novel, Chichicov, is, however, not nearly so well des-
      cribed as Cervantes' Don. Nor are the two characters
      at all similar, for the Russian is guided only by greed.
      The characters in *Dead Souls*, like those in the *Quijote*,
      are great talkers. But there is a marked difference in
      the dialog technique of the two writers. Cervantes is
      influenced by the Lucianesque dialog in which there is

an actual interchange of thoughts between characters. Gogol's "dialogs" are more nearly parallel and intertwined monologs, and the characters remain isolated from each other. But both Cervantes and Gogol love people, and the satire in the *Quijote* and in *Dead Souls* is saved by humor. Both writers use a form of irony, a bittersweet irony, which is really the basis of the intrinsic affinity between the two writers. There is one distinction, however, in the technical use of irony by the two novelists. Cervantes is, generally speaking, ironic only toward his two protagonists, and the personalities of other characters are not usually described in detail. Gogol, however, does not describe his central figure well, but examines many other characters and deals with them ironically.

400. Ferrer, Olga Prjevalinsky. "Un Cide Hamete Benengeli ruso." In *Homenaje a Rodríguez-Moñino: estudios de erudición que le ofrecen sus amigos o discípulos hispanistas norteamericanos.* Vol. 1, pp. 173–188. Madrid: Editorial Castalia, 1966.

[This article deals largely with the Russian writer K.K. Sluchevsky, 1837–1904, who wrote "Un capítulo del *Quijote* recientemente descubierto." In this episode, Ferrer points out, Sancho is the real hero, and is a figure who seems genuinely both Spanish and Russian. The critic examines previous attempts to Russianize Sancho and notes that Catherine II ordered Sancho's proverbs copied down. Ferrer briefly discusses two plays based on the *Quijote* by N.N. Sandunov, 1768–1832, one play dealing with Sancho's government of Barataria.]

401. Giusti, Wolfgango. "Sul 'donchisciottismo' di alcuni personaggi del Dostojevskij." *Cultura* 10 (February 1931):171–179.

[Giusti begins by noting various highly favorable references by Dostoevski to the *Quijote*: in a letter dated January 1, 1868; in *The Diary of a Writer*; and in *The Idiot*. As for the so-called *quijotismo* of certain of Dostoevski's characters, the critic cautions the reader that one must distinguish between the direct influence of Cervantes' novel and the inherent tendency of the great Russian novelist to create a new type of antihero. Giusti finds that Djevushkin (*Poor Folk*) and Golyadkin (*The Double*), while they have certain traits in common with Cervantes' Knight, are actually too pitiful

to be truly quixotic. Myshkin (*The Idiot*), however, is
said to be more similar to the Knight, though Myshkin
is more humble.
The critic notes the influence of E.T.A. Hoffmann on
Dostoevski's characters. Giusti also discusses the possible influence of Turgenev's essay *Hamlet and Don
Quixote* on the change of Dostoevski's characters from
weakhearted figures into humanly complete ones like
Myshkin.]

402. Khatchadourian, Haig. "*Dead Souls* & *Don Quixote*: A
      Comparative Sketch." *Visvabharati Quarterly* 26 (1961):
      8-20.

Both Cervantes' *Quijote* and Gogol's *Dead Souls* have
a picaresque atmosphere. The heroes in each work, the
Knight and Tchitchikov, travel widely, and this traveling reflects the restlessness of spirit and unceasing
quest in both novels. But there is a great difference
between the quest and the motives of each hero. Tchitchikov is materialistic; Don Quijote has lofty ideals,
in spite of his weakness for glory. Tchitchikov surren-
ders to the world of the senses, while the Knight believes that the apparent world is an illusion and that
his vision is reality.
Cervantes looks upon his hero's ideal with some irony,
but sees that the ideal was an historical reality. This
is not true in Gogol's novel. Here the ideal is not of
the past, least of all of the present; it is only of the
future. Gogol planned to purify Tchitchikov in Part II
of *Dead Souls* and redeem him in Part III. This was never
accomplished. Therefore, the extant portion of Gogol's
work remains a powerful portrayal of a dark reality, un-
illuminated except faintly by the light of an ideal.
Don Quijote is a tragic figure in the classical sense,
and his "fall" on his deathbed is tragic. Tchitchikov
is *not* a tragic figure and could never be one; he is
mediocre even when he falls; he has no zeal even for
evil. Tchitchikov is more like Sancho, but he lacks the
Squire's drollery and simplemindedness.
The Don's plight is deeper than Tchitchikov's, and
we feel it more deeply because it is humanity's plight
and tragedy in finding itself enslaved by poor reality.
Tchitchikov's plight lies in not knowing that there is
a contrast between the ideal and what he considers real.
That is why he is a dead soul and does not know it.
Both *Don Quijote* and *Dead Souls*, like the *Odyssey*,
are books that present "the whole truth," as Aldous

Huxley would say, not merely the tragic. As we read
these works we laugh and feel sad at the same time. The
lyric and the matter-of-fact are juxtaposed, giving a
more rounded picture of life.

403. Maldonado de Guevara, Francisco. "Cervantes y Dostoyev-
      ski." *Revista de Ideas Estéticas* 6 (1948):123-136.

      [This article does *not* study the possible influence
      of Cervantes' Knight on other abnormal figures such as
      Shakespeare's Hamlet, Goethe's Faust, or Dostoevski's
      Raskolnikov (*Crime and Punishment*). Instead these fig-
      ures are merely compared and contrasted, and Maldonado
      concludes that the Don lacks the curiosity and demonic
      characteristics of Hamlet and Faust. The Knight's arro-
      gance is said to be angelic in its mercy. Comparing and
      contrasting Don Quijote and Raskolnikov, Maldonado points
      out that both are superindividuals and that both feel
      superior to kings and judges. But, continues the critic,
      Raskolnikov lacks the Knight's Christianity and moral
      humanism. At the end, Maldonado states, the Don returns
      to sanity; he matures though he retains a childlike
      simplicity.]

404. Maldonado de Guevara, F. "Dostoievski y el *Quijote*."
      Anales Cervantinos 3 (1953):367-375.

      Dostoevski, in 1877, maintained that Don Quijote sought
      to rationalize magic, but the Russian writer was not
      correct. The Knight never questioned magic until his
      renunciation just before death. Possibly Dostoevski
      interprets magic in the *Quijote* through magic in *Faust*,
      but this is a false approach. The enchanters are pur-
      suing Don Quijote; they are on the hero's side in *Faust*.
      In reality, it is not the Don but Cervantes who thinks
      like Dostoevski.

405. Malkiel, Yakov. "Cervantes in Nineteenth-Century Rus-
      sia." *Comparative Literature* 3 (Fall 1951):310-329.

      Only for a few decades did Russia's best artists have
      an opportunity to understand Cervantes' secret. While
      Pushkin, Gogol, Turgenev, and Dostoevski were, to an
      extent, affected by the Spaniard, Cervantes is not Push-
      kin's sole, or even main, source of inspiration. The
      Spaniard's principal influence on Gogol was in motifs
      and techniques rather than in characters and ideas; and
      Dostoevski produced "quixotic" characters *before* he was
      acquainted with the writings of Cervantes. All in all,

the influence of the author of the *Quijote* has at no
time been overly great in Russia.

406. Marrero, Vicente. "*El Idiota*, Don Quijote y Cristo."
     Índice de Artes y Letras 12 (February 1958):4.

     [Marrero discusses Dostoevski's letter to his niece
     Sofia, dated January 1, 1868, concerning the difficul-
     ties in writing *The Idiot*, a work in which the central
     idea is the presentation of a noble and positive man.
     Dostoevski, states Marrero, found that the spirit of
     Christ was best represented in Western literature by
     Don Quijote, and to a lesser extent by Dickens' Pick-
     wick.
         Marrero also observes that Dostoevski discussed the
     Quijote in his *Diary of a Writer*, where he referred to
     it as sublime, as the highest expression of human
     thought, yet the bitterest irony which man could formu-
     late. The critic compares and contrasts Myshkin and
     the Knight, and notes that the former is meek while the
     latter is aggressive; yet neither can adjust to society.
     Marrero finds that both the *Quijote* and *The Idiot* have
     a disconcerting ambiguity about them. The critic ad-
     mits that Myshkin and the Don have a certain superficial
     resemblance to Christ. Marrero, however, does not fol-
     low those who would make them Christ figures, for Christ
     was neither ridiculous nor insane nor idiotic; his hu-
     manity was perfect and he had a superhuman side, lacking
     in Prince Myshkin and the Knight, who are incomplete
     beings.]

407. Montero Díaz, Santiago. "Cervantes en Turguénief y
     Dostoyewski." *Cervantes, compañero eterno*, pp. 21-28.
     Madrid: Aramo, 1957. [See also *Estudios* (Santiago de
     Chile), no. 173 (June 1947), pp. 3-27.]

     [Montero Díaz disagrees with Turgenev's assertion
     that Don Quijote and Hamlet are poles apart, since,
     states Montero, Hamlet was capable of action and Don
     Quijote was at times melancholy. The critic contrasts
     the reaction of Cervantes toward suffering with the re-
     action of Dostoevski, finding that Cervantes reacted
     with dignity while the Russian did not. After examining
     Dostoevski's figure Myshkin in *The Idiot* Montero con-
     cludes that he is not at all like Don Quijote.]

408. Portnoff, George. "Cervantes and Dostoyevsky." *Modern
     Language Forum* 19 (1934):80-86.

Cervantes does not seek evil in the human heart. All
his characters are good, and his art is human in essence
and form. In Dostoevski's art, on the other hand, the
cruel, the tragic, the mysterious hold first place,
even though it aspires in essence to the ideal. To
understand the *Quijote* is to understand life itself; to
understand Dostoevski fundamentally is to understand
the intrinsic nature of a sick, complex soul.

Prince Myshkin, the chief character of *The Idiot*,
was inspired by Cervantes' Don. Dostoevski's hero has
inherited the spirit, the illusion, and the inner faith
of the Knight of La Mancha. Aglaia, who falls in love
with the prince, clearly sees the quixotic nature of
Myshkin. He is an undoer of wrongs and is unconscious
of danger. His platonic love affairs are like the love
of Don Quijote for Dulcinea. Myshkin, like the Knight,
is a reformer. His dream of regenerating Russia is as
noble as the Don's ideal of restoring chivalry. What
the Idiot bears within himself of the eternal of Don
Quijote is purity and inner faith, thanks to which he
lives according to his truth, as did Don Quijote.

409. Selig, Karl-Ludwig. "Cervantes and Dostoyevski: Some
      Observations on *The Idiot*." *Arcadia* 1 (1966):312-318.

      Dostoevski read the *Quijote* and was profoundly influ-
      enced by it. He refers to Cervantes' masterpiece both
      in *The Idiot* and in his *Diary*. Dostoevski also read
      Turgenev's essay "Hamlet and Don Quixote," 1860, and,
      in general, agreed with Turgenev's interpretation. There
      are many similarities between Dostoevski's Prince Mysh-
      kin (the Idiot) and Don Quijote: both are innocent,
      chivalrous, impractical, comical, charitable, generous,
      discreet, sincere, and simple-hearted with a touch of
      the absurd. Both figures have excess imagination and
      fantastic inclinations. Dostoevski uses Pushkin's poem
      The Poor Knight as a starting point for an interpreta-
      tion of the figure Myshkin, as a blend of Christ and
      Don Quijote.

410. Serrano Plaja, Arturo. *Realismo "mágico" en Cervantes;
      Don Quijote visto desde "Tom Sawyer" y "El idiota."* Ma-
      drid: Editorial Gredos, 1967. Pp. 236. [Translated
      into English as *"Magic" Realism in Cervantes; Don
      Quijote as Seen Through "Tom Sawyer" and "The Idiot."*
      Berkeley, Los Angeles, and London: University of
      California Press, 1970. Pp. 216.]

[Serrano Plaja considers the Don *not* as insane but as
merely a play-actor, like Tom Sawyer. The critic notes
that neither Cervantes' Knight, nor Twain's Tom Sawyer,
nor Dostoevski's Myshkin (the Idiot) have an immediate
family and that there are thus no outside restraints on
these protagonists; all three are infants and have a
quest for justice on the fringe of the law.]

411. Serrano Poncela, Segundo. "Don Quijote en Dostoievski."
      Insula 23 (1968):19-20.

The first influence of the *Quijote* on Russian literature was on Pushkin's *The Poor Knight*, a poem that was
later used by Dostoevski in *The Idiot*. The hero of
that novel, Myshkin, has quixotic characteristics which,
while secondary, are significant. He also has something of Hugo's Jean Valjean and something of Christ.
Both Myshkin and Don Quijote clash with reality, but
Dostoevski's hero realizes his lack of common sense and
knows how to make fun of himself. Don Quijote does not.
    Stefan Trofimovich Verjonevski, the protagonist in
Dostoevski's *The Possessed*, is also a quixotic figure,
a supreme liberal, vain and candid, a utopian. He flees
from reality in a search for beauty, and at the end
abandons liberalism for Christianity.
    On two occasions in his *Diary* Dostoevski praised the
Quijote, in one instance as the highest expression of
human thought and the bitterest of ironies. On the
other occasion he compared the Russian people to the
Knight of La Mancha. In an article, "La mentira se
salva por la mentira," Dostoevski discussed self-decep-
tion and its existential value in a way that is similar
to Unamuno's later approach to the *Quijote*.

Twentieth-Century Russia

412. Arconada, César M. "Cervantes en Moscú." *Revista de
      Revistas*, 12 October 1947, pp. 22-23.

[Arconada tells of entering Parnassus and speaking
with Cervantes. Together they visit Moscow. The critic
notes Russian radio and theatrical adaptations of the
Quijote, and pictures Cervantes praising Russia as a
place where arms and letters are not in conflict, but
serve one another harmoniously.]

413.   Claver, José María. "Don Quijote en el país de las
       maravillas." *Diario de Yucatán*, 6 December 1947.
       [This item could not be located. For a brief sum-
       mary, see Rafael Heliodoro Valle and Emilia Romero,
       Bibliografía cervantina en la América española (425),
       p. 66.]

       [This article deals with the Russian interpretation
       of the *Quijote*, especially by Lunacharski in his *Don
       Quijote libertado*. The critic finds that Lunacharski
       turns the Knight into something of a scarecrow.]

414.   Núñez y Domínguez, Roberto. "Lunacharsky y Don Quijote."
       Revista de Revistas, 18 February 1934; *Repertorio
       Americano* 7 April 1934, p. 208. [Based on a summary
       by Rafael Heliodoro Valle and Emilia Romero in *Biblio-
       grafía cervantina en la América española* (425), p.
       193. This item could not be obtained.]

       [Núñez y Domínguez finds that Lunacharsky's *Don Qui-
       jote libertado* was written to impress the masses and
       has a tendency to defend the politics of violence of
       the Bolsheviks.]

415.   Richie, Donald. "Don Quijote, Russian Style." *His-
       pania* 41 (September 1958):388. [From *The Japan Times*,
       14 November 1957.]

       [Richie approves of certain structural changes made
       in the Russian film of *Don Quijote*: moving the windmill
       episode to the end, thus making this scene the climax,
       and having the galley slave adventure take place during
       the Knight's final homeward journey. However, the cri-
       tic severely condemns the doctrinaire-minded Soviet film-
       makers. Particularly resented is the blowing up of the
       wineskin episode into a "tedious and tasteless five-
       minute sequence." Richie also criticizes the Russian
       version of the adventure of the lions in which the Don
       is forced by the *Duques* to challenge the lion rather
       than act of his own free will.]

416.   Tijan, Pablo. "*Don Quijote* para la juventud rusa."
       Revista de Literatura 8 (October-December 1955):313-
       318.

       [Tijan discusses a 1952 shortened edition of Ljubimov's
       translation of the *Quijote*. The critic observes that
       this edition was designed for high school students. He
       takes note of the portions expurgated (such as the Mari-
       tornes bedroom scene and the interpolated episodes).

Detailed attention is devoted to Konstantin Derzhavin's
introduction to this edition, which introduction praises
the universal value of the *Quijote*, describes the life
of the Spanish masses, and discusses Cervantes' realism,
his sympathy for the humble, and his protest against
the wealthy and the grandees. Derzhavin, notes Tijan,
also points out both the ridiculous and the noble side
of the Knight's personality, and pictures Sancho Panza
as a man who gives up his egoism and acquires a higher
sense of justice.]

417. Turkevich, Ludmilla Buketoff. "N. Lyubimov's tr. from
the Spanish [of *Don Quijote*]." *Hispania* 39 (September 1956):384-385.

The influence of the *Quijote* on Russian literature has
been the profound type of influence: the philosophy, the
tragic irony, the essential qualities of the heroes.
Therefore, it is not surprising, in spite of the low
state of Hispanic scholarship in Russia today, that the
350th anniversary of the *Quijote* was marked by the publication of a new Russian edition of Cervantes' masterpiece. This latest Russian rendering, by N. Lyubimov,
is excellent. The poetry in the novel is well translated by M.N. Luzinsky, and the illustrations are extremely good. An exhibition was also held to honor the
Quijote, and the 1605 Valencian edition was on display,
along with numerous other editions. Illustrations by
Coypel, Doré, Johannot, and Chodowiecki were also to be
seen. The Soviet press claims fifty editions of the
Quijote during the Soviet era, in the fourteen languages
of the U.S.S.R., with total issues exceeding one mil-
lion copies.

418. Turkevich, Ludmilla Buketoff. "Status of Spanish Studies in the Soviet Union." *Hispania* 41 (December
1958):485-490.

The recent deaths of B.A. Krzhevsky and U.S. Uzin cut
deeply into the sparse ranks of Spanish scholars in the
U.S.S.R. In the 1870's Storozhenko taught the masterpieces of the *Siglo de oro* at Moscow University, and at
the turn of the century L. Shepelevich carried Spanish
literature to the University of Kharkhov where he devoted a great deal of attention to Cervantes. World War
I set Hispanic studies back considerably, and in the
1920's scholars, out of hunger, were forced into other
jobs. In the 1920's and the 1930's only a small number
of zealots were left; private and university libraries

were in poor condition and often out of date. Neverthe-
less, this era saw a series of fine translations of
Spanish classics, including the 1929 translation of the
Quijote by Krzhevsky and Smirnov.

   World War II interrupted the work of Spanish scholars
who were living in Russia, and the post-war period has
been so utilitarian that there is little room for the
finer things, such as research in Spanish literature.
Currently, courses on Spanish literature at any level
are practically non-existent, and there is little like-
lihood of change, since replacements for the few aging
professors of Spanish are not being trained.

VIII. *DON QUIJOTE* IN LATIN AMERICA

General
(*See also* item 5)

419. Carilla, Emilio. *Cervantes y América*. Buenos Aires:
Impr. de la Universidad, 1951. Pp. 70.

[Various Latin American adaptations of the *Quijote*
are noted in Chapter I: *Semblanzas caballerescas o las
nuevas aventuras de Don Quijote*, by Luis Otero Pimentel,
1861, a story set in a Cuban environment; a rare work,
Don Quijote en América, 1905, by the Venezuelan writer
Tulio Febres Cordero, which attacks the foreign influence on Latin American literature; the drama *Miguel de
Cervantes*, 1849, by José Caicedo Rojas; poems by José
Asunción Silva ("Futura" and "La razón de Don Quijote")
and by Ricardo Nieto ("¡Oh Sancho!"); José Joaquín Fernández de Lizardi's *La Quijotita y su prima*, written in
the early nineteenth century; Heriberto Frías' *El triunfo de Sancho*; several works by Manuel José Othón, including a one-act play, *El último capítulo*; Rubén Darío's
Letanías de Nuestro Señor Don Quijote; and Alberto Gerchunoff's *Jofaina maravillosa*.
The second chapter of Carilla's study is devoted to
an examination of Juan Montalvo's *Capítulos que se le
olvidaron a Cervantes*, published in 1895. Carilla
states that the Ecuadorian Montalvo joins polemic ar-
dor with a passion for language and a cult of Cervantes
in an attack on the tyrants of Ecuador.
The third chapter is devoted to Juan Bautista Alberdi's
work, *La peregrinación de luz del día*, finished in 1871,
which is a satire of the political situation in America,
especially of Argentina and its ruler Sarmiento.
The fourth chapter discusses Rubén Darío's *Letanías
de Nuestro Señor Don Quijote* and examines the general
tendency to deify the Don, which tendency began in the

Romantic epoch and has maintained itself sporadically
in commentators of very diverse origin and tendencies.
Carilla points out other writers who deify Cervantes'
Knight: Emilio Becher, Dostoevski, Unamuno, Evaristo
Carriego, José Enrique Rodó, and Alberto Gerchunoff.]

420. Rodríguez Marín, Francisco. "El *Quijote* y Don Quijote
      en América." *Estudios cervantinos*, pp. 93-137. Ma-
      drid: Patronato del IV Centenario de Cervantes, 1947.
      [Conferencias leídas en el Centro de Cultura Hispano-
      Americana en los días 10 y 17 de Marzo de 1911.]

      [This work begins with a discussion of the shipment
      of copies of the *Quijote* to America. Rodríguez Marín
      states that the records of the Archivo General de Indias
      reveal that in 1605 at least 346 copies of Cervantes'
      masterpiece were shipped to America. The critic be-
      lieves that almost all the *príncipe* edition went to the
      New World. Rodríguez Marín also discusses the general
      popularity of the *Quijote* and points out an early Spanish
      adaptation, *Los invencibles hechos de Don Quijote de la
      Mancha*, 1617, by Francisco de Avila. Celebrations in
      which the figure Don Quijote appeared are described,
      and particular attention is devoted to a fiesta at
      Paussa, Peru, in 1607.]

421. Torres-Ríoseco, Arturo. *Grandes novelistas de la
      América Hispana*. Vol. 1: *Los novelistas de la tierra*.
      Berkeley and Los Angeles: University of California
      Press, 1941. Pp. ix + 280.

      [The critic notes (pp. 54 and 57) several similarities
      between Rómulo Gallegos' *Doña Barbara* and the *Quijote*:
      the simple, clear, national, robust style; the frequent
      use of idiomatic expressions; the multiple symbolical
      possibilities (idealism-materialism, civilization-
      barbarity).
      Later (pp. 99-100) Torres-Ríoseco finds a kinship be-
      tween Ricardo Güiraldes' *Don Segundo Sombra* and Cervan-
      tes' masterpiece. The critic considers Güiraldes' story
      a return to the classical Spanish novel, in which the
      characters are more important than the episodes, and in
      which the protagonists acquire a separate existence
      which is developed in exterior form in their adventures.
      To Torres-Ríoseco both works contain adventures which
      are separate from one another, and there is lacking the
      true linkage of a sustained and systematic intrigue.
      The use by both authors of the complementary-character
      technique is also noted. The critic further observes

that both Don Quijote and Don Segundo Sombra are knights
who feel the call of the road, who hate idleness, who
are confident in their own strength. Torres-Ríoseco
also compares the pranks of the "muchacho" in Güiraldes'
novel to the rascalities of Lazarillo and Sancho Panza,
and concludes that Güiraldes must have had the *Quijote*
and *Lazarillo de Tormes* in mind when he composed *Don
Segundo Sombra*.

Analogies between Carlos Reyles' *El Terruño* and the
Quijote are discussed (p. 204). The critic finds that
Reyles' character Tocles has a bit of the Knight in him,
and that the utilitarian and prosaic Mamagela is a good
bit like the Squire. Torres-Ríoseco finds traces of the
Quijote in several episodes of *El Terruño*: the discourses
of Mamagela surrounded by sheep, the successful lance
attack by Papagoyo, the slaughter of sheep by Primitivo.]

422. Uribe-Echevarría, Juan. *Cervantes en las letras his-
    pano-americanas, antología y crítica*. Santiago de
    Chile: Edit. Universitaria, 1949. Pp. 231.

[Uribe-Echevarría examines in great detail the possible influence of Cervantes on such writers as José
Joaquín Fernández de Lizardi, Antonio José de Irisarri,
Juan Bautista Alberdi, Daniel Barros Grez, Emilio G.
Quintanilla, Juan Montalvo, Egidio Poblete, Juan Francisco Bedregal, Carlos Bolívar Sevilla, Julián Motta
Salas, and Jorge Luis Borges. The critic compares
the *Quijote* to José Hernández' *Martín Fierro* and notes
that the heroes in both works fight against a materialistic, non-heroic society. Cervantes' masterpiece is
compared with Ricardo Güiraldes' *Don Segundo Sombra*. Uribe-Echevarría also points out theatrical adaptations of the *Quijote* by Hispano-Americans, for example, Ventura de la Vega's *Don Quijote en Sierra Morena*,
1832, Antonio de Sojo's *Don Quijote en Buenos Aires*,
1885, Leopoldo Lugones' "Dos ilustres lunáticos o divergencia sentimental," Leonardo Eliz' *Apoteosis de Cervantes en el Parnaso*, 1916, and Horacio H. Dobranich's
Don Quijote de la Mancha.

Verses dedicated to Don Quijote, Sancho, and Cervantes
are studied, including those of Esteban Tarralla y
Landa, Ventura de la Vega, Amenodoro Urdaneta, Rubén
Darío, Luis Fors, and Ricardo Palma.

The chapter "Cervantes y el pensamiento hispano-
americano" is a lengthy chapter devoted to Spanish American critics and interpreters of Cervantes' works.]

423. Valle, Rafael Heliodoro. "Cervantes en las letras de
      Hispano-américa." *Memorias de la Academia Mexicana*
      12 (1955):43-51.

      [Valle briefly mentions the possible influence of the
      Curious Impertinent on Juan Ruiz de Alarcón's *El seme-
      jante a sí mismo*. The critic also notes several Latin
      American works based on the *Quijote*, including *La
      Quijotita y su prima* by José Joaquín Fernández de Li-
      zardi. Critical works on Cervantes by Latin Americans
      are pointed out, including Pablo Moreno's *Algunas ob-
      servaciones críticas sobre Don Quijote*, 1841. Valle
      discusses other disciples of Cervantes, including Al-
      berto Gerchunoff, Augusto D'Halmar, and José Enrique
      Rodó. Poems dedicated to Don Quijote are briefly
      examined, and Rubén Darío's *Letanías de Nuestro Señor
      Don Quijote* is particularly praised. The critic lists
      several plays based on the *Quijote*: a zarzuela, *Don
      Quijote en la venta encantada*, 1871, by A. García and
      Miguel Planas; Manuel José Othón's *El último capítulo*,
      1905; and Jesús Urueta's tragedy *Dulcinea*, 1905.]

424. Valle, Rafael Heliodoro. "Cervantes en la América es-
      pañola." *Cuadernos Hispanoamericanos*, no. 93 (Septem-
      ber 1957), pp. 369-381.

      [Valle tells of the arrival of the *Quijote* in the New
      World in 1605. He also notes Cervantes' allusions to
      America and things American. The critic discusses the
      possible influence of the *Curious Impertinent* on the
      Mexican Juan Ruiz de Alarcón's *El semejante a sí mismo*.
      Definitely affected by the *Quijote*, states the critic,
      are José Ignacio Bartoloche's *El mercurio volante*, Li-
      zardi's *La Quijotita y su prima*, and Francisco Meseguer's
      dialog between Sancho and Bonaparte, written in Spain
      and reproduced in Mexico in 1809. Valle finds an in-
      fluence of the style of the *Quijote* on the following
      works: *El cristiano errante* (Antonio José de Irisarri,
      1847); *Peregrinación de luz del día* (Juan Bautista Al-
      berdi, 1871); and *Capítulos que se le olvidaron a Cer-
      vantes* (Juan Montalvo). The critic next lists various
      Latin-American *cervantistas* and also notes poets who
      were enamored of Cervantes. Valle points out two zar-
      zuelas based on the *Quijote* or on Cervantes' life, a
      tragedy, *Dulcinea* (Jesús Urueta, 1905), and a drama,
      El último capítulo (Manuel José Othón, 1905). Cervantes
      celebrations and *Quijote* editions and collections are
      briefly noted.]

425. Valle, Rafael Heliodoro, and Romero, Emilia. *Biblio-grafía cervantina en la América española.* México: Imp. Universitaria, 1950. Pp. 313.

[This helpful work lists, and often briefly summarizes, books and articles printed in Latin America on the sub-ject of Cervantes and his literary productions. Editions of the *Quijote* and other of Cervantes' *obras* done in Latin America are pointed out.]

Argentina

426. Azorín [Martínez Ruiz, José]. "Cervantes y Hernández." *Obras completas.* Vol. 5, pp. 884–888. Madrid: Agui-lar, 1960. [From *En torno a José Hernández*, Buenos Aires: Edit. Sudamericana, 1939.]

Both Miguel de Cervantes and José Hernández thought that they were writing works of social utility. For-tunately both were wrong. These two writers also pro-duced a second part to their masterpiece, in which sec-ond part sorrow is more obvious than in the first. Early readers considered both the *Quijote* and *Martín Fierro* to be festive in nature. Only later did the public come to regard them as basically melancholy. Time in both stories is marked by departures and arri-vals. How great are the departure scenes in both works! There is also a basic similarity between the heroes of the two masterpieces: neither is a person who can remain still.

427. Carilla, Emilio. "Cervantes y la crítica argentina." *Cuadernos Hispanoamericanos* 8 (September–October 1951):197–208.

[Carilla begins by criticizing Adolfo Saldías' *Cervan-tes y el Quijote*, 1893, which treated the *Quijote* as primarily a political work written to combat absolutism. Saldías regarded the Knight as a symbol of the conserva-tive aristocracy and Sancho as pure democracy. Luis R. Fors' *Criptografía quijotesca*, 1905, is dis-cussed, as is his *Vida de Cervantes*, 1904, and Ricardo Monner Sans' works (*Ensayo de antología* and *Valor docente del Quijote*) are briefly dealt with. More attention is devoted to Paul Groussac and his dispute with Menéndez y Pelayo in regard to the identity of the

true author of the 1614 spurious *Quijote*. (Groussac
also adopted the theory that the 1605 *Quijote* was originally a *novela ejemplar* and that Cervantes was uncertain
of his goal while writing the 1605 *Quijote*.)

Ricardo Rojas' studies on Cervantes are examined, and
Carilla finds that Rojas, in his *Cervantes*, 1935, gives
too much importance to the biographical elements in Cervantes' life, and that he is too critical of Cervantes'
language. Several works by Arturo Marasso are noted,
as well as studies by Jorge Luis Borges, Carlos Alberto
Leumann, José Gabriel, Ángel J. Battitessa, and Juan
Millé y Giménez. Carilla devotes some attention to Arturo Giménez Pastor's *El mundo de Don Quijote*, 1927.]

428. Carilla, Emilio. "Cervantes en la Argentina." *Revista
      de Educación* 3 (1958):471-492.

[This article is dedicated almost entirely to nineteenth-century Argentine criticism and adaptations of
the *Quijote*. Carilla notes an article dated December 27,
1801, in *El telégrafo mercantil* regarding the Canon of
Toledo's discussion of the Spanish drama. Note is also
taken of the traditionalist Padre Castañeda, who used
passages in the *Quijote* in his attacks on Rousseau and
Voltaire. Carilla also points out José Echeverría's
comments on Cervantes' style: "festivo, agudo y verboso,"
and notes Sarmiento's observations on Cervantes' language and thought. Attention is devoted to Juan Bautista
Alberdi's *Peregrinación de luz del día*, in which the
Knight and Squire appear. Carilla also discusses the
Generation of 1880, and briefly notes allusions to the
Quijote by Eduardo Wilde, Santiago Calzadilla, and Rafael Obligado. More attention is devoted to José
Manuel Estrada's "El *Quijote* y el quijotismo," a discussion concerning talent divorced from common sense,
and to Eduardo Sojo's play *Don Quijote en Buenos Aires*,
in which appear a pallid Don Quijote and Sancho Panza.]

429. Coll, Edna. "Aspectos cervantinos en Julio Cortázar."
      Revista Hispánica Moderna 34 (1968):596-604.

Cervantes' *Quijote* initiated the modern novel, while
the Argentine Cortázar's *Rayuela* seeks to begin the
novel of the future. Both writers attempt to renovate
fiction. Both works contain the literary currents of
their respective eras, from the crudest to the most ex-
quisite. Both Cervantes and Cortázar present confused
worlds; both mingle poetry and music in their prose.
Cervantes and Cortázar mock pseudo-writers of bad taste

who use high-sounding words. Both condemn the common
reader, *el vulgo*. The author of the *Quijote* and the
author of *Rayuela* laugh in the midst of the most tragic
and pathetic moments. Both deal with multiple perspectives in that each character clings to his own truth.
To both writers, the authentic reality is always the
world of the diverse and the contrary. In both novels
life is a tenacious process in progress, which causes
characters to become formed and unformed.

Both writers take advantage of life's contradictions
to conceive their works with a plan of antithesis, where
opposites are harmonized and extremes are brought into
balance: poetry and reality; madness and bravery; the
world of fiction and the world of the abstract. Furthermore, in both novels the double truth of faith and reason is found, and in both works the seriousness of certain scenes is covered over by comicness.

Both Cervantes' Don and Cortázar's Horacio fail; each
discovers that he does not have the liberty which he
yearned for. Love is a central theme in *Rayuela* and
the *Quijote*, love at all its levels. Both heroes create
their own amorous ideal in order to possess it; both are
Platonic and will only surrender to perfection. In
spite of the fact that there are many factors which
separate Cervantes and Cortázar, since each reflects a
different epoch, still there is a definite kinship between the two writers.

[Coll also compares the descent of Don Quijote into
the cave of Montesinos to Horacio's descent into the
Morgue: both heroes live their poetic truth in an under-
ground world; both have a crisis and an awakening.]

430. Díaz-Plaja, Guillermo. *Don Quijote y el país de Martín
     Fierro*. Madrid: Ediciones Cultura Hispánica, 1952.
     Pp. 186.

Argentine *Cervantismo* has three epochs: (1) the colon-
ial; (2) the period of independence, in which writers
sought to avoid Spanish models; and (3) the return to
Spanish values of universal dimension.

The founding fathers of Argentina's independence ob-
jected to Spanish literature in general, but not to Cervantes, whom they regarded as a liberal. Juan Bautista
Alberdi praised Cervantes' language and even used the
Don as a character in his curious work *Peregrinación de
luz del día*. Bartolomé Mitre, about 1837, praised the
harmony of Cervantes' sentences and emphasized the importance of *quijotismo* in the human soul. Domingo

Faustino Sarmiento, author of *Facundo*, recommended that
the *Quijote* be placed on the list of books which could
serve as a popular library. Sarmiento considered the
Quijote to be a didactic work. He further believed that
Cervantes wrote during the peak of the Spanish language,
and that later the Spanish tongue dried up and became
mummified in Cervantes' honor.

Among the Romanticists, Ventura de la Vega (born in
Argentina) used Cervantes as a character in his play
Los dos camaradas, 1861. He also wrote a play entitled
Don Quijote en Sierra Morena and certain *décimas* dedi-
cated to Cervantes.

The post-Romanticist Rafael Obligado wrote a poem entitled *El alma de Don Quijote*, 1905. In 1926 appeared
the curious fictional work of Carlos Bosque called *Don
Quijote en Sudamérica*, which deals with the supposed
arrival of the first copy of the *Quijote* in Argentina
in 1612. José Hernández was influenced by Cervantes'
masterpiece, and *Martín Fierro* has often been compared
to the *Quijote*.

Though Leopoldo Lugones was not greatly influenced
by Cervantes, he did, in 1918, present a dramatic work
in which Don Quijote and Hamlet speak to one another
(*Dos ilustres lunáticos o divergencia sentimental*), and
also wrote a work entitled *El triunfo de Don Quijote*.
Here Lugones concludes that the Knight lived and died as
he desired; he died when he should have, when he had
done all that he had set out to do.

Arturo Giménez Pastor, in 1916, presented poems to
the Don and his Squire in his *Convocatoria a la apoteosis de Cervantes*. In 1927, in his "El mundo de Don
Quijote," he contrasts the Don with Ariosto's Orlando.

[Díaz-Plaja notes numerous other works on Cervantes
by writers from Argentina. For example, he points out
Adolfo Saldías' *Cervantes y el Quijote*, 1893, which regarded Cervantes' novel as a hidden attack on the aristocracy of the author's time and as a work of democra-
tic exaltation. Díaz-Plaja also discusses Eleutoria F.
Tiscornia's *Representación ideal del Quijote*, 1916, and
finds that work to be an important forerunner of Américo
Castro's *El pensamiento de Cervantes* in that it seeks
to depict Cervantes' renaissance ideas and his cultural
outlook. The critic further observes that Tiscornia,
like Castro later, rejects the idea that Cervantes was
an uncultivated writer, an "ingenio lego."]

431. Gates, Eunice Joiner. "A Note on the Resemblances Be-
      tween *Don Segundo Sombra* and *Don Quijote*." *Hispanic
      Review* 14 (October 1946):342-343.

Dr. Arturo Torres-Ríoseco (421) has noted general similarities between Güiraldes' *Don Segundo Sombra* and Cervantes' *Don Quijote*, namely that both works were hardly more than a series of episodes. But other similarities between these masterpieces may be noted: both stories contain great philosophical truths throughout, particularly on the subject of personal liberty; both works are rich in proverbs; the heroes in both novels are symbolical and represent rugged individualism; and Güiraldes' episode of the *seco* and *arrugado* Don Sixto Gaitán's hallucination bears a sharp resemblance to the Knight's dream adventure with the wineskins.

432. Ross, Waldo. "Don Quijote y los símbolos estructurales del *Martín Fierro.*" *Cuadernos Hispanoamericanos* 78 (May 1969):502-512.

Cervantes' Don Quijote and José Hernández' Martín Fierro are both strugglers in conflict with the reality which surrounds them. Yet there is a great difference between them. The Don struggles to impose his ideals. Martín has few ideals; he merely wishes to protect gauchos, not to undo wrongs; he does not consider himself the arm of God like Don Quijote; Martín Fierro does not have the Knight's moral glow.

Don Quijote's life unfolds in a harmonious circular movement; he goes out and returns to the same place. Martín Fierro describes an enormous parabola. At the end of the Knight's career he dies; Martín disappears. The Don is a tree that dies; Martín Fierro is a seed that, dragged along by the wind of destiny, struggles desperately to cling to the land.

Don Quijote reveals to us the function of one of his archetypes, Dulcinea, his own *anima*; she allows him to die serenely. Martín Fierro's spiritual activity is almost non-existent.

Brazil

433. Macedo Soares, José Carlos. "Cervantes en el Brasil." *Boletín de la Academia Argentina de Letras* 16 (1947): 589-613.

[Macedo notes early Lisbon editions of the *Quijote* and various Portuguese translations of Cervantes' works in the eighteenth and nineteenth centuries. Mention is

made of the well-known adaptation of the *Quijote* by the
Brazilian Jew José António da Silva in 1735: *Vida do
grande D. Quixote e do gordo Sancho Pança*. Other adaptations are noted. Macedo points out the praise which
the Visconde de Taunay, author of *Inocencia*, had for
Cervantes' novel. Comments by various Brazilian critics
are presented, and bibliographical works on Cervantes
by Brazilians are discussed. Tributes paid to Cervantes
by poets of Brazil are set forth. Various Brazilian
editions of the *Quijote* are examined, including two in
1898, and editions of Cervantes' works in Brazilian
libraries are listed. In his conclusion the critic
finds that the *Quijote* has had great influence in Brazil,
especially on such writers as Silvio Romero, Machado de
Assis, Olavo Bilac, Ruy Barbosa, Augusto Lima, Euclides
da Cunha, Juan Ribeiro, and Afraino Peixoto.]

434. Ziomek, Henryk. "Parallel Ingredients in *Don Quixote*
     and *Dom Casmurro*." *Revista de Estudios Hispánicos* 2
     (1968):229-240.

     Cervantes and Machado de Assis are similar in choosing
     names for their heroes, names with humor and meaning.
     Also, Machado follows the technique used by Cervantes
     at the beginning of the *Quijote*: the vague place of ac-
     tion, the time (in both cases "not long ago"), the in-
     definite description of the character introduced. In
     both novels a definite division separates the first
     happy-go-lucky part from the more serious half, which
     is full of self-analysis. Both writers change to a
     third-person style and assume the role of second author:
     in *Don Quijote* at the end of Chapter 8; in *Dom Casmurro*
     in Chapter 97. Both also switch to the past tense.
     The humor in the two works is similar. Part I of the
     Quijote is slapstick; Part II contains refined humor.
     Similarly, in the earlier chapters of Machado's novel
     a whimsical, plebian type of humor flowingly bursts
     forth, but after the midpoint of the book an ironic
     brand of humor with satiric power is exhibited. Cer-
     vantes' Knight and Machado's protagonist Bentinho are
     similar in several ways. Both are motivated by a de-
     sire to love and to enjoy life.

Chile

(*See also* item 5)

435. Eliz, Leonardo. *Apuntes para una bibliografía chilena
      sobre Cervantes.* Valparaíso: Imp. Royal, 1916. Pp.
      10.

      [In his introduction Eliz urges closer ties between
      Chile and Spain. He notes the great influence of Cer-
      vantes on literature and the popularity of the leading
      characters in the *Quijote*. The main body of Eliz' work
      consists of a listing of approximately fifty works on
      Cervantes printed in Chile.]

436. Medina, José Toribio. "Cervantes en las letras chile-
      nas." *Estudios Cervantinos*, pp. 565-600. Prólogo
      del Dr. Rodolfo Oroz Scheibe. Santiago de Chile:
      Fondo Histórico y Bibliográfico José Toribio Medina,
      1958. [First published in 1923, Santiago de Chile,
      Imprenta Universitaria.]

      The *Quijote* was not really known in Chile until the
      late eighteenth century, for in the middle of that cen-
      tury there was only one known copy of Cervantes' master-
      piece in Santiago. Furthermore, the *Quijote* was not
      truly read in Chile until the middle of the nineteenth
      century when the bookdealer Santos Tornero offered no
      fewer than eight different editions of Cervantes' novel
      in his 1858 catalog.
      In 1863 an abbreviated edition of the *Quijote* was
      published in Valparaíso; in 1878, Cervantes' death was
      specifically honored in Chile. Between that date and
      1906 various articles on Cervantes and his works ap-
      peared in Chilean newspapers and journals. Between 1906
      and 1916 numerous works in Chile praised Cervantes. In
      that latter year Leonardo Eliz prepared a bibliography
      (435) of Cervantine articles and books published in
      Chile. [Medina adds a supplement to Eliz' bibliography
      consisting of 93 items, some of which are briefly sum-
      marized.]

437. Molina, Julio. "Cervantes en Chile." *Atenea* 24 (1947):
      136-147.

      [The critic notes prior studies on the subject of Cer-
      vantes in Chile and particularly praises the work of
      José Toribio Medina, 1923 (436). Molina points out
      critical works on the *Quijote* by Chileans as well as

Chilean adaptations of Cervantes' novel. A brief discussion of the world reception of the *Quijote* is included. The critic briefly discusses the first Chilean
editions of the *Quijote* in the second part of the nineteenth century.]

438. Sánchez, Porfirio. "Aspectos quijotescos del *Niño que
        enloqueció de amor.*" *Romance Notes* 12 (1970):55-61.

[Sánchez compares the *Quijote* with the Chilean Eduardo Barrios' *Niño que enloqueció de amor*, 1915, and notes
the following similarities between the heroes of each
novel: both are carried away by books and neglect their
duties, the Don his property and the "niño" his school-
work; both are idealistically in love, the Knight with
Dulcinea, the "niño" with Angélica; both figures are
prepared to suffer for love; each has an intense self-
domination and faith in himself; both the Don and the
"niño" have a common-sense figure in whom they can con-
fide (Sancho Panza-Don Carlos Romeral); both figures
are misunderstood by the world; both are held to be insane and scoffed; the books of both heroes are burned.]

439. Sullivan, Maurice W. "La influencia de Cervantes y su
        obra en Chile." *Anales Cervantinos* 2 (1952):287-310.

In his *Martirios de amor* and in his *Alboroto en el
cotarro* the Chilean writer Antonio Espiñeira, 1885-1907,
was heavily influenced by Cervantes. The first work is
based on the Ezpeleta episode in Cervantes' life; the
second deals with Cervantes and several of his characters in Parnassus. Both Rafael Allende, 1850-1909, and
Egidio Poblete, 1860-1940, drew upon Cervantes, the latter writing a continuation of the *Quijote* in 1905 (*Don
Quijote en Chile*). Continuations of the Spaniard's
masterpiece were also written by Juan Barros and Julio
Alemparte.

440. Uribe-Echevarría, Juan. "Cervantes en la obra de An-
        tonio Espiñeira." *Atenea* 24A (October 1947):132-135.

[Uribe-Echevarría notes the Chilean Espiñeira's work
Alboroto en el cotarro, 1878, a fantasy in prose, dealing with the arrival of Cervantes, Don Quijote, Sancho,
and other figures in Parnassus. The critic points out
other works dealing with Cervantes in Parnassus: Leonardo Eliz' play *Apoteosis de Cervantes en el Parnaso*,
1916, and Carlos Bolívar Sevilla's novel *Don Quijote en
la Gloria*, 1928. Uribe discusses another play by

Espiñeira, *Martirios de Amor*, 1887, which deals with
the Ezpeleta episode. The critic examines still another
play by Espiñeira, *Cervantes en Argel*, 1886, based on
Cervantes' life, on *El trato de Argel*, and on "La Historia del Cautivo" found in the *Quijote*.]

Colombia
(*See also* item 5)

441. González, Alfonso. "Elementos del *Quijote* en la carac-
terización de *La Vorágine*." *Romance Notes* 15 (1973):
74-79.

[González compares the figure Cova in the Colombian
José Eustasio Rivera's *La Vorágine* with Cervantes'
Knight, especially in his chivalresque manner and in
his tendency to offer spontaneous and unconditional
help to the needy. The critic also compares the harmony
of the Age of Gold in the Don's speech (*D.Q.* I, ch. 11)
to Cova's attempt to restore harmony between nature and
man in the jungle; and Cova's idealistic attitude
toward women is compared to the ideas of the Knight.
The frequent use by Rivera of such words as *hidalguía*,
enamorado, and *idiosincrasia caballeresca* is observed,
as is his use of names from the *Quijote*: Zoraida, Mari-
tornes, Clarita. González points out that the character-
narrator Don Clemente Silva also has quixotic features.
All in all, the critic finds that *La Vorágine* is somewhat like *Don Quijote* told from the Knight's point of
view.]

442. Nieto Caballero, Luis Eduardo. "Don Quijote en Colombia." *Memorias de la Academia Mexicana* 12 (1955):
201-213.

[This work is intended as a supplement to the bibliography of Valle and Romero (425). Numerous Colombian
cervantistas are listed.]

443. Ortega Torres, José J. "Cervantes en la literatura
colombiana." *Boletín del Instituto Caro y Cuervo*
(superseded by *Thesaurus*) 5 (1959):447-477.

[This article is intended as a supplement to the essay
of Rafael Torres Quintero (445). The bibliography contains 212 items (poems, studies, articles, speeches)

written by Colombians on Cervantes or on his works. At
the end are listed official acts honoring Cervantes.]

444. Pérez Silva, Vicente. *"Don Quijote" en la poesía colom-
      biana*. Bogotá: Editorial Guadalupe, 1962. Pp. 206.

      [This work is a compilation of poems by Colombians
      dedicated to Cervantes or to the characters in his works.
      The collection of poems is divided into three parts:
      (1) "Sonetos," by fifty poets, plus three "sonetos dia-
      logados"; (2) "Otros poemas," by thirty poets; (3) "Poe-
      mas a Cervantes," by sixteen poets. Brief biographical
      information is given for each poet. There is a short
      introduction ("Limen") by Pérez Silva and a prolog by
      Noel Estrada Roldán. The total number of poems is 111.]

445. Torres Quintero, Rafael. "Cervantes en Colombia: ensayo
      de bibliografía crítica de los trabajos cervantinos
      producidos en Colombia." *Boletín del Instituto Caro
      y Cuervo* 4 (1948):29-89.

      [The critic states that, in spite of the low opinion
      in which Cervantes was held by his early readers, there
      were some in Colombia during the colonial era who ap-
      preciated the elegance of his style and who saw in him
      something other than merely a writer of burlesque ad-
      ventures. Antonio Ossorio de las Peñas and Carlos Mar-
      tínez Silva are listed as early appreciators of Cervan-
      tes' writings. Torres Quintero points out a drama based
      on Cervantes' life, written during the Romantic epoch by
      José Caicedo Rojas. The increasing popularity of the
      Quijote is discussed, and the critic concludes that at
      times the praise of Cervantes' masterpiece is excessive.
      Leading Colombian *Cervantistas* are mentioned: M.A. Caro,
      José Ignacio Escobar, and Rafael Maya. The bibliography
      consists of 144 entries by 113 writers, all works pub-
      lished in Colombia. Each entry is followed by a summary
      of content.]

                                   Cuba

446. Pérez Beato y Blanco, Manuel. *Cervantes en Cuba. Es-
      tudio bibliográfico con la reproducción del "Quijote"
      en verso de don Eugenio de Arriaza*. La Habana: Imp.
      de F. Verdugo, 1929. Pp. 120. [This item could not
      be obtained in spite of considerable effort.]

[Pérez Beato's work is highly praised by Rafael Heliodoro Valle and Emilia Romero at page 204 of their *Bibliografía cervantina en la América española* (425). It is
also noted with approval by Juan J. Remos in his "Tradición cervantina en Cuba" (447). Pérez Beato also
published an earlier work, *Bibliografía comentada sobre
los escritos publicados en la Isla de Cuba, relativos
al "Quijote,"* La Habana, 1905. This earlier bibliography, unfortunately, was likewise unavailable to us.]

447. Remos y Rubio, Juan J. "Tradición cervantina en Cuba."
Revista Cubana 22 (1947):170-205.

[This work contains a wealth of information on Cuban
critics and adaptors of the *Quijote*. Remos condemns
Luis Otero Pimentel's *Semblanzas caballerescas o las
nuevas aventuras de Don Quijote de la Mancha*, 1886, as
lacking in logic and artistic sense, and finds Eugenio
Arriaza's *Don Quijote de la Mancha en Octavas*, 1849, to
be in bad taste. Toward the end of this article (p.
203) poems, music, and paintings inspired by the *Quijote* are briefly discussed.]

Ecuador
(*See also* item 5)

448. Agramonte y Pichardo, Roberto. *Cervantes y Montalvo.*
La Habana: "Universidad de la Habana," 1949. Pp. 48.

[This work consists of five short chapters. The critic concludes that Juan Montalvo, 1832-1889, in his
Capítulos que se le olvidaron a Cervantes, identified
with Cervantes' Knight's ideals and believed that every-
one should have something of the Don in his personality
in order to be appreciated and loved.

Montalvo, continues Agramonte, believed the *Quijote*
to be a book of *living* philosophy and a work that is a
classic in its language. The *Capítulos*, the critic
asserts, follows the *Quijote* in the literary form of its
thoughts, in that it deals with great matters through
humorous dialog, not through abstract principles. Yet,
Agramonte is quick to add, Montalvo did not view the
Quijote as a mere book of gaiety, but as a work which
presented the tragic side of life.

A chapter is devoted to the duality of the Knight and
Squire, a duality which is compared to Heidegger's

duality of genuine versus non-genuine experience, imagination versus sensation. Also, a chapter is dedicated
to Montalvo's moral precepts as reflected in his *Capítulos*. To Montalvo, the critic states, sin originates
in selfishness and in the lack of noble sentiments.
The final short chapter deals with Montalvo's ideas
on death and the vanity of human life, as reflected in
his figure Don Quijote, a man who, like the original,
pictures the miracle of the struggle for the ideal.]

449. Anderson Imbert, Enrique. "Sobre el *Quijote* de Mon-
      talvo." *Sur* 14 (1944):112-117.

      [The critic finds that Juan Montalvo, author of
      Capítulos que se le olvidaron a Cervantes, was essen-
      tially a man out of tune with his times both in politics
      as well as in style of writing. Anderson Imbert states
      that Montalvo rejected the speech of his own land, Ecua-
      dor, and copied that of Cervantes without understanding
      its original meaning. To the critic, in short, Montalvo
      did not know how to write a novel; he was too much an
      essayist, too verbose, too artificial.]

450. Arias, Augusto. "El Quijote de Montalvo." *América* 23
      (1947):199-228.

      [Arias begins with a lengthy praise of Cervantes'
      Quijote. He states that almost all the episodes of
      Montalvo's *Capítulos que se le olvidaron a Cervantes*
      have their origin in Cervantes' masterpiece. The critic
      discusses the style used by both writers, finding several
      similarities such as the same gradual rhythm. However,
      Arias notes, there are other possible influences on
      Montalvo's literary technique: Cicero, Quevedo, and var-
      ious French writers. On the whole, the critic finds
      Montalvo to be more like Don Quijote than like Cervan-
      tes: a battler who is never conquered, a moralist with
      a deep concern for justice. In praising Montalvo's
      Capítulos, Arias states that it is the most finished
      imitation of the *Quijote*, leaving aside the work of
      Avellaneda. The critic further concludes that Montal-
      vo's introduction ("Buscapié") is one of the most per-
      spicacious studies of Cervantes' novel. The *Capítulos*
      is also praised as an excellent study of the Spanish
      language.]

451. Dessau, Adalbert. "Montalvo und Cervantes." *Beiträge
      zur romanischen Philologie*, Sonderheft (1967), pp.
      148-160.

[Dessau discusses Juan Montalvo's *Capítulos que se
le olvidaron a Cervantes* (posthumous, 1895). The critic
follows Roberto Agramonte (448) in finding this work to
be the most original and idealistic imitation of Cervantes' masterpiece. For Montalvo, states Dessau, the
Quijote was a "curso de moral," the hero a philosopher
and a disciple of Plato, guided by virtue. In Montalvo's
work, the critic observes, the action is revealed by
conversation, which gives the hero an opportunity to
discuss many questions about life. The *Capítulos* is
discussed as a manifesto of liberalism and as an attack
on various enemies of the author. Dessau notes an earlier tract by Montalvo in 1866, entitled *Capítulo que
se le olvidó a Cervantes*, an attack on a political enemy.
The critic examines Montalvo's use of Cervantes as a
stylistic guide and points out Montalvo's elimination
of Americanisms from his work in order to achieve a
purer, more classic style.]

452. González, Manuel Pedro. "La más afortunada imitación
del *Quijote*." *Hispania* 9 (October 1926):275–283.

[González examines Juan Montalvo's continuation of
Cervantes' *Don Quijote* entitled *Capítulos que se le olvidaron a Cervantes*, 1895. The critic concludes that
there is a great distance between the original Don and
Squire and the heroes of Montalvo's work, the Don of
the continuation having few lucid intervals, and the
new Sancho being an overuser of proverbs and a man
without ideals. González further observes that Cervantes is an artist, while Montalvo is basically a moralist.]

453. Guevara, Darío. *Quijote y Maestro: Biografía novelada
de Juan Montalvo o el Cervantes de América.* Prólogo
de Augusto Arias. Quito: Edit. Ecuador, 1947. Pp.
308.

[As the title indicates, this item is a rather poetic
biography of Juan Montalvo, author of *Capítulos que se
le olvidaron a Cervantes*. Guevara's work contains
forty-two short chapters, a posthumous dialog, plus an
epilog entitled "El Cervantes de América," plus material
of a bibliographical nature. Of particular interest is
the epilog (pp. 223–249), which discusses the similarities between Cervantes and the nineteenth-century Ecuadorian writer. Both, states Guevara, were creative
writers who immersed themselves in their characters;
both were great stylists; their heroes are similar in

their idealism; both writers present life-like characters, some of whom, nevertheless, have a symbolic value;
both novelists satirize customs; both are great users
of irony; both seek to teach virtue. Guevara notes
that Montalvo's work was basically a satire against political tyrants, whereas the stated purpose of the *Quijote* was to attack the popularity of the decadent chivalresque novel.]

454. Revilla, Manuel Gustavo. "Un feliz imitador de Cervan-
     tes." *El Tiempo Ilustrado*, 21 May 1905. [This item
     could not be obtained. It is summarized by Rafael
     Heliodoro Valle and Emilia Romero, in *Bibliografía
     cervantina en la América española* (425), p. 215.]

     [Revilla discusses Juan Montalvo's novelistic adapta-
     tion of Cervantes' masterpiece, *Capítulos que se le ol-
     vidaron a Cervantes*. The critic finds that Montalvo
     falsifies the hero somewhat, making him too irascible,
     and overdoes Sancho as a user of proverbs.]

455. Rodríguez García, José A. *Vida de Cervantes y juicio
     del Quijote*. 3ª ed. La Habana: "Cuba Intelectual,"
     1916. Pp. 169.

     [This third edition, in a short chapter entitled
     "Imitadores" (pp. 147-150), discusses two continuers of
     the *Quijote*: Avellaneda and Montalvo. The critic points
     out that these two imitators are quite different: the
     former seeks to humiliate Cervantes, while the latter is
     a true disciple. By way of criticism of Montalvo, Rod-
     ríguez states that his *Capítulos que se le olvidaron a
     Cervantes* is much more artificious and less intuitive
     than the original.]

456. Zaldumbide, Gonzalo. "El Don Quijote de América o
     'Capítulos que se le olvidaron a Cervantes.'" *Boletín
     de la Academia Argentina de Letras* 16 (1947):651-658.

     [Zaldumbide's article is one of general praise for
     Juan Montalvo's adaptation of Cervantes' masterpiece.
     The critic does not find *Capítulos que se le olvidaron
     a Cervantes* to be a systematic reconstruction of Cervan-
     tes' vocabulary, but a free and masterful use of classic
     Spanish writing. Zaldumbide particularly praises Mon-
     talvo for preserving the Knight from degradation, for
     depicting Sancho as a tender servant and not as a glut-
     ton, and for the general moral tone of the *Capítulos*.
     The critic finds Montalvo's novel to be more a natural

development and continuation of the *Quijote* than an imitation or reproduction of that work.

In spite of the moral, justice-seeking tone of Montalvo's work, Zaldumbide finds *Capítulos que se le olvidaron a Cervantes* to be a story full of freedom and vivacity, of realism and realities. The critic contests Montalvo's assertion that he had written a *Quijote* for Spanish America, because Zaldumbide finds nothing peculiarly American in *Capítulos*. Instead, the critic considers the story more universal than local in its episodes and characters.]

Mexico

457. Amo, Julián. "El *Quijote* en México." *Memorias de la Academia Mexicana* 12 (1955):267-313.

[Amo discusses the early popularity of Cervantes' masterpiece in Mexico, and points out the use of the *Quijote* as a theme for a masquerade in 1621. In regard to the influence of the *Quijote* on Mexican writers, the critic notes the possible use of the plot of *El curioso impertinente* in a play by the Mexican-born Juan Ruiz de Alarcón entitled *El semejante a sí mismo*. Imitations of Cervantes' *Novelas ejemplares* by Luis de Belmonte Bermúdez are briefly noted. Amo finds that José Fernández de Lizardi (1776-1827) was definitely influenced by the *Quijote* both in *Periquillo* and in *La Quijotita y su prima*. The critic lists fourteen Mexican editions of Cervantes' masterpiece and discusses briefly the reception of the *Quijote* by Mexican critics.]

458. González-Cruz, Luis F. "Influencia cervantina en Lizardi." *Cuadernos Hispanoamericanos*, no. 286 (April 1974), pp. 188-203.

[González-Cruz takes issue with the view that the Mexican José Joaquín Fernández de Lizardi's *El Periquillo Sarniento* is really a picaresque novel. Instead, the critic finds that work to be more similar to the *Quijote* in structure and to be heavily influenced by Cervantes' style. González-Cruz notes that there are more references to the *Quijote* in Lizardi's story than to any other work except the Bible. The critic points out the following examples of Cervantine influence: (1) Lizardi defends his moralizing tendency by referring

to Don Quijote; (2) the description of characters is
similar in that each author begins with praise, then immediately follows with a jest; (3) both writers fail to
follow a rigorous order of events, and instead double
back and rectify; (4) Lizardi compares Perico to the
Knight; in fact Perico even compares himself to the
imaginative Don; (5) both heroes repent at the end,
make their wills, and die; (6) there are poems to the
hero at the end of both works; (7) both authors claim
to be merely the simple depository of the story; (8)
the interpolated episodes in each work have a function,
and there is a thematic connection between the interpolation and the main plot; (9) both writers interrupt
their interpolations.]

Nicaragua
(*See also* item 5)

459. Sánchez, Alberto. "Cervantes y Rubén Darío." *Seminario
      Archivo Rubén Darío* 6 (1962):29-44.

      [The critic notes Darío's allusions to the *Quijote*
      and his use of certain phrases from it. Sánchez also
      points out Rubén Darío's essay "Hércules y Don Quijote,"
      in which the author contrasted the Knight and Hercules
      and compared the Squire with Plautus' figure Silenus.
      Two poems by Darío on the *Quijote* are briefly discussed:
      "Caballero andante de los caballeros" and "Letanías de
      Nuestro Señor Don Quijote." Sánchez concludes that
      Darío, inspired by the *Quijote* and penetrated with its
      stylistic quintessence, produced his "Letanías" with
      the two wings of Cervantes' novel: idealism and humor.]

Uruguay

460. Baig Baños, Aurelio. *El primer "Quijote" suramericano
      y el uruguayo Arturo E. Xalambrí*. Madrid: Impr. de
      Unión Poligráfica, 1934. Pp. 30.

      [After a brief foreword Baig Baños includes an article
      by Xalambrí: "La primera edición suramericana del *Quijote*
      es uruguaya--Cervantes en la literatura nacional--
      aspiraciones y anhelos." Xalambrí asserts that the

first complete South American edition of the *Quijote*
is a two-volume edition published in 1880 in Montevideo,
not the 1904 La Plata edition as claimed by Julián
Apraiz (in "Cervantes y America," *Crónica del tercer
centenario de la publicación del Quijote*," 1905). The
title page of the 1880 edition is reproduced, at page
10. Numerous Uruguayan Cervantistas (critics, authors,
poets, and others) are briefly discussed, including
José Enrique Rodó and Juan Zorrilla de San Martín.]

461. Forero Ruiz, Carlos E. "El Quijote americano (Ensayo
sobre *Tabaré* a la luz del *Quijote*)." *Revista Javer-
iana* 28 (September 1947):132-141.

[The critic finds that the Uruguayan Juan Zorrilla de
San Martín's poem *Tabaré* is authentically Latin American
and that the hero, Tabaré, is a direct descendant of Don
Quijote. Forero also notes a similarity between Dulcinea and Zorrilla de San Martín's heroine, Blanca.]

Venezuela

462. Bosch, Juan. "De Don *Quijote* a *Doña Bárbara*." *Human-
ismo*, no. 22 (1954), pp. 31-35.

The crux of the *Quijote* and of the Venezuelan Rómulo
Gallegos' *Doña Bárbara* is found in the contrast between
the two central characters. The leading figures in
both novels are all Spanish and are well portrayed. In
addition, the two protagonists in both novels are symbolical. In Cervantes' novel and in that of Rómulo
Gallegos the secondary figures are well described, though
they are more vivid in *Doña Bárbara*. Also, these minor
characters in both novels often determine the events in
the story (Sansón Carrasco in the *Quijote* and Pajarote
in *Doña Bárbara*). There are other parallels between
the two works. In both, landscape has a function. In
both stories the author makes the reader laugh, though
Gallegos does not use a ridiculous character to do so.
Finally, one should note that neither writer considered
his true masterpiece to be his best work: Cervantes preferred the *Persiles* and Gallegos preferred *Cantaclaro*
and *Canaima*.

463. Grases, Pedro. "Cervantes y Bello." *Cultura Universitaria*, no. 3 (September-October 1947), pp. 17-26.

[Grases notes the admiration of the Venezuelan Andrés
Bello for the *Quijote* and discusses the influence of the
Age of Gold speech (*D.Q.* I, ch. 11) on certain of Bello's
works, such as *Venezuela consolada*, *Alocución a la poesía*, and *Carta escrita de Londres por un americano a
otro.*]

General

464. Coe, Ada M. "Don Quixote on the American Stage."
     Bulletin of Hispanic Studies 28 (July–September 1951):
     167–173.

     [Starting with Henry Fielding's *Don Quixote in England*
     (performed in Philadelphia in 1767) Mrs. Coe traces the
     adaptations of Cervantes' masterpiece on the American
     stage. Mrs. Coe is of the belief that the *Quijote*, in
     view of its complexity and subtlety, will never be suc-
     cessfully adapted to the stage.]

465. Harkey, Joseph Harry. *"Don Quixote* and American Fiction
     Through Mark Twain." Ph.D. dissertation, University
     of Tennessee, 1967. Pp. vi + 205.

     [After seven chapters of detailed examination of the
     influence of the *Quijote* on the American novel, its
     adaptations on the American stage, and its reception by
     critics in the United States, Harkey concludes:] A
     study of *Don Quijote*'s influence in America always leads
     one to an interesting paradox, that Americans have al-
     ways treasured the Knight and rejected him at the same
     time. There are in this nation definite tendencies to-
     ward both idealism and pragmatism. The love of idealism
     caused William Dean Howells to overlook the fact that
     Cervantes found Don Quijote an ineffective agent of
     good who cut a ludicrous figure. Brackenridge, the
     author of *Modern Chivalry*, loved Farrago for his mis-
     guided idealism even as Washington Irving loved the
     crusty, old, quixotic Peter Stuyvesant in *Knickerbocker
     History of New York*. This same mood has made Dale Was-
     serman's play *Man of La Mancha*, 1965, a favorite of in-
     telligentsia and businessman alike. At the same time,

however, American empiricism has always dictated that
we ridicule the impractical idealist. Don Quijote and
Peter Stuyvesant are loved for their quixotism, but re-
jected because the national experience demands that
idealism be tempered by practicality. Another major
Quijote was cast in this image--Tom Sawyer. Despite
his dreams and wild schemes, Tom's actions are ultimately guided by practicality. Furthermore, the Sancho-
like Sir Boss of *A Connecticut Yankee in King Arthur's
Court* is pictured as the practical man *par excellence*,
but he is also an idealist, though holding ideals radi-
cally different from those of Don Quijote, Farrago, Peter
Stuyvesant, or Tom Sawyer.

[At the end of his thesis Harkey points out that the
influence of the *Quijote* in America does not end with
Twain, since this influence is still a factor in Richard
Powell's *Don Quixote, U.S.A.* (an elaborate yarn about a
quixotic Peace Corpsman) and in the continued success of
the play *Man of La Mancha.*]

466. Heiser, M.F. "Cervantes in the United States." *Hispanic
      Review* 15 (October 1947):409-435.

The first review of *Don Quijote* in the United States
is contained in Joseph Dennie's short biography of Cervantes, published in 1802. Washington Irving's *Knickerbocker History of New York* is heavily indebted to the
Quijote, and Longfellow, in 1843, drew upon Cervantes'
La Gitanilla in writing his *Gypsy Student*. However,
Longfellow never came to grips with the *Quijote*. During
the Romantic period the satirical element of Cervantes'
masterpiece was forgotten, but American Romanticists
were not stampeded into highly subjective, emotional,
and impressionistic reactions to the novel. In the
Realistic Age Lowell studied the *Quijote* and found little
national in it. He also saw two morals in the novel:
(1) don't quarrel with the nature of things; and (2)
only a spirit like Don Quijote's can accomplish great
results. Mark Twain was greatly influenced by the *Quijote*. Tom Sawyer is the equivalent of the imaginative
Knight, and Huck Finn is the earthy Sancho.

467. Nikoliukin, A.N. "Cervantes en la literatura norte-
      americana." In *Servantes i vsemirnaîa literatura*,
      pp. 141-149. Edited by N. Balashof, A. Mijailof,
      and I. Terterian. Moscow: Nauka, 1969.

[Nikoliukin discusses the influence of the *Quijote*
on Hugh Brackenridge's satirical novel *Modern Chivalry*

and on Washington Irving's *Knickerbocker History of New York.* The critic briefly mentions the early knowledge of the *Quijote* in the United States, and notes the performance of various plays based on the *Quijote.* Also discussed here is the influence of Cervantes' novel on Herman Melville's *Moby Dick* and on the dialogs in Mark Twain's *Tom Sawyer* and *Huckleberry Finn.* Nikoliukin quotes the ideas of William Dean Howells on the worth of the *Quijote.*]

468. Romera-Navarro, M. *El hispanismo en Norte-América. Exposición y crítica de su aspecto literario.* Madrid: Renacimiento, 1917. Pp. xii + 451.

[The index lists (at page 438) twenty-eight references to Cervantes by American critics, biographers, and writers. In the text are found allusions to Cervantes by such men as William Prescott, George Ticknor, Henry Wadsworth Longfellow, Rudolph Schevill, and William Dean Howells.]

469. Williams, Stanley Thomas. *The Spanish Background of American Literature.* 2 vols. Hamden, Conn.: Archon Books, 1968. [First published in 1935, Yale University Press, New Haven, Conn.]

[The critic observes that the *Quijote* was quite well known to such Americans as Cotton Mather, Jared Sparks, and Thomas Jefferson. Williams discusses in some detail the influence of Cervantes' masterpiece on H.H. Brackenridge, Herman Melville, Bret Harte, Mark Twain, and Washington Irving. The critic concludes that Melville was not greatly affected by the *Quijote*, although he was quite interested in the Knight's monomania. Remarks by North American critics are quoted from time to time. Williams points out a poem of 1878 by William Cullen Bryant entitled "Cervantes" and a play, *Sancho Panza*, 1923, by Melchior Lengyel.]

Eighteenth-Century United States

470. Hendrickson, John R. "The Influence of *Don Quixote* on *Modern Chivalry.*" Ph.D. dissertation, Florida State University, 1959. Pp. ii + 132.

[Chapter One of this thesis deals at length with the life of Hugh Henry Brackenridge, who was born in

Kintyre, Scotland, in 1748, and migrated to Pennsylvania
with his family.

Chapter Two examines Brackenridge's reading of the
Quijote and studies prior critics who have noted the
resemblance between the *Quijote* and *Modern Chivalry*.

Chapter Three deals with the plan, the characters,
and the incidents of Brackenridge's novel, the loose
structure of which is said to resemble that of Cervantes' masterpiece. In addition, notes Hendrickson,
Brackenridge follows Cervantes in using the technique
of a dual point of view: Captain Farrago stands in the
place of Don Quijote, and Teague O'Regan and Duncan Fer-
guson stand in the place of Sancho Panza. In both
novels, Hendrickson observes, the hero goes aimlessly
off into the world, mounted on a palfrey that is no-
table for its poor qualities; each protagonist is accom-
panied by a squire. Further comparing Captain Farrago
with the Knight, Hendrickson points out that both are
bachelors about fifty years of age; both are gentlemen
and farmers; each is well-read and enjoys a certain
prestige in his respective community; neither is satisfied to be a mere spectator; each wishes for his own
ideals to prevail, the Captain's ideals, like those of
the Don, being largely derived from reading; and both
heroes are naive about worldly affairs.

In Chapter Four Hendrickson seeks deeper similarities
between the *Quijote* and *Modern Chivalry*. Both works,
he concludes, adopt the same vital theme: the clash between lofty idealism and the mundane established order
of society, the theme of the modern novel. The critic
notes that both works follow a realiotic technique, and,
more importantly, both authors use exceptional characters who are at one and the same time individuals as
well as types.]

471. Roades, Sister Mary Teresa. *"Don Quixote* and *Modern
      Chivalry."* *Hispania* 32 (August 1949):320-325.

      Hugh Henry Brackenridge was born in 1748 and died in
      1816. His novel *Modern Chivalry* was published between
      1792 and 1815 in six volumes. Brackenridge, like Cer-
      vantes, tried to laugh away the absurdities in thought
      and conduct which he observed in his fellow man. Like
      Cervantes, too, he used as the vehicle for his satire
      the story of a wandering master and his dull, roguish
      squire.

      There are numerous other likenesses between the *Qui-
      jote* and *Modern Chivalry*. The hero of Brackenridge's

story, Captain Farrago, is about fifty-three, of good
natural sense, and a voracious reader. He occasionally
uses fictional characters as pretended authorization
for his speech and actions. Teague, the Irishman, is
Sancho's counterpart until the latter part of the novel
when the Scotsman Duncan takes over that function.
Other similarities between the *Quijote* and *Modern
Chivalry* are: burlesque descriptions of women; literary
criticism; advice to servants; a visit to a cave; mala-
propisms; a yearning for power by the squire; the
squire's fear of physical pain; the hero's sympathy
for unfortunate lovers. But there are serious differences between Don Quijote and Farrago. Brackenridge's
hero is basically a realist who strives to be practical.

Nineteenth-Century United States

472. Aguirre, José L. *"Moby Dick de Herman Melville."*
     Atlántico, no. 5 (1957), pp. 33-48.

     [Aguirre asserts that all great books are adventure
     books, in one way or the other, and that all are sym-
     bolical in spite of the author's intention. The critic
     finds similarities between Melville's and Cervantes'
     sense of humor ("amargo y delicioso") and between their
     lives: poor aristocrats, petty government jobs, wander-
     ings, lack of success during their lifetimes. Both
     Moby Dick and the *Quijote*, states Aguirre, are works of
     erudition, humor, and adventure; both have an insane
     hero who dies in his third sally; and both novels attack
     the customs of the day.]

473. Clark, Harry Hayden. "Mark Twain." In *Eight American
     Authors: A Review of Research and Criticism*, pp. 319-
     363. Edited by Floyd Stovall. New York: M.L.A. of
     America, 1956.

     [Clark discusses Twain's use of contrasting figures:
     the imaginative Tom Sawyer (Don Quijote) and the delight-
     ful Huck Finn (Sancho), and concludes that Twain may
     have used this technique as early as 1866-1867.]

474. Gilman, Stephen. "Cervantes en la obra de Mark Twain."
     In *Cuadernos de Insula*. Vol. 1: *Homenaje a Cervantes
     en el cuarto centenario de su nacimiento, 1547-1947*,
     pp. 207-222. [Madrid]: Insula, [1947].

Mark Twain and Cervantes have many factors in common.
Both imitate themselves; both examine and resolve the
problem of a continuation; both Tom Sawyer and Don Quijote become aware of themselves as literary figures in
prior works. In the novels of Twain and Cervantes each
character has a point of view, a most important factor
in the modern novel. In the continuation of the *Quijote*
and of *Tom Sawyer* conversations are no longer linked to
an adventure frame, for topics of discussion range far
and wide. Also one finds in the second parts of Twain's
and Cervantes' masterpieces that life is no longer
taken for granted; life becomes problematical, and people must constantly re-evaluate themselves.

475. Levin, Harry. "*Don Quixote* and *Moby Dick*." In *Cervan-
      tes Across the Centuries ... A Quadricentennial Volume
      Edited by Ángel Flores and M.J. Benardete*, pp. 217-
      226. New York: The Dryden Press, 1947. [1969 reprint,
      Gordian Press, pp. 227-236; for the Spanish version
      see "*Don Quijote y Moby Dick*," *Realidad* 2 (1947):254-
      267.]

Herman Melville's comments on *Don Quijote* display a
set of attitudes which he himself had crystallized five
years before in *Moby Dick*: a questioning of the nature
of reality and an affirmation of the brotherhood of Man.
Moby Dick is a roaming novel like the *Quijote*, and deals
also with a monomaniac hero who dominates all around
him. Both works contain a wide variety of styles of
language, and in both novels the library is the point
of departure. However, *Moby Dick* is not a mock-epic
like the *Quijote*. Furthermore, while Cervantes under-
mines romance with realism, Melville lures us from a
literal to a symbolic plane. Thus the relation of *Moby
Dick* to *Don Quijote* is neither close nor similar; it is
complementary and dialectical. The *Quijote* proposes
worldly wisdom in place of worn-out ideals. *Moby Dick*
goes questioning after a transcendental fate.

476. Moore, Olin Harris. "Mark Twain and Don Quixote."
      PMLA 37 (1922):324-346.

Although Mark Twain is generally considered a purely
American writer, this is not so, for he was clearly influenced by European writers. For example, it is most
likely that he read *Don Quijote* early in his career, as
early as *Innocents Abroad*, and while composing *Huckleberry Finn* he went so far as to use Cervantes as a
standard-bearer against Walter Scott and the Romantic

writers, whom Twain considered frauds. The influence
of the figures Don Quijote and Sancho Panza on Twain's
masterpieces is clear. Twain substitutes a dreamy boy,
Tom Sawyer, for the romantic Knight, and Huckleberry
Finn takes over the role of the prosaic Sancho Panza.
Thus the humor of Twain and of Cervantes lies to a great
extent in the contrast between imaginative and unimagi-
native characters.

Other humorous devices employed by both writers are
similar. For example, Twain and Cervantes both make
frequent use of the "misunderstanding-of-terms" technique. That Twain had Cervantes in mind when writing
his *Huckleberry Finn* can be gleaned from his specific
reference in Chapter III of that work to evil enchanters
who intervene to thwart the glory of a hero.

One should note that Twain also wrote a satire against
chivalric novels, *A Connecticut Yankee in King Arthur's
Court.*

477. Morgan, Sophia Steriades. "Death of a Myth: A Reading
      of *Moby Dick* as Quixotic Literature." Ph.D. disser-
      tation, University of Michigan, 1972. Pp. v + 177.

[Morgan defines a quixotic work as a work marked by a
conscious and manifest preoccupation with the problem
of the relationship between books and reality, or, in
other words, between reality and its representation.
This is the central problem of both the *Quijote* and
Moby Dick, the critic states, and there can be no consistent reading of Melville's novel which does not take
this into account. Nor, continues Morgan, is there any
valid critical dilemma which is not resolved once this
is taken into consideration; therefore, all other rele-
vant problems are subsumed under this one.

The dissertation contains a Preface, three chapters,
and a brief conclusion. Chapter One deals with the
Melville-Ishmael-Ahab relationship, together with the
relationship of Melville and Ishmael to Cervantes. The
second chapter is concerned with Ahab: his plight, his
quest, his monster, and his relationship to Ishmael.
In this chapter the critic seeks to negate a number of
interpretations of Ahab, particularly the archetypal or
mythical interpretation. The final chapter returns to
Ishmael and discusses how "the entire character of this
quixotic enterprise has been cast. It talks about
language."

Morgan finds that Melville knew and understood Cervantes profoundly. Yet, she continues, one cannot by

any means talk of a Cervantine influence on Melville,
because the latter most resembles the Spaniard where he
(Melville) most departs from Cervantes or inverts his
formulas.]

478.   Roades, Sister Mary Teresa. "Was Mark Twain Influenced
       by the Prolog to *Don Quixote*?" *Mark Twain Quarterly*
       9 (Winter 1952):4-6, 24.

       Twain read the *Quijote* many times and alludes to it on
       several occasions, as in *A Horse's Tale* and in *Huckle-
       berry Finn*. Both Cervantes (Prolog to the 1605 *Quijote*)
       and Twain (*The Gilded Age*) refuse to make the usual
       apologies for their work, and both writers ridicule the
       custom of quoting unknown or pretended sources. The
       evidence seems to favor the conclusion that Twain was
       influenced by Cervantes' prolog to *Don Quijote*, Part I.

479.   Santayana, George. "Tom Sawyer and Don Quixote." *Mark
       Twain Quarterly* 9 (Winter 1952):1-3.

       The ghost of Don Quijote stalks in the background of
       Huckleberry Finn. Tom Sawyer's plans for the escape of
       the Negro slave show the same mission and disinterested
       bravery as that of the Knight of La Mancha. Tom, like
       the Don, loves ceremonies, vigils, and exacting labors,
       and at times blames his failures on witches. But Tom's
       playacting is accompanied by a wink, for basically he is
       a realist. The problem of artificial madness will not
       be solved in him quite as it was in the Don, because
       the root of fantasies in Tom had been only adolescence,
       not, as in Don Quijote, a settled vital demand for the
       supremacy of the spirit.

*   Serrano Plaja, Arturo. *Realismo "mágico" en Cervantes;
       Don Quijote visto desde "Tom Sawyer" y "El idiota."*
       Madrid: Editorial Gredos, 1967. Pp. 236. [Translated
       into English as *"Magic" Realism in Cervantes; Don
       Quijote as Seen Through "Tom Sawyer" and "The Idiot."*
       Berkeley, Los Angeles, and London: University of
       California Press, 1970. Pp. 216.] Cited above as
       item 410.

       [Serrano Plaja regards Cervantes' Knight as more an
       actor than a madman. The critic points out numerous
       similarities between the Don and Tom Sawyer: neither
       has an immediate family; both have a quest for justice
       on the fringe of the law; both have a craving for fame;
       the Don fears his housekeeper as Tom fears Aunt Polly;

both heroes make use of "magic" (Don Quijote simply de-
clares his helmet to be ready, while Tom insists that
his pick is a case knife, as in adventure stories).]

480. Templin, E.H. "On Rereading Mark Twain." *Hispania* 24
(October 1941):269-276.

[Templin states that the *Quijote* is second only to
the Bible among the literary influences on Mark Twain.
Indeed, the critic continues, it might be said that
Mark Twain is a sort of adolescent Cervantes, and a man
steeped in the *Quijote*. Templin compares the personality and style of the two writers and notes that both
are embellishers and idealists in sexual matters. The
critic points out the use by both authors of the ideal-
real dualism and concludes that Twain is an amateur in
this area, whereas Cervantes is masterfully subtle.
The latter portion of this article deals with *A Connecticut Yankee in King Arthur's Court*. Its kinship to
the *Quijote* is briefly noted.]

481. Vázquez-Arjona, Carlos. "Spanish and Spanish-American
Influences on Bret Harte." *Revue Hispanique* 76 (1929):
573-621.

[Vázquez-Arjona states that the figure Don José Sepúl-
veda of Bret Harte's *A Knight-Errant of the Foothills*
is like Don Quijote in character and attitude. The
critic also suggests an influence of Cervantes' Knight
on the character Enríquez in *The Devotion of Enríquez*.]

Twentieth-Century United States

482. Adams, Mildred. "Don Quijote, arquetipo para america-
nos." *Revista de Occidente* 22 (August 1968):199-204.

While some say we should not be quixotic in foreign
affairs, others take a different view of *quijotismo*, as
far as the theatre is concerned. George Balanchine, in
his ballet version of *Don Quijote*, views the Knight as
tragic, blind, and betrayed by friends. In the conception of Dale Wasserman (*Man of La Mancha*), Cervantes,
Don Quijote, and Alonso Quijano are three distinct
facets of the same man and are represented in successive
scenes by the same actor. The action begins in Seville,
where Cervantes is in jail, and ends with the death of

Alonso Quijano as Dulcinea sings a hymn defying destiny
and praising the victory of the human soul. Both the
ballet by Balanchine and Wasserman's *Man of La Mancha*
emphasize the fact that the Don's apparent defeat is
only the point of a new beginning.

483. Bocaz, Sergio H. "*El Ingenioso Hidalgo Don Quijote de
      la Mancha* and *The Old Man and the Sea*: A Study of the
      Symbolic Essence of Man in Cervantes and Hemingway."
      *Bulletin of the Rocky Mountain Modern Language Asso-
      ciation* 25 (1971):49-54.

Both Cervantes and Hemingway deal with the essence of
man. Their heroes, Don Quijote and Santiago (the Old
Man), are archetypes with similar characteristics which
tend to measure the essence and meaning of the eternal
idea of universal man. Why are Cervantes' and Hemingway's heroes purveyors of the most important human
values? Because they say that the essence of man stems
from the importance of a human endeavor applied toward
the fulfillment of a morally good idea. They are men
of action, and action gives meaning to their morality,
and ultimately to their essence. They know that life
is cruel yet do not despair or grow cynical.
The Knight and the Old Man are similar physically and
psychologically; they are old yet youthful; both are inspired by positive ideals; both show stamina and are
self-denying; neither can be satisfied by being just
another man; both are in a state of nature, of primi-
tive innocence; both seek silence in order to reinforce
their active morality; both are of a true mystic nature.
Cervantes and Hemingway reach their peak dealing with
death, the apparent death of their respective old men.
Both writers use the technique of sleep to create their
common symbolism, the immortality of the Knight and of
the Old Man. And both Cervantes and Hemingway, to bring
out the vital essence of their old men, use contrasting figures (Sancho-Manolin) who become spiritual sons
of their teachers.

484. Floan, Howard R. "Saroyan and Cervantes' Knight."
      Thought 33 (Spring 1958):81-92.

Needless to say, there is no one character in Saroyan's writing who embodies a full complement of quixotic
qualities. But there is a rather large group of people
who share with Don Quijote the inability to reconcile
their private, imagined world with that of their daily
affairs. The ones who remain passive before the

seemingly impossible demands of their dream tend invar-
iably to be pathetic, and, as fictional characters,
nearly always fail. The others (and they are more prop-
erly called quixotic), who refuse to compromise their
private visions in order to meet the demands of an in-
tractable world, are successful as fictional characters,
even when they are only sparingly sketched. The paradox of these persons is that their failure in the
practical, measurable order is an essential ingredient
of their particular kind of achievement. Amid both
tragic and comic aspects of man's inability to realize
his dreams Saroyan implies that human suffering has a
certain efficacy of its own. The playwright invests
human misery with a sense of beauty.

485. Gross, Theodore L. *The Heroic Ideal in American Litera-
      ture.* New York: The Free Press; London: Collier-
      Macmillan, Limited, 1971. Pp. xvi + 304.

      [Gross studies the tension between idealism and au-
      thority in five heroic figures in American literature:
      the Emersonian hero; the Southern hero; the Black hero;
      the Disenchanted hero; and the Quixotic hero. Chapter
      Five (pp. 243-295) is devoted to the last-named figure.
      The critic finds the leading characters of Saul Bellow
      to be, for the most part, quixotic, vacillating, gro-
      tesque figures who tremble before the particular choice
      they must make, who wish to act idealistically and to
      transcend the constrictions of their lives but find
      themselves crippled by their own frailty. The heroes
      of J.D. Salinger are regarded as anxiety-ridden figures
      who are driven to the point of madness and suicide.
      Norman Mailer, states Gross, rebels against totalitarian
      America and refuses to relinquish the heroic ideal. Yet
      his figures are defeated by materialism. Ernest Heming-
      way's heroes are described (p. 220) as disenchanted
      figures who are somewhere between the Emersonian hero
      and the quixotic hero.]

486. Hassan, Ihab Habib. *Radical Innocence: Studies in the
      Contemporary American Novel.* New York: Harper & Row,
      1961. Pp. vi + 361.

      [Hassan notes the strange quixotic gestures of the
      characters of J.D. Salinger. The critic also points out
      the obstinacy of several of Saul Bellow's creations,
      and finds that their bilious or quixotic gesture saves
      them from a Prufrockian fate of genteel cynicism.]

487. Light, Martin. *The Quixotic Vision of Sinclair Lewis.*
      West Lafayette, Ind.: Purdue University Press, 1975.
      Pp. xiii + 162.

      [The critic states (at p. 143):] Lewis's use of
      quixotism brought to us a view of ourselves which we
      needed--and still need. Quixotes remain among the
      archetypes of American literature, along with the Ada-
      mic innocent and the Faustian rebel--from *Modern Chi-
      valry* and *The Connecticut Yankee* to *The Adventures of
      Augie March, The Catcher in the Rye,* and Faulkner's
      trilogy. They are useful in portraying our fanciful
      vision, our chivalric impulses, our foolhardiness, our
      compulsion to aid the world and to fight its battles
      everywhere, our ambition to right all wrongs. We are
      befuddled into embarking on crusades; we undertake im-
      probable wars; we are duped into our generous trade
      deals. Our idealism is admirable in motive, yet would
      benefit from reexamination. The national quixotism
      needs its cure. In his time Lewis made an effort to
      heal it (not always successfully). Lewis tried to
      undertake to do again "that good work done by Cervantes"
      (as Mark Twain put it) in purging the national culture
      of its foolishness once more.
      [However, Light notes (at p. viii) that Lewis suf-
      fered from a significant disadvantage that made his
      attitude self-contradictory, namely that he loved ro-
      mance, succumbing to it even as he fought it.]

488. Pérez, Louis C. "Wilder and Cervantes: In the Spirit
      of the Tapestry." *Symposium* 25 (1971):249-259.

      [Pérez begins with a general discussion of the influ-
      ence of Lope de Vega, Calderón de la Barca, and Miguel
      de Cervantes on the works of Thornton Wilder. In re-
      gard to the influence of the *Quijote* the critic finds
      that the character Brush, in *Heaven's My Destination,*
      has noticeable quixotic traits. Pérez also points out
      that in *The Eighth Day* one of the main characters,
      Beata Ashley, reads to her children from the *Quijote.*
      Pérez notes the use by both authors of the image of the
      tapestry (by Cervantes in the *Quijote* and by Wilder in
      The Eighth Day). Both writers, states the critic, re-
      late the novel to the tapestry in their technique, in
      that all episodes are somehow related.
      Pérez concludes that both the *Quijote* and *The Eighth
      Day* have the same philosophic thread: the secret of a
      full and happy life is in creating, in carrying out a
      program, for to do nothing is to die spiritually. The

figure Constance in *The Eighth Day* is compared to the
Knight in her desire to know people, to be part of a
design. Pérez also concludes that Cervantes wrote to
counteract the negative, cynical spirit of the picaresque and that Wilder, similarly, wrote to contradict
the aesthetic implications of Sartre's existentialism.
To Pérez, both Cervantes and Wilder believed that we
are all involved in mankind, and that our acts influence
directly or indirectly the lives of others; and both
writers use the tapestry image to convey this message.]

489. Tudisco, Anthony. "Don Quixote, U.S.A." *Revista His-
      pánica Moderna* 34 (1968):457-461.

[Tudisco briefly notes Balanchine's ballet entitled
Don Quixote and Dale Wasserman's recent musical *Man of
La Mancha*. This article, however, is primarily concerned with Thornton Wilder's *Heaven's My Destination*
and Richard Powell's *Don Quixote, U.S.A.* These two
works are discussed in some detail and compared to
Cervantes' masterpiece. Tudisco concludes that the
heroes of Powell's and Wilder's stories only remotely
resemble the Don, and that these authors did well in
not imitating Cervantes closely.]

490. Tull, John F., Jr. "*Man of La Mancha*: una nueva inter-
      pretación del *Quijote*." *Duquesne Hispanic Review* 8
      (Spring 1969):37-43.

This play, as Wasserman has stated, was written as a
deliberate denial of the prevailing spirit of our time,
that of aesthetic masochism which finds its theatrical
mood in the deification of despair. The play opens in
the dungeon of the Inquisition. Cervantes defends his
manuscript against those who seek to confiscate his
property. Next he puts on a play about Don Quijote for
the benefit of his fellow prisoners, and takes the role
of the Knight. At the end of the drama Cervantes adopts
the bravery of the Knight as his own. He no longer
fears his inquisitors. Wasserman finds Cervantes and
Don Quijote to be, in all essential ways, the same
person.

Eastern Europe and the Balkans

491. Englebert, Jo Anne. "A Sancho for Saint Francis."
      Hispania 46 (May 1963):287-289.

      The hero in Kazantzakis' *Saint Francis* (Greek version
      1956, English version 1962) is, like Don Quijote, a mix-
      ture of violence and gentleness, fierce passion and un-
      speakable tenderness. Brother Leo is quite similar to
      Sancho Panza. He struggles with his dull wits to under-
      stand his master. The figure Leo, like that of Sancho,
      facilitates the continuity of the story, the creation
      of dramatic situations, even the exposition of important
      ideas. The intimacy of the servant with his master is,
      in both novels, the most important means of showing not
      only the master's "human" character but of revealing
      spiritual insights as well.

492. Freiberg, Medeea. "Los primeros ecos de la obra de
      Cervantes en la literatura rumana." *Cahiers Roumains
      d'Études Littéraires* 3 (1974):84-94.

      [Freiberg's study of the influence of Cervantes in
      Rumania ends at the mid-nineteenth century. The critic
      points out that the *Quijote* was well-known in Rumania
      long before it was translated into Rumanian in 1840.
      Prior to such a translation, states Freiberg, Cervantes'
      masterpiece was of great influence on Ion Budai-Deleanu
      in his *Trei Viteji* (c. 1812-1820), and in *Tiganiada*,
      the hero of which, as Budai-Deleanu himself stated, was
      "a sort of Transylvanian Don Quijote." The critic finds
      that the comical preparations of the protagonist Desche-
      ric Istov are similar to those of the Knight, and that
      the Squire Craciunel is similar to Sancho. The heroine
      Anghelina is compared and contrasted with Dulcinea, the

critic finding that Budai-Deleanu's heroine is treated
more realistically.

Freiberg examines in some detail the partial translation of the *Quijote* into Rumanian in 1840 by Ion Heliade
Radulescu. The critic states that it is based on Florian's French version.

The popularity of the *Curioso impertinente* in the
mid-nineteenth century is discussed.]

493. Frunzetti, Ion. "Cervantes en Roumanie." *Europe*, nos.
      121-122 (January-February 1956), pp. 50-54.

      [Frunzetti notes the various Rumanian translations of
      the *Quijote* and alludes to his own translation (with
      Edgar Papu) in 1956. Several critical works on Cervan-
      tes and the *Quijote* by Rumanians are noted. A four-act
      play by M. Sorbul is examined briefly.]

494. Hampejs, Zdenek. "Tradiciones y estado actual del
      hispanismo en Checoslovaquia." In *Actas del Primer
      Congreso Internacional de Hispanistas*, pp. 315-318.
      Oxford: The Dolphin Book Co., Ltd, 1964.

      Czech Hispanism goes back to the first part of the
      nineteenth century when the *Novelas ejemplares* were
      translated into Czech in 1838. The *Quijote* was first
      rendered in Czech in 1864, and now there are twelve
      different translations in that language. There have
      been six editions of Cervantes' masterpiece since 1945,
      the latest edition containing a 120-page sociological
      study of Spain.

495. Hatzantonis, Emmanuel. "Captain Sole: Don Quijote's
      After-Image in Kazantzakis' *Odyssey*." *Hispania* 46
      (May 1963):283-286.

      In *Traveling-Spain* Kazantzakis praises Cervantes'
      life and sympathizes with the ill treatment the Spaniard
      received as a writer. Here one has the impression that
      he is reading Kazantzakis' own experiences up to the
      publication of *Zorba the Greek*, the novel which brought
      him belated recognition. Kazantzakis adopts Unamuno's
      interpretation of *Don Quijote* as the "libro máximo de
      la raza," as a book that urges Spaniards to live up to
      the essence of their race. In Book XX of his *Odyssey*
      Kazantzakis introduces the figure Captain Sole, a figure
      modeled after Don Quijote. Sole is similar in charac-
      ter and appearance to the Knight and rides a bony and
      ancient camel called Lightning. Kazantzakis was

particularly anxious to have the reader see the similarity between Sole and the Knight; for Captain Sole
was the name he had given for Don Quijote in a poem
written in 1934 (four years prior to the *Odyssey*), in
which poem Kazantzakis pictured the divinity of Don
Quijote's madness.

496. Iordan, Iorgu. "Los estudios hispánicos en Rumania."
In *Actas del Primer Congreso Internacional de His-
panistas*, pp. 328-334. Oxford: The Dolphin Book Co.,
Ltd., 1964.

Between 1868 and 1870 the critic Stefan Vîrgolici
wrote several articles on Lope de Vega, Cervantes, and
Calderón. This same critic published his translation
of the 1605 *Quijote* in 1890 and 1891, but the translation is not complete. After World War I Alexandru
Popescu-Telega wrote several works on Cervantes. Since
World War II Rumanian Hispanism has grown to such an
extent that there is interest in Latin American writings
as well as in Spanish Peninsular literature.

497. Marković, Milan. "Cervantes dans la littérature yougo-
slave." *Revue de Littérature Comparée* 14 (1934):68-
95.

In 1856 or 1857 the first partial translation of the
Quijote appeared in Serbian, that of Djordje Popović
Danicar. It was not until some forty years later that
Danicar's work was completed and published. In 1864,
eight chapters from Part I of the *Quijote* were rendered
into Slovenian by an unknown translator. In 1879, at
Zagreb, there was published an abridged edition of the
Quijote in Croatian, by Jos. Eugen Tomic. The *Quijote*
was of considerable influence on Jovan Rajić and Jovan
Sterija Popović. The latter followed Cervantes' tech-
nique of contrasting the real and the ideal, and, like
the Spaniard, often used digressions. At times the
Quijote was used as a basis for political satire: for
example, Zarnik's four-act tragicomedy directed against
Ljudevit Gaj's and Stanko Vraz' Illyrian movement.

498. Orgaz, Manuel. "Don Quijote en Grecia." *Cuadernos
Hispanoamericanos* 34 (March 1958):368-370.

[Orgaz briefly discusses the modern Greek author Nikos
Kazantzakis and several of his works, including *Alexis
Sorbas* and *Odisea*. The critic concludes that Cervantes
was Kazantzakis' greatest literary love. Orgaz further

points out that the novel *Alexis Sorbas* was dedicated
to Sancho Panza, who was of great influence on Kazantzakis in the creation of his hero Alexis Sorbas, a Macedonian peasant.]

499. Tudorica, Olga. "Un eco cervantino en la poesía de
      Mihail Eminescu." *Beiträge zur romanischen Philologie.*
      Sonderheft (1967), pp. 189-194.

      [Tudorica discusses the possible influence of the
      Quijote on the Rumanian Eminescu's poem *Diamantul Nor-
      dului*, first written in 1873-1874 in Berlin. The critic
      notes that there are two later versions of this poem
      which contain changes, and that in the final version,
      1877, the author added the following to the title:
      "Utopia lui Don Quixotte y Viziunea lui Don Quixotte."
      Similarities between Cervantes' novel and Eminescu's
      poem are pointed out: (1) Don Quijote goes out into the
      world to conquer it for Dulcinea, while Eminescu's
      Caballero goes forth to conquer the diamond of the north
      for his beloved Inés; (2) both heroes resist the advan-
      ces of women, Don Quijote in the Altisidora episode and
      the Caballero in his dealings with the princess; (3)
      both heroes are scorned by their lady-loves; (4) in both
      works there is an atmosphere of enchantment which each
      hero must break; (5) both protagonists awake to cruel
      reality at the end and realize that they were heroes
      only in their dreams.]

500. Velcev, Petr. "Obraz Don Kixota v sovremnnoj bolgarskoj
      poèzii." *Izvestija Akademiia Nauk S.S.S.R., Serija
      Literatury i Jazyka* (Moscow) 30 (May-June 1971):240-
      248.

      [Velcev quotes from the works of various Bulgarian
      poets who have dealt with Don Quijote, including Kon-
      stantin Belichkov, Nikolai Rainov, Pirvan Stephanov,
      and L. Levchev.]

501. Vîscan, Silvia. "Cervantes en Rumania." *Beiträge zur
      romanischen Philologie.* Sonderheft (1967), pp. 195-
      200.

      The first attempts to translate the *Quijote* into
      Rumanian were by Ion Eliade Radulescu, who in 1840 pub-
      lished fifty chapters of Part I. This text is based on
      a French version of the *Quijote* and is written in Slavic
      letters. In 1881 Stefan C. Vîrgolici published in Ru-
      manian a version of the *Curioso impertinente*, based on

a Spanish text. In 1936, the first complete Rumanian edition of the *Quijote* was published by Al. Iacobescu, based on a French version; and in 1944 Al. Popescu Telega partially translated Part I of the *Quijote* into Rumanian directly from the Spanish. In 1965, E. Papu and Ion Frunzetti published a full edition based directly on the Spanish.

[Vîscan briefly examines the interpretation of the *Quijote* by Rumanian critics, and points out several of his countrymen who have adapted Cervantes' novel: Il. Cargiale, Constantin Iorgulescu, and M. Sorbul. The influence of the *Quijote* on the poems of I.B. Deleanu, M. Eminescu, and Lucian Blaga is also discussed. Vîscan concludes that Rumanians, in general, have oversimplified the figure of the Knight. However, the critic praises the interpretation by Lucian Blaga in his poems, especially in *Footsteps of the Prophet*.]

502. Zimic, Stanislav. "Cervantes en Eslovenia: Estudio bibliográfico." *Boletín de la Real Academia Española* 48 (January-April 1968):101-115.

In 1934 Marković (497) studied Cervantes' influence in Yugoslavia, but this study is incomplete, as the author freely admits. Between 1935 and 1937 Stanko Leben published the first complete Slovenian edition of the *Quijote* based on Rodríguez Marín's 1927-1928 Spanish edition. Leben's version is illustrated by N. Pirnat. [In his appendix Zimic lists the Serbian, Croatian, and Macedonian editions of the *Quijote*.]

China

503. Chang, José. "*El Quijote* en China y sus influencias en la literatura del país asiático." *ABC* (Madrid), 4 October 1955.

[Chang notes three Chinese translations of the *Quijote*: the 1917 version by Lin-Chin-Nan; the 1939 translation by Fon-Ton-Hua with sketches by Yon et Perrichon; and a 1942 version which uses the Jarvis English translation as a basis. In briefly discussing the influence of the *Quijote* on Chinese works, Chang mentions Lu Siun's *Biografía de A-Q* during the Communist era, a work which the critic finds to be anti-quixotic in spirit.]

504. Yao Hua. "Whitman and Cervantes in China." *People's*
      China, no. 24 (16 December 1955), pp. 15-17.

      [Yao Hua calls attention to a meeting held to cele-
      brate the anniversaries of *Leaves of Grass* and of the
      Quijote. Cervantes, he states, is no stranger to China.
      The critic further notes the first Chinese translation
      of Cervantes' masterpiece at the beginning of the cen-
      tury, in classical Chinese, by Lin Shu, but states that
      the popular edition used at this time is one by Wu Shih,
      written in the vernacular, though containing recondite
      passages. Yao Hua mentions another translation in prog-
      ress but does not give the name of the translator.
      The critic also refers to remarks by Chou Yang, who
      stated that the *Quijote* embodies the best thinking and
      emotions of the literary renaissance, that its greatness
      lies in its reality, and that it paints an unforgettable
      panorama of sixteenth-century Spain. At the end of his
      article Yao Hua mentions the recitation by César Arco-
      nada of his poem "Don Quixote in China."]

                          The Low Countries

505. Arents, Prosper. *Cervantes in het Nederlands; Biblio-*
      graphie. Gent: Koninklijke Vlaamse Academie voor
      Taal-en Letterkunde, Secretarie der Academie, 1962.
      Pp. xlviii + 474.

      [In his introduction Arents seeks to refute the idea
      that Cervantes' works have been little known and poorly
      understood in the Low Countries. The critic lists, by
      work, the numerous editions and versions of Cervantes'
      obras published in Holland and Belgium. All types of
      adaptations are noted, and selections are listed as
      well. Arents furnishes pictorial interpretations of
      Cervantes' works and describes critical articles on
      Cervantes published in the Low Countries. Pages 1-32
      are devoted to separate editions of the *Quijote* in
      Dutch, beginning with the edition of Lambertus van den
      Bos in 1657.]

506. Roose, Roland. "*Don Quichotte* dans la littérature
      néerlandaise aux XVIIe et XVIIIe siècles." *Les Let-*
      tres Romanes 2 (February 1948):45-59; 2 (May 1948):
      133-149.

[Roose notes several seventeenth-century editions of
the *Quijote* published in Spanish in Brussels and other
cities in Flanders. Next he points out editions in
Spanish published in Holland. The Dutch translation of
Don Quijote published by Bos at Dordrecht in 1657 is
discussed in great detail. Later editions of this
translation are listed. Roose notes various adaptations
of Cervantes' novel, including several farces. A play
by Van der Cruyssen, 1681, based on Sancho's government,
is briefly examined, as is a popular play by Pieter
Langendijk, 1711, dealing with Camacho's wedding. Roose
concludes that the *Quijote* has been little exploited in
the Low Countries and that it has had less influence
there than the works of Lope de Vega and Calderón.]

507. Vandercammen, Edmond. "De Don Quichotte à Thyl Ulen-
       spiegel." *Bulletin de L'Académie Royale de Langue et
       de Littérature Françaises.* 32 (March 1954):78-84.

       [The critic compares Cervantes' *Quijote* to the Belgian
       Charles de Coster's *Légende d'Ulenspiegel*, noting simi-
       larities between Ulenspiegel and the Don, and between
       Lamme Goedzak and Sancho Panza. The critic concludes
       that both authors were realistic writers, but of an in-
       terior realism, and that both were fascinated with
       justice, goodness, and love.]

                              Portugal

508. Ares Montes, José. "Cervantes en la literatura portu-
       guesa del siglo XVII." *Anales Cervantinos* 2 (1952):
       193-230.

       [The critic states that allusions to Cervantes by
       seventeenth-century Portuguese writers are scarce: (1)
       Francisco Manuel de Melo in *Hospital de letras* and in
       two other instances; (2) Sousa de Macedo in *Flores de
       España* and in *Exelencias de Portugal*; and (3) Faria y
       Sousa in his commentaries on *Os Lusiadas*.]

509. Ares Montes, José. "Don Quijote en el teatro portugués
       del siglo XVIII." *Anales Cervantinos* 3 (1953):349-352.

       There were several plays in eighteenth-century Portu-
       gal based on *Don Quijote*: (1) António José da Silva's
       Vida do grande D. Quixote de la Mancha e do gordo Sancho

Pança; (2) *Entremés de Don Quixote*; (3) *O grande governador da Ilha dos lagartos*; (4) *As tres cidras do amor ou O cavalleiro andante*; (5) a farce by Francisco José Montero Mayo entitled *El Quijote renacido*, about which little is known. The *Entremés de Don Quixote* is attributed to one Nuño Niseno Sutil, a pen name for an unknown playwright. The action of this farce takes place in the main inn. Maese Pedro reappears and, with the innkeeper, plays a trick on the Knight, convincing him that the inn is a castle, that all are in captivity and can only be saved by a certain Don Quijote. *O grande governador da Ilha dos lagartos* was published anonymously in 1774. It is based on two scenes from da Silva's *Vida do grande D. Quixote*. As *tres cidras de amor* consists of three short scenes involving the antics of Camelião, a quixotic old man who seeks to marry off his daughters to knights-errant. This farce appeared anonymously in 1793.

510. Figueiredo, Fidelino de. "O thema do *Quixote* na litteratura portuguesa do seculo XVIII." *Revista de Filología Española* 7 (January–March 1920):47–56.

[This article discusses two Portuguese works of the eighteenth century which deal with the *Quijote*: (1) an operetta presented in 1733 by António José da Silva, *Vida do grande D. Quixote de la Mancha e do gordo Sancho Pança*. Figueiredo insists that this play exaggerates the comic element in Cervantes' novel; (2) a satire, *Quixotada*, by Nicolau Tolentino, 1740–1811, against the Marqués de Pombal. Figueiredo concludes that the *Quijote* is merely an external flame for this satire.]

511. Figueiredo, Fidelino de. "O thema do *Quixote* na litteratura portuguesa do seculo XIX." *Revista de Filología Española* 8 (April–June 1921):161–169.

[This article notes the following works based in part on Cervantes' life or on his masterpiece: (1) José Joaquim Leal's play *D. Quixote na cova de Montesinhos*, 1813; (2) an anonymous play of fantasy which appeared in *Panorama* in 1840, in which work the young Cervantes appears as a character; (3) three poems by Gomes Leal; (4) Gonçalves Crespo's "A morte de D. Quixote," 1882; (5) Thomas Lopes' sonnet "D. Quixote," printed in 1904; (6) Ramos Coelho's poem concerning the transcendental significance of the *Quijote*; (7) three poems by Filinto de Almeida about the Knight and the Squire, published in 1915; (8) two poems by Joaquim de Araujo; and (9) three poems by Abilio Maia.]

512. Glaser, Edward. "The Literary Fame of Cervantes in
      Seventeenth-Century Portugal." *Hispanic Review* 23
      (July 1955):200-211.

      The *Quijote* was not generally appreciated in Spain or
      Portugal in the seventeenth century, for it was not con-
      sidered a serious book. Portuguese writers, like other
      Iberian intellectuals, saw only the comic elements in
      Cervantes' masterpiece. What is striking is that in
      spite of their professed disdain for the artistic merits
      of the *Quijote*, the Portuguese were among the most atten-
      tive and enthusiastic readers of the work. Their fail-
      ure to eulogize the novel in their writings may be
      attributed to a lack of aesthetic perspective and to
      nationalistic prejudices. The Portuguese, who claimed
      for themselves the honor of having given the world such
      novels of chivalry as the *Amadís de Gaula* and *Palmerín
      de Inglaterra*, could hardly be expected to defend the
      perfection of a work which admittedly aimed at rele-
      gating to oblivion these national glories of Lusitania.

513. Glaser, Edward. "More About the Literary Fame of Cer-
      vantes in Seventeenth-Century Portugal." *Anales
      Cervantinos* 5 (1955-1956):143-157.

      The seventeenth-century Portuguese dramatists had too
      simplified a view of the *Quijote*, for they pictured the
      Don as either an example of gratuitous bravery or of un-
      warranted devotion to a lady-love. Sancho was depicted
      as largely simpleminded. Cervantes' two protagonists
      had some influence on the playwright Jacinto Cordeiro
      (died 1646) in his depiction of Delfín and Pinalvo in
      El hijo de las batallas. This same dramatist, in the
      Famosa comedia del mal inclinado, refers to the Knight
      as an exemplary lover. [Other playwrights of seven-
      teenth-century Portugal who refer either to Don Quijote
      or Sancho are noted.]

514. McPheeters, D.W. "El *Quijote* del judío portugués An-
      tónio da Silva (1733)." *Revista Hispánica Moderna*
      34 (1968):356-362.

      The play *Vida do grande D. Quixote de la Mancha e do
      gordo Sancho Pança*, by the Jewish dramatist António José
      da Silva, was performed in the Teatro do Bairro Alto in
      Lisbon in October, 1733. It is one of the most curious
      adaptations of Cervantes' masterpiece.
      Da Silva was born in Rio de Janeiro on May 8, 1705.
      He was taken by the Inquisition to Portugal along with

his parents in 1712. His mother was convicted and imprisoned for practicing Judaism and was not freed until
July 9, 1713. Thirteen years later, both mother and
son were arrested. She was imprisoned for three years
and exiled to Castro Marim for an additional three
years. António was tortured and confessed to Judaism.
He was freed in 1726. Later he became a lawyer and a
playwright. António José da Silva married Leonor Maria
de Carvalho in 1734 or 1735 and had a daughter, Louren-
ça, in 1735. In 1737, da Silva, his wife, and his
mother were taken into custody, having been denounced
by servants and others. The dramatist was garroted and
his body burned on October 18, 1739.

  Da Silva's play is based on the *Quijote*, Part II. It
contains, in the mouth of Sancho, a lengthy discussion
of justice, a preoccupation of the dramatist. The ac-
tors were sixteen life-sized puppets made of cork. Although da Silva's play is humorously crude, there is a
tragic ambiguity under the surface.

515. Peixoto, Jorge. "Bibliografia das ediçõens e tradu-
     çõens do *D. Quixote* publicadas em Portugal." *Boletim
     Internacional de Bibliografia Luso-Brasileira* 2
     (January-March 1961):597-622.

  [Peixoto, in his introductory remarks, states that
Cervantes' masterpiece has not had wide divulgation in
the Portuguese language, largely because the educated
classes in Portugal were able to read the *Quijote* in
the original. Nevertheless, he adds, that novel has
been translated into Portuguese more often than one
would expect. Peixoto briefly mentions the three *Quijote* editions of 1605 published in Spanish in Lisbon
and also discusses the Portuguese translations of 1794
and 1853. The critic comments at some length upon the
1954-1955 free translation of Cervantes' novel by Aqui-
lino Ribeiro. Peixoto includes a diagram of Portuguese
translations (p. 600) and a chronological listing and
discussion of each edition of the *Quijote* published in
Portugal from 1605 to 1959 (pp. 601-622). Numerous
photocopies of covers are to be found in this work.]

516. Xavier, Alberto. *Dom Quixote (Análise crítica)*. Lisboa:
     Livraria Portugália, [194-?]. Pp. 339.

  [This book is summarized in Volume Two of this bibliography (item 335, pp. 223-224). The latter portion of
this work deals with the diffusion of the *Quijote*, its
imitations and adaptations. A special chapter at the

end is devoted to the reception of the *Quijote* in Portugal by dramatists, poets, novelists, and critics. Special attention is devoted to two plays: António José da Silva's *Vida do Grande Dom Quixote e do Gordo Sancho Pança*, 1733; and José Joaquim Leal's *D. Quixote na cova de Montesinhos*, 1813. Both plays, states Xavier, are mediocre, because the former deforms and ridicules the Knight, and the latter fails to present the psychology of the cave episode. Numerous Portuguese critics are briefly discussed, including Oliver Martins, who saw the *Quijote* as a condemnation of Spanish society.]

Scandinavia

517. Bugge, Alexander. "Litteraere forbilleder, Cervantes-Holberg." *Edda* 14 (1920):118-132.

[The likely influence of the *Quijote* on the comic epic *Peder Paars*, by the Norwegian-Danish writer Ludvig Holberg, 1684-1754, is the principal subject of this article.]

518. Fredén, Gustaf. *Don Quijote en Suecia*. Madrid: Insula, 1965. Pp. 112.

[Fredén discusses the influence of the *Quijote* on Olof Dalin's *Den Svenska Argus*, 1732, and upon the writer Jacob Wallenberg. The various Swedish versions of the *Quijote* are noted, beginning with the partial translation of C.C. Berg in 1802, and including the first complete Swedish version in 1818-1819 by J.M. Stiernstolpe. Fredén points out the use by August Strindberg of the characters Don Quijote and Sancho Panza in *Himmelrikets nycklar*, 1891. Numerous critical works by Swedes on the *Quijote* are noted.]

AUTHOR INDEX

(References are to items, not pages)

Adam, Antoine 146
Adams, Mildred 482
Adams, Robert M. 40
Agramonte y Pichardo,
    Roberto 448
Aguirre, José L. 472
Alarcos Llorach, E. 164
Alonso, Dámaso 7
Alter, Robert 8, 274
Ames, Van Meter 165
Amo, Julián 457
Anderson Imbert, Enrique
    449
Arconada, César M. 412
Arents, Prosper 505
Ares Montes, José 508-509
Arias, Augusto 450
Armas y Cárdenas, José de
    220
Ashbee, H.S. 314
Astrana Marín, Luis 235
Auburn, C. 295
Avalle-Arce, Juan Bautista
    41
Ayala, Francisco 90, 236
"Azorín" 91, 136, 331, 361,
    426

Babinger, Georg 57
Bahlsen, Leopold 237
Baig Baños, Aurelio 460
Bailey, John 9
Balanzat, Luisa 81
Balashof, N. 385

Balseiro, José A. 122
Baquero Goyanes, Mariano 166
Bardon, Maurice 137, 167-168
Barton, Erika R.S. 350
Basdekis, Demetrios 126
Bawcutt, N.W. 238
Beall, Candler B. 159
Becker, Gustav 221, 239
Belza, S.E. 386
Bergel, Lienhard 336
Berger, Tjard W. 337
Bertrand, J.-J.A. 169-171,
    362-364, 378
Bickermann, Joseph 365
Bidou, Henry 146
Blasco Ibáñez, Vicente 10-11
Bocaz, Sergio H. 483
Bond, R. Warwick 240
Booth, Wayne C. 12, 304
Borbón, La Infanta María de
    la Paz 42
Boring, Phyllis Z. 82
Bosch, Juan 462
Bosdorf, Erich 275
Bourne, Marjorie A. 184
Boynton, Mary Fuertes 324
Bradford, Gamaliel, Jr. 241
Brooks, Douglas 276
Brüggemann, Werner 338
Brunetière, Ferdinand 139
Buck, Gerhard 277
Bugge, Alexander 517
Burton, A.P. 222
Busi, Frederick A. 332

Campos, Jorge 43
Carilla, Emilio 419, 427–
  428
Casalduero, Joaquín 92
Castro, Américo 13, 215
Catena, Elena 123
Caus, Francisco A. 72
"Cervantes en la URSS" 387
Chaix-Ruy, J. 172, 216
Chang, José 503
Chtein, A. 388
Clark, Harry Hayden 473
Claver, José María 413
Clavería, Carlos 44
Close, Anthony 268
Coburn, William Leon 278
Coe, Ada M. 58, 464
Coll, Edna 429
Colón, Germán 1
Conner, John Joseph 45
Consiglio, Carlo 217
Correa, Gustavo 93
Cotarelo y Mori, Emilio
  69, 78
Cox, Ralph Merritt 302–303
Croce, Benedetto 195–197
Crooks, Esther J. 147–148
Cruz Rueda, Ángel 124

Davison, C.F. 149
Derjavin, Const. 389–390
Derzhavin, K.N. 389–390
Descouzis, Paul Marcel 119
Dessau, Adalbert 451
Díaz-Plaja, Guillermo 430
Diego, Gerardo 59
Dimler, G. Richard 351
Dorer, Edmond 339
Driskell, Leon V. 279
Durán, Manuel 46, 73
Durand, Frank 94
Durand, René L.F. 173

Efron, Arthur 29
Elistratova, A.A. 280
Eliz, Leonardo 435
Ellis, Havelock 14
Ellis, Keith 131

Englebert, Jo Anne 491
Entwistle, William J. 15, 242
Espinós Moltó, Víctor 60–61

Falconieri, John V. 95
Farinelli, Arturo 47, 139,
  188, 340, 366
Fernández Cuenca, Carlos 62
Ferrer, Olga P. 399–400
Figueiredo, Fidelino de 510–511
Fitz Gerald, Thos. A. 2
Fitzmaurice-Kelly, James
  223–224, 243–245
Flaccomio, Rosaria 189
Floan, Howard R. 484
Forero Ruiz, Carlos E. 461
Frazier, Harriet C. 297–298
Fredén, Gustaf 518
Freehafer, John 246
Freiberg, Medeea 492
Frunzetti, Ion 493
Fucilla, Joseph G. 190–191,
  205–206
Fürst, Rudolf 48

Gale, Steven H. 247, 315
García Blanco, M. 63
García Lorenzo, Luciano 132
García Morejón, Julio 120
Garrone, Marco A. 202
Gates, Eunice Joiner 431
Gendre, Jean 309
Getto, Giovanni 207
Ghiano, Juan Carlos 16
Gillespie, Gerald 96
Gilman, Stephen 74, 474
Giraldi, Enzo Noè 208
Girard, René 174
Giusti, Wolfgango 401
Glaser, Edward 512–513
Goldberg, Homer 281–282
González, Alfonso 441
González, Manuel Pedro 452
González-Cruz, Luis F. 458
Graham, Walter 299
Grases, Pedro 463
Green, Otis 17, 97
Greene, J. Lee 283

Greene, Thomas 379
Gross, Theodore L. 485
Gross, Wilbur 269
Guevara, Darío 453
Gutiérrez-Noriega, Carlos 18
Hämel, Adalbert 341
Hainsworth, Georges 185
Hammond, John H. 75
Hampejs, Zdenek 494
Hannay, David 225
Harkey, Joseph Harry 465
Harland, Frances 159
Hassan, Ihab Habib 486
Hatzantonis, Emmanuel 495
Hatzfeld, Helmut 175, 209
Hayes, Elizabeth Gentry 310
Haywood, Charles 64
Hazard, Paul 49-50, 140
Heiser, M.F. 466
Hendrickson, John R. 470
Herman, Jack Chalmers 98-100
Herrero-García, Miguel 70
Hinz, John 325
Hobbs, Edna Earle 249
Hoffmeister, Gerhart 342
Howell, Stanley E. 83
Huebener, Theodore 367
Hübner, E. 343
Hume, Martin 226
Huszár, Guillaume 141, 150

Icaza, Francisco A. de 30
Iordan, Iorgu 496

Jackson, Robert M. 84
Johnson, Maurice 284
Jouglard, Madeleine 176

Kaplan, David 151
Kayser, Wolfgang 285
Keele, Alan Frank 380
Kent, W.H. 326
Khatchadourian, Haig 402
King, Willard F. 127
Knowles, Edwin B. 227, 249

Koeppel, Emil 250-252
Krutch, Joseph Wood 19
Kurth, Lieselotte E. 358

LaGrone, Gregory Gough 71
Lanson, Gustave 152-153
Lathrop, Henry Burrowes 228-229
Latorre, Mariano 101
Lebois, André 20
Levin, Harry 21-22, 177, 475
Light, Martin 487
Lott, Robert E. 85
Lugli, Vittorio 178
Lussky, Alfred Edwin 368-369

Macedo Soares, José Carlos 433
Mack, Maynard 286
Maldonado de Guevara, Francisco 403-404
Malkiel, Yakov 405
Markovitch, Milan 179, 487
Marrero, Vicente 406
Martínez, Armando 133
Martínez Ruiz, José 91, 136, 331, 361, 426
Matthews, Brander 51
Maxwell, Baldwin 253
Mays, Jack Thurston 296
McDonald, W.U., Jr. 322, 327-328
McPheeters, D.W. 514
Medina, José Toribio 436
Meier, Harri 31
Mele, Eugenio 198-201
Meregalli, Franco 32-33, 192
Mijailof, A. 385
Mirabent, F. 370
Mitchell, Jack 52
Molina, G. 86
Molina, Julio 437
Monner Sans, José María 218-219
Montero Díaz, Santiago 407
Montesinos, José F. 102
Moore, Olin Harris 476
Morgan, Sophia S. 477

Morley, S. Griswold   154
Muir, Kenneth   300
Murch, Herbert S.   254

Nava, Ernesto   203
Navarro González, Alberto
  76, 311
Neumann, Max-Hellmut   143,
  344
Neuschäfer, Hans-Jörg   155
Niehus, Edward Lee   270
Nieto Caballero, Luis
  Eduardo   442
Nimetz, Michael   103
Nokoliukin, A.N.   467
Núñez y Domínguez, Roberto
  414

Obaid, Antonio Hadad   104-
  107
O'Connor, Frank   329
O'Donovan, Michael   329
Orgaz, Manuel   498
Orgill, Douglas Harold   255
Ortega Torres, José J.   443
Outumuro, María de las
  Mercedes   53
Overmans, Jakob   345
Ovidio, Francesco d'   210

Palacín Iglesias, Gregorio
  B.   54
Palau y Dulcet, Antonio   3
Palmer, Melvin D.   156
Parker, A.A.   287
Parker, J.H.   55
Patterson, Malcolm Howie
  271
Pedraz García, Margarita
  María   108
Peers, E. Allison   230
Peery, William   256
Peixoto, Jorge   515
Penner, Allen Richard
  288-289
Pérez, Louis C.   488
Pérez Beato y Blanco, Manuel
  446

Pérez Capo, Felipe   65
Pérez de Ayala, Ramón   109,
  290-291, 316-318, 371
Pérez Firmat, Gustavo   333
Pérez Silva, Vicente   444
Perniola, Mario   381
Petriconi, Hellmuth   34, 372
Pinilla, Norberto   186
Plaskacz, Bohdan   391
Pollin, Alice M.   79
Pons, Émile   292
Popescu-Telega, Al.   193
Portnoff, George   408
Predmore, Richard L.   35
Pujals, Esteban   392
Puppo, Mario   211

Quilter, Daniel Edward   36

Rabizzani, Giovanni   204
Ramírez-Araujo, Alejandro   80
Randall, Dale B.J.   257
Rausse, Hubert   373
Real de la Riva, César   37
Remos y Rubio, Juan J.   447
Reparaz-Ruiz, G. de   187
Revilla, Manuel Gustavo   454
Richie, Donald   415
Rius y de Llosellas, Leopoldo
  4
Roades, Sister Mary Teresa
  471, 478
Robert, Marthe   56, 382
Rodríguez, Antonio   38
Rodríguez Chicharro, César
  110
Rodríguez García, José A.
  455
Rodríguez Marín, Francisco
  420
Rogers, Paul Patrick   143
Romera-Navarro, M.   468
Romero, Emilia   425
Rondani, Alberto   212
Roopnaraine, Rupert   319
Roose, Roland   506
Ropa, Denis L.   144
Rosenbach, Abraham S. Wolf
  258

Rosenheim, Edward W., Jr. 312
Ross, Waldo 431
Rubinos, José 117
Russell, P.E. 259

Sackett, Theodore A. 111
Salgues Cargill, Maruxa 134
Salinas, Pedro 23
Sánchez, Alberto 77, 125, 135, 459
Sánchez, Porfirio 438
Sánchez-Castañer y Mena, Francisco 66
Sánchez Escribano, Federico 334
Sanín Cano, Baldomero 112
Santayana, George 479
Sanvisenti, Bernardo 213
Sarmiento, Edward 330
Sarrailh, Jean 160, 180
Schevill, Rudolph 39, 260, 301
Schneider, Adam 352
Schnelle, Kurt 353
Schubart, Walter 393
Schweitzer, Christoph Eugen 354-355
Schwering, Julius 346-347
Seda-Rodríguez, Gladys 121
Sedó Peris-Mencheta, Juan 67
Sedwick, B. Frank 194
Selig, Karl-Ludwig 383, 409
Serrano Plaja, Arturo 410
Serrano Poncela, Segundo 411
Showalter, English, Jr. 161-162
Shroder, Maurice Z. 24
Siler Salinas, Jorge 394
Siles Artés, José 261
Simón Díaz, José 5
Singleton, Mack 313
Slavín, León 181

Small, Miriam Rossiter 272
Smith, Paul C. 113
Smoot, Jean J. 157
Socorro, Manuel 118
Soler Godes, E. 395
Spilka, Mark 293
Spitzer, Leo 25
Starkie, Walter Fitzwilliam 231-232
Staves, Susan 273
Stedmond, John M. 305
Steiner, Arpad 356
Stout, Gardner D., Jr., 309-310
Struyk, John 374
Sullivan, Maurice W. 439
Suñé Benages, Juan 6
Suñé Fonbuena, Juan 6

Tamayo, Juan Antonio 87
Tave, Stuart M. 233
Templin, E.H. 480
Terraguso, Antoinette Mahieu 158
Terterian, I. 385
Thibaudet, Albert 182
Thomas, H. 262
Thompson, Clifford R., Jr. 88
Tiemann, Hermann 348
Tijan, Pablo 416
Todd, F.M. 263
Torner, Florentino M. 183, 234
Torraca, Francesco 214
Torres Quintero, Rafael 445
Torres-Ríoseco, Arturo 421
Trilling, Lionel 335
Tropsch, Stephan 359
Tudisco, Anthony 489
Tudorica, Olga 499
Tull, John F., Jr. 490
Turkevich, Ludmilla B. 396-398, 417-418

Unamuno, Miguel de 128-130, 294
Underhill, John Garrett 264

Uribe-Echevarría, Juan   422, 440
Urzidil, Johannes   384

Valencia, Gerardo   68
Valle, Rafael Heliodoro 423-425
Vandercammen, Edmond   507
Van Maelsaeke, D.   349
Vaughan, C.E.   308
Vázquez-Arjona, Carlos   481
Velcev, Petr.   500
Vianna Moog, Clodomir   26
Vîscan, Silvia   501
Vortriede, Werner   360, 375

Wagner, Horst   320
Wagner, José   376
Wann, Louis   265
Warshaw, J.   114

Welsh, Alexander   321
Weydt, Günther   357
Williams, Stanley Thomas   469
Willis, Raymond S.   27
Wilson, Edward M.   266-267
Wolf, Martin   163
Wolfe, Clara Snell   323
Woodbridge, Hensley C.   115
Wouk, Herman   28

Xavier, Alberto   516

Yao Hua   504

Zaldumbide, Gonzalo   456
Zeidner, Betty Jean   116
Zeydel, Edwin H.   377
Zimic, Stanislav   502
Ziomek, Henryk   434
Zúñiga, Ángel   89

SUBJECT INDEX

(References are to items, not pages)

A bordo con Don Quijote 38
Abenteuerliche Simplicissi-mus, Der 351
Account of the English Dramatick Poets, An 256
Adams, Parson (*Joseph Andrews*) 51, 225, 229, 269, 275, 277, 279, 282, 284, 286, 288-289, 291-292, 317
Adaptations, see esp. 36
Addison, Joseph 225, 228, 280, 337
Adimari, Alessandro 189
Adventures of Augie March, The 487
Adventures of Sir Launcelot Greaves. See *Sir Launcelot Greaves*
Adventures on the Black Mountains 301
Advice to Sancho. See Consejos to Sancho
Agramonte's camp 213
Alain-Fournier 144
"Alamir, Prince de Tharse" 151
Alarcón, J.R. de 423-424, 457
Alas, Leopoldo 82, 84, 88
Alberdi, J.B. 419, 422, 424, 428, 430
Alboroto en el cotarro 439-440

Alcalde de Zalamea, El 77
Alceste (*Le misanthrope*) 157
Alchymist, The 226
Alcidalis et 'Zélide 149
Alcides de La Mancha y famoso Don Quijote, El 87
Alegría del capitán Ribot, La 81
Alemparte, Julio 439
Alexis Sorbas 498. See also *Zorba the Greek*
Algunas observaciones críti-cas sobre Don Quijote 423
Alice in Wonderland 9, 324-325
Allende, Rafael 439
Alma de Don Quijote, El 430
Almeida, Filinto de 511
Alocución a la poesía 463
"Alphonse et Bélasire" 151
Altisidora 289, 323
Amadís de Gaula 41, 130, 174, 196, 254, 322, 512
Amante liberal, El 149
Amends for Ladies 57, 249, 256-258
Amicable Quixote, The 271-272
Amor y Ciencia 91
Amor y pedagogía 121
Amorous Prince, The 236, 297
Amphitryon (Molière) 137, 150

Andrés 267
Angel (*Nazarin*) 93
Anselmo 151, 258
Antiquary (See Oldbuck,
   Jonathan) 51
Anti-roman 21. See also
   Berger extravagant
Antón, Francisco 129
Anton, Robert 239, 257
Apologia de Cervantes 79
Apolonio (*Belarmino y Apo-
   lonio*) 134
*Apoteosis de Cervantes en
   el Parnaso* 422, 430
Apraiz, Julián 460
Arabella (*The Female Qui-
   xote*) 272
Araujo, Joaquim de 511
Arbuthnot, John 224
Arca de Noé, El 75
Archer (*The Beaux' Strata-
   gem*) 309
Arconada, César 504
Argenis 342, 356
Argens, J.B. d' 302
Argentina, *D.Q.* in 419,
   426-432
Ariosto, Ludovico 213, 389,
   430
Arriaza, Eugenio de 446-
   447
Ashley, Beata (*The Eighth
   Day*) 488
Asino, L' 189, 192
Astarac, M. d' (Anatole
   France) 180
Asunción Silva, José 419
Audiguier, Vital d' 147
Auerbach, Erich 378
Auger, Simon 142
Aulnoy, Mme. d' 145, 156
Austen, Jane 9, 21, 273,
   329
Authorial attitude 16, 285
Autonomous characters 20,
   53, 68, 216
Avellaneda 73-74, 118, 137,
   160, 163, 221, 362, 427,
   450, 455

Avila, Francisco de 71, 420
Avisso di Parnaso 201
Avse(y)enko 392, 396
Ayala, Francisco 131, 135
Azarena, Cristóbal de
   (pseud.) 69
Azorín 63, 119-125

Balanchine, George 482, 489
Ballet de D. Quichot (Saute-
   nir) 59
Ballets, see esp. 64
Balzac, Honoré de 56, 90, 92,
   96, 166-167, 170, 173
Banchieri, Adriano 198
Banished Man, The 273
Baños de Argel, Los 265
Barataria episode 67, 249-
   251, 255, 283, 306, 324
Barbarosa (*The Knight of the
   Burning Pestle*) 260
Barbe (Anatole France) 180
Barber's tale (Neptune) 251,
   255
Barbosa, Ruy 433
Barclay, John 342, 356
Barco, Juan 130
Bardon, Maurice 185
Baretti, G. 303
Baroja, Pío 121
Baroque (German) 349-350
Barrios, Eduardo 438
Barros, Juan 439
Barros Grez, D. 422
Barth, John 8, 52, 274
Bartoloche, J.I. 424
"Basilio und Quiteria" 340
Battitessa, A.J. 427
Baty, Gaston 63, 67, 186
Baudouin, Jean 148, 258
Beaumont, Francis 50, 57,
   65, 232, 237, 242, 247-251,
   253-254, 258, 260, 264, 266
Beaux' Stratagem, The 309
Becher, E. 419
Beckett, Samuel 8, 319, 331
Bécquer, Gustavo 87
Bedregal, J.F. 422
Behn, Aphra 236, 297

Belarmino (*Belarmino y
    Apolonio*) 134
Belarmino y Apolonio 121,
    134
Belgium, *D.Q.* in 505-507
Belichkov, K. 500
Belinski, V. 387, 392, 396
Belle par accident, La 48
Bello, Andrés 463
Bellori, Antonio 198
Bellow, Saul 274, 485-486
Belmonte Bermúdez, Luis de
    457
Benjumea, Nicolás Díaz de
    338
Berger extravagant 21, 48,
    55, 137, 143, 147-148
Bergeret, M. (Anatole France)
    180
Bergson, Henri 20
Berta (*Doña Berta*) 82
Beschreibung eines Kampfes
    383
Bickermann, J. 336
Bilac, Olavo 433
Bildungsroman 22
Biografía de A-Q 503
Blaga, L. 501
Blanchelande, Georges de
    (Anatole France) 180
Blanket-tossing episode 206
Blechtrommel, Die 319
Bloom, Leopold (*Ulysses*)
    274
Boccaccio, Giovanni 196
Bodas de Camacho, Las (Grau)
    132
Bodas de Camacho, Las
    (Menéndez Valdez) 68
Bodmer, Johann G. 336-337,
    339-340, 343, 347, 349
Böttiger, K.A. 340
Boiardo, Mateo Maria 389
Bolívar Sevilla, C. 422,
    440
Bonnard, Sylvestre (*The
    Crime of Sylvestre Bon-
    nard*) 180

Booby, Lady (*Joseph Andrews*)
    289
Borachio (*The Cruel Brother*)
    250
Bordelon, Abbé 162
Borges, Jorge Luis 8, 422, 427
Bosdorf, Erich 277
Bosola (*The Duchess of Malfi*)
    238
Bosque, Carlos 430
Bougeant, Guillaume H. 162
Bouhours, P. 137
Bourgeois gentilhomme, Le
    150, 154, 158
Bouterwek, Friedrich 55,
    142, 168, 302, 339
Bouvard et Pécuchet 136,
    164, 167, 178
Bovary, Emma. See *Madame
    Bovary*
Bowle, John 55, 231-232,
    302-303, 328
Bracciolini, Francesco 199
Brackenridge, H.H. 272, 465,
    467, 469-471
Bradwardine (*The Antiquary*)
    225, 229
Bramble, Matthew (*Humphry
    Clinker*) 225, 229
Braying village episode 189
Brazil, *D.Q.* in 433-434
Bretón de los Herreros, M.
    83
Brooke, Arthur 328
Brooke, Dorothea (*Middlemarch*)
    274
Brooke, Henry 223
Brosse, N. de 57, 137, 143
Brothers Karamozov, The
    319
Brüggemann, Werner 378
Brunello (*Orlando furioso*)
    213
Bruno, Guillermo (*Amor y
    Ciencia*) 91
Brush (*Heaven's My Destina-
    tion*) 488
Bryant, William Cullen 469
Budai-Deleanu, Ion 492

Bulgaria, *D.Q.* in 500
Bulwer-Lytton, Edward 269
Burne, William 258
Burton, Robert 250
Butler, Samuel 50, 55, 78,
  223-224, 226-227, 232,
  261, 266, 270
Buxton, George 271-272
Byron, Lord 227, 232, 336,
  338

"Caballero andante de los
  caballeros" 459
"Caballero del Verde Gabán,
  El" 121, 281
Caballero encantado, El 99,
  116
Caballero puntual, El 69,
  72
Cadalso, José 80
Caicedo Rojas, José 419,
  445
Calderón, Pedro 20, 71, 77,
  215, 343, 488, 496, 506
Calloandro 196
Calzadilla, S. 428
Camacho's wedding 67-68
Camus, Albert 41
Canaima 462
Cantaclaro 462
Cantù, Cesare 55
Capaccio, G.C. 190, 195,
  198
Capek, Karel 20
"Capítulo del *Quijote* re-
  cientemente descubierto,
  Un" 400
*Capítulo que se le olvidó a
  Cervantes* 451
*Capítulos que se le olvi-
  daron a Cervantes* 69,
  419, 424, 448-456
Cappozzoli, Raffaele 217
Captive's tale. See Cautivo
  episode
Cardenio 223-224, 234-235,
  241, 243, 245-246, 249,
  253, 255, 262, 297, 299-
  300

Cardenio episode 67-69, 87,
  137, 146, 206, 223-224, 241,
  253, 267, 297-298, 300-301
Cargiale, Il. 501
Carlos VI en la Rápita 92
Caro, M.A. 445
Carrasco, Bruno (*Episodios
  Nacionales*) 106
Carrasco, Sansón 213
Carriego, E. 419
Carroll, Lewis 324-325, 379
*Carta escrita de Londres por
  un americano a otro* 457
Cartaret, Lord 232
Cartoons of *D.Q.* 58
Carus, C.G. 339
Casona, Alejandro 133
Castañeda, Padre 428
Castle, The 379, 381
Castro, Américo 49, 121,
  123, 267, 336, 430
Castro, Guillén de 36, 57,
  71, 87
Castruccio (*The Double Mar-
  riage*) 240, 251, 255
Catalan, *D.Q.* in 1
Catcher in the Rye, The 487
Cautivo episode 67, 252,
  298, 440
Cazotte, Jacques 48
Celelí, Padre (*Episodios
  Nacionales*) 106
Celestina, La 7
Celoso extremeño, El 155
Ceñudo (*El necio bien afor-
  tunado*) 72
Cerretani, Arturo 53
"Cervantes" (W.C. Bryant)
  469
"Cervantes" (Merezhkovski)
  392
Cervantes (Rojas) 427
Cervantes en Argel 440
Cervantes in Frankreich 185
Cervantes o la casa encantada
  63
Cervantes y el Quijote 427,
  430
Challe, Robert 161-162

Chapelain, Jean 137
Chapman, George 252
Charlotte Summers 12
Chartreuse de Parme 167
Chateaubriand, François René
de 170
Chatillion (*The Noble Gen-
tleman*) 240
*Chevalier hyponcondrique,
Le* 137
Chichikov (*Dead Souls*) 392,
399, 401
Chile, *D.Q.* in 435-440
China, *D.Q.* in 503-504
Chodowiecki, Daniel 417
Chou Yang 504
Choulette (Anatole France)
180
Christ-figure, D.Q. as a
35, 227
Chucks, Mr. (*Frederick
Marryat*) 225
Chulkov, G. 392
Cibber, Colley 277
Cid, El 7, 76
Cid, Pío (*Ganivet*) 121
Cisneros, E. 57
"Clarín" 82, 84, 88
Clemencín version 169, 302
Coelho, Ramos 511
Coffee-House Politician 277
Coignard, Abbé 180
Coleridge, Samuel Taylor
232
Collier, Jeremy 224
Colombia, *D.Q.* in 441-445
Combe, William 224
*Comical History of Don Qui-
xote* 60, 257, 297
Commedia dell'Arte 158, 332
Confessions of Felix Krull
21
Congreve, William 12
*Connecticut Yankee in King
Arthur's Court, A* 465,
476, 480, 487
*Conquista del reino de Maya,
La* 121
Conrad, Joseph 25, 333

Consejos to Sancho 266
Constance (*The Eighth Day*)
488
*Continuation de l'histoire de
l'admirable Don Quichotte*
162
Cooper, Anthony Ashley 278
Cordeiro, Jacinto 513
Corneille, Pierre 144
Cortázar, Julio 429
Coster, Charles de 507
Counterfeiters, The 21, 319
Cousin Pons 167
Coverley, Sir Roger de 225
Coxcomb, The 57, 248, 251,
255, 258
Coypel, Antoine 55, 417
Crespo, Gonçalves 511
Crime and Punishment 403
Criptografía quijotesco 427
Cristiano errante, El 424
"Cristo a la jineta, El" 35
Critics, *D.Q.* and the, see
esp. 29-39, 55
Croatia, *D.Q.* in 497, 502
Croaxall, Samuel 301
Crooks, Esther J. 185
Crowne, John 236
Cruel Brother, The 236,
250-251, 257
Cruyssen, Simon van der 506
Cuba, *D.Q.* in 419, 446-447
"Cultura literaria de Miguel
de Cervantes y elaboración
del Quijote" 38
Cunha, E. da 433
Cunningham, John William 271
Curieux impertinent, Le 143
*Curioso del suo propio danno,
Il* 57
Curioso impertinente, El 47,
57, 67-68, 71, 121, 132,
137, 148, 151, 155, 199,
213, 220, 236, 248-249, 251,
255-256, 258, 276, 281-282,
309, 336-337, 346, 352, 368,
373, 423, 457, 492, 501
Curioso impertinente (Guillén
de Castro) 57

Cyrano de Bergerac   141
Czechoslovakia, D.Q. in   494

Dalin, Olof   518
Dalrymple, William   328
Dancourt, Florent   143
Dandinardière (Nouveau-
    gentilhomme bourgeois)
    156
Darío, Rubén   35, 419, 422-
    423, 459
Daudet, Alphonse   43, 46,
    51, 55, 136, 143, 171,
    178, 180
D'Avenant, William   236,
    249
David Copperfield   316
De claris mulieribus   189
Dead Souls   392, 395-396,
    399, 402
Defoe, Daniel   221, 280, 311
Deleanu, I.B.   501
Denmark, D.Q. in   55, 517
Dennie, Joseph   466
Derzhavin, K.   392, 416
Des arts   159
Des Frans (Les illustres
    françoises)   162
Desheredada, La   94, 96,
    103, 116
Desmond   273
Destouches, Phillipe N.   57
Details, use of   7, 19
Devotion of Enríquez, The
    482
Devuchkin (Poor Folk)   392,
    401
Dialog in D.Q.   7
Diamantul Nordului   499
Diary of a Writer, The   392,
    401, 406, 409, 411
Dickens, Charles   13, 26,
    28, 46, 50, 92, 224, 226,
    228-229, 232-233, 269,
    290, 314-321, 406
Dickens, John   316
Diderot, Denis   8, 136
Dillon, John Talbot   328

Disappointment or the Mother
    in Fashion, The   57, 236,
    257
Discorsi Morali   200
Djevushkin (Poor Folk)   392,
    401   .
Dobranich, Horacio   422
"Doctor Sutilis"   88
Doctor Syntax   224
"Documento, Un"   88
Dodgson, Charles   324-325, 379
Dom Casmurro   434
Dom Juan   150
"Dom Quixote" (Crespo)   511
Dom Quixote de la Manche
    (Guérin de Bouscal)   143, 146
Dom Quixote na cova de Monte-
    sinhos   511, 516
Don Abbondio   213
"Don Alvaro de Tarfe"   121
Don Bilioso de l'Estomac   224
Don Chisciotte della Mancia
    (Limosino)   206
Don Chisciotte della Mancia
    (Morosini)   198
Don Chisciotti e Sanciu (Meli)
    189, 202, 204
Don Ferrante (I promessi
    sposi)   207, 210, 212, 214
Don Gil de la Mancha   71
Don Juan (Unamuno)   129
Don Lazarillo Vizcardi   79
Don Mendo (El alcalde de
    Zalamea)   77
Don Quichotte (Jamiaque)   184
Don Quichotte en France au
    XVIIe et au XVIIIe siècle,
    1615-1815   185
Don Quichotte in Köln   380
Don Quijote (Chulkov)   392
"Don Quijote and the Rela-
    tivity of Truth"   267
Don Quijote de la Mancha
    (Dobranich)   422
Don Quijote de la Mancha en
    octavas   447
Don Quijote en América   419
Don Quijote en Barcelona   65

Don Quijote en Buenos Aires 422, 429
Don Quijote en Chile 439
Don Quijote en la Gloria 440
Don Quijote en la venta encantada 423
Don Quijote en Sierra Morena 422, 430
Don Quijote en Sudamérica (Bosque) 430
Don Quijote, his Critics and Commentators 230
Don Quijote libertado 63, 392, 396, 413-414
Don Quijote o el amor 38
Donquijotismo y demonismo 389, 396
Don Quixote (Balanchine) 482, 489
"Don Quixote in China" 504
Don Quixote in England 272, 280, 282, 289, 292, 464
Don Quixote, U.S.A. 465, 489
Don Segundo Sombra 13, 421-422, 431
Don Sylvio von Rosalva 48, 337, 340, 342, 347, 358-359
Doña Barbara 421, 462
Doña Berta 82, 88
Doña Perfecta 95, 116
Doña Rodríguez 266
Doré, Gustave 42, 417
Dorotea 238
Dos camaradas, Los 430
"Dos ilustres lunáticos o divergencia sentimental" 422, 430
Dostoevski, Feodor M. 13, 21, 38, 41, 44, 46, 50, 52, 321, 387, 392-394, 396-397, 401, 403-405, 407-411, 419
Dottori, Carlo de' 189, 192
Double, The 396

Double Falsehood, The 241, 255, 297-301
Double Marriage, The 240, 249-251, 255-257
Du Bail, L.M. 137
Ducal palace 67
Duchess 252
Duchess of Malfi, The 238, 263
Dufresny, Charles 146
Duke of Milan, The 252
Dulcinea 104, 186, 206, 250, 261, 333
Dulcinea (Baty) 63, 67, 186
Dulcinea (Urueta) 423-424
Dulot vaincu 153
Duques 113, 158
Du Verdier, G.S. 137

Eça de Queiroz, J.M. 84
Echegaray, J. 57
Echeverría, José 428
Ecuador, *D.Q.* in 419, 448-456
Editions 1-6, 56, 425
Eichendorff, Joseph 339, 342, 362
Eighth Day, The 488
Eliot, George 45
Eliz, Leonardo 422, 436, 440
Elizabeth I 264
Eminescu, Mihail 499, 501
England, *D.Q.* in 1-2, 29-33, 36-37, 44, 46-47, 49-50, 55, 58, 61, 220-335
Enlightenment (German) 355
Ensayo de antología 427
Entremés de Don Quixote 509
Entremés de los romances, El 71
Episodios Nacionales 104, 106-108
Escobar, José Ignacio 445
Espiñeira, Antonio 439-440
Esplandián 196
Essai sur les moeurs 159

Estafeta del dios Momo,
  La 72
Estrada, J.M.   428
Estragon (*Waiting for*
  Godot)   332
Étranger, L'   319
Eugene Onegin   392, 396
Eugenio   131, 281-282
Excelencias de Portugal   517
Eximeno, Padre Antonio   79
Existentialism   488

Facundo   430
Fair Penitent, The   236
Falla, M. de   59, 61
Falstaff   245, 262
Familia de León Roch, La
  116
Famosa comedia del mal
  inclinado   513
"Fantasía de un delegado de
  Hacienda, La"   88
Faria y Sousa, Manuel de
  508
Farinelli, Arturo   55
Farquhar, George   309
Fatal Dowry, The   57, 236
Faulkner, William   8, 487
Fausse Clélie   162
Faust   194, 365, 367, 403-
  404
Faux-Monnayeurs, Les   21,
  319
Febres Cordero, Tulio   419
Female Quixote, The   48,
  223-224, 271-273, 280, 310
Female Quixotism   272
Ferdinand Count Fathom   296
Fernández, Santiago (*Epi-*
  sodios Nacionales)   107
Fernández de Lizardi. See
  Lizardi
Fernando-Dorotea episode
  87, 238
Fictitious historian   9
Field, Nathan   57, 244,
  249, 256, 258, 261

Fielding, Henry   12, 21, 43,
  46-47, 49-51, 55, 220, 223-
  225, 227-229, 232-234, 268-
  270, 272, 274-294, 296,
  317-318, 337, 464
Fiera, el rayo y la piedra, La
  77
Filadar   395-396
Fitzgerald, F. Scott   45
Fitzmaurice-Kelly, James   55,
  230
Flaubert, Gustave   9, 13, 21,
  25, 40, 82, 84, 136, 163-
  164, 166, 167-169, 171-177,
  181-182, 216
Fletcher, John   60, 65, 215,
  223, 226, 232, 235, 237,
  241-244, 246, 248-251, 253-
  255, 258, 260, 264, 266,
  280, 299-301
Florentina (*Marianela*)   97
Flores de España   508
Florian, Jean   143, 222
Floridor (pseud. for Soulas,
  Josias de)   395
Folies de Cardenio, Les   143,
  146, 297
Fontana de oro, La   99, 100,
  116
Fool of Quality   222
Footsteps of the Prophet   501
Forastiero   189, 195
Ford, John   252
Formalistic criticism   389,
  396
Forns, José   128, 130
Fors, Luis   422, 427
Forster, John   321, 335
Fortunata y Jacinta   111, 116
Foscolo, Ugo   192, 211
Foulché-Delbosc, R.   55
France, Anatole   180
France, *D.Q.* in   1-2, 30-31,
  33, 36, 50, 55, 57, 61,
  136-187, 249, 302
Francoeur (Anatole France)
  180

Franz Sternbald 338
Fray Gerundio 69
Frenzel, Karl 42
Freund und Frau 373
Frías, Heriberto 419
Furetière, Antoine 162
"Futura" (Asunción Silva) 419

Gabriel, José 427
Gal, G. 386
Galatea, La 375
Galdós, Benito Pérez 13, 53, 84; see esp. 90-116
Gallegos, Rómulo 421, 462
Galley slaves adventure 67, 159, 206, 238
Gamelin, Evariste (Anatole France) 180
Gamelin, Mme. (Anatole France) 180
Ganivet, Ángel 112, 119-121
García, A. 423
García Luna, Luis 87
Gascon extravagant, Le 137
Gautier, Théophile 169
Gayton, Edmund 232, 249, 257, 266-267
Generation of 1880 428
Generation of 1898 119-130
George II 283
Gerchunoff, Alberto 419, 423
Germany, *D.Q.* in 1-2, 30, 33, 37, 44, 47, 49, 55, 57, 61, 336-384
Gerstenberg, Heinrich W. von 47
Geta (*The Prophetess*) 251, 255
Gide, André 21, 25, 40-41, 53, 144, 319
Gilded Age, The 478
Gili, G. 189
Giménez Pastor, Arturo 427, 430

Gissing, George 334
Gitanilla, La 143, 466
Göchhausen, A. von 337
Goethe, Johann Wolfgang von 38, 44, 47-48, 338-339, 342, 344, 349, 361-362, 365-368, 375-376, 403
Gogol, N.V. 43-44, 50, 387, 392, 395-397, 399, 402, 405
Goldsmith, Oliver 51, 228-229, 269-270
Golfín (*Marianela*) 97
Golyadkin (*The Double*) 401
Gomes Leal, A.G. 511
Gómez, Alejandro (*Nada menos que todo un hombre*) 121
Gómez Bas, Joaquín 53
Gonsalve de Cordue 143
Gorchs edition 42
Gorki, Maxim 387
Gottsched, Johann C. 347
Gouvernement de Sanche Pansa, Le 143, 146, 154
Gran teatro del mundo, El 20, 77, 215
Grande Governador da Ilha dos lagartos, O 509
Grandison der Zweite 48, 337, 340, 342
Grau, Jacinto 20, 132
Graves, Richard 220, 224, 234, 270-273
Great Gatsby, The 45
Greece, *D.Q.* in 491, 495, 498
Grilparzer, Franz 336, 339, 366, 377
Grimmelshausen, H.J.C. 350-351, 357
Grisóstomo episode 137, 148
Groussac, Paul 427
Gual, Adriá 132
Guérin de Bouscal, G. 50, 137, 143, 146, 154
Guía del lector del Quijote 38, 267
Guinart, Roque 336, 340, 342, 364, 378

Güiraldes, Ricardo   13, 421-
422, 431
Gulliver's Travels   270,
325
Gumpelino (H. Heine)   373
Guzmán de Alfarache   145

Haldudo, Juan   267
Halm, Friedrich   373
Halma   92-93, 103, 116
Halmar, Augusto d'   422
Hamlet   245, 262, 297,
345, 403, 407
"Hamlet and Don Quixote."
See "Hamlet y Don Quijote"
"Hamlet y Don Quijote"   35,
38, 389, 391-392, 396,
401, 409
Hanska, Eveline   173
Happy Captive, The   298
Hardenberg, Friedrich von.
See Novalis
Harsdörffer, Georg P.   355,
357
Harte, Bret   469, 481
Haus an der Veronabrücke,
Das   373
Hazlitt, William   233, 277,
327
Heart of Darkness   333
Heaven's My Destination
488-489
Hegel, Georg W.F.   338-339
Heidegger, Gotthard   340
Heine, Heinrich   38, 55,
336, 338-339, 342, 344,
346, 349, 361-362, 366-
367, 371-373, 376
Heinse, W.   360
Hemingway, Ernest   483, 485
Henry IV   262
Henry VIII   299
Heptameron   155
"Hércules y Don Quijote"
459
Herder, Johann G.   47, 339-
340, 342, 349, 360, 362

Hernández, José   422, 426,
430, 432
Herodotus   131
Hesperus   374
Heyse, Paul   47
Hijo de las batallas, El   513
Himmelrikets nycklar   518
Hinsch, Heinrich   340
Histoire des littératures du
midi de l'Europe, L'   49
Historia de D. Pelayo Infan-
zón de la Vega   69
Historia del valeroso D.
Rodríguez de Peñadura   69
Historia verdadera de César
Nonato, el avieso: Caballero
manchego de Relance   86
History of Cardenio. See
Cardenio
History of Don-quixot, The
257
History of Sir George War-
rington, or the Political
Quixote   272
History of Sir Launcelot
Greaves. See Sir Launcelot
Greaves
"History of Two Friends, The"
276, 281
History of Western European
Literature   392
Hoffmann, E.T.A.   401
Holberg, Ludvig   517
Holland, D.Q. in   1-2, 55,
505-506
Horse's Tale, A   478
Hospital de letras   508
Howells, William Dean   465,
467-468
Huckleberry Finn   46, 466-
467, 473, 476, 478-479
Hudibras   50, 55, 78, 223-
224, 226-227, 232, 261,
266, 270, 272, 280
Huet, Pierre Daniel   347
Hugo, Victor   141, 168-169,
411

Humboldt, Wilhelm von 362, 366
Humphry Clinker 296
Hurtado, A. 57
Huxley, Aldous 40, 402
Hyazinth (H. Heine) 373

Idiot, The 21, 46, 52, 392-393, 396, 401, 406-411
Illustrations 55
Illustres françoises, Les 161-162
Ilustre fregona, La 77
Immermann, Karl 336, 342
Imperfecta casada, La 49
"Incarnation in Don Quixote" 13
Incognita 12
Infernal Quixote, The 271-273
Infidèle confident, L' 143
Influence of Cervantes in France in the Seventeenth Century 185
Inglis, Henry David 328
Inner man 15
Innocents Abroad 476
Inocencia 433
Insarov (*Nakanune*) 391
Intended, the (*Heart of Darkness*) 333
Interpolated episodes; see esp. 370
Intruding narrator 12, 304
Invencibles hechos de Don Quijote, Los 68, 71
Iorgulescu, C. 501
Irisarri, A.J. de 422, 424
Irving, Henry 331
Irving, Washington 51, 321, 465-467, 469
Isidora (*La desheredada*) 96
Isla, Padre F.J. de 69
Italy, *D.Q.* in 1, 20, 46, 55, 57, 61, 188-219

Jacinta (*Fortunata y Jacinta*) 113

Jacques (*Jacques le fataliste*) 136
James, Henry 9, 335
Jamiaque, Ives 184
Jaques (*Noble Gentleman*) 240
Jarnés, Benjamín 63
Jefferson, Thomas 469
Jofaina maravillosa 419
Johannot, Tony 417
Johnson, Samuel 34, 227, 302, 313
Jonson, Ben 220, 226, 232, 250-251, 260, 312
Joseph Andrews 12, 21, 55, 271-272, 275-289, 291-295, 317-318
Jourdain, M. (*Le bourgeois gentilhomme*) 158
Joyce, James 16, 25, 319
Julita (*El rapto*) 131, 135
Jungdeutschen 338

K. (*The Castle*) 274
Karamzin, N.M. 386
Karelin, V. 389, 392, 396
Kazantzakis, Nikos 491, 495, 498
Keller, Gottfried 47
Kierkegaard, Søren 20
"Knickerbocker" 51
Knickerbocker History of New York 51, 465-467
Knight of the Burning Pestle 65, 223, 226, 232, 237, 242-243, 247-251, 253-255, 257-258, 260
Knight-Errant of the Foot-hills, A 481
Knighting ceremony 68, 206
Koenig, Johann U. von 340
Kogan, P. 389, 396
Komet, Der 374
Kommerell, Max 336, 378
Koskarov (*Dead Souls*) 399
Kotzebue, August von 366
Kurtz (*Heart of Darkness*) 333

Lafayette, Mme. M.-M. de
    151, 155
La Fontaine, Jean de 144
Lamb, Charles 227, 232
Langbaine, Gerard 256
Langendijk, Pieter 506
La Rochefoucauld, Fran-
    çois de 306
Latin America, D.Q. in 30,
    419-463
Lawrence, D.H. 379
Lazarillo de Tormes 77,
    137, 354, 421
Lázaro (Rambles in the Foot-
    steps of Don Quixote)
    328
Leal, José J. 511, 516
Leandra 135
Leaves of Grass 504
Légende d'Ulenspiegel 507
Lennox, Charlotte 48, 220,
    223-224, 270, 273, 280,
    310
León, Arias de 69
Leonhardt, B. 266
Leré (Nazarín) 93
Lesage, Alain René 137,
    160, 163, 282
Lessing, Gotthold E. 47,
    337, 340
"Letanías de Nuestro Señor
    Don Quijote" 35, 419,
    423, 459
Letters from an English
    Traveller in Spain in
    1778 328
Leumann, C.A. 427
Levchev, L. 500
Lewis, Sinclair 478
Libro de Buen Amor, El
    7
Licenciado Vidriera, El
    75
Licurgo, Tío (Doña Per-
    fecta) 95
Life of Charles Dickens
    (Forster) 321
Life of Jonathan Wild, The
    293

Lima, Augusto 433
Limosino, Nicola 206
Lizardi, J.J.F. de 419, 422-
    424, 457-458
Locke, John 302, 313
"Loco-cuerdo" theme 13, 75
Longest Journey, The 335
Longfellow, H.W. 466, 468
Lopes, Thomas 511
López de Ayala, A. 57
Lothario 236, 250
Louis XIV 146, 162
Louis XV 147
Love and a Bottle 309
Lowell, James Russell 466
Lozinski, G. 387
Lu Siun 503
Lucas, Charles 271-273
Lugones, Leopoldo 422, 430
Luis (Pepita Jiménez) 85
Lukacs, Georg 22, 336
Lunacharski, A.V. 63, 387,
    392, 396-397, 413-414
Lusiadas, Os 508
Luzinzky, M.N. 417
Lvov, A. 389

Macedo, Sousa de 508
Macedonia, D.Q. in 502
Machado de Assis, J.M. 26,
    433-434
Mackenzie, Henry 270
Madame Bovary 21, 40, 45,
    47, 52, 82, 84, 165, 167,
    175, 177-178, 182, 274
Madariaga, Salvador de 38,
    120, 267
Maeztu, Ramiro de 38, 119-
    121, 128, 338
Maia, Abilio 511
Mailer, Norman 485
Maison du Berger, La 176
Malamud, Bernard 274
Mambrino's helmet 206, 307
Man of La Mancha 465, 482,
    490
Mancha, La 107
Mandas, Duque de 331
Mann, Thomas 21, 38, 336,
    378

Manzoni, Alessandro 21,
207-210, 212-214
Marasso, Arturo 427
Marcela episode 55, 83,
137, 148, 158
*Marcela, o ¿cual de los
tres?* 83
Mariander (*The Infernal
Quixote*) 273
Marianela 97
Marine (*Noble Gentleman*)
240
Marivaux, Pierre de 12,
48, 50, 55, 141, 143,
162, 282
Marmorel 142
Marquina, Eduardo 129
Married Beau, The 236,
257
Marryat, Frederick 225
Marston, John 251
Martín Fierro 422, 426,
430, 432
Martínez Silva, C. 445
Martins, Oliver 516
Martirios de amor 439-440
Maruján, Juan 338
Marxist interpretation
389, 392, 394, 396
Mascardi, Agostino 200
Massinger, Philip 57,
236, 249-253, 265
Mather, Cotton 469
Matos, Juan de 71
"Matrimonio di Don Chis-
ciotte della Mancia e di
Donna Dulcinea, Il" 205
Maupassant, Guy de 56, 82
May, Thomas 250
Maya, Rafael 445
Mayáns y Siscar, G. 222,
338
Medina, J.T. 437
Medvedev, P.N. 396
Meier, Harri 378
Meister, Leonhard 337
Mélancolique, Le 153
Mele, Eugenio 55

Meléndez Valdés, Juan 68
Meli, Giovanni 189, 192, 202-
204, 217
Melo, Fr. Manuel de 508
Melville, H. 43, 45-46, 467,
469, 472, 475, 477
Melville, Renaldo (*Ferdinand
Count Fathom*) 296
Menéndez Pidal, Ramón 74
Menéndez y Pelayo, M. 38,
117-118, 427
"Mentira que se salva por la
mentira, La" 411
Mercurio volante, El 424
Meredith, George 232
Merezhkovski, D. 389, 392,
396
Mérimée, Prosper 169
Meseguer, F. 424
Meursault (*L'étranger*) 41
Mexico, *D.Q.* in 424, 457-458
Meyer, C.G. 358
Micawber, Mr. (*David Copper-
field*) 312, 316
Middlemarch 45
Middleton, Thomas 226
Miguel de Cervantes (J. Cai-
cedo Rojas) 419
Milagro, José (*Episodios
Nacionales*) 106
Milford, John 328
Millé y Giménez, J. 427
Milton, John 389
Minaev, D.P. 386
Miranda, Diego de 123, 281
Misanthrope, Le 150, 157
Miseries of Infant Marriage
226
Mitre, Bartolomé 430
Moby Dick 45-46, 467, 472,
475, 477
Modern Chivalry 272, 465,
467, 470-471, 487
Molière (pseud. for J.B.
Poquelin) 144, 150, 154,
157-158, 312
Monde qui finit, Un 168
Monner Sans, R. 427

Monsieur Oufle 162
Montaigne, Michel de 9
Montalvo, Juan 69, 419,
    422, 424, 448-456
Montero Mayo, Fr. J. 509
Montesinos' cave 323-324
Moor, Karl (*Die Räuber*) 378
Mooreland, Catherine 273
Morel-Fatio, Alfred 55
Moreno, Pablo 423
Moreno, Vincenzo 217
Morhof, Daniel 337
Moriomachia 239, 257
Morosini, Marco 217
Morris, Corbyn 233
Morrison, E.G. 227
"Morte de D. Quixote, A"
    511
Moseley, Humphrey 246, 300
Motta Salas, J. 422
Mouchemberg, A.M. de 356
Movie adaptations of *D.Q.*
    43, 62, 398
Müller, J.G. 48, 337,
    340, 356
Münchhausen 342
Mundo de Don Quijote, El
    (Giménez Pastor) 427,
    430
Murch, Herbert 266
Musaeus, Johann 48, 337,
    340, 342
Musical adaptations of *D.Q.*
    59-60, 62-64, 66-67
Myshkin (*The Idiot*) 21,
    392-394, 401, 406-411

Nabokov, Vladimir 8
*Nada menos que todo un
    hombre* 121
Nakanune 391
Napoleón en Chamartín 90
Nappi, Emmanuele 217
Navarra, Marguerite de 155
Navarrete, Martín F. de
    302
Nazarín 91-93, 103, 116
Nazarín, Nazario 91, 93

Necio bien afortunado, El 72
Netherlands, *D.Q.* in the 1-
    2, 55, 505-506
Neugebauer, W.E. 342, 358
Neumann, Max-Hellmut 185
"New Christians" 13
Newcome, Colonel (*The New-
    comes*) 225, 229, 269, 326
Newcomes, The 225, 326
Nicaragua, *D.Q.* in 459
Nicolás 247
Nicolini, Francesco 189
Niebla 121, 126-127, 215
Nieto, Ricardo 419
Nietzsche, Friedrich 336,
    376
*Niño que enloqueció de amor,
    El* 438
Nivola 127
Noble Gentleman, The 240, 253
Northanger Abbey 21, 273, 329
Norway, *D.Q.* in 517
Nouveau-gentilhomme bourgeois
    156
Novalis (Hardenberg, Fried-
    rich von) 342
Novelas ejemplares 143, 147,
    192, 218, 226, 237, 248,
    259, 346, 457
*Novelas españolas contempo-
    ráneas* 116
Novitski, P.I. 392, 396
Novo, Salvador 68

Obligado, Rafael 428, 430
Odisea (Kazantzakis) 495, 498
Odyssey (Homer) 402
Odyssey (Kazantzakis) 495,
    498
"¡Oh Sancho!" (Nieto) 419
Old Man and the Sea, The 483
Old Manor House, The 273
Oldbuck, Jonathan (*The An-
    tiquary*) 269
Oliver Twist 315
On the Eve 391
Opera, *D.Q.* in the 64, 194
Opitz, Martin 342, 356

Orlando furioso 213
Oronaro (*Triumph der Emp-findsamkeit*) 375
Ortega y Gasset, José 38, 112, 120, 122, 338
Otero Pimentel, Luis 419, 447
Othón, Manuel José 419, 423-424
Ouverture pour un Don Quichotte 60
Ovillejo verse form 7
Ozores, Ana (*La Regenta*) 84

Pabst, G.W. 63
Palacio Valdés, A. 81
Paladio (*La estafeta del dios Momo*) 72
Palémon (Anatole France) 180
Pallol, B. 338
Palma, Ricardo 422
Palmerín de Inglaterra 512
Pamela 286
Pangloss, Dr. (*Candide*) 312
Panurge (Rabelais) 305
Paphnuce (Anatole France) 180
Paradise Lost 389
Pariati, Pietro 189
Parker, A.A. 267
Partridge (*Tom Jones*) 288
Pasamonte, Ginés de 21
Pascal, Blaise 10
Pathé Frères film 62
Paysan parvenu, Le 12
Peder Paars 517
Pedro, Maese 323
Peixoto, Afraino 433
Péladan, J. 171
Pellicer, Juan A. 302
Penáguilas, Pablo (*Marianela*) 97
Peñas, A.O. de las 445
Pensamiento de Cervantes 13, 49, 267, 430
Pepita Jiménez 85
Percy, Walker 274

Peregrinación de luz del día, La 419, 424, 428, 430
Peregrine Pickle 296
Peregrino en su patria, El 255
Perequillo el de las Gallineras 75
Perequillo Sarniento, El 457-458
Pérez, Augusto (*Niebla*) 127
Pérez Capo, F. 65
Pérez de Ayala, R. 121, 134
Pérez Galdós, Benito 13, 53, 90-116, 134
Perrault, Pierre 137
Persiles, El 122, 248, 462
Perspectivism 13, 144
Peru, *D.Q.* in 420
Pessimistic interpretation of *D.Q.* 49, 140, 142, 344
Petronius 145
Petruchio (*Taming of the Shrew*) 262
Pfandl, Ludwig 336
Pharsamon, ou le Don Quichotte moderne 12, 48, 55, 145, 147, 162
Pheander, The Maiden Knight 239
Philinte (*Le misanthrope*) 157
Philip II 283
Phillips, John 257
Philosophical Quixote, The 271
"Philosophy of Don Quixote, The" (Storozhenko) 396
Picaresque novel 315
Pichou 137, 143, 146, 297
Pickwick Papers 46, 51, 226, 229, 232, 314-317, 319-321, 406
Pilgrim, The 150, 152
Pirandello, Luigi 16, 20, 25, 172, 215-216, 218-219
Pirnat, N. 502
Pistol (*Henry IV*) 262
Planas, Miguel 423

Pleasant Notes Upon Don
    Quixot 249, 266
Poblete, Egidio 422, 439
Poems to D.Q. 66
Poetic adaptations, see
    esp. 68
Political Quixote, or, the
    Adventures of the Renowned
    Don Blackibo, Dwarfino,
    and his Trusty "Squire,"
    Seditonio 271-272
Pombal, Marqués de 510
Poor Folk 392, 396, 399
Poor Knight 392, 396,
    409, 411
Pope, Alexander 313
Popescu-Telega, A. 496,
    501
Popović, Jovan S. 497
Portugal, D.Q. in 1, 30,
    61, 508-516
Portuguese editions 433,
    515
Possessed, The 411
Postel 340
Powell, Richard 465, 489
Prelude, The 330
Prescott, William 55, 468
Primrose, Dr. (Vicar of
    Wakefield) 51
Princess Casamassima, The
    335
Princesse de Clèves, La
    151, 155
Princesse lointaine, La 141
Private Papers of Henry
    Ryecroft 334
Promessi sposi, I 207-
    210, 212, 214
Prophetess, The 251, 255
Proust, Marcel 8, 25, 144,
    174
Pucelle, La 159
Puppet-show episode 79
Purbeck, Jane 271-272
Purcell, Henry 60, 224
Pushkin, Alexander 387, 392,
    396-397, 399, 405, 409, 411

Quevedo, Francisco 36
Quijano-Quijana (Galdós) 94
Quijote del siglo XVIII, El
    69
Quijote y el quijotismo, El
    69
Quijotita y su prima, La 419,
    423-424, 457
Quin, Michael J. 328
Quintanilla, E.G. 422
Quitóles, Agapito (Don
    Lazarillo Vizcardi) 79
Quixotada 510
Quixote renacido, El 509

Rabelais, François 137, 141,
    222, 305-306
Radomski (The Idiot) 394
Radushev, A.H. 386
Räuber, Die 336, 340, 342,
    347, 364, 378
Ragionamento sopra la poesía
    giacosa 201
Rainov, N. 501
Rajić, Jovan 497
Ralph (The Knight of the
    Burning Pestle) 260
Ralpho (Hudibras) 224, 261,
    266
Rambles in the Footsteps of
    Don Quixote 328
Rang, F.C. 336
Rapin, René 142, 222
Rapp, Moritz 251
Rapto, El 131, 135
Raskolnikov (Crime and Punish-
    ment) 41, 274, 403
Rastignac (Le père Goriot)
    274
Rayuela 429
"Razón de Don Quijote, La"
    (Asunción Silva) 100, 419
"Recent Rambles in the Foot-
    steps of Don Quixote" 328
Recherche de l'absolu 167
Recio, Pedro 250
Recteur Leterrier (Anatole
    France) 180

Redgauntlet 323
Réflexions sur la poétique d'Aristote ... 222
Regenta, La 84
Reisebilder 344
Renan, Ernst 26
Renegado, The 252, 265
Representación ideal del Quijote, La 423
Retablo de las maravillas, El 77
Retablo de Maese Pedro, El 59, 63
Rey, Pepe (*Doña Perfecta*) 95
Rey Candaules, El 132
Reyles, Carlos 421
Ribeiro, Juan 433
Ribero y Larrea, A. 69
Ribot, capitán (*La alegría del capitán Ribot*) 81
Richardson, Samuel 275, 277, 286, 318, 337, 366
Richer, Jean 148
Richter, J.P.F. 47, 339, 342, 349, 366, 370, 374
Ríos, V. de los 79
Rius, Leopoldo 217
Rivera, José E. 441
Rivier, J. 60
Robarts, Henry 239
Robbe-Grillet, Alain 319
Robinson Crusoe 311
Robles, Juan de 76
Roca, Vicente de la 131, 135
Rocinante 266
Roderick Random 295-296
Rodó, Enrique 35, 419, 423, 460
Rojas, Ricardo 427
Roman à clef, D.Q. as a 142
Roman bourgeois, Le 12, 164
Roman comique, Le 162
Romanesques, Les 141
Romanticists, *D.Q.* and the 44, 46, 49, 96, 165-171, 336-339, 342-343, 360, 377

Romero, Silvio 433
Rostand, Edmond 141
Rouge et le noir 13, 40, 167
Rousseau, J.J. 144, 366, 389
Rowe, Nicholas 236
Rucio 266
Rüegg, August 378
Rumania, *D.Q.* in 492-493, 496, 499, 501
Ruskin, John 232, 321
Russia, *D.Q.* in 30, 46, 50, 55, 385-418
Ruta de Don Quijote, La 121-122

Sagrario, Ido del (*Fortunata y Jacinta*) 113
Saint Francis 491
Saint-Amant, M.A. 145
Sainte-Beuve, C.A. 55, 169
Saint-Évremond, Charles 145, 302
Saint-Martin, F. de 55
Saint-Pierre, B. de 137, 142, 302
Sajon, Carlo 198
Salas Barbadillo, A.J. 36, 69, 72
Saldías, A. 427, 430
Salinger, J.D. 485-486
Sallet, F. von 345
Salmón, Padre (*Episodios Nacionales*) 106
Sancho, or the Proverbialist 271
Sancho Pança (Dufresny) 146
Sancho Panza 27, 104, 106, 123, 130, 134, 137, 150, 158, 161, 212, 240, 245, 250-251, 261-262, 275, 288-289, 317, 321
Sancho Panza (Filadar) 396
Sancho Panza (M. Lengyel) 469
Sancho Panza, gobernador de la ínsula Barataria 395
Sancho Pança gouverneur 143
Sancho's government. See Barataria
Sand, George 56

Sandunov, N.N.   400
Santa Cruz, Juanito (*Fortu-
   nata y Jacinta*)   113
Santos, Francisco   75
"Sar, le" (pseud. for J.
   Péladan)   171
Sarasin, J.F.   153
Sarmiento, Domingo F.   428,
   430
Saroyan, William   484
Sarriette (Anatole France)
   180
Sartre, Jean-Paul   488
Sastre del Campillo, El
   75
Savoiano, Valerio Fulvio
   201
Scandinavia, *D.Q.* in   517
Scardeone, lo   189
Scarron, Paul   12, 162, 282
Schallück, Paul   380
Scheel, Peter (*Don Qui-
   chotte in Köln*)   380
Schelling, Friedrich von
   38, 55, 336, 339, 342,
   344, 362
Schevill, Rudolph   55, 468
Schiebeler, Daniel   340
Schiller, Friedrich   336,
   340, 342, 347, 364, 378
Schlegel, A.W. von   169,
   336, 338, 344, 349, 362
Schlegel, Dorothea von   366
Schlegel, Friedrich von
   169, 336, 338-339, 342,
   344, 349, 362
Schleiermacher, Friedrich
   E.D.   362
Schmitz, Anton (*Don Qui-
   chotte in Köln*)   380
Schopenhauer, Arthur   20,
   38, 339, 376
Schürr, Friedrich   378
Schulmeisterlein Wutz   374
Schulz, J.G.   337
Schwab, Raymond   20
Schwering, Julius   378

Scott, Sir Walter   9, 21, 28,
   51, 214, 225, 228-229, 269,
   273, 322-323, 476
Secchia rapita   189, 192,
   195, 198
Second Maiden's Tragedy   57,
   236, 249, 257-258
Segrais, J.R. de   142
*Sei personaggi in cerca
   d'autore*   215, 218-219
Self-aware characters.   See
   Autonomous characters
Self-conscious narrator   12
*Semblanzas caballerescas o
   las nuevas aventuras de Don
   Quijote*   419, 447
Semejante a sí mismo, El   423-
   424, 457
Sentimental Journey, A   306-
   307
Serbia, *D.Q.* in   502
Servantes i Don Kokhot   392
Servien, Jean (Anatole France)
   180
Sévigné, Mme. de   145
Sganarelle (*Dom Juan*)   150
Shaftesbury, third Earl of
   278
Shakespeare   9-10, 42, 223-
   224, 234-235, 241, 243,
   245, 249, 258, 262, 297,
   299-301, 387, 403
Shandy, Walter (*Tristram
   Shandy*)   308
Sheep-army adventure   206
Shepelevich, L.   389, 418
Shklovsky, V.   389, 396
Siegfried von Lindenberg   48,
   337, 342
Sierra Morena   67
Silent Woman, The   226
Silva, António José da   343,
   509-510, 514, 516
Silva, F.N. de   76
Simplicius Simplicissimus
   351, 357
Simson (H. Heine)   372

Siñeriz, J.F. 69
Sir George Warrington 271
Sir Launcelot Greaves 55,
78, 232, 271-273, 296
Sismondi, Jean C.L.S. de
49, 55, 168-169, 302
*Six Characters in Search of
an Author* 215, 218-219
*Sketches in Spain and
Morocco* 328
Slovenia, *D.Q.* in 497, 502
Sluchevsky, K.K. 400
Sly (*Henry IV*) 262
Smith, Charlotte 273
Smollett, Tobias 46-47,
50, 55, 78, 220-225, 228-
230, 232, 234, 295-296,
318-319
Soden, Friedrich 366
Sojo, Antonio de 422
Sojo, Eduardo 428
Sollogul, V.A. 392
Sorbul, M. 493, 501
Sorel, Charles 20, 48, 50,
52, 55, 137, 143, 147,
158, 357
Sorel, Julien (*Le rouge et
le noir*) 13, 274
Sosie (Molière) 137, 150
Sot-Weed Factor, The 52
Soulas, Joseph. See
Floridor
Southerne, Thomas 57, 236
Spain, *D.Q.* in 30, 36-37,
57, 61, 69-135, 302
Spain in 1830 328
Sparks, Jared 469
Spiritual Quixote 224,
271-272
Spitzer, Leo 336
Stage Coach, The 309
Steele, Richard 221, 233,
278, 280, 337
Stendhal (pseud. for Beyle,
M.H.) 13, 21, 40, 56,
96, 167, 170, 174, 177
Stephanov, P. 500

Sterne, Laurence 8, 46, 50,
220, 224, 228-229, 232-233,
269-270, 273, 296, 304-308,
368, 374
Storozhenko, N.I. 389, 392,
396, 418
Strindberg, August 518
*Studien über das englische
Theater* 251
Subligny, A.P. de 162
Suite de Don Quichotte, La
154
*Summer's Ramble of Geoffry
Wildgoose*. See *Spiritual
Don Quixote*
Sutil, Nuño Niseno (pseud.)
509
Svenska Argus, Den 518
Svevo, Italo 319
Sweden, *D.Q.* in 518
Swift, Jonathan 12, 43, 55,
224, 270, 312
Swinburne, Henry 328
Switzerland, *D.Q.* in 61
Symbolists 338

Tabaré 461
Tailhade, Laurent 168, 171
Tale of a Tub, A 12, 55,
270
Taming of the Shrew 262
Tarantas 392
Tarfe, Alvaro 123
Tarralla y Landa, E. 422
Tartarin de Tarascon 46, 51,
55, 136, 144, 179, 181
Tassoni, Alessandro 189,
192, 195, 198
Tatiana (*Eugene Onegin*) 392
Taunay, Visconde de 433
Tchitchikov (*Dead Souls*) 392,
399, 402
Temple, William 221, 233
Tenney, Tabitha 272
Terruño, El 421
"Testamento de Don Quijote,
El" 36

Teutsche Don Quichotte, Der
342, 358
Thackeray, William 224–
225, 228–229, 269, 326
Theatrical adaptations,
see esp. 57–68
Theobald, Lewis 241, 246,
255, 297–301
Theorie des Romans 22
Thomasius, Christian 347,
353, 355
Thompson, Francis 227
Through the Looking Glass
324
Tía fingida, La 141
Ticknor, George 55, 468
Tieck, Ludwig 38, 55, 336,
338–342, 344, 349, 362,
368–370, 376–377
Tiganiada 492
Tío Mamuco, El 78
Tirante el Blanco 7
Tiscornia, E.F. 430
Titan 374
Tobias Knaut 342
Toby, Uncle (*Tristram
Shandy*) 231, 269, 305,
308
Toledo, Juan de (*El caba-
llero puntual*) 72
Tolentino, N. 510
Tolstoi, Leo 42, 56
Tom Jones 12, 21, 49,
232, 272, 277, 280, 283,
287–289, 295, 304, 318
Tom Sawyer 49, 410, 465–
467, 473–474, 476, 479–
480
Torquemada 90
Tournebroche, Jacques
(Anatole France) 180
*Trabajos del infatigable
Pío Cid, Los* 121
"Tragedy of Idealism, The"
396
*Tragödie vom unzeitigen
Fürwitz* 57

*Traité de l'origine des
Romans* 347
Translations of *D.Q.* See esp.
1–6. See also individual
translators: Basinin 395;
Bataillon 187; Berg, C.C.
518; Bertuch 337, 340,
342, 348, 367; Biehl 55;
Bos 55, 505–506; Danicar
497; Duffield 230; Florian
492; Fon-Ton-Hua 503;
Franciosini 55, 189, 195,
198, 217; Frunzetti 493,
501; Iacobescu 501; Jarvis
221, 230; Joukovski 389;
Krjevski 388, 418; Leben,
Stanko 502; Lin-Chin-Nan
503; Lin Shu 504; Lockhart
230; Lyubimov 388, 416–417;
Motteux 55, 221, 227, 230,
309; Ormsby 230; Osipov
55, 389; Oudin 55, 137,
147, 398; Pahsch Bastel von
der Sohle 337, 339; Papu
493, 501; Radulescu 492,
501; Ribeiro 515; Rosset
55, 137, 147, 152; Shelton
55, 221, 224, 230, 234, 238,
243, 245–246, 256, 258–260,
280, 299, 301; Smirnov 388,
418; Soltau 342, 377;
Stiernstolpe 518; Tomic
497; Viardot 169; Watson
388, 395; Wilmot 221; Wu
Shih 504
Trastulli della villa 198
Trato de Argel, El 440
Traveling-Spain 495
*Travels Through Spain and
Portugal in 1772 and 1773*
328
*Travels Through Spain and
Portugal in 1774* 328
*Travels Through Spain in the
Years 1775 and 1776* 328
Trei Viteji 492
*Tres cidras do amor ou O
cavalleiro andante, As* 509

Trifaldi episode 68
Trim, Corporal (*Tristram Shandy*) 308
Tristram Shandy 232, 272, 295, 302, 303, 319
Triumph der Empfindsamkeit, Der 48, 375
Triumph of Peace, The 257
Triunfo de Sancho, El 419, 430
Tu prójimo como a ti 77
Turgenev, Ivan 35, 38, 50, 55, 389, 391-392, 396-397, 401, 405, 407, 409
Twain, Mark 43, 46, 51, 410, 465-467, 469, 473-474, 476, 478-480, 487
Twiss, Richard 328
Two Noble Kinsmen 299

Último capítulo, El 419, 423-424
Unamuno, Miguel de 20, 35, 38, 53, 96, 119-121, 123, 126-130, 215, 338, 411, 419, 495
"Unfortunate Jilt, The" 276, 281
United States, *D.Q.* in the 29-30, 54, 272, 464-490
Unsichtbare Loge, Die 374
Urdaneta, A. 422
Urfey, Thomas d' 60, 224, 227, 297
Urueta, Jesús 423-424
Uruguay, *D.Q.* in 460-461
Uzin, U.S. 413

Valera, Juan 85, 89, 112, 122
Valéry, Paul 144
Valjean, Jean (*Les misérables*) 411
Valle-Inclán, Ramón del 119
Valor docente del Quijote 427

Vargas Machuca, Alonso (pseud.) 86
Vega, Lope de 17, 122, 255, 343, 488, 496, 506
Vega, Ventura de la 87, 422, 430
Velázquez, Diego 175
Venezuela, *D.Q.* in 419, 462-463
Venezuela consolada 463
Venta encantada, La 87
Verjoncvski, Stefan (*The Possessed*) 411
Vicar of Wakefield, The 229
Víctor (*Cervantes o la casa encantada*) 121
Vida de Cervantes (Fors) 427
Vida de Don Quijote y Sancho 38, 126, 130
Vida do grande D. Quixote de la Mancha e do gordo Sancho Pança 433, 509-510, 514, 516
Vida y empresas del ingeniosísimo Caballero Don Quijote de la Manchuela 69
Vie, Une 82
Vigny, A.V. de 176
Villani, Nicola 201
Vîrgolici, Stefan 496, 501
Viviana y Merlín 63
Vladimir (*Waiting for Godot*) 332
Voiture, V. 145, 149
Voltaire, François 137, 159, 386, 428
Voluntad, La 121
Vorágine, La 441
Voyage merveilleux du Prince Fan-Férédin 162

Wahlverwandschaften, Die 367
"Wahrheit über Sancho Pansa, Die" 383-384
Waiting for Godot 332
Wallenberg, Jacob 518
Ward, Edward 224, 230, 234, 267

Wasserman, Dale 465, 482, 489-490
Waverley 273, 321, 323
Webster, John 238, 263
Weinrich, H. 378
Weller (*Pickwick Papers*) 315, 317, 321
Werther 375
Wezel, J.K. 336, 342
Whitman, Walt 504
Wieland, Christoph M. 47-48, 78, 337, 340, 342, 347, 349, 358-359, 366
Wilde, Eduard 428
Wilde, Oscar 56
Wilder, Thornton 488-489
Wildgoose, Geoffry (*Spiritual Don Quixote*) 273
Wilhelm Meister 44, 338, 366-367
Wilkins, George 220, 226
William Shakespeare (Hugo) 168-169
Wilson, Mr. (*Joseph Andrews*) 281

Windmill adventure 206
Wluiki, Lafcadio (*Les caves du Vatican*) 41
Woolf, Virginia 8, 25
Wordsworth, William 330
Wycherley, William 309

Yorick (*Sentimental Journey*) 306-308
Young Philosopher, The 273
Your Five Gallants 226
Yugoslavia, *D.Q.* in 497, 502
Yuste (*La voluntad*) 121

Zalacaín (*Zalacaín el aventurero*) 121
Zarnik 497
Zayde, histoire espagnole 151
Zeno, A. 189
Zola, Emile 56, 92
Zorba the Greek 495, 498
Zorrilla de San Martín, Juan 460-461